Global Politics
as if People Mattered

NEW MILLENNIUM BOOKS
IN INTERNATIONAL STUDIES

SERIES EDITORS
Eric Selbin, Southwestern University
Vicki Golich, California State University, San Marcos

FOUNDING EDITOR
Deborah J. Gerner, University of Kansas

NEW MILLENNIUM BOOKS issue out of the unique position of the global system at the beginning of a new millennium in which our understandings about war, peace, terrorism, identity, sovereignty, security, and sustainability—whether economic, environmental, or ethical—are likely to be challenged. In the new millennium of international relations, new theories, new actors, and new policies and processes are all bound to be engaged. Books in the series are of three types: compact core texts, supplementary texts, and readers.

Titles in the Series

Global Backlash edited by Robin Broad

Globalization and Belonging by Sheila Croucher

The Global New Deal by William F. Felice

The Information Revolution and World Politics by Elizabeth C. Hanson

Sword & Salve by Peter J. Hoffman and Thomas G. Weiss

International Law in the 21st Century by Christopher C. Joyner

Elusive Security by Laura Neack

The New Foreign Policy, 2nd ed. by Laura Neack

Negotiating a Complex World by Brigid Starkey, Mark A. Boyer, and Jonathan Wilkenfeld

Global Politics as if People Mattered, 2nd ed. by Mary Ann Tétreault and Ronnie D. Lipschutz

Military-Civilian Interactions, 2nd ed. by Thomas G. Weiss

Global Politics
as if People Mattered

Mary Ann Tétreault and Ronnie D. Lipschutz

ROWMAN & LITTLEFIELD PUBLISHERS, INC.
Lanham • Boulder • New York • Toronto • Plymouth, UK

ROWMAN & LITTLEFIELD PUBLISHERS, INC.

Published in the United States of America
by Rowman & Littlefield Publishers, Inc.
A wholly owned subsidiary of The Rowman & Littlefield Publishing Group, Inc.
4501 Forbes Boulevard, Suite 200, Lanham, Maryland 20706
www.rowmanlittlefield.com

Estover Road, Plymouth PL6 7PY, United Kingdom

British Library Cataloguing in Publication Information Available

Library of Congress Cataloging-in-Publication Data

Tétreault, Mary Ann, 1942–
  Global politics as if people mattered / Mary Ann Tétreault and Ronnie D. Lipschutz. -- 2nd ed.
      p. cm. -- (New millennium books in international studies)
  Includes bibliographical references and index.
  ISBN-13: 978-0-7425-6657-6 (pbk. : alk. paper)
  ISBN-10: 0-7425-6657-9 (pbk. : alk. paper)
  ISBN-13: 978-0-7425-6658-3 (electronic)
  ISBN-10: 0-7425-6658-7 (electronic)
  1. International relations--Social aspects. I. Lipschutz, Ronnie D. II. Title.
  JZ1251.T468 2009
  327--dc22
                                                    2008052642

Printed in the United States of America

♾™ The paper used in this publication meets the minimum requirements of American National Standard for Information Sciences—Permanence of Paper for Printed Library Materials, ANSI/NISO Z39.48–1992.

Contents

1

Global Politics
Because People Matter

"The time has come," the Walrus said, "To talk of many things: Of shoes—and ships—and sealing wax—Of cabbages—and kings."

—Lewis Carroll

This book is about how people behave as actors in world politics. In most international relations (IR) textbooks, nearly all the people you are likely to read about are political leaders. Leaders populate this book too, but so do people living normal lives in what are ordinary settings by the standards of their time and place. Our focus here is on what we call the "social individual." We chose this term to emphasize two things: the free will and agency of the individual and the social structures that set limits to human thought and action.

The Western tradition emphasizes individual free will over social constraints, but it does so in peculiar ways. For example, in his seventeenth-century work *Leviathan*, Thomas Hobbes imagines that people living before the invention of society existed in what he calls the "State of Nature."[1] But his image of human beings in that State of Nature serves to remind us that all of us, in reality, are social products. Hobbes writes as though people never were born; never had families, friends, or neighbors; never went to school; and never worked together. As Christine Di Stefano observes, Hobbes's human beings "spring up like mushrooms."[2] They appear as fully adult and autonomous, able to speak, reason, and perform complex tasks like hunting, gathering, and even agriculture, without any education or history, and in total isolation from one another. Yet Hobbes's people show emotions—fear, which he calls "diffidence"; competitiveness, or the drive to be better than others; and a desire for glory. All these emotions presume either knowledge of others, a desire to impress them, or both.[3]

How do people learn to fear others? How do they learn ways to make others fear them? This is where the "system" comes in. In Hobbes's world and ours

1

people are hemmed in by structures, not only physical constraints but also social conventions, rules, and common practices. Although it is presented as being without rules, Hobbes's world has very strict rules. Every person is an individual player in a "game" whose objective is to survive. To eat, find shelter, and live for another day, she must locate what she needs and defend it from others ready to take it from her. Everyone is forced to behave in similar ways because the rules of the game demand it. Any player who trusts another is likely to end up dead or at least robbed of whatever she has managed to wrest from her harsh world. In Hobbes's own words, life in the State of Nature is "solitary, poor, nasty, brutish, and short."[4]

Hobbes lived during the period of the English civil war, a time when religious conflict was tearing the country apart, the king was beheaded, and the country was taken over by Protestant fanatics led by Oliver Cromwell. Hobbes was a royalist who invented the State of Nature in part to persuade his fellow countrymen to accept the necessity of a strong central government. His solution to the terrors of the State-of-Nature game is for every individual player to surrender her autonomy in return for protection from the other players. The frontispiece to *Leviathan* included a picture, a kind of political cartoon, illustrating this message. It shows a king holding a sword and a mace (instruments symbolizing the coercive power of the state). His body is packed with tiny little persons, all of whom presumably have agreed to a "social contract," surrendering their individual rights. There are no little people in the king's head—unlike his subjects, the king is fully autonomous. He is the only actual player (agent) in the Leviathan game, the one who makes all the moves for the "body" of the nation.[5]

This sketch of a philosopher's imaginings would be amusing if the hidden assumption in them, that people are inherently uncooperative and in need of strict regimentation, were not contradicted by logic and by what we see around us every day. Yet it is a powerful image and, in spite of what is around us, it is widely held. This odd article of faith explains why so many texts about world politics ignore persons. If, as Hobbes says, people are fundamentally alike in their capabilities and desires—and if states are just "heads" that reason and behave like people—then you don't have to think about any of them as individuals or examine the rules of the games they are playing. Instead, you can talk about identical units filling various roles: parental units, student units, professor units, farmer units, consumer units, and, in the case of the state, national [leader] units. All are playing one or another version of the State-of-Nature game, in which "choice" is nonexistent because the system forces each unit to do the same thing in any given situation.[6]

Decisions and Actions: The Agent-Structure Puzzle

Our perspective in this book is neither that people (or states) are identical units, nor that personality or "character" is the only determinant of human action. We conceive of the social individual as capable of acting on her own volition, but with the proviso that no one acts in a vacuum. Each person has a history (upbringing, family-supplied resources such as emotional security, nutrition, and education), individual capacities (intelligence, health, energy, and attractiveness), interests (social and economic), and temperament (optimism/pessimism, initiative/passivity). We think that people, even though similarly situated persons face similar choices, bring different human and other resources to the act of choosing: different ambitions, ethics, likes, and dislikes; more or less zest for life; different amounts of money, ideas, support from friends and family; and good or bad luck. Here we emphasize the interplay between the structure of situations, the intentions a person forms, and the efforts she makes to achieve her goals.

We start with the premise that every person is a potential agent, someone "able to make a difference to the world . . . [someone who has] power (where power means transformative capacity) . . . [and] the ability to carve out spheres of autonomy of [her] own."[7] We also believe that the human capacity for autonomy is constrained by structures. Structures are such things as systems of rules and values, resource endowments, and what sociologist Anthony Giddens calls the "'containment' of resources," by which he means the capacity to control the settings in which groups of people use those resources for collective ends.[8] Some of this capacity is innate, but much of it is the product of social position and prior learning. A child whose caregivers show her that she is entitled to claim resources, and teach her how to use them to achieve her goals, will have more power as an adult than one whose experience is of deprivation and abuse.[9]

What about States?

Even if people have individual talents and unique abilities to use them—a proposition that most of us can accept on the basis of personal observation—why should we expect collective actors to be similar? Here we are most interested in the state as a collective actor. A state is a political system or regime that governs a bounded territory and the people who live there. It usually includes the institutions that claim the authority to make and enforce the rules for society. States are governed by persons; some people—for example, historians—believe that states behave like people because what they do is the result of leaders' choices and actions. IR theorists rarely hold such a view, most believing instead that states are functionally similar units governed by systemic pressures, along the lines that Hobbes describes, with differences among them accounted for by the different resources they have to work with.[10]

Some people imagine states themselves as having individual qualities, a perspective that has its own history. Until the last fifty or so years, it was common in popular culture and in academic writings to treat states as though they had personalities, a "national character" based on history, climate, economic activities, and even cultural artifacts like cuisine, music, and writing. The state's personality was imagined as shared by its citizens. So Germans were thought of as regimented, tidy, and precise; the French as logical, romantic (we didn't say that these characteristics were consistent!), and lovers of good food; Italians as religious, excitable, and talking with their hands; and so on. Much of the national-character literature was based on geographic determinism, the idea that climate and topography determined significant aspects of culture and history.[11]

Whole theories were built around ethnocentric views of how geography shapes people and their states. One is the hydraulic culture model. Analysts from Karl Marx on the left to Max Weber and Karl Wittfogel on the right were convinced that nations whose agriculture depended on large-scale irrigation were bound to have governments ruled by dictators.[12] They argued that such states would develop Leviathan-style governments to force people to work on the irrigation infrastructure on the assumption that no one would work voluntarily on something owned by everybody. Anthropologists like Clifford Geertz have found real-world examples of participatory politics in states with large irrigation networks,[13] but some continue to believe that the societies that grew up around large systems of irrigated agriculture are naturally biased toward authoritarianism, while societies supported by rain-fed agriculture are naturally biased toward democracy. Geographers like J. M. Blaut call this perspective plain and simple prejudice, identifying it as part of the widespread "Eurocentrism" that dominates most theories of world politics.[14] Such theories present the states and populations of northern Europe and its former settler colonies (like the United States and New Zealand) as inherently better than others.[15]

A new theory of national character takes a somewhat different tack. Instead of identifying "good" states by their geography and weather, it advocates the moral qualities of states according to the type of political regime they have. One currently popular example holds that democracies are less aggressive than other regimes. People who share this point of view suggest that important characteristics of democratic states, such as regular elections, keep leaders from declaring war without clear provocation. This "democratic peace" thesis became popular during the Clinton administration, under a president who believed that "democracies rarely wage war on one another."[16]

Upon investigation, however, there seem to be holes in this theory, too. Joanne Gowa finds evidence supporting the democratic peace thesis only during an anomalous period in world politics, the cold war, when democratic states banded together in formal and informal alliances to oppose Soviet expansion. She argues that it was not democracy but rather shared interests that kept these states from declaring war on one another during that time.[17] Ido Oren comes to a similar conclusion based on a careful analysis of the writings of prominent U.S. political scientists prior to and following the start of World War I. He shows that democracy was defined differently during these two periods. Before the war, qualities such as constitutionalism and electoral participation, in which Germany scored higher than Britain, France, and the United States, were regarded as the most important indicators of democracy. After the United States found it-

self allied with France and Britain in a war against Germany, what made a country democratic or not changed in Americans' minds to reflect the political characteristics shared by the United States and its major allies.[18]

Who's Really in Charge?

Why is so much effort expended to explain the behavior of states—the decisions
of their leaders—as though the states and not the leaders are in charge? There
are several reasons. One is so that leaders can avoid responsibility for their
thoughtless, stupid, or dangerous decisions and actions. A classical example of
a person who took this "Pontius Pilate" approach to political responsibility was
Sir Edward Grey, Britain's foreign minister on the eve of World War I. In his
book on that war, historian Niall Ferguson presents Grey as a man with a private political agenda vastly different from the position of his party and prime
minister.[19] Grey disdained the official position of the Liberal Party, which was
to take a neutral stance toward France and Germany. Grey, who disliked Germans and Germany, instead engaged in secret negotiations with French leaders,
hinting that Britain would come to the support of France in the event of a war
on the continent of Europe.

Did the resulting uncertainty about what Britain actually would do encourage the Germans to "consider a pre-emptive strike," thereby making "a continental war more rather than less likely," as some historians believe?[20] It's a
plausible assumption. Yet to whatever extent Grey's confusing actions contributed to turning the conflict between Germany and France into a world war,
he refused to associate himself with the results. In his memoirs, Grey presents
himself as a tragic figure caught up in events he could not control. He recalls a
friend saying that Grey had greeted the coming of war with the observation
that the lamps were going out all over Europe and would not come on again
during his lifetime without acknowledging that his own hand was on one of the
switches. A second reason for presenting state actions as inevitable is linked to
the first. It lets observers avoid confronting the effects of past policies and practices whose outcomes, whether consciously intended or not, turn out to be bad
for the national interests of the state whose leaders chose them. One example is
the nurturing and arming by U.S. and Saudi Arabian policy makers of the Taliban and persons who later became the nucleus of the al-Qaeda network. Mujahideen (holy warrior) groups were embraced as Saudi and U.S. proxies in the
war that raged throughout most of the 1980s between Afghanistan and the Soviet Union. Both governments sent support to the mujahideen, directly and via
intermediaries such as Pakistan, and the United States provided military training. At the behest of then-CIA director William Casey, high-tech armaments
such as Stinger missiles were provided by the U.S. Congress to the mujahideen.
Casey also committed the Central Intelligence Agency (CIA) to support Pakistan's intelligence agency, Inter-Services Intelligence (ISI), in its efforts to re-
cruit Muslims to fight along with the Afghan mujahideen. Among the ISI's

recruits were the Saudi Osama bin Laden and other young Arabs from places as far away as Algeria and the United States.[21]

When the Soviet Union withdrew from Afghanistan in the late 1980s, the United States turned its back on the devastation that a decade of war had inflicted there. The CIA offered to buy back leftover Stinger missiles, but it was oblivious to the situation of the human beings trained to operate them. Young fighters who had been mobilized from across the Arab and Islamic worlds suddenly lost their mission and the material and status rewards that came with it. They did hold on to their weapons, however, along with their training and their desire to be powerful figures in their respective countries and in the world. Within a few years, one group of mujahideen, the Taliban, took over most of the Afghan state. Meanwhile, al-Qaeda turned into a terrorist organization. Its leader, Osama bin Laden, and many core members, were from Saudi Arabia. When their government rejected their offer to keep Saddam Hussein out of Saudi Arabia following his invasion of Kuwait, they became very angry. They mounted attacks in their home country and elsewhere in the world, including the United States, which they saw as a nation of infidels who had usurped their rightful role as defenders of their country. The most spectacular of these attacks took place on September 11, 2001, in New York and Washington. But when Republicans look back with nostalgia at the "Reagan legacy," they never mention the Reagan administration's support of the mujahideen or the "blowback," the repercussions, it provoked.

A third reason why the fingerprints of specific actors on the policies they make are so frequently overlooked is because many people see bad outcomes as unavoidable products of economic and other systemic conditions outside anyone's control as though political economies were merely accidents or forces of nature. But they are not. They are structures produced by rules and practices established and enforced—or violated—by powerful governments and their agents, intentionally or not. Yet the conditions imposed by the World Bank on developing-country borrowers and by the International Monetary Fund (IMF) on developing countries experiencing trade deficits are discussed as though the actions and ideologies of powerful countries had nothing to do with the nature of these policies,[22] how they are implemented, or to what effect—and the effect can be devastating. Peter Uvin traced the impact of IMF demands for structural adjustment on one case, Rwanda. He concluded that the deep cuts in employment and social services contributed directly to the massive genocide that Rwanda's Hutu government perpetrated against the Tutsi minority during one hundred horribly bloody days in the spring of 1994.[23] Rodwan Abouharb and David Cingranelli considered many countries when they studied whether "structural adjustment" policies imposed under agreements with the World Bank affect governments' human rights behavior. Looking at measures of a government's treatment of citizens with respect to their rights to be free from torture, political imprisonment, extrajudicial killings, and disappearances, they concluded that these agreements do indeed "worsen government respect for physical integrity rights."[24]

Agents in *Structures*

In spite of our belief that structures are important causes of outcomes, we acknowledge that accounting separately for the contributions of agents and structures is hard work. Structures help to shape agents, who, in turn, alter structures to give themselves greater power and more choices in the future. Sir Edward Grey, who was able to undermine the stated policy of his party and the government it led, started out with structural advantages that enhanced his agency. He was from a wealthy family whose prominence increased the likelihood that he would get a university degree, even though he had been "rusticated" (suspended) by two Oxford colleges for laziness. Social connections smoothed Grey's path into politics in spite of what one contemporary, Lloyd George, called his lack of vision. The political environment also worked for Grey. While he was foreign minister, his Liberal Party was divided. Leaders worried more about keeping the party together than about how Grey was directing foreign affairs. Meanwhile, the Conservative Party agreed with Grey's pro-France policy and had no reason to encourage anyone to look too closely at what he was doing. As a result, "the detail of Grey's policy (and the devil lay there) was not subjected to close enough parliamentary scrutiny."[25] What Jane Mansbridge calls "adversary democracy"[26] depends on just that—scrutiny, which today we call "transparency"—and open debate. In this case, neither party was fulfilling its obligation to scrutinize and publicize the actions of policy makers and thereby hold them accountable.[27]

Adolf Hitler was another agent who used favorable structural conditions to pursue destructive policies. After World War II, what amounts to a scholarly industry grew up to explain how a lower-middle-class, indifferently educated, and undistinguished Austrian rose to become the leader of the German state, initiated a global conflict, and masterminded the extermination of a majority of the Jews of Europe. Daniel Goldhagen does make Hitler responsible for mobilizing what he calls Germany's "willing executioners" of the Jews. But he also argues that Germans followed Hitler and supported the Holocaust because they grew up in an anti-Semitic culture that defined Jews as evil and deserving to be killed.[28] This is a structural thesis that removes responsibility from individual Germans—after all, if they had been socialized in a virulently anti-Semitic culture, how could they help being anti-Semitic? Some scholars who emphasize Hitler's agency point to personal qualities to account for his behavior: an abusive father, the horrific death of his mother, his alleged drug addiction, his sexual problems, and an evil soul are suggested as causes of Hitler's anti-Semitism and his lethal policies.[29] The tacit message in these studies is that anyone with such problems couldn't avoid growing up to be a mass murderer and therefore could not be fully responsible for his actions.

How would we navigate through explanations that focus on culture and personality, two factors that we do believe supply partial explanations for action? Let's start with culture. Anthropologist Eric Wolf also explains the rise of the Nazis in terms of German culture, but he draws the connection between culture and behavior differently than Goldhagen. Wolf argues that the German middle class, unlike the middle classes of France and England, developed without a tradition of citizenship, that is, the belief that citizens have the right to participate in the decisions of the state. Rather, Germany took shape as fragments prior to unification in 1871, each with a middle class cut off both from the autocratic "petty princelets" who ruled the many little German states and from the masses of illiterate peasants and workers. During the founding period of the modern German state, all that unified German social groups was a common written language and a common "high culture" of music and literature (indeed, Germans spoke many, often mutually unintelligible, local dialects). Germans had no shared memories of a unique common history defining them as members of a community in which they had earned rights and to which they owed obligations.[30] German autocracy left intellectuals without any role in politics, so none of them had practical experience in governance. Wolf tells us that German revolutionaries in Europe's year of revolution, 1848, couldn't even agree on how the state they were fighting for should be organized. As a result, it was relatively easy for Prussian and Austrian troops to close down their assemblies, parliaments, and "security committees" and reinstate autocratic rule.[31]

German activists failed to democratize their politics in 1848, but they did succeed in making their fellow Germans see themselves as a united people. Germans did not feel united because they were fellow citizens, but because they all were related as members of the same ethnic group or tribe—in German, a *Volk* (folk). A political community is based on values and goals that citizens choose together and alter when they wish; it is imagined as an ongoing joint project always under construction. In contrast, a Volk is "natural" and unchangeable, shaped by "vital forces driving physiological and psychological life, binding individuals to the Volk, people to the landscape, landscape to nature, nature to cosmos."[32] As a Volk, Germans were unified by their Germanness, by blood, rather than because they were a responsible political community. Even after Prussia unified Germany from a collection of smaller states, continued autocratic rule retarded the development of institutions in and through which citizenship and political responsibility could develop as normal social practice.

The strongest institution in the new Germany's narrowly based state was its large professional army. The army's needs took priority over everything else. Before Germany was united, people used to joke that Prussia, the statelet that became Germany's nucleus, was little more than an army with a state. Unified Germany was Prussia writ large, and the now-German army began its existence with a spectacular early success. Its defeat of France in the Franco-Prussian War (1870–1871) made Germany a world power, and the army took full credit for the new state's achievement.

But as U.S. president John Kennedy observed after his first major foreign policy act, an invasion of Cuba, had crashed and burned, "victory has 100 fathers and defeat is an orphan."[33] After Germany was defeated in World War I, army leaders refused to take responsibility for the loss, arguing that the military had been "stabbed in the back."[34] They looked for scapegoats, and Jews and socialists, categories with substantial overlap, became the favored targets for the army's defenders. Ian Kershaw traces how ruthlessly the army put down postwar movements attempting to create a socialist democracy in Germany.[35] As part of its campaign, the German army funneled arms and ammunition to right-wing paramilitary groups like the Freikorps, and later to the Nazis, who shared the army's views on the desirability of a militarized Germany and the undesirability of a social revolution. These groups opposed the disarmament provisions of the Versailles Treaty outlining the postwar settlement and argued that the authority of military leaders should be preserved.

The Nazi Party, like other *volkisch* parties, capitalized on Germany's postwar economic collapse and popular dissatisfaction with the democratic but weak national government that had replaced the Kaiser after his sudden abdication at the end of the war. The government of Bavaria, the state where these right-wing parties were strong, rarely arrested party members for their violent behavior. In 1923, one of the Nazi Party leaders, Hitler, was arrested for a failed attempt to lead an armed, right-wing, populist rebellion (the "Beer Hall Putsch"). Sentenced to a year in prison, he was treated like a king by prison authorities. After he was released, he was even more popular and more powerful than he had been before.[36]

The Nazi Party was good at manipulating structures. It used the electoral system to run candidates for the national parliament; and it avoided criminal penalties from the justice system after it used terrorist tactics against its opponents. Ron Rosenbaum describes how Nazis intimidated and even killed some of their "enemies," not only candidates who ran against them (on the right and on the left) but also newspaper reporters and publishers who dared to criticize them and expose their activities.[37] Protected by their connections in the army and by a Bavarian state that looked the other way when their brand of politics led to violence, Hitler and other Nazis were elected to the German parliament. They were not effective legislators, however, and the Nazis soon lost their appeal. The proportion of the German vote that went to the Nazi Party was already declining when, in 1933, a government crisis prompted the country's president, former army general Paul von Hindenberg, to tap Hitler to become chancellor (prime minister). Von Hindenberg thought that Hitler was so insignificant that he would be easy to control. This is how a politician who might have ended his career as a mere curiosity found himself at the helm of the German state.

Hitler came to power in Germany in part because German culture ensured that racist appeals were acceptable in a "mainstream" political platform. But Nazi successes also depended on the support the party received from the army and the Bavarian government. Guns, money, and impunity allowed Nazi leaders to swagger in front of unemployed young male voters and buy them drinks at party meetings (which usually were held in beer halls). Meanwhile, Nazi thugs could eliminate critics and opponents by beating them up or killing them without worrying that they would be punished for these actions. Hitler himself was an energetic agent and used his position to manipulate and transform structures in his favor. A talented speaker, he used his year in jail to make an end run around his rivals for Nazi Party leadership. He held court from prison and also wrote a book—*Mein Kampf*, "my struggle." The book impressed his followers, whether they read it or not, and chilled his opponents, who read it very carefully. When Hitler was offered the position of chancellor, he surprised his backers, taking control of the state, changing the laws, and altering the constitution to carve himself a unique and unchecked position as the führer (leader) of the German people.

Even though the Nazi Party was in decline by the time that Hitler was invited to head the government, his position still allowed him to be in the right place at a time when powerful, behind-the-scenes manipulators were looking for a front man. Hitler's anti-Semitism was integral to his personality and shaped what he did with the German state when he was put in charge of it. Even so, the actions of the army and national leaders in a state lacking democracy and a tradition based on the rule of law explain more about the rise of Hitler and the Nazis than either culture or personality.

The Creation of the Social Individual

The stories of Edward Grey and Adolf Hitler illustrate the importance of institutions like parties, parliaments, and armies in creating what sociologists call "opportunity structures," situations through, against, or within which individuals can exercise their agency. The household is one of several powerful institutions that shape opportunity structures for social individuals. Households are where people are produced, the place where children are reared (socialized), educated, and prepared for adult life by the people who live with them. Although every child has her own talents and temperament, what she can do—and what she can get away with—is first learned at home.

A household also is an economic unit. Children receive money, goods, and services produced or earned by the adults in their households and some children contribute money, goods, and services to their households. The home, its inhabitants, their collective resources, and the rules they adopt for sharing resources are part of the legacy of every human being. There is an African saying that "it takes a village to rear a child." This reflects an understanding that the road from the infant's dependency to the adult's autonomy is necessarily populated by caregivers in and outside of the household. Each caregiver provides or withholds resources from persons and institutions that depend on them, including the household itself as a productive and reproductive unit. As a result of how and how many resources are provided or withheld, children learn who they are and what kind of claims they can make on their world.

Some caregivers teach children by hitting them or humiliating them in front of others. Their philosophy of education is to punish so that children will avoid what is forbidden. If punishment is made into a spectacle, even children who are not punished directly might be terrified enough to refrain from the activities that caused suffering to their siblings or peers. The technical term for this strategy is "deterrence." Similar tactics, applied to adults, are concrete manifestations of the philosophy behind state terrorism. They include ritual torture and murder by governments and their agents,[38] and capital punishment, whose advocates believe that killing criminals can deter others from becoming criminals.

Michel Foucault, a twentieth-century analyst of knowledge and power, argues that the standardization of punishment by legal means, along with the development of institutions that rely on regimentation, surveillance, and isolation, together increase states' capacity for social control. When he speaks of "institutions" Foucault refers not only to prisons but also to schools and workplaces, and the beliefs and practices they embody. Here individuals are taught to discipline themselves by authorities who subject them to routines presented as the results of "laws" or universal systems, and punish them when they fail to conform. Forced conformity and the loss of individuality shape the mind to submit to the will of others, a will that is disguised by presenting its demands as objective laws (such as supply and demand in the market) or even as divine commands ("Spare the rod and spoil the child").[39] Philip Greven offers the example of Susanna Wesley, an eighteenth-century parent who applied her own version of Foucault's model to the rearing of her children.

> Susanna Wesley recalled that her infants had been "put into a regular method of living" from the outset, in their patterns of sleeping, eating, and dressing. . . . [She] was insistent upon harsh physical punishment from a very early age: "When turned a year old (and some before) they were taught to fear the rod and to cry softly, by which means they escaped abundance of correction which they might otherwise have had: and that most odious noise of the crying of children was rarely heard in the house."[40]

The regime imposed by Wesley resembles Foucault's description of disciplinary institutions, illustrating how much the technique if not the technology of discipline and punishment predates "modernity." Modernity is a worldview associated with the Enlightenment in which human reason and rationality are regarded as superior to religion and custom as sources of guidance for life decisions.[41] But as Anthony Giddens emphasizes, it is the application of surveillance in a complex system defined by industrialization and militarization, along with its coordination by the nation-state, which gives modernity its unique qualities.[42]

The modern state is often described as an institution that monopolizes the legitimate use of violence but, as with the violence inflicted by Susanna Wesley on her children, we should question how legitimate this violence is and what the source of that legitimacy might be.[43] By presuming states' or parents' use of violence to be legitimate from the outset, we deny ourselves the right to withhold or withdraw our consent to their actions, and the right to hold those in charge responsible for any atrocities they might commit.[44] We substitute "the law" for the truth. Elaine Scarry makes this point in her examination of torture and how it is justified by being paired with interrogation.

> Pain and interrogation inevitably occur together in part because the torturer and the prisoner each experience them as opposites. The very question that, within the political pretense, matters so much to the torturer that it occasions his grotesque brutality will matter so little to the prisoner experiencing the brutality that he will give the answer. For the torturers, the sheer and simple fact of human agony is made invisible, and the moral fact of inflicting that agony is made neutral by the feigned urgency and significance of the question.[45]

That there is a question, even though "everyone knows" that a person being tortured will say anything to stop the infliction of pain, removes moral responsibility from the torturer and those in whose name he works. As we have seen with U.S. and British torture of prisoners in Afghanistan, Iraq, and Guantánamo Bay, torturers deny what they are doing by recasting it as necessary for "reasons of state."[46] Similarly, parents who beat their children justify that as necessary to make them obey, for "until a child will obey his parents, he can never be brought to obey God."[47]

Stanley Cohen argues that denial allows adults to observe and even participate in the abuse of children, and allows persons in authority to order, observe, and participate in the abuse of their fellow citizens as well as foreigners.[48] Denial requires knowing and not knowing at the same time.[49] Persons in denial know what is happening and what they are doing, but they distance themselves from responsibility. Some do this through "normalization," a claim that the violence inflicted on others is deserved, either because of the actions of the victim or because that is the routine way that things are done. Others "turn a blind eye," not really failing to see but being indifferent to the harm inflicted on others as long as there is no danger that similar harm will come to themselves. Some select particular atrocities as blameworthy and shut others out completely.

> Why . . . was the My Lai massacre—the deliberate killing, one by one, of unresisting women and children—viewed as more repugnant than achieving the same results by the standard mechanical means of smart bombs dropped invisibly from a distance? Perhaps because knowledge of impersonal mass killing is much like the background knowledge that children are starving while you eat.[50]

Thus we use boundaries to close off the world we "see" from the worlds we turn a blind eye to.

Much of the creation of the social individual is concerned with defining boundaries. Boundaries, which we discuss in more detail in chapter 6, allow us to feel safe and protected by marking places where we can feel secure enough to "be ourselves." Boundaries mark off those whom we can trust from those who are not obligated to be especially kind to us or sympathetic to our interests. They also indicate our "communities of obligation," the people who are obligated to assist us and whom we are obligated to assist, and in what ways that assistance is to occur. "Those X-group members always stick together," some grumble, and yet one of the most important benefits of group membership is being able to call on someone else in your group—your mom, the person who sits across from you in class, a helpful neighbor, or your nation's embassy in a foreign country—to do something that you need to have done.

There is no magic formula for deciding how to navigate the distance between "us" and "them." One way to look at the problem comes from Immanuel Kant. In his essay "Perpetual Peace," Kant talks about obligations to "the stranger," the person who is not a member of our community. Kant says we should show "hospitality" to strangers by being polite and offering what they need to be safe and comfortable while they are with us. But Kant also says that we should not treat strangers as though they were members of our community. He wants both to preserve diversity, which includes the right of strangers to be different and to make claims and confer benefits on other strangers, and also to preserve the integrity of each group. Mutual obligations, the things that members of a group owe to one another, are the key to Kant's distinction between the stranger and the community of obligation. Neither the stranger nor the community is obligated to the other except with regard to being courteous, and neither should be punished for being who or what she or it is.

The problem in today's world is that the stranger lives in constant peril if she cannot mobilize others to come to her aid when she is attacked by her family, her employer, or her state. It is the denial of personhood to "the other": by the parent to the child, by the firm to the worker, by the torturer to the victim, by the state to the citizen, that gives the agent-structure problem its moral urgency. Those who make the rules must take responsibility for them and for their effects, and for this to happen, the rules must apply equally. As Stanley Cohen writes,

> There is only one way to include the distant stranger: to define the threshold of the intolerable as *exactly the same for everybody*. The starting point is not pseudo-universalism or touchy-feely empathy, but a recognition of the radical and irreducible differences that do matter. These differences derive not from my ethnicity, culture, income, world-view, age, sexuality or gender, but from the primeval facts that my children have not and will not die from hunger and *that I have not or will not be forced from my home after watching my wife be hacked to death with a machete*.[51]

The Social Individual and World Politics

The fact that multiple forms of political and other communities exist indicates that people are not alike. There is neither a single way to be human nor a single way to organize human communities.[52] This is a liberating thought. It means that we as human beings build our own institutions and can design them to suit a wide variety of needs and desires. At the same time, we shouldn't feel too liberated. The institutions that support the powerful and the rules they make are insulated from agents who would challenge their legitimacy. Talented young socialists like Rosa Luxembourg had little opportunity to take charge of Germany after World War I given the large, demobilized army dispersed among the population. With plenty of weapons and a desire to deny its responsibility for having lost a long and terrible war, this army lavished structural supports on those who sought to crush leftist dissidents and created structural impediments to those who wanted to control rightist dissidents. Although these structures did not guarantee that Hitler would come to power in Germany, they made it far more likely that social movements would push Germany's postwar government toward an authoritarian state because they created conditions under which right-wing groups were favored. Unusually gifted leaders might have been able to navigate around those biased structures but, sadly, Germany's postwar leaders were mediocre at best and only modestly committed to democratic governance. There was no German George Washington or Carrie Chapman Catt, or Mohandas Gandhi to champion the democratic institution building that could have made a paper constitution into a reality of democratic practice, and no German Alexander Hamilton powerful enough to ensure that the life savings of middle-class Germans would be protected against hyperinflation and their spirits thereby protected against impoverishment and bitterness.

Social fragmentation also discouraged the kind of unified popular uprising in post–World War I Germany that Iranians from across the social and political spectrum successfully mounted against the shah (king) in 1978–1979.[53] We "remember" Iran's struggle as a religious revolution, but the clergy took over only after bitter battles among the many and highly varied people and groups who had joined together to overthrow the shah. Iran's revolution was a model "united front" against an authoritarian regime, and the revolutionaries were so idealistic that many couldn't even imagine that their revolution would be hijacked—until it actually happened. But as in Germany, in Iran there were few legitimate institutions outside the state, and almost no experienced leaders other than among the clergy. A different situation operated in the postrevolutionary United States, where long-standing local governments and revolutionary institutions like the Committees of Correspondence and the Continental Congress generated scores of leaders across social and geographic divisions, and served as foundations for new representative institutions after the British were defeated. Few other former colonies or dependencies were left such an institutional legacy because colonial powers learned from the British experience in the United States that competent local governments could undermine their power. As a result, many subsequent postcolonial states foundered after liberation because the imperial powers had destroyed or so deformed local governing structures that they no longer were able to generate strong leaders or strong institutions that could check their power.

We emphasize the simultaneous need for good leadership and strong social organization. Outcomes that are democratic and fair depend on both. A gifted leader can overcome poor institutions by creating better ones, just as effective social organizations can compensate for poor leaders by training better leaders. But both patterns are rare. It is more common for talented leaders to use their positions as opportunities to do whatever they think is best. (After all, aren't they their nation's "best and brightest"[54] and entitled to do as they like?) Some might use their talents to devise authoritarian structures to make that possible. Social organizations with poor leaders are usually ineffective because poor leaders avoid making tough decisions and cannot earn the respect that would enable them to coordinate and mobilize members to achieve the organization's goals. In consequence, the organization either finds itself unable to attract necessary resources and gradually becomes even less capable, or it is captured by opportunists to serve ends likely to be very different from the ones it started with. An example is contemporary Zimbabwe, where the corrupt and destructive government of Robert Mugabe looted the state and destroyed its economy.

Opportunities come to those who are prepared. Following the democratization of the French army, Napoleon is supposed to have said that every soldier carried a marshal's baton in his backpack. Although it was almost as unlikely then as before that a common soldier from a peasant or working-class background could become a field marshal, this saying encapsulates the concerns that brought us to write this book. People prepare for lives of action by learning how to evaluate situations and mobilize others to help them work for what they desire. The image of the common soldier is useful because it carries with it the image of an army and thus the importance of coordinated collective action. It also reminds us that action can be dangerous. The young soldier promoted on the battlefield stands among the dead and dying and risks the same fate if she fails to use her opportunities wisely to preserve her life while striving to achieve her objectives.

The capacity for human agency is itself the product of prior choices, chance events, and the ability of human beings to see and understand how they can be effective. Embedded in webs of relationships and structures, some that enable action and others that constrain it, each social individual is part of many different groups that intersect and overlap at every human point. This is how social individuals create and occupy the various opportunity structures from which they act. In the chapters that follow, we hope to show you how such social individuals participate, whether they realize it or not, in decisions that affect their own lives and the lives of others in the world.

What Is in the Rest of This Book?

Our intention in this book is to offer a different perspective on and analysis of what we call "global" politics, a politics that leaps over state borders and other boundaries to encompass the world. Global politics presumes a network of communication and human relations that allows people to connect with one another on their own volition, forming myriad communities linked by discourse—a kind of conversation among people who share a common way of knowing. We do this by considering global politics from a perspective far broader than the state and relations among states, or economies and relations among states, corporations, and other "economic" bodies. Indeed, in chapter 2, we begin with people and households, one of the basic building blocks of human social organization, and the first place that people learn to speak to, understand, and live with one another.

2

People, Households, and the World

"Who are you?"
"I'm fine, thanks, who are you?"

—Chico Marx to interlocutor (*Monkey Business*, 1931)

Think about the household in which you grew up. How many people lived in it? Were you "native born" or did you immigrate to the country where you live? What kind of work did household members do? Did anyone work at home? How were you educated? From whom did you learn how to behave "properly"? Are you the "product" of nature or nurture? How do you know who you are? Where did your water and food come from? How did your household articulate with the world? Did you and your household have anything to do with global politics? And what does such knowledge have to do with global politics?

Especially in the United States, we tend to think of ourselves in individual terms. Each of us is an individual different from every other individual, with a fate different from that of every other person. This belief is largely a myth. It is a myth because every human being is born into a social setting, into a network of social relations. Conception is a biological process, of course, as is birth, but both result from relations between human beings, and both are fraught with social and symbolic significance. Even before birth, even before conception, a potential new person is already enmeshed in these social and economic webs. We call this person—and every other person—the *social individual*.

This chapter is about the social individual and what makes her who she is. It is also about the role of the social individual in the household—and in the family—and the place of the family and household in global politics and global political economy. We don't ordinarily think of these two institutions—the household and the family—as playing a significant role in global politics,

17

but, as we shall see, they are foundational in ways that are very important even if they are almost invisible.

We begin by defining what we mean by the terms "liberal individual" and "social individual." We then turn to a discussion of the household and family, and the ways in which they are constituted by society and economy, on the one hand, and the ways in which they contribute to the constitution of society and economy, on the other. In the third part of the chapter, we address the relationship between the social individual and global politics.

Defining the Liberal Individual

In mainstream liberal political theory,[1] there are two primary agents: the individual and the state. Classically and historically, the first theorists of liberalism as we understand it today could not explain how the state came into being. In chapter 1, we saw how Hobbes applied logical reasoning to the problem and proposed a solution. He argued that men (never women) came together out of mutual fear, selected a ruler (sovereign), and gave that man the authority to govern and maintain a social order in which every man could enjoy his possessions without fear that he might lose them to another. It's a nice story, but badly flawed and wholly fictional. Nevertheless, it has influenced many generations of political theorists and scholars of international politics and provides the basis for the theoretical approach usually called "realism." Why has Hobbes been so influential?

To provide a fully developed explanation would require several books and an intimate knowledge of seventeenth-century English history.[2] Hobbes wrote *Leviathan* during his exile in Paris, at a critical juncture in European political and economic development. Feudalism had largely disappeared from England, and capitalism was in its early stages of development. The English civil war between the Puritans and Royalists had ended with the victory of the Puritans, led by Oliver Cromwell, but Hobbes feared a rekindling of the passions and hatreds that had killed a king and torn the country apart. He was determined, moreover, to root the sources of the sovereign's authority in some kind of natural law as a way to limit conflict over the form of England's government. He also wished to illustrate what could happen if men did not willingly yield up their freedom to a sovereign and remained in a "warre of all against all." Whether Hobbes actually believed that men had ever lived in a State of Nature as he had imagined it is less than clear; what is clear is that his notion later came to be applied to relations among states, which were said to exist as isolated individuals in an environment without a world sovereign.[3]

It is curious to note, therefore, that Hobbes had little to say about international relations.[4] In fact, his analysis hardly applied at all to the European world of his time, which was largely constituted through alliances concluded on the basis of royal marriages, and whose territories were, for all practical purposes, the property of kings, queens, princes, popes, and various other landlords. Not until the beginning of the nineteenth century, after the American and French Revolutions, the Napoleonic Wars, and the first stirrings of nationalism and state sovereignty, did interstate relations actually begin to resemble Hobbes's State of Nature.[5] International relations (IR) came into its own as an area of study separate from international law only in the twentieth century.[6] But, whereas international law conceives of states as existing within a society of states, however underdeveloped, in its more vulgar forms IR denies the existence of any sort of interstate society.[7]

IR theories and, to some degree, IR practices, were thus developed around the idea of the state as an isolated agent in a condition of constant danger from other, similar agents, each of which constantly threatened war and death. This condition is called "anarchy." Within states, it is only by virtue of a "social contract"[8] among men and with the sovereign that a similar condition of danger and fear is avoided, according to this line of reasoning (whether correct or not). Therefore, continues the argument, a modern (European) polity or community is constituted by isolated individuals who willingly contract with the state and one another to live peacefully in society. The law—both as it is written and as it is embodied in policemen and judges—ensures that the contract is kept, and it deals harshly with those who violate it. Because there is no social contract among states, and no sovereign to force them to behave in a civil manner, states are like Hobbes's uncivilized men.[9] They must always be on guard against other states.

A little reflection on the story of the State of Nature forces us to ask some difficult questions. After all, how do we know that men ever existed in a State of Nature like the one Hobbes envisioned? And just when did this condition exist? How could men have reproduced? Who would have taken care of babies or provided food? How could language have developed, and why would it, especially if men had nothing to do with one another?[10] For Hobbes, such questions were neither germane nor especially interesting; he was concerned with providing a naturalized narrative that would prevent internecine warfare in England. Theorists of liberalism following Hobbes, however, saw individual consciousness and self-interest as evident characteristics of every person and, consequently, thought they must be the starting point of any theory of politics. Further, to ensure the continuity of this materialist conception of the individual, a disciplinary structure of legal documentation was necessary.

Indeed, the legal construction of the individual is one result of the exercise of the policing power of the state. Western legal and political systems are organized around the notion of the *liberal individual* (historically a male citizen) to whom obligations, rights, duties, and liabilities are made manifest through legal documents whose material existence constitutes a blueprint describing each particular individual. John Locke (like Aristotle) argued that a man could not truly be a reasoning, political being unless he owned Property (normally land).[11] In the modern world, the ownership of property is attested to by legal title. Hence, according to Locke's reasoning, title constitutes the citizen. Or consider the matter of work. In the United States, as in many other countries, to work one must possess and present on demand legal documents that show property rights in the self that we call "citizenship." Without such documents, one is not legally permitted to sell one's labor for wages. It is also understood that without such authorization one cannot collect entitlements from the state, such as unemployment benefits. In fact, without such documents, one does not even *exist* in the eyes of the state.[12]

In order to present herself as a "real" person, the liberal individual must generate the documents that testify to her legal and material existence. To travel outside U.S. territorial borders (an abstract right), a citizen must obtain a passport (material documentation) testifying to that right. To obtain the passport, the prospective traveler must produce a birth certificate (or comparable document) "proving" the occurrence of a specific historical and material event (that she was born in the United States). But any single individual's birth certificate exists only by virtue of the duty of parents to register her birth legally as the issue of two liberal individuals—spaces on the birth certificate name both mother and father. (Until recently, the child without a documented father was regarded as somehow less than fully legitimate.) The parents' registration of the child generates the material document proving the future adult's existence. (A failure to register a birth might result in the paradox that one does not exist legally and has no identity.) Moreover, *this very act of registration by two liberal individuals, an act required by law, produces in the eyes of the law the object whose material existence is undeniably (but not legally) demonstrated by virtue of her having been born.* The puzzling questions become: How is it that such documentation has come not only to signify but also to substitute for the individual's physical existence? And what has been lost or ignored in this construction of a liberal individual?

Defining the Social Individual

What if, contra the theorists, there is no such thing as the "individual" of liberal theory? What if a human being born alone and left in isolation never develops into a person? What if the "individual" is constituted by society rather than society being no more than the simple summation of the actions of many individuals? What if we can't have one without the other(s)?

That is the premise of this chapter. By using the term "social individual," we recognize people as *social beings* born with and socialized into relationships that grow over a lifetime. Each person creates and relies on mutual relations with and responsibilities to other persons. All develop along their own life trajectories with those around them, together manifesting historical, material, and collective properties. What does this mean? The material reality of the social individual is almost never in doubt; the very event of birth is an occasion of pain and joy, to be shared, and often witnessed, by those close to the new infant's parents. Hearing them recount the event, even decades later, who can question its reality? And birth is only the beginning of a lifetime of such social experiences. People are born into their social situations and, for the most part, every social individual develops as a result of interactions with other social individuals, especially those who are older, more authoritative, more powerful, and—usually, but not always—parents (indeed, those who are largely isolated during the first formative months of life don't develop in this way and often never recover).[13]

Our initial concept of ourselves is microsituational, generated by the practices and structures of everyday life. Ultimately, we are who we are not because of our beliefs, actions, and self-ascribed "identities," but by virtue of our being embedded in webs of social relations that form our sense of self and our identities. The fully autonomous and atomized individual, however well documented on paper, is not a human being except in the legal sense; we become and remain human by virtue of our sociality. Whereas the liberal individual is an object produced through rational law—a law that is so deeply naturalized as to be regarded as inviolate and unremarkable—the social individual is constituted by emotional and material relations among people acting as active subjects rather than by contractual relations among people existing as passive objects.

The Household and the Family

Evidently, then, social individuals do not live isolated lives, and very few are able or want to live in anything approaching Hobbes's mythical State of Nature. Even the hermit who has rejected society can be committed to her mission only by virtue of her relationships to the others from whom she separates herself. The social individual is both a political and an economic actor, engaged in production and reproduction of the conditions necessary for both individual survival and social maintenance. Thus, the fundamental unit of social organization is not the social individual; it is the *household*. In ancient Greece, the household was called an *oikos*, a word that is the root of both *economy* and *ecology*. A household has both an economy of production and an ecology of reproduction. As Immanuel Wallerstein and Joan Smith point out, "most individuals live on a daily basis within a 'household' which is what we term the entity responsible for our basic and continuing reproduction needs (food, shelter, clothing)." [14] To this we would add "socialization," which involves internalizing rules, roles, and relationships characteristic of households and cultures. Wallerstein and Smith make a clear distinction between the household and the family: "The former refers to that grouping that assures some level of pooling income and sharing resources over time so as to reproduce the unit," the latter to a group of individuals, generally related by biology, law, norms, or custom. A family may constitute a household, but it is not necessary that a household be constituted by a family. Indeed, a household may include one person or many.

Although the biological family appears to be a "natural" formation, functionally organized to enable survival and nurture children, it is actually a very political institution. Historically, which is to say for as long as we have evidence of what happened in the past, human beings were organized into kin groups, that is, extended families of persons related by blood, and others whom they treated as blood relations.[15] Within these groups, there were normally hierarchies of authority and power based on age, lineage, and gender. The survival of the kin group depended on members fulfilling their roles within that hierarchy. While "nuclear" families of parents and children existed in some societies, they were not in themselves political units. That is, the *social* organization of the kin group did not dictate the *political* organization of the family.[16]

This changed radically with the coming of the modern state. Recall Hobbes's vision of the state as described in chapter 1: the sovereign's body filled with his people. In fact, the sovereign occupied a position in relation to his people akin to that of the husband and father, or patriarch, to his wife, children, and servants. People were the "property" of the sovereign; wife, children, and servants were the property of the husband.[17] ("A man's home is his castle" is not just a saying.) The rule of law exercised by the patriarch over his family was precisely like that exercised by the sovereign over his "family."

The famed "nuclear family" of 1950s America served to exaggerate this parallel, for its isolation from extended kinship groups meant that power was concentrated in the male head, and all of the subordinate roles—servant *and* wife— were loaded onto the woman. The iconic representation of this family form was *Leave It to Beaver* (*LITB*), a sitcom featuring Ward Cleaver, the wise father who worked outside the family domain in some never-revealed occupation; June Cleaver, the servant-wife who wore pearls while she vacuumed the carpets; and

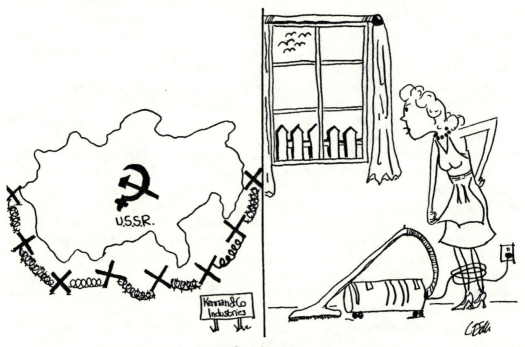

Containment

Wally and Theodore (aka the Beaver), the two male children whom June served and for whom she acted as an intermediary with their father. The family's isolation from the extended kinship group made it difficult for the woman in the family to challenge Ward's authority: June was contained.[18]

The nuclear family also served a broader political purpose in the post–World War II (WWII) United States. There is a parallel between the patriarchal organization of the family, with its internal relations of power and property, and the organization of the American state: pay close attention to the importance of family relations in political campaigns, especially the family of the president, which is held up as a desired model. This is evident in myriad articles about candidates' spouses, their speeches, appearance, education, children, how "strong" they are, how "outspoken," even what they wear on the campaign trail. Consider an example from the 2008 U.S. presidential campaign:

> Michelle Obama, the wife of Senator Barack Obama, discovered this [about speaking out] last week, if not before, when news reports truncated a comment she made about keeping one's house in order. Her comment was quickly interpreted as a swipe at Mrs. Clinton. Fox News' "Fox & Friends," for example, showed a picture of Mrs. Obama juxtaposed against Mrs. Clinton over the caption: "THE CLAWS COME OUT."[19]

Moreover, just as the father was deemed to be the primary authority in the family when political opinions and decisions were involved, so is the president the primary authority acting on behalf of the country (and candidates' management of their children somehow reflects on their potential for managing the country). Another reporter wrote that

> All of the candidates use their children to charm voters. The children are the tiny Ed McMahons of the race, warming up the audience before the main pitch. This summer, Mr. Brownback's children introduced him over the bus public address system at campaign stops. . . . Mr. Thompson, a former Republican senator from Tennessee, made a video for an antiabortion group that began with cameos by his 3-year-old daughter, Hayden, and Samuel, his 9-month-old.[20]

Historically, the father's authority relationship was stabilized by its parallelism to the source of political stability—at least, in theory—allowing family members to be socialized into the essential "rightness" of patriarchal authority structures. The structure of authority was materially reinforced by a system of entitlements that were of particular benefit to nuclear families. In the United States, examples are the home mortgage tax deduction and, more recently, the tax credit for children seventeen or younger. In Kuwait, an example is the family allowance based on the number of dependent children paid to every male head of household.

Thus, while the terms "family" and "household" are often used interchangeably, they are identical only under very specific conditions. More generally, the

internal organization of a household is contingent and depends on the relationships among the household's members. The American concept of the "normal" household constituted by the nuclear family is very much a product of
post–WWII politics and political economy, not a God-given or natural institution. A household of four men or six women is likely to be organized very differently depending on the needs and desires of particular members, and so is
one consisting of an extended, multigenerational group of related individuals.

The key point is that each household should be seen as a unit of social *reproduction.* Its members are engaged in *production* to generate the resources necessary for the household to maintain itself. This is how members supply their basic material needs, as noted above, and also how they reproduce various kinds
of social relations. These social relations don't always involve the rearing of
children. Some households form and remain in existence for decades. Others
form and dissolve after weeks or months. The stability and longevity of any
household depends on the internal and external relations that shape the continuing ability and willingness of its members—who, in some instances, are coerced and compelled—to engage in the productive activities necessary to ensure its reproduction. In every society, there are social customs, norms, and
laws that encourage the establishment and maintenance of some kinds of
households and discourage other kinds. As we saw, the reasons have less to do
with the ability of the household to reproduce itself than with the maintenance
of social discipline and structure in the larger society. Often, there are both political and economic reasons for this favoritism, as when one party or another
seeks laws that forbid some kinds of familial organization and behavior (e.g.,
families with two parents of the same sex) while encouraging others (e.g., a
"teen age" minimum wage). Even so, and in spite of such political efforts,
changes in capitalism, technology, and social relations can make some forms of
household quite dysfunctional, such as when the primary breadwinner loses
her job. If sufficiently widespread, such disruptions may trigger changes in the
dominant form of organization at other levels. An example is an economy that
shifts from industrial production to service provision.[21]

Life, American Style

To illustrate some of these propositions, let us consider examples from the
United States. The *Leave It to Beaver (LITB)* nuclear family became the idealized
form of household in the mid-twentieth century. This was a result of U.S. economic expansion following WWII and elite intentions that consumer demand
continue to support the growth of businesses and the economy.[22] Earlier, household reproduction had relied largely on the direct production of food, clothing,
and other needs within and by household members, supplemented by goods
obtained via weak market relations to producers in the larger economy. Farmers, like peasants, usually controlled the means of production (land), and provided for their own subsistence (food, shelter, water), while depression and war

encouraged families living in towns and cities to cultivate gardens to supplement food supplies. People in similar circumstances living in developing countries practice the same sort of subsistence agriculture today—if they can. One consequence of the spread of industrial agriculture has been to limit the land available for families to produce food for their own use, often forcing them more deeply into the labor market.[23]

After World War II, Americans found themselves with extra money to spend, some for the first time in their lives. Enforced savings, thanks to high-paid employment and rationing during the war, and coupled with various benefits to returning veterans, gave American families ready cash at the same time that U.S. industry had to switch from producing war matériel to making consumer products. Single-family houses in newly constructed suburbs were filled with labor-saving appliances, and their garages held the cars needed to carry men to their jobs in the cities.[24] Smaller households tend to consume more goods per capita relative to large ones and, not surprising, as appliances, automobiles, and other consumer products became cheaper and more widely available, more households acquired them. As suburbanization took hold and spread, the single-family dwelling packed with furniture and appliances came to be seen as the norm. The nuclear family became the economic ideal and, therefore, the social ideal.[25]

Not that this idealized family was a stable structure. As is the case with most social institutions, the *LITB*-style nuclear family was the product of the social relations and economic organization contingent on and unique to a particular era: apparently autonomous, individualized households occupied by different "classes" of family members mirrored blue- and white-collar workers subject to hierarchical authority in factories and offices. The nuclear family depended on parents fulfilling roles specified by that political economy—one high-wage earner bringing home enough to support spouse and children, one home worker who was unpaid but nonetheless worked sixteen hours per day—and children educated and trained for eventual employment in the industrial economy and military forces of the time. There were mothers working outside the home even in the 1950s—especially among minority groups—but it was possible for most "average" families to live on a single income.[26]

Reproduction of the nuclear family as an institution also relied on a U.S. foreign policy that ensured a continual flow of cheap raw materials, such as oil, while U.S. foreign policy was buttressed by the American nuclear family as an exemplar for the rest of the world.[27] Stories of collectivized life in China and distasteful images of families crammed into crowded communal apartments in the Soviet Union loomed in the public mind as part of the narrative of communist rule.[28] Fear that the broadly based material prosperity of that time might be lost to war or depression made family support for containment of both communism abroad and dissent at home seem all the more critical.[29] Inevitably, however, the emerging contradictions of national and international politics and economics also affected the fate of the nuclear family.

As we can see in films from the 1950s such as *Rebel Without a Cause* (Nicholas Ray, 1955), the *LITB*-style nuclear family was (and remains) a structure of discipline and power. Both were exercised not in direct fashion, but through obedience to implicit rules and fear of the chaos that might follow from breaking those rules (and escaping containment). Total discipline is difficult to achieve under any circumstances. Marriage is not a conflict-free institution, and children are both sensitive to and opportunistic toward power struggles between parents. Social and economic pressures also undermine this fragile regime. What if a father loses his job and the mother has to seek outside employment? The need for income produced contradictions that engendered resistance, and adaptations that failed to conform to social ideals.

These effects reverberated from home life to international affairs. During the 1950s, resistance to nuclear-family discipline appeared as the Beat generation, while rock and roll challenged race relations and conventions governing sexuality. Such explicit rejections of America's internal social relations were almost as frightening to those in power as the external threat posed by communism. Elvis Presley was condemned because he moved his hips too much; comic books were censored for corrupting innocent youth. During the 1960s, the Beatles mounted a further challenge, questioning gender categories with their long hair and social assumptions with their subversive lyrics. Politically, the failure of the U.S. war in Vietnam undermined the authority structure of the American state and eroded the broader disciplinary arrangements that fostered obedience. That decade became a time of social experimentation and opposition to authority. Perhaps paradoxically, the relative prosperity of the time also made the nuclear family seem less necessary. The 1960s supported all kinds of innovations in household organization, sexual practices, and gender relations. Divorce became more common, and some couples didn't bother to get married at all.[30]

Not until the 1970s, however, was the economic base of the nuclear family undermined. Rampant inflation resulted from wartime budget deficits and spikes in fuel prices. Nuclear families increasingly found that they could not maintain a middle-class lifestyle, with children, on the income of only one wage earner. Soon the rising costs of owning a house or just running a household pushed and pulled more mothers into the job market. Despite the Civil Rights Act of 1964 and other laws addressing workplace equity, however, employers found they could still pay women less for comparable work (a phenomenon hardly unique to the United States).[31] As a result, households became more complex, and new forms of familial relations began to acquire social legitimacy.

Ultimately, the impact of economic changes in the 1970s, 1980s, and through the 1990s made the "traditional" *LITB* family almost impossible to maintain. Today, not only is the two-income family virtually the norm—and required to maintain anything like a "middle-class" lifestyle, but the constant restructuring of economic units—factories, offices, corporations—and relations of production within those units also means that the average wage earner will have to change jobs often and relocate several times during her working life.[32] This phenomenon is not unique to developed countries, either. For example, the vast increase in wealth as a result of the oil boom of the 1970s generated floods of migration throughout the Middle East and other parts of the world, as wage earners in poor countries left their homes for employment opportunities in the booming economies of oil-exporting countries. Periods of global economic growth over the past twenty years have had similar effects everywhere.[33] The movement of Spanish-speaking immigrants toward and across the U.S.-Mexican border, from areas of intense poverty to regions where jobs, however poorly paid, are available, has been similarly motivated. None of this is conducive to the stability of nuclear, or other forms, of families.

The decline of the nuclear family has not been regarded as a positive development by those with a vested interest in maintaining the old power relations, such as men in working-class families and privileged social groups and elites.[34] Their oppositional response to such changes was fierce, and it continues today. After all, if the maintenance of social discipline and authority relations throughout society is dependent on their reproduction within the household, and if a particular family form, such as the *LITB* model, helps to maintain a broad acceptance of elite dominance, then the collapse of that family form threatens elite domination and its ability to accomplish its political and economic objectives.

During the 1970s, the political emergence of the Religious Right, in coalition with neoconservatives, was motivated in no small part by this perceived threat.[35] These forces worked hard to establish a link in the popular mind between discipline in the family and broader social stability and American power. Their appeal to working-class men, who otherwise might have been tempted to get involved in progressive labor politics, was based on triggering men's fears of losing power in the family.[36] The irony in this strategy was, perhaps, that it is the very economic institution to which the neoconservatives are most loyal—the laissez-faire market—that is most erosive of the nuclear family they profess to revere.

But note carefully: the household continues to be essential to the global economy. Indeed, work within the household—especially work by women—constitutes a major subsidy to that economy. It is said that working women hold two jobs (often called "the double shift") because, even in households with two or more wage earners, important tasks that *someone* must do, such as caring for children and elderly parents, cooking, and cleaning, are mostly performed by women.[37] Except where servants are involved, no wages are paid for this work, and no records are kept of its value. Nonetheless, by some estimates, the value of "housework," which is not measured or recorded, is equal to one-third or more ($25 trillion) of the world's estimated economic output ($60 trillion to $75 trillion).[38] This unpaid labor is a subsidy to the global economy, an "articulation" made possible because capitalism is a mode of production uniquely able to extract value generated by other modes of production, such as kin-based housework.[39]

One such pattern of extraction can be seen in the common practice among well-off families, in which women who work in high-paying professional jobs rely on low-paid (and sometimes undocumented) immigrants to watch their children and clean their houses.[40] While their high wages make important contributions to family income, many professional women are paid less than men in comparable positions. Hence, employers impose the costs of housework on their employees even as they benefit from the lower wages they pay women.[41] If the holders of capital had to pay the full value of housework, many now-profitable industries would lose money. Recognition of the role of this now-unrecognized labor in industrial and postindustrial economies also brings into question the bias in capitalist systems favoring capital over labor through such practices as taxing capital gains at lower rates than wages and salaries, and limiting family leaves for births, illness, and deaths.[42] It is hardly surprising, therefore, that proposals to pay women for housework are usually dismissed as ridiculous, impractical—and far too expensive.[43]

Despite all attempts to hide this fact, the household is integral to the global economy. It subsidizes capitalism. It educates and socializes children to become the workers of the future. It is a locus of consumption that produces the next generation of consumers. It is the most important institution responsible for the reproduction of social, political, and economic relations. As such, it ensures that the global political economy will continue. At the same time, however, the excessive exploitation of the household as a means to extract value from its members degrades it by transforming its internal "moral economy"—the household as a "community of obligation" and mutual support—into just another unit bound together by contracts among its members.

The Social Individual and Global Politics

We all are members of a household, whether it consists of one person or one hundred. But how do we, as social individuals, fit into global politics and the world economy? Or, rather, what is our unmediated relationship to both? Few of us are directly involved in the business of running countries, attending international conferences, managing transnational corporations, or fighting in foreign wars. Even fewer hold positions in which they can directly influence the course of present-day politics and economics. But we are all "global"; as geographer John Agnew has noted, "[People] are *located* according to the demands of a spatially extensive division of labour, the global system of material production and distribution, and variable patterns of political authority and control,"[44] a claim that suggests we don't have a great deal of choice in the matter. Nonetheless, without the active involvement of billions of people, our political and economic systems could not function. So, how much autonomy (or agency) *do* we have?

Considering the liberal individual as conventionally conceived, very little. Inasmuch as the global economy is organized according to certain rules and practices that must be followed if one is to have any hope of success, economic autonomy extends only as far as being able to choose a field of specialization (with the hope that it will not become obsolete), a job (with the hope that some are available), and a place to live (assuming that housing is affordable somewhere close enough to that job to make commuting possible).[45] The so-called private sphere—household, family, religion, civic associations, personal consumption—is generally treated as though it were untouched by such external constraints. This heroic assumption relies on the belief that the individual is fully autonomous in the private sphere. But because activities in the private sphere are essential to social reproduction, which, in turn, is necessary to system stability, autonomy begins to look pretty limited here as well. The state is not shy about regulating such personal and private relations and practices in order to ensure production and reproduction.

To put this point another way, the much-vaunted freedom of the individual in a liberal society is a highly structured freedom. It is not that people do things because they are directly threatened or coerced (although this does happen). Rather, it is that available choices are limited in particular ways; in many realms, alternatives are practically nonexistent. This can be illustrated by a story from Harvard economist Amartya Sen. In *Development as Freedom*, he tells about the Muslim man who continued to work in a Hindu neighborhood during the worst of the intercommunal violence accompanying the partition of India in 1948.[46] One day, the violence was particularly intense, but he went to work as usual because it was the only way he could earn money to feed his family. As a result, he was killed in the fighting. We could say that he should have stayed at home where he was safe, but it is easy to see why that was not among his choices. If he had not gone to work, his family would have gone hungry. For most of us, options are neither so stark nor so extreme, but consider carefully the kinds of freedoms you possess and how they might limit or discipline the choices you do make.

The social individual does not necessarily possess greater autonomy—after all, to paraphrase Karl Marx, we live in the world as it is given to us.[47] Much of that world today is a liberal one, emphasizing individualism, self-interest, wealth, and freedom to consume—but the social individual lives in a somewhat different cognitive and physical world, motivated by ideas, emotions, and conditions that bind people to one another.[48] Thus, an awareness of the social and emotional relations that constitute the social individual can help us to understand her relationship not only to household, family, and community but also to global politics and the world economy. This awareness also opens up new possibilities for action and autonomy. Autonomy and freedom should not be understood merely as choices to be exercised in the private sphere but rather as the kind of politics that becomes possible through social power exercised by tightly knit groups. The suppression of such social bonds and alternative social relations, and the relegation of relations between human beings to the "private sphere," are constitutive of the liberal individual, global politics, and capitalism. Just as the household is central to the global order, so too is the social individual, albeit one who is "liberally educated" about the necessity of separating the realm of emotion from the realm of interests.[49]

What, exactly, do we mean by this jargon? As we saw earlier, no one is born into the world as an isolated individual; yet, in a society marked by capitalism and markets, the newborn is almost immediately inducted into a matrix of commodity relations (think about how relentlessly maternity and baby accessories are advertised and sold). In the ideology of capitalism, the baby's primal desire for self-satisfaction at the mother's breast is transformed into the psychological basis for liberal self-interest: *I want!* But a child's basic wants and needs conflict with the demands of the modern political economy. Because it costs money to maintain a household, parents must work, making time a scarce resource. Things are offered to replace the absent parent but, because things cannot satisfy a child's emotional needs, ever new and ever more things are demanded to compensate. Those parents who do not, or cannot, fulfill their child's desires through the accumulation of things—even as they are bombarded with constant messages to buy more stuff—feel they are shortchanging their child. They feel like inadequate parents.

Paradoxically, as the child matures, the deferral of gratification from shared time with beloved adults is treated as a critical moral lesson—gratification deferred is all the sweeter and builds self-control—while, at the same time, a constant barrage of advertising encourages the immediate fulfillment of desires for commodity goods and services. The message is that property relations to things that can be acquired only through purchase in the market are an adequate substitute for emotional relations among people. Even emotional relations within the private sphere can be commodified and sold; there is much money to be made from love, hate, envy, desire, and passion, and the consumer is led to believe that she can and should experience these emotions via the market: "Diamonds are forever"; nannies are a necessity; trophy wives are evidence of a man's power.[50]

Marx wrote about the alienation of the worker from the products of her work; today, we face alienation of emotion through the endless consumption of goods. Is such alienation a necessary and inevitable corollary to the global expansion of capitalism? Is it necessary to democracy? Benjamin Barber argues that it is not, that consumerism actually destroys democracy by persuading us that shopping malls are the moral equivalent of public space.[51] This is why Bill McKibben urges people to reconstruct their neighborhoods and towns along the relational lines that were common in subsistence societies based on limited exchange, where production and reproduction are closely tied to trust and mutual obligation. Survival is still paramount but it goes beyond self-interest to the survival and prosperity of the community. Otherwise, neither the group nor the individual can survive. Members of such communities rarely think in terms of "interests," Rousseau's parable of the hunter[52] notwithstanding. Rather, one does what one does because that is what one is relied upon to do.

In a society with more extensive exchange (say, early capitalism), markets foster a division of labor and provide things not easily produced within the household.[53] Nonetheless, trust and obligation within the household remain important. Adam Smith wrote about the importance of long-term, face-to-face relationships between consumers and the providers of goods and services as a way to keep transactions honest on both sides.[54] As capitalism developed in Eu rope during the eighteenth and nineteenth centuries and whole populations were detached from their accustomed localities,[55] much of this emotion was transformed into nationalism and patriotism. The individual was still obligated to family, but his [*sic!*] love was for his country. Both production and consumption were directed, in part, toward national ends.

Only in very rich societies motivated by consumption rather than production as traditionally understood, do such emotions and bonds of trust and obligation become a drag on the economy.[56] National(ist) capitalism is limited by the size of a country's domestic markets,[57] and even a consumption-driven society cannot accommodate an infinite number of refrigerators and cars. But manufactured emotional need that seeks satiation through the market is virtually a bottomless pit, especially if one's sense of self-worth comes to depend on one's level of accumulation and consumption rather than on the strength of one's relations with others.[58] Under these conditions, human attachment is relegated to the private sphere where it becomes an appendage of, and even an obstacle to, the main business of life: consumption.

Consider one example already alluded to: diamonds. Diamonds—jewels, more generally—have long been associated with wealth and royalty, and their relative scarcity made them very costly. Moreover, they had no practical use. They were signifiers of "conspicuous consumption" associated with high status.[59] The demand for them *as jewelry* was limited, too, although diamonds were sometimes acquired as an easily portable store of wealth. It was not until diamond mining became a large-scale endeavor, following the discovery of enormously productive mines in southern Africa, that the supply of diamonds began to exceed demand by a significant margin. As we are told repeatedly, in an oversupplied market the price of a commodity will fall, perhaps even below the cost of production. Some sellers will go bust, supplies will decrease, and a new equilibrium will be found.

But there is an alternative. Sellers can restrict supply. Fearful of a diamond glut, corporations involved in the diamond trade set up an international cartel—the Central Selling Organization (CSO), based in London and often associated with the De Beers family—to limit supply and keep prices high. Every year the CSO would decide how many diamonds would be put on the market and at what price.[60] But cartels are difficult to sustain. When the market price of a commodity is maintained by restricting supply, there is an incentive for others outside the cartel to search for new sources to sell it at a lower price.[61] This is what has happened with diamonds. The CSO managed to bring some, but not all, producers into the association, and so the uncontrolled product puts downward pressure on prices.[62]

There is, of course, another way to keep prices high: stimulate demand. This can be done by advertising diamond jewelry not only as beautiful and status oriented (and a store of wealth) but also as a signifier of *heterosexual* love. No matter that diamonds are simply lumps of carbon, possessing little intrinsic value or utility;[63] artificially maintained scarcity and high retail prices become the basis for consuming, as a constant and relentless advertising campaign transforms diamonds from sparkly rocks into an emotionally charged symbol portrayed as unique to a particular relationship. Indeed, women are all but warned by these advertisements that only through diamonds can love be truly consummated, implying that their absence from a relationship indicates an absence of "real" love. In this way, an emotion that is social, if not instinctual, and found in every human society, is commodified, sold, and even managed.

The reader should not think that she is the victim of conspiratorial forces beyond her control. These forces can be resisted, although peer pressure to conform and the potentially high costs of nonconformity are powerful incentives to go with the flow. Moreover, trying to resist as a liberal individual by limiting one's own consumption while everyone else does not, makes the effort even more difficult and also unlikely to be effective.[64] For the social individual, the task is somewhat easier, because emotions such as love and respect for others can become the basis for group resistance to commercial entreaties and a highly valued substitute for commodity fetishism, as exemplified in the film *Sex and the City*.

We are all familiar with, and may even belong to, groups held together by a sense of shared emotion (gangs, punks, Goths, bird watchers, bikers, drag racers, even students and professors). Such groups are sometimes regarded as threats to the society around them, not because they have the power to destroy that society, but because their members do not seem to be motivated by the interests and desires of the larger society in which they live (even—perhaps especially—bird watchers, who are entirely too concerned with environmental protection).[65] Consequently, they cannot be controlled (or their ideas and activities normalized) by society's disciplinary apparatus. It is ironic to note that many of these alienated groups are nevertheless deeply engaged in consumption, and that their affectations often become commodified and quite profitable—think of tattoos, big pants, and gangsta rap (and, for those bird watchers, fancy binoculars and ecotourism trips to Costa Rica).[66]

Social groups organized into activist modalities or "social movements," motivated by political objectives and bound together by emotional commitments, are a primary locus of resistance to the unreasonable demands of politics and markets in the world today.[67] Social movements should be distinguished from interest groups whose members are bound by class, or other groups characterized by conferring or withholding privilege. Such associations lack emotional commonality; their members are motivated primarily by what they can gain for themselves from their membership.[68] Social movements vary greatly in terms of size, formality, focus, spatial reach, and influence, but they all share one characteristic: their basis is the *social* individual who has decided to make commitments on the basis of affection rather than reason or self-interest (the latter two are not excluded, but they are not primary). And while emotions are easy to manipulate, they are difficult to organize and control. For those in positions of power and authority whose primary desire is to maintain their control of the status quo, the social individual presents a constant challenge.

Conclusion

In this chapter, we have attempted to situate people, households, and families in a global context. Most mainstream writers on global politics and economics focus primarily on the effects of structures and processes on individuals depicted as "free to choose" within the narrow confines of liberal democracy and markets.[69] Many critical observers point out that the disciplinary structures of globalized capitalism leave little wiggle room for autonomous action and, short of a major crisis, it is not clear how opposition can ever become general and motivate social change (but see chapter 10). We acknowledge the limits to freedom implicit in contemporary liberal societies and the low probability of a mass breakout from this "iron cage."[70] But we are very far from thinking that all is lost.

We observed that one key element in the creation of the liberal individual is replacing emotional ties with reason, self-interest, and commodified relationships among people. This move is essential to liberal society as it makes political organization more difficult and subjects it to high transaction costs because people must seek out others who share their particular interests.[71] A focus on interests also is essential to capitalism, because it allows value to be measured in terms of money rather than meaning or a person's commitments or obligations. In this scheme of things, the household—idealized in the form of the *LITB* nuclear family—becomes an economic unit responsible for reproduction and subsidizing capital, and the microlevel model of a social and global order characterized by atomization and hierarchy. As we have shown, however, households need not be nuclear families. Indeed, changes in familial and household organization required by globalization often undermine the preferred social order of governing elites.

We also argued that emotional relations can be commodified, as in the equation of love with diamonds, but this is another move that is neither necessary nor inevitable. It arises from systemic pressures for growth and accumulation, which encourage putting a monetary value on *everything*. By cultivating consumption without constraints, capitalism fosters the development of interest-based associations and discourages collective action by social movements acting according to ideas or affections. There are strong disincentives to the creation of solidary groups based on affective bonds and commitments; Mancur Olsen argues that they do not serve individual self-interest and, therefore, ought not to exist.[72] Solidary groups nevertheless remain a powerful basis for a politics of resistance and social change. What this means is that we must bring emotions into the open and treat them not as dangers to the political order but as essential to political freedom.

In the next chapter, we examine the role of power in contemporary global politics and political economy. Power plays a central role in structuring the patterns discussed above, while it also offers extensive and creative means for resisting and changing them. Most international relations texts look at power in terms of force and influence, but here we take a much more nuanced view. Power serves to structure institutions, but it is not a substance that can be commodified and measured. Rather, it is a relational concept. Emotion is as much a form of power as suppression of emotion in the pursuit of rationality and self-interest. As a form of power, emotion can be abused and manipulated, but the same is true of interest-based forms of power. The task is not to fall into that trap—easier said, perhaps, than done.

3

People and Power

One dark night, a passer-by offered to help an obviously inebriated man who was searching for something under a lamppost. "What are we looking for?" asked the volunteer helper. "My keys," answered the drunk. "Did you lose them right here?" asked the helper. "No," answered the drunk. "I lost them down the street." "Then why are we looking here?" asked the bewildered helper. "Because the light is better," the drunk replied.

—Anonymous

Defining Power

Political scientists frequently look for power under the intellectual equivalent of lampposts. What they see is stuff: territory, populations, soldiers, guns, bombs, tanks, money, food supplies, oil—all of which are visible and, more important, can be measured and counted. Soldiers, weapons, and the money to buy more of them match up with what political scientists like Kenneth Waltz and Robert Dahl define as power: "the ability of A to make B do what A wants when B would prefer to do something else."[1] Those who look at power more comprehensively see this as only one of its aspects, calling it "power-over," or power based on the threat or use of force.[2] This is the image of power in war: power is what A can bring to bear to destroy B. It equates power with violence.

Others disagree. Philosopher Hannah Arendt argues that violence erases power.[3] If you have to maim or kill people to make them do what you want, they probably won't be able to do it very well after the dust settles. We remember an American soldier during the Vietnam War who explained why his company had obliterated a village by saying, "We had to destroy the village in order to save it." But what was saved? Violence eliminated the village and its people. Nothing material survived. Arendt would take that a step further to point out that power itself wasn't saved: the destruction of the village revealed that the Americans, despite all their bombs, guns, and chemical weapons, could not change the perceptions and choices of large numbers of Vietnamese people. Similar stories could be told about the application of force against villages in Afghanistan, Iraq, Georgia, and Pakistan.

Arendt's definition of power is very different from the power-over model. She thought of power as what political scientists like Robin Teske call "power with," the ability to join forces to achieve a common goal.[4] Arendt imagined power as generated by people acting together in what she called "spaces of appearance," public spaces in which "I appear to others as others appear to me, where men exist not merely like other living or inanimate things but make their appearance explicitly."[5] In such locations—examples include legislatures, boardrooms, clubhouses, and family councils held around the dining room table—power is not an attribute of individuals. As we suggested in chapter 2, it grows out of an ensemble of persons who empower one another when they decide to act.

Theoretically, people are more or less equal in spaces of appearance, but some are more capable than others of shaping the final outcome of deliberations. So stuff is important in this understanding of power, too. Everyone knows who has land, money, networks, servants, and clients, and they probably have pretty good estimates of how much. But stuff is not everything. The space of appearance and the power it generates also depend on the personal qualities of the participants. How tall are they? (Powerful leaders from King David to George Washington were admired for their imposing size as well as for their military reputations.) How smart are they? (Alcibiades and Bill Clinton impressed their friends with their intelligence, even though they also irritated their friends by their sexual behavior.) How well do they speak in public? (Hitler and Franklin Roosevelt could mesmerize multitudes.) How well did their earlier ideas turn out? (This is how James Madison got to be president despite being short and a terrible speaker.) Do they have friends who stick up for them to create a "bandwagon" in favor of their proposals, or do they have enemies who make their ideas look ridiculous, reducing confidence in them and drawing their followers away? This is how a lot of people did or did not get to be leaders.

It's clear that power is not merely how much stuff anyone has but what happens when people with different collections of stuff get together and decide what to do with it all—the quintessential image of collective decision making, from town meetings to caucuses to international organizations. This image describes both how citizens agree to levy taxes on themselves or choose candidates to run for office, and how groups like the Concert of Europe decided to intervene anywhere that revolution threatened early nineteenth-century Europe, or how the late twentieth-century United Nations decided to eradicate smallpox or liberate Kuwait. It also explains why, although all participants have equal access, their voices do not carry equal weight.

Formal and Informal Rules

Our discussion of the social individual as an agent embedded in structures leads to another way to think of power: as the authority of agents to create and enforce rules. Following the Italian political theorist Antonio Gramsci, we call this kind of power "hegemony."[6] Rules alone are frail supports for desired action: laws against stealing and murder have not made these crimes obsolete. But this doesn't mean that *enforcement* is nothing more than *force*. Think of the laws that define property rights or rules that spell out appropriate behavior in a household or a classroom. Theoretically, parents and teachers can hit kids (or one another) to force them to obey the rules, but, as Arendt observed, such behavior is a better indicator of power failure than of power. Most of the time, most people obey rules voluntarily. They believe in them; they believe in the people and institutions that made them; and they care what other people think. It's only when law givers and rule enforcers demonstrate that they are not worthy of respect and trust that they have to resort to force to get people to do what they want (and even then, often fail).

We don't want such "consent of the governed" to seem too benign, however. Consent rests on a large measure of invisible—structural—coercion. Think of the Fourteenth Amendment to the U.S. Constitution. It was ratified after the Civil War to give former male slaves the same protections, privileges, and immunities that white male citizens enjoyed (the Fourteenth Amendment is the first place in the Constitution where the sex of citizens is mentioned). But in exchange for resolving the disputed 1876 election in their favor, the mostly northern Republicans agreed to end Reconstruction, along with federal enforcement of the post–Civil War constitutional amendments and the laws to implement them, if the mostly southern Democrats would support the loser of the popular vote, Republican Rutherford B. Hayes. The special commission set up to decide the election agreed to this "compromise of 1877," after which Reconstruction began to be dismantled.[7]

The Supreme Court was an important tool for liquidating Reconstruction. Its representative on the election commission, associate justice Joseph Bradley, was also chair of the commission. Bradley wrote a series of opinions that first asserted and then drew back from an energetic interpretation of the three Civil War amendments setting out the rights of former slaves. Among these were the "due process" and "equal protection" rights embedded in the Fourteenth Amendment. The court redefined these rights in steps that withdrew them from former slaves and applied them to corporations.[8] Soon corporations were defined as "persons" under the law and were accorded the same rights as white men. Not incidentally, both were treated equally under the law, even though corporations are larger, richer, and more powerful than persons. Americans' respect for the Supreme Court and the law still supports this rule change. Today, despite massive corporate scandals that lost thousands of workers their jobs and pensions, millions of stockholders billions of dollars of their investments, and hundreds of thousands of homeowners their houses through mortgage foreclosures, most Americans continue to think it would be unfair to deny corporations "their" constitutional rights.

A corporation can claim all the rights accorded to persons under the Fourteenth Amendment, including privacy rights. This let tobacco companies argue that "proprietary" information, such as evidence that nicotine is addictive, should be protected from disclosure.[9] Pharmaceutical corporations do the same, even when their drugs can be shown to be ineffective or to have nasty side effects. Corporate rights are enforced by the U.S. government unless a plaintiff can "show cause" why they should not be. Even when we get down to life-or-death issues, corporations almost always have the advantage over people.[10]

Sovereign Rights and Wrongs

A similar attachment to rules made it hard for nations to come together to stop genocide in Bosnia in 1991, Rwanda in 1994, and Darfur and the Congo today. As we discuss in chapter 5, the usual understanding of the rules governing behavior among states emphasizes sovereignty over human rights. Sovereignty is defined in part as a government's right to do as it likes on its home territory. The United Nations, whose members all are states, thought it would be unfair, even illegal, to intervene against the governments of Yugoslavia[11] and Rwanda—even to save the hundreds of thousands of citizens they could see agents of these governments displacing, imprisoning, raping, and murdering every night on their TV screens. After these horrible crimes were halted, war-crimes tribunals were set up to punish the ethnic cleansers and *genocidaires*, but critics called these tribunals "victors' courts," and claimed that they violated state sovereignty. The United States used similar arguments in 2001 to take back its signature on the 1998 Rome Treaty setting up a permanent International Criminal Court (ICC), even though the United States had led those demanding that war-crimes tribunals be established after the genocides in Bosnia and Rwanda—and also in Germany and Japan after World War II.[12]

As these inconsistencies demonstrate, views of sovereignty often depend on whether the critic is among potential interveners or those likely to be intervened against.[13] Many who accused the United Nations of callousness for ignoring the genocides in Bosnia and Rwanda while Security Council members demanded that the sovereignty of these states be upheld, had earlier accused the Security Council of interfering where it wasn't wanted when it voted to intervene after Kuwait had been invaded by Iraq. To great human rights activists like Václav Havel, a new era appeared to have dawned with the 1999 NATO intervention in Kosovo. Havel believed that Kosovo signaled that human rights are beginning to supersede the values protecting nation-states.[14] U.S. policy since then makes this assessment appear optimistic. Halfhearted peacekeeping in Afghanistan following the 2001 defeat of the Taliban, a preemptive war against Iraq grounded in a controversial new strategic doctrine that contradicts provisions of the United Nations Charter, and the systematic use of torture against U.S. prisoners taken in the "war" against terrorism,[15] put hopes for the rapid evolution of an international rule of law in doubt.

Yet there are plenty of advocates opposing "negative" sovereignty—the idea that states can do what they like inside their own borders—and from a variety of perspectives. Hegemonic ideologies and their associated institutions are not invincible. One example comes from U.S. domestic politics: the twentieth-century restoration of civil rights to the descendants of former U.S. slaves in spite of the nineteenth-century reconstruction of the Fourteenth Amendment to award these rights to corporations instead of citizens. There are international examples, too. War-crimes tribunals in Arusha and the Hague, the prosecution of war criminals like Chile's former president Augusto Pinochet, and (back to the United States) the twenty-first-century trials of old Ku Klux Klanners in Birmingham, Alabama, also reflect a growing conviction that the rule of law should operate everywhere, including against criminals authorized and pro-tected by their governments.[16] These courts pursued, tried, and even convicted some of these murderers who long had believed that they would suffer no ad-verse consequences for their actions.[17] Because their governments did not stop them at the time—as we noted, some of the killers were actually working for their government—they had come to believe that no one would ever be able to bring them to justice. But minds change and, with them, the consensus on rules and how they should be enforced.

Powerful Ideas

Making counterhegemonic ideas concrete is how people fight what Antonio Gramsci calls a "war of position."[18] Alternative ideas and different ways of doing things undermine the normalization of hegemonic values and practices by creating what East European dissidents during the cold war called "the parallel polis." *Polis* is the Greek word for a political community. Anticom-munists in Eastern Europe wanted to change their political communities, but they were barred even from talking or writing about reform. Step by step, dis-sidents created shadow political communities, parallel universes/*poleis* that embodied their desires for democratic life.[19] They wrote, read, talked about, and did things by their own rules, just as if their actions were legal even when they were not.

At first the dissidents faced constant danger, and their parallel universes had to be kept secret. In Czechoslovakia, scores of dissident women used manual typewriters and carbon paper to type essays, poetry, and stories and distribute this forbidden samizdat literature through underground networks.

Mothers put whole typed books in their babies' carriages when they went out for walks, and delivered them to the next person in the chain of transmission by switching grocery bags in food markets. "I left my place in the line apparently with the same bag, but the contents were different," reports Czech dissident Jiřina Siklová about her life at that time. "Instead of cauliflower there were correspondence texts—and once a carrot which I did not intend to buy."[20] When their activities were revealed, dissidents were arrested and tried. Many were imprisoned under conditions that shortened or ended their lives. But their persistence and the justice of their cause attracted new adherents from among their fellow citizens in the other—the "real"—polis, and hollowed out those authoritarian regimes.

Dissident movements also had help from abroad. Samizdat writings left Czechoslovakia via a courier service manned by foreign embassy personnel, and were taken where they could be published. Dissidents used special signals to let couriers know when a package of writings was ready to go. One was a small piece of a postage stamp pasted on the window of a Prague bar called the Blue Duck. When he saw the stamp fragment on the window, a young Swedish diplomat knew to walk by a certain apartment house and pick up an envelope of samizdat that he would take to be sent abroad by diplomatic pouch. Other external assistance came from new nongovernmental organizations (NGOs) like Helsinki Watch and Amnesty International, which, with Human Rights Watch, shine an international spotlight on the brutal actions of "real" governments. These actions kept the imprisonment of dissidents on the political agenda of Western states and prevented these men and women from being "disappeared" as so many dissidents were in Latin America during the same period. In Czechoslovakia, prominent dissidents eventually signed a manifesto, Charta 77, that declared openly the existence of their parallel polis. The government gradually crumbled, giving us a new concept, "velvet revolution"—the nonviolent collapse of an old regime when the people withdraw their belief in the authority of the state and stop complying with its strictures.

Remaking Reality—Power "as-if"

Powerful ideas and actions are not the sole property of democrats. Authoritarians are equally energetic in thinking about how their ideas and political preferences can be embedded in structures that will live beyond their time in power. One example that has cascaded into other states is the pursuit of the idea of the "unitary executive" in the United States.[21] Under this theory, presidential power is seen as absolute. In the words of President Richard Nixon, "When the President does it, that means it is not illegal."[22] This view was contested by Congress, which was in the process of crafting a resolution of impeachment when Nixon resigned rather than risk having to answer for the many crimes he had committed in office. Since then, advocates of the unitary executive have sought to limit congressional oversight and, when they were in power, to pack the federal courts with judges they thought were sympathetic to their perspective. The most egregious assertion of presidential supremacy is the practice of issuing "signing statements," presidential directives published in *The Federal Register* that list the parts of a law that the president has just signed that he will not enforce. Signing statements were infrequent before the presidency of George W. Bush, who has issued well over seven hundred, more than all previous presidents combined.[23]

We might ask why presidents have been able to free themselves from congressional checks and balances in this way. Signing statements began innocuously enough, as indications from presidents that parts of laws written by Congress might be unconstitutional. When they were not challenged, the courts began to consult them for guidance in deciding cases, just as courts traditionally have used the records of congressional debates to determine "legislative intent." Without ever being confronted directly in a legal case, signing statements have acquired a patina of legitimacy. Even presidents who were not particularly authoritarian were quite happy to use the powers arrogated by their less democratic predecessors when it was convenient for their own purposes.[24] Precedents of questionable legality become accepted ways of doing things if they are not contested by alert citizens.[25]

Similarly, democratic precedents can be established through what political scientist Diane Duffy calls the exercise of "power-as-if," the creation of "facts on the ground" that the state finds difficult to ignore—or destroy. In postcommunist Poland, women's human rights, along with social services for families, were severely curtailed by the regime. In response, a handful of Polish women's organizations set out to create structural power for themselves by providing social services such as family planning, job training, and health-care education, which the government no longer offers. Members of these feminist NGOs also participate in meetings of international organizations with counterparts from other countries, reporting on domestic conditions facing women and families and suggesting how poorly performing countries could improve.[26]

The Polish government would like to eliminate these feminist groups, both to avoid their demands and to be spared the embarrassment they cause by reporting accurately how badly the government is treating Poland's most vulnerable citizens. Yet too many families and local governments depend on the services the women's groups provide, and too many potential investors and foreign aid donors would be angry to see them suppressed. A similar situation constrains the ability of the government of Egypt or the Palestine National Authority to close down completely those Islamist organizations that provide schools, feeding programs, jobs, and disaster relief to populations the governments cannot serve because of their own limited resources. These groups can claim some protection under Islamic law, which requires devout Muslims to contribute 2 percent of their wealth every year to charity. By acting as if they have power, well-organized and dedicated groups can acquire power. In a relatively open society, groups like Hezbollah in Lebanon can engage in legitimate political competition. In harshly repressive societies like Egypt's, the moderate

Muslim Brotherhood suffers from recurrent police actions and its representatives often are banned from the ballot, not only in state elections but also in student government elections at public universities.[27]

"Facts on the ground" are favored tools of repressive governments. After Israel almost accidentally captured territory populated by Palestinian Arabs during the Six-Day War in 1967,[28] its leaders decided that, in spite of UN resolutions demanding an end to the occupation, Israel would try to keep the territory. "Settlements" of Jews were planted throughout the Occupied Territories, creating armed enclaves of Israeli-held Palestinian land. The settlements had two major structural effects. First, they dispersed Israelis throughout Palestinian territory, justifying military intervention by the state to protect them and preventing Palestinians from moving freely from place to place within the Occupied Territories. The West Bank was carved up into islands of Palestinians, an archipelago separated by highways connecting the settlements to one another and to Israel proper. Palestinians can travel from one island to another or to and from Gaza only by passing through checkpoints protected behind concrete barriers and barbed wire. There they are stopped and searched before being allowed to cross Israeli-held roads and lands. Second, the settlements gave more than four hundred thousand Israeli settlers a vested interest in keeping "their" land part of Israel rather than returning it as part of a peace settlement, while the settlement program convinced many Palestinians that they could never have their own state without destroying Israel first.[29] This is a clear example of how structures constrain agency and influence thinking.

Structures of Power in the International System

Each definition of power we've discussed is built on a set of ideas about the world and how it works. Each definition also is partial: the world is a complicated place, and power exists and operates differently in different places and at different times. Power-over operates where force is the primary authority. Some political scientists see the whole nation-states "system" as that kind of world. If all states have negative sovereignty—if there is no external authority to make them "behave"—then they exist in a state of "anarchy" or "no government," a "self-help" universe where might makes right. Stuff is integral to this vision of power because it is what you need to crush your opponents as you try to make them do what you want. From this description, we can classify systemic theories or ideologies like "realism" as power-over models.

Balancing Acts

Anarchy is the image of the world that people have in mind when they talk about "the balance of power." It reflects the assumption that because no one is in charge of the world, every state must defend itself from attacks by other states. Some versions of this model assume that the most powerful states are self-conscious actors, interested not only in preserving themselves but also in upholding "the system," the current division of power and rules of the game that put them in charge. This view adds to power-over an element of power-with, and is reflected in the proposition that, for most states, the primary objective of international relations is to avoid war. In this variation of the balance-of-power model, states use diplomacy, alliances, payoffs, persuasion, and appeasement to keep the peace. In contrast, the standard version of balance-of-power theory assumes that no state is committed to the system; each is committed only to itself. Here, the threat of war is the ultimate power-over mechanism that keeps the balance among the dominant states, and war itself the creator of a new balance that the losers are cautioned not to challenge.[30]

Why does a power system become unbalanced? Political scientist Robert Gilpin offers a simple and elegant answer: because things change, and, when they do, they don't change evenly.[31] Powerful states inevitably become weaker—maybe their militaries become fat and self-satisfied and their governments become so complacent that they allow their clients to loot the state and steal its capacity to provide and protect. Perhaps citizens refuse to pay taxes or rebel against how the state spends the money it takes from them. But even if a powerful state maintains huge armies and weapons stockpiles, says Gilpin, other states can still beat it. They can invent better weapons systems; their economies can expand because they innovate more successfully than their rivals in commercial markets; they can acquire colonies that produce valuable materials and offer strategic bases. Any state that convinces its people that it is under threat can devote a disproportionately large share of national production and wealth to increase its power as an international competitor. This is another way in which the military is used as a tool of the government, and not just when it becomes the only way to protect populations because all else has failed.

When we look at real cases, however, it becomes clear why balance-of-power theory by itself is not a useful predictor of the future. Perhaps the best example is the mental image analysts have when they think of "classical" balance-of-power theory, the states system envisioned as operating from about 1820 to the start of World War I (WWI) in 1914. Prior to WWI, Britain, the dominant world power in a multipolar international system (one with more than two major powers) throughout much of the nineteenth century, suffered a relative decline in its economy. New competitors, especially the United States and Germany, developed more efficient industries that undermined British products worldwide, including in its home markets. Although the British navy remained the most powerful in the world, Britain had not fielded a large army, even during wartime, since the seventeenth century. Meanwhile, the armies of Germany, France, and Russia were large and growing, while Japan surprised all the European powers by demonstrating excellent war-fighting ability against Russia in 1905 (Japan won that war).

This brings us to another problem with applying balance-of-power theory: depending on which version you use, you get different answers. Historian Niall

Ferguson, basing his analysis on the self-conscious "balancer" model (power-over plus power-with), argues that Britain should have allied with Germany, which became the continent's weaker power/coalition following the alliance between France and Russia. Had Britain done so, Ferguson suggests, there would not have been a world war. There might not have been a war at all if Germany had not seen itself as being in a "now or never" position, fearing it would have to face all three of the strongest powers in Europe on the battlefield in the not-too-distant future. Even if Germany had continued to feel surrounded by what former U.S. diplomat George Kennan called the "fateful alliance" between France and Russia, Ferguson asserts, a war between the alliance and Germany (with or without its allies, Austria and the Ottoman Empire) would have been limited if Britain had delayed sending its Expeditionary Force (BEF) until the defeat of France was imminent.[32]

Most historians take the opposite view, arguing that whatever Britain did or did not do, war in Europe was inevitable. A combination of the militarization of German politics and the way the German military prosecuted the war from the beginning—invading neutral Belgium and purposely targeting civilians along with cultural monuments from cathedrals to the library at Louvain—would have persuaded Britain to send the BEF regardless and to the same effect.[33] Even this explanation, with its stress on the actions of the weak Austrian-Hungarian empire, contradicts balance-of-power expectations. Indeed, the persistence of Germany's convictions that it would win were so strong (until the summer of 1918) that it made plans for the territories it would claim in Europe and Africa and argued about what it would demand as reparations from its defeated foes. This shows how little the balance of power matters in real life, as well.

In response to difficulties in applying standard balance-of-power models to real situations, some theorists have built models based on the "mitigation" of anarchy, strategies for modifying anarchy to give agents more scope. These models add more dimensions to balance-of-power theory. They also offer better explanations of events and, analysts hope, better predictions of what might happen in the future. Most still focus on the nation-state, but many include nonstates as agents in their descriptions of the international system and how it works.

Political scientist Hedley Bull looks at what he calls "international society," mostly heads of state and their relationships with one another.[34] U.S. presidents are notoriously eager to establish face-to-face relationships with other heads of state. Recall how George W. Bush said that he had looked into the eyes of Vladimir Putin and saw his soul. Being able to call another leader on the telephone in the middle of an emergency, as George H. W. Bush did following the Iraqi invasion of Kuwait in August 1990, gives a president a rapid reading on how potential allies might respond to the range of actions he is considering.[35] Yet the real society composed by the European ruling class—like "dear Nicky" and "dear Willie," the emperors of Russia and Germany respectively—was powerless to stop a war pressed by the arrogant generals who controlled the armies and weapons of Austria-Hungary and Germany.[36]

The history of secret agreements offers equally ambiguous evidence about how much or little international society mitigates anarchy. In Niall Ferguson's story about Sir Edward Grey, we recall that Edward Asquith, the prime minister Grey served, wished to pursue a neutral policy vis-à-vis a Europe that seemed to be moving toward war. Yet Grey made informal, secret agreements with representatives of France and behaved rudely to German representatives, rejecting their overtures toward closer relations with Britain at a time when diplomacy might have blocked the ambitions of the German army.[37] Whether Britain would or would not have sent the BEF to Europe in response to German aggression in the absence of Grey's ventures into international society, France had been led to expect British assistance. A counterexample is Richard Nixon's secret agreement with Nguyen Van Thieu, president of South Vietnam, in November 1972, saying that he would send military assistance to keep North Vietnam from taking over Saigon. In the end, his successor, Gerald Ford, could not fulfill this pledge because Congress forbade any assistance to be sent to the South Vietnamese government after the peace treaty formally ending the war went into effect in 1973.[38] An even more complex piece of evidence that "international society" is ambiguous at best in mitigating anarchy is the policy of Ronald Reagan. Under a similar congressional ban on aid to the contras (a U.S.-supported paramilitary force based in El Salvador trying to bring down the government of Nicaragua), President Reagan solicited funds for the contras from private donors. When these sources proved to be insufficient, he sent a delegation to Iran to sell arms in exchange for money for the contras and Iran's assistance in freeing U.S. hostages held by Hezbollah in Lebanon.[39] These transactions were only marginally useful in freeing U.S. hostages, and did nothing to mitigate the conflict in Central America or the ongoing war between Iran and Iraq.

Market Power

Other theories describing the mitigation of anarchy focus on economic actors. Prior to WWI, British writer Norman Angell wrote a popular book, *The Great Illusion,* suggesting that British investments throughout Europe might inhibit a major war because British policy makers would not want these investments to go up in smoke. A counterpoint to that book was published by another Englishman, Edward Hallett Carr, shortly before WWII. Angell's analysis was ambiguous regarding whether he thought foreign investments actually could keep the peace. Carr's book, *The Twenty Years' Crisis*, was openly critical, even scornful, of the idea that economic interdependence was a deterrent to war. It dripped with sarcasm at what the author described as the utopian notion that markets promote a harmony of interests either among nations or among social classes within a nation.[40]

Carr identifies fundamental contradictions in the widely held assumption that markets keep the peace. Looking closely at market theory and basic balance-of-power theory, we can see that they are based on similar assumptions about motivations and behavior. Each assumes the existence of a universe of unitary competitive actors all trying to maximize their individual power and wealth. If basic (power-over) balance-of-power theory predicts that war, as the regulator of the balance among states, will be frequent, why should we assume that market competition, especially nationally based market competition, won't also regulate the balance through war? This, after all, is the message of most standard theories of industrial organization. Like nations seeking hegemony, firms seek monopoly. In a competitive market, big firms lower prices below costs, hoping to drive out smaller companies, which they can either take over or simply allow to die. Economist Joseph Schumpeter called this "creative gales of destruction," but the targets of hostile takeovers are less cheery about this process; they call it "cut-throat competition."[41]

The "harmony of interests" theory thus has the same flaw as balance-of-power theory. Both rely on events and behaviors coming from outside the model. Will firms avoid cutthroat competition by sharing markets? According to the theory, we shouldn't count on it. Will policy makers avoid balance-of-power wars through accommodation—a strategy that was called "appeasement" before it failed so spectacularly with Hitler in 1938?[42] These are "empirical" questions that can be answered only by looking at actual cases and figuring out why things happened as they did.

Complex Models

Other theories incorporate elements of hegemony and power-as-if. As we noted earlier, a hegemonic system is directed by a single major-power authority that makes the rules for the world as a whole. In his analysis of the role of power in war and change, Gilpin devotes substantial attention to just that kind of authority. He calls it "prestige" and defines it as a reputation for being powerful that a state earns by winning the last big war. The winner gets to make the rules for the postwar international system and thereby alters international structures to reinforce its own dominance. The winner persuades other states to go along because it has so much prestige that it rarely has to use direct force to get its own way.

The coalition that won WWI consisted of Britain, the United States, and France.[43] The Versailles Treaty ending the war established a new international system based on German disarmament, arms limitations on all the major powers, a revived gold standard, and a relatively open trade regime. It also imposed reparations on Germany for having started the war, requiring the country to pay damages. However, these arrangements were not successfully enforced. The United States refused to ratify the treaty, and the other winners were too weak to make it stick on their own. Meanwhile, Germany's rule-imposed disadvantages allowed its government to justify avoiding, evading, and actually defying those rules, even in the minds of non-Germans. German policy makers were able to persuade a prominent British economist, John Maynard Keynes, that the reparations were unjust; Keynes quickly became one of the most influential advocates of reducing them.[44] Just as the perception that a system of rules is legitimate makes enforcement easier, Germany's successful campaign to make the post-WWI rules look unfair undermined the victors' ability to extract reparations, enforce free-trade relations in Eastern Europe (where Germany had an advantage that free trade would have eliminated), and stop Germany from rearming openly after the world economy had collapsed into depression.

Individual countries were not solely responsible for the management of the post-WWI system. At the urging of U.S. president Woodrow Wilson, the major powers set up the League of Nations, an international organization that they hoped would prevent another disruption of the balance of power like the one they thought had led to "the Great War." The League of Nations was charged with applying a special understanding of balance-of-power theory, "collective security," to future occasions of conflict. Under collective security, if any country or alliance were to attack another, all the rest would band together against the aggressive power(s) and defend the one that was attacked. In practice, the League of Nations did not work any better than the anti-Germany measures (disarmament and reparations). Having spurned the Versailles Treaty, the United States also refused to join the League of Nations. The powers that did join refused to defend nations and territories that were attacked by a fellow European state. The pattern was set when Italy invaded Ethiopia in 1935. The League of Nations expressed disapproval but did not unite against Italy and force it to withdraw, as the U.S.-led "coalition" governments did when they united against Iraq after it invaded Kuwait in 1990.

Indeed, with the exception of Germany and Italy, throughout the 1930s the governments of Europe were reluctant to go to war for any reason and, even in Germany and Italy, a majority of their populations were equally war-weary.[45] Having sustained huge losses in the trench warfare of 1914 to 1918, they had little stomach for another exhausting conflict. When a general war in Europe became unavoidable in 1939, the countries opposing the European Axis powers (Germany and Italy—Japan was the third member of that axis) were unprepared to fight, and nearly all were rapidly defeated and occupied. Only two major European powers escaped German conquest. The Soviet Union, which started out as a signatory to a treaty with Germany that theoretically bound each partner to nonaggression toward the other, survived Hitler's unexpected 1941 invasion, just as Russia had survived Napoleon's invasion more than a hundred years earlier. The Soviet Union was so huge that the Germans were forced to extend their logistical lines too far to fight effectively, although they did manage to kill more than twenty million Soviet citizens during nearly four years of fighting.

Britain survived the bitter air battles of 1940 and after with the help of massive arms transfers from the United States through a program called Lend-Lease—the product of an agreement between U.S. president Franklin Delano Roosevelt and the British prime minister, Winston Churchill. But even after Germany declared war on the United States following Japan's attack on Pearl Harbor in December 1941, the prospects for an Allied victory were far from assured; this changed only with the successful June 1944 invasion of occupied France. Yet the Allied victory in WWII was tainted. The carnage of the war was unprecedented, with both sides targeting civilians, cities, and cultural monuments with nearly every weapon at their disposal, ending in the dropping of two atomic bombs on Japanese cities. Despite his argument that World War II was not merely an extension of World War I, historian Alan Kramer sees the brutality of military strategy and tactics in that war as logical extensions of "the dynamic of destruction" that had begun in a small way in eastern Europe during the Balkan wars (1912–1913) and bloomed so malignantly in WWI.[46]

The colossal failure of both parts of the post-WWI settlement forced the winners of WWII to think more broadly as they organized the postwar international system. Once again, a relatively open trading regime was a prime objective. Another was a "League of Nations II," the United Nations (UN), based on new rules governing intervention against aggression. These rules provided that if all five of the designated major-power victors agreed, and were able to persuade a few additional countries to support them, they could intervene legally, even with military force, against another sovereign state. This is the UN Security Council system, of which these winners —the United States, Britain, the Soviet Union (now once again Russia), China (now with "communist" China replacing Taiwan), and France—are the only permanent members. There are ten rotating members of the Security Council, but only the "big five" have veto power. If just one of them disagrees with a measure, it is defeated.

How that post-WWII system worked in practice was altered abruptly as relations between the two biggest winners, the United States and the Soviet Union, deteriorated after 1945. Each gathered allies in Europe and elsewhere. Each "superpower" created and sustained its own "international" economy, one capitalist and one centrally planned, and knitted its alliance together by forging strategic and economic dependencies with its allies. Each bloc operated as if the other were totally evil in every way and, in the process, each superpower exacted a high price from its allies and its own population in lives, money, and environmental degradation (most of the nuclear waste that infects the world today came not from power plants but from U.S. and Soviet weapons production and deployment). Today, pieces of nuclear and other so-called weapons of mass destruction that the superpowers developed for use against each other are traded and deployed in the murky world of thieves, defectors, and terrorist organizations.[47] Current concerns about chemical weapons, "dirty bombs," anthrax, smallpox, and other deadly infectious diseases arise directly from the detritus of those cold war arms races, while continued production of nuclear weapons has created a huge stockpile of "depleted uranium" now used by the United States and Britain to make "conventional" bombs. Scientists and legal specialists are only beginning to understand the devastating impact the use of these weapons has had on the health of populations and soldiers.[48]

The end of the cold war between the United States and the Soviet Union, and the subsequent collapse of the Soviet Union itself, left the United States as the only major world power. It has the world's largest military, deadliest weapons, and one of the largest economies. The more than $600 billion (and still rising) the United States spends each year on "defense" is equal to what the entire rest of the world spends for the same purpose.[49] The United States presides over a system of international rules that tilt the playing field in its favor, including revamped post-WWII economic rules that operate through institutions like the International Monetary Fund (IMF) and the World Bank to give the United States disproportionate influence over international finance.[50] The United States is a global hegemon.

Before Americans celebrate, however, we should recall that hegemony has three parts, not only lots of military stuff and economic rules that favor the dominant actor but also the agreement of others that the dominant actor has the right to rule. Hegemonic theory and practice include elements of power-with, making hegemony dependent on consent. With regard to the current U.S. hegemony, this consent is under stress. Consent has been damaged by U.S. decisions to act unilaterally having failed to persuade others that its decisions were being taken in pursuit of good for all. Many disapprove of the U.S. refusal to honor the Kyoto Agreement to fight global warming; at the December 2007 UN Conference on Climate Change held in Bali, Indonesia, U.S. pronouncements were booed from the floor.[51] President Bush's "unsigning" of the Rome Treaty, which established a permanent international criminal court to try persons charged with war crimes and genocide, and his rejection of treaties designed to organize and implement inspection systems for biological weapons, limit international trade in small arms, and ban land mines, convince allies and adversaries alike that the United States has no respect for international law and no desire to treat other nations with respect. His decision to put weapons into space led Bush to abrogate (back out of) another treaty, the Anti-Ballistic Missile Treaty with the old Soviet Union; this is perhaps the most potentially damaging of the U.S. decisions listed here, for both the global environment and world peace. Since then, Russia has suspended all participation in a treaty limiting conventional forces in Europe, a decision triggered by NATO expansion and U.S. plans to deploy elements of a new anti-ballistic missile system in Eastern Europe.[52] Meanwhile, the war in Iraq, undertaken in spite of UN objections, alienated most U.S. allies and provided a platform in the heart of the Middle East for anti-American terrorists. Such decisions parallel how previous hegemonic powers undermined their authority by estranging allies and degrading significant parts of the physical, economic, and political environment in which they and everyone else must live.

Who Has International Power?

From under the lamppost, power seems to be concentrated in the hands of large states, firms, and other corporate bodies such as churches and international organizations that control vast physical and monetary resources. How this power can be wielded in quiet ways was revealed during the Soviet war in Afghanistan, in which U.S. economic sanctions were critical to the withdrawal of Soviet forces, over the objections of the nation's military leaders, by a new general secretary whose program for reforming his country depended on a strong economy.[53] Yet, as Anthony Giddens points out, no one is without power. Even the weakest person can resist a tyrant, if only by refusing to obey. Other examples of "weapons of the weak" are described by journalist James William Gibson in a book about the American war in Vietnam. Gibson writes of the ingenuity of impoverished Vietnamese who mounted ambushes against U.S. troops, threw stones into the rotors of helicopters to make them crash, and tunneled under military installations to spy on, steal from, and destroy U.S. forces.[54] In the Vietnam War, the country that looked the most powerful under the lamppost was defeated by a smaller and militarily weaker adversary. In the wars in Iraq and Afghanistan, insurgents cobble together roadside bombs and set them off with mobile telephones. Yet there is never a guarantee that agents will be able to alter structures in the ways they envision. The defeat of the United States in Vietnam did not change overall U.S. power and prestige or diminish bipolarity in the international system. In contrast, the defeat of the Soviet Union in Afghanistan did hasten the Soviet collapse, changing the structure of the international system from bipolarity to hegemony.

States are not alone in their ability to exercise political power. Individuals also can check tyrants. Mohandas Gandhi led hundreds of thousands of Indians in nonviolent protests against British colonialism and mobilized them to refuse to buy British products. Similar movements, such as the civil rights movement in the United States and the antiapartheid movement in South Africa, also used nonviolent protest successfully against armed and dangerous adversaries. When opponents used violence against these movements, such as by assassinating Martin Luther King Jr. and Malcolm X in the United States, and murdering Steven Biko in a South African prison, it focused popular opinion domestically and internationally against these racist governments and their policies, and hastened the pace of progressive social change.

A single individual who acts successfully against a powerful adversary seldom acts alone. The example that proves the rule is the young man who stood in front of the tanks rolling into Tiananmen Square in June 1989. The tanks all stopped. Not one ran him down. But this was not a single-handed victory. This very brave man stood in front of cameras as well as tanks; whatever happened to him would have been witnessed by millions worldwide, and the officers directing the tanks knew this. Similarly, Gandhi was effective not only because he persuaded Indians to give money to the nationalist cause, boycott British textiles in his famous buy-Indian campaigns, and engage in selective marches and strikes, but also because he took his stand in front of the world press at a time when the British government was reluctant to be seen treating a tiny, elderly, unarmed man with brutality. Still, the main requirement for success in a long campaign is effective organization. Although Martin Luther King Jr. stood at the head of the civil rights parade, Rosa Parks, Ralph Abernathy, Fred Shuttlesworth, Jesse Jackson, Ella Baker, Andrew Young, and many others marched alongside him and kept the movement going. Tens of thousands followed their leadership. Luckily for some of them, cameras often were there too.[55]

Publicity is crucial for the survival of dissident movements. Charta 77 could keep hope alive in the knowledge that news of dissidents was getting out, leading to pressure on governments that served to keep those arrested alive.[56] Dissidents who fight without the benefit of publicity must either pare their activities down to ambiguous actions that offer little excuse for repression,[57] or take to the hills prepared for a long struggle against an oppressive state. Thus, effective power lies in the capacity of the social individual to mobilize and participate in a social network, appeal to "public opinion"—an even larger social network—and ensure transparency—public visibility—for her work. An individual can resist by herself but individual resistance (and the resister) can be easily ignored, ridiculed, marginalized, and even eliminated. Publicity is a crucial tool of effective action. It was not until the domestic political hegemony established by Stalin had been eroded, first by Nikita Khrushchev's 1956 revelations of his myriad abuses and then by the success of Mikhail Gorbachev in opening the entire Soviet system to public scrutiny and criticism, that the government of the Soviet Union could be brought down. When its population stopped believing in the Soviet Union, it disappeared.

Collective action also is crucial to protect individual dissidents. The limits of small-scale action were evident in Nazi Germany. Resistance to the Nazis was minimal and dispersed throughout a population that either feared retaliation or actually agreed with the Nazi program.[58] Small dissident groups like the White Rose, a student movement, were discovered and liquidated. Dissent within the Nazi Party was not tolerated. The "Night of the Long Knives" in 1934 saw the murder of as many as four hundred followers of Ernst Roehm, himself a Nazi but one who was too independent and too popular for Hitler's taste. Stalin also was a ruthless pursuer of dissidents, arresting some twenty million Russians he feared had or might turn against him during his long reign of terror in the Soviet Union. Some were executed, but most were taken to prison camps in remote areas of the country where they were worked to death instead. Evgenia Ginzburg's memoirs recount not merely the loss of her freedom but also the loss of her family and her health after more than twenty years in the gulag.[59] Internationally known writer-dissidents like Anna Akhmatova, Boris Pasternak, and Andrei Sakharov were variously imprisoned, denied work, and, in Akhmatova's case, hounded to death by the Soviet secret police.

Totalitarian systems are built on force, on structural power—jobs, schools, and housing are all controlled by the state so that dissenters risk not only themselves but also their children and parents if they continue their activities. These systems also depend on a hegemonic ideology that puts the state and its leader at the pinnacle of power. Ginzburg relates an experience at a movie theater several months after her release from prison. The film included a sequence showing part of a Roman Catholic mass. Two women were sitting behind her. "Fancy that," said one. "[T]hey used to worship God! Just as if he were Stalin!"[60]

Power and Democracy

The Afghanistan war, spreading dissidence, and the subsequent collapse of the Soviet Union show the difficulty of maintaining a power-over system in the modern world. As Charles Tilly notes, the evolution of Europe during the modern period is a story about the gradual imposition of accountability on governments. Kings became "constitutional monarchs," encouraged by various means to share power with parliaments, courts, and voters.[61] As we shall see in chapter 5, even the most powerful kings had to accommodate at least some of the demands and needs of the economic actors who produced the wealth on which their rule depended. Towns and cities within their territories, along with firms and banks whose activities transcended boundaries between town and country and between realms, negotiated concessions from kings in return for gains from trade and loans to support the kings' military adventures.

The power of moral authority and its capacity to mobilize public opinion was foreshadowed in the challenges by popes, bishops, and priests to the authority of "temporal" rulers. Even after the Protestant Reformation had erased the empire of the Catholic Church from vast swaths of Europe, clergy and "holy" persons still managed to criticize kings and mobilize people to oppose them. Indeed, scholars like Michael Walzer see the Reformation not only as initiating structural changes in relations among European states but also as the primary generator of social movements, the long-term effects of which included the democratization of much of Protestant and Catholic Europe.[62]

The democratic-peace thesis we discussed in chapter 1 makes a special claim for democracy as a structural deterrent to war, but, despite its attractiveness in theory, it doesn't hold up in practice. Democracy is a political system that incorporates the wishes of masses of people in decisions affecting the whole community and has many positive (and some negative) effects on conditions other than war and peace among states. Democracy is empowering. Going back to Hannah Arendt's vision of power as something that happens when people get together to accomplish a common goal, democracy enables groups, communities, and states to mobilize active participation in the formation of and consent to a chosen policy. As Jane Mansbridge observes in the case of town meetings in Vermont, however, this does not mean that everyone is treated equally or that every alternative is debated—democracy is a process, not an outcome.[63]

Democracy also supports entitlements to a nation's collectively produced goods and services. All states take money from people to finance the government. Democracies force governments to haggle with citizens over how much will be taken and what will be given back: good governance, social services, protection from harm (this is the theory, at any rate). Above all, democracies entitle their populations to demand a high standard of conduct and performance, whether they actually do so or not. Their entitlement is guaranteed by regular and peaceful opportunities to dismiss leaders and replace them with others who might do a better job.

Like most of the other terms we use in this book, "democracy" means different things to different people. In the United States today, we believe that we live in a democracy, but the Greek citizens of fifth-century Athens would disagree. They (like Rousseau) would see our representative institutions as making us "democrats for a day" every few years when elections are held and, the rest of the time, mere subjects of the state. Eighteenth-century supporters of the U.S. Articles of Confederation (which preceded the Constitution) would agree with the Athenians. They saw the consolidated state outlined in the Constitution as the end of democracy, which they understood as empowering citizens to govern their own communities.

Kevin Phillips, the man who designed the "southern strategy" used by Richard Nixon's successful 1968 presidential campaign, also has serious doubts about the nature of democracy in the United States, where, he argues, the very rich and their busy interest groups crowd the rest of us out of politics.[64] There is much truth in all of these critiques. But let us end this section with an acknowledgment of the power of citizens in a democracy as compared to the lack of power among subjects of an autocratic regime—including one that holds regular elections. This affirmation comes from Hamid Zangeneh, an Iranian who now lives in the United States:

> [U]nelected American Lobbies (hired guns) who try and do influence American policies [are] quite different from the unelected political organs of Iran who . . . control and make policies without much accountability. If the

"But I'm the Leviathan"

American citizenry do find a policy, regardless of how it became law, repugnant and repulsive enough, they have a choice. They [can] go to the
polls and remove the politicians who were responsible. In Iran, there is no
such mechanism, with real enforcement. No one could seriously suggest
that the unelected organs of the political system in Iran are accountable to
the people [or that they] are in any "peaceful" danger. As a matter of fact,
the paralysis of the Iranian political system at this time is due to this very
fact, that there is no accountability other than through violence.[65]

Zangeneh argues that power remains with the people as long as they can act
politically without violence.

International Power Today

Today we say we are living in an age of "globalization." Nations and cultures
engage in increasing contact with one another and are transformed by it. As we
describe in chapter 9, globalization also causes power to shift from states and
their agents to individuals and their agents. Nonstate agents include NGOs, religious organizations, social movements, international media, labor unions and
professional organizations, firms and banks, and the myriad other organizations and methods used by social individuals to create "societies" that tran-
scend differences between people and borders between states. Some believe
that globalization is creating a new international "civil society"; others believe
there is no such thing; still others believe that civil society always existed and
always has been international. Among the last, Alex Colás argues that the international system itself is a product of civil society, however much twentieth-
century IR theorists chose to ignore civil society to concentrate on states.[66]

The civil society debate, which we examine more closely in chapter 5, is
part of the struggle to assert international power, whether as power-over by
those trying to limit civil society and bring it under control or through power-
with by activists pursuing strategies to achieve human rights and a better life
for themselves and others. In this struggle, however, we should not assume
that states are negative forces in civil society any more than we should assume
that nonstate organizations and institutions are good or that attractive elements of cultures of protest cannot be used by entrepreneurial victimizers of
citizens and states alike.[67] All actors embody positive and negative qualities.
Churches send missionaries overseas to overturn the values, beliefs, and practices of other cultures, however generous the motives of individual missionaries might or might not be. International firms bring new investment and job
opportunities, and they also bring pollution, corruption, and ways of changing values, beliefs, and practices different from the missionaries' but no less
destructive. At the most extreme, activist organizations like the Red Army
Faction, al-Qaeda, and the Irish Republican Army all are or were parts of international civil society—and at the same time they are terrorist groups. As
Colás makes clear, states also are part of international society. Hannah

Arendt's observations about the incompatibility of violence and power offer a better way to distinguish between mostly constructive and mostly destructive international actors and organizations: death and empowerment are mutually exclusive states of being; an organization that is powerful is the one that can accomplish its goals without force.

International civil society offers an even better model for examining power than one that includes only nation-states, but it is far more complicated to specify and use. As we discussed in chapter 1, states are imagined as functionally similar and juridically equal even though they have widely different resource endowments, capacities, and internal organizations. The nation-state system is conceived as fundamentally egalitarian, in part because of the theoretical homogeneity of the states that are its constituent parts. In contrast, international civil society has many different parts that no one even pretends are homogeneous. Its units are not only different but also overlap in a way that nation-states, imagined as territorially distinct agents, cannot. Consequently, imagining power in civil society is a lot more complicated than imagining it in an "international system." But it is not impossible. We'll start by looking at the economy, another theoretically egalitarian system that, in practice, inscribes hierarchies within, between, and across nation-states.

4

People and Economy

If the U.S. market slows down or goes into a recession, the rest of the world is going to feel the pinch, too. . . . A sneeze in the United States can cause a flu around the rest of the globe.

—Mellody Hobson, president of Ariel
Capital Management, January 22, 2008[1]

The structure of our economy is sound.

—U.S. Treasury Secretary Henry Paulson speaking
to the U.S. Chamber of Commerce, January 22, 2008[2]

You only find out who is swimming naked when the tide goes out.

—Warren Buffett, letter to Berkshire Hathaway
shareholders, February 28, 2002[3]

In chapter 2, we examined how people form households, and how households constitute both economy and politics. Chapter 3 discussed the relationship between people, power, and global politics, and how particular forms of power locate people in the global political economy (we return to this topic in chapter 9). This chapter addresses how the global economic system—that is, globalized capitalism—functions to *produce* human needs and desires, and to *reproduce* individuals and societies. The framework we present here strongly emphasizes three points. First, we distinguish *political economy*—the arrangement and operation of the economy—from *moral economy*—the social relations and obligations among people—as an important, but rarely discussed consideration. Second, we note that in a market-based or "marketized" society—a capitalist one—the individual is "free to choose" among a great number of goods and services for sale. This tends to create the illusion that a similar freedom extends to all aspects of life, including politics. Third, the very real limits to choice in a capitalist society are obscured by the plethora of available goods and services, but these limits serve to maintain a high degree of political and social order.

The paradox here is that "freedom" has the effect observed by John Agnew (cited on this point in chapter 2) that "[people] are *located* according to the demands of a spatially extensive division of labour, the global system of material production and distribution, and variable patterns of political authority and control."[4] We propose that the "freedom to decide" is more important, and meaningful, than the "freedom to choose" but, if we are to decide, we'd better understand choice. Providing the necessary tools for analysis of such freedoms is one of the central goals of this chapter.

We begin the chapter with a review of the dual roles of the individual in production and reproduction. Recall that *production* refers to making goods and providing services essential to individual and social survival. *Reproduction* refers not only to producing the next generation of producers but also to those activities and institutional practices that give meaning to action, reinforce collective belief systems, and maintain the social order.[5] The distinction between production and reproduction is not so clear as it might at first appear. Many people make their living through cultural activities—writing, reporting, teaching, singing, dancing, acting—that reproduce meanings, beliefs, and social order. At the same time, funding of cultural activities by wealthy individuals, organizations, and the state enables people to pursue cultural projects rather than doing other things to make a living.

Next, we examine the concept and reality of *modes of production* and all that entails. This term offers a useful way to conceptualize contrasting forms of economic organization and their social impacts. We need to ask three questions about any mode of production: First, how is it organized and by whom? Second, who operates it and who provides the labor? Third, who benefits from it and in what ways? In the third part of this chapter, we turn to a discussion of the contemporary global economy and its capitalist arrangements, which leads to the phenomenon called *globalization*. We have already used the last term in earlier chapters (and will return to it in detail in chapter 9). Here we define it more carefully, all the while recognizing that it is a highly contested concept, as well as examine the relationship between the individual and the global economy. This section elaborates the distinction and relationship between the "freedom to decide" and "the freedom to choose," and, in particular, the ways in which the latter tends to obscure and even eliminate the politics implicit in the "freedom to decide." In effect, and drawing on the conceptions of power discussed in chapter 3, we argue that highly liberalized capitalist markets—an outgrowth of an ideology commonly known as "neoliberalism"—eliminate politics from much of everyday life, replacing it with consumer choice as the most significant act in social life.

The fourth and final part of this chapter asks whether there are different—and better—ways to understand and act in terms of "people and economy." To put this in terms of contemporary events and movements, does putting people back into economics require that globalization be stopped in its tracks, as protesters in Seattle, Washington, Geneva, Goteborg, and Genoa tried to do? Are there other ways of humanizing capitalism to make it more just, fairer, and more transparent? Can we facilitate the freedom to decide rather than merely providing growing supplies of goods and services to some, while leaving shelves empty for others?

People, Production, and Reproduction

Production is at the heart of every social system and of the institutions and political arrangements that enable that system to "operate" in a particular way. The word *production* literally means the making of things, but it is useful to recall a second meaning: the creation and display of an intentionally designed arrangement of people, objects, and actions, as in plays, exhibits, and even theme parks. For our initial purposes, the first meaning is more relevant: the manufacture and delivery of basic necessities, such as food, water, and clothing, and various nonessential goods, such as pots, pans, cars, books, and so on. While we tend to take for granted the ready availability of these things (for a price), several *billion* of the world's people struggle every day, and not always successfully, to meet these needs.[6] At the same time, the second meaning is also important: we all fill roles in society and our daily public performances in those roles produce and reproduce the social arrangements that make possible the provision of necessities and luxuries (consider, for example, how the role of "professor-producer" requires a certain type of performance in delivering services to "student-consumers").

Without the ability to produce or acquire basic necessities, the individual and household can neither survive nor reproduce, in either biological or social terms. What might be less obvious is that a bare minimum of necessities can support only the bare minimum of social development. When all of a household's time and energy must be devoted to procuring food, water, and shelter, reproduction means little more than maintaining the labor supply through giving birth to children, socializing them to the arrangements that allocate responsibilities among household members, and sending them out to work. Many people in many parts of the world still live at this very basic level.[7]

In accounting for the origins of society and state, Thomas Hobbes was not troubled by this dilemma. Even though people in the State of Nature did not live in the Garden of Eden, food and shelter were available as needed, and no one possessed much more than anyone else (this was also John Locke's view of the State of Nature). It was only when someone did manage to accumulate an excess of goods that she had reason to worry that others might become jealous and resort to theft—or even murder—to take what she had. Theft is not, of course, a legitimate means of acquiring basic necessities (although it might sometimes be a necessary means). In this light, Hobbes suggested that the state should be seen not only as the provider of security and law to men but also the guarantor and protector of the property and property rights of those who have, against those who do not.

Anthropologists speculate that it was the ability to accumulate food and goods beyond subsistence levels, accompanied by a "division of labor" that allocated tasks among members of a social order and supported increasingly complex social arrangements that enabled the development of cities and states.[8] The emergence of professional classes (kings, priests, managers) not engaged directly in production became possible only when surplus food could be expropriated for the needs of these ruling classes. Although such expropriation might be done with force, it could not be done willy-nilly—that would be theft. It had to be justified on the basis of the centrality of the professional classes to household security and societal survival. This could be expressed as religious doctrine, but it was always couched in legal terms.[9]

In addition to explaining the sources of life, death, and other natural phenomena, and resolving conflicts without overt violence, religion legitimated the ruling hierarchies through which the production of social necessities and the reproduction of social arrangements and relations were organized.[10] The ruler was imagined as a blood relation of one or more gods; the gods ensured the provision of those natural elements (land, water, sun, seeds) that gave and sustained life. It followed, therefore, that the ruler bore major responsibility for seeing that those elements continued to be provided through propitiation of the gods.[11] Peasants worked the land, raised the crops, and relied on the good will of the ruler and the gods to maintain the cycle of life that allowed them to survive. Rulers and priests did not raise their own food because their work was to connect the material world to the cosmos. Therefore, peasants provided the food so that the professional classes could eat as well as perform the rituals necessary to continue the cycle of life and the reproduction of the hierarchy, rules, and practices that maintained the social order. Thus the circle was closed.

Although capitalism is a materialist rather than a spiritual ideology—for the most part it focuses on provision of goods rather than succor to the spirit[12]—it is similar to earlier modes of production in that production of goods is central to system maintenance. What is different is how little of what is produced is required for subsistence and survival. Consequently, because basic needs can be so readily supplied, capitalism requires the continuous transformation of products into "necessities." For example, in Los Angeles, a car is a basic requirement for finding and keeping a job that enables a person to buy food and shelter, and to pay the bills. But two cars? Each costing $40,000? Why such expensive cars? And how do cars maintain the legitimacy and hierarchy of the social system within which the individual and household are embedded? Aren't there less costly and less frustrating ways of living and getting around? Such questions are rarely asked, much less answered.[13]

There are a few important points to note here. First, as noted, within capitalism, the distinction between production and reproduction is not always clear. Many things that seem to be part of reproduction—such as art, foods prepared in special or "traditional" ways, or even music—are produced and sold like food and shelter. Clearly, large and growing numbers of people "produce" goods and services that individuals do not produce by and for themselves—Happy Meals, houses, clean laundry, air travel, and so on. This frees up time for those served to engage in other occupations. Some of these people produce "intellectual goods," such as books, music, films, laws, research papers, video games, newspapers, and so on, that support the cultural infrastructure necessary to social reproduction.[14] Second, consumption of such "luxury" goods is integral to sustaining the production through which people earn the income required to pay for both necessities and luxury goods (we return to this point later in this chapter). Third, rising rates of consumption of nonnecessities are required for the reproduction of contemporary "consumer" capitalism, which must either grow or stagnate.[15] If capitalism stagnates, not only will the economy fail to prosper, but people may also have trouble finding employment enabling them to acquire both necessities and luxuries. Finally, the smooth operation of all these arrangements plays an important role in maintaining political legitimacy and social stability. As in the religious system outlined previously, the circle must be closed to avoid social and political crises. If too many people are out of work, or if a small fraction of society becomes much wealthier than the majority of people, delegitimation and instability may follow.[16]

Modes of Production: Which Way Do the Arrows Point?

As we noted earlier, a mode of production constitutes the basic organization through which a society acquires the material requirements necessary for social reproduction. Karl Marx argued that a society's mode of production determines the relations of authority within it. In a capitalist economy, a factory requires an appropriately skilled group of workers who will follow the orders of the owner or manager. These relationships tend to mirror others outside the factory wall. A capitalist society also depends on people who must sell their labor power for wages as well as those who, owning the means of production (such as factories) must pay wages to workers. Owners (capitalists) and workers (labor) constitute distinct *classes*, groups of people whose similar economic situations give them common interests. Marx thought that conflict between classes would ultimately lead to the replacement of capitalism by communism, a system characterized by a different mode of production and different social relations. Others, such as Friedrich Hayek, found such distinctions nonsensical and argued that all that was required to sustain capitalism and its social relations was the unfettered right of individuals to conclude contracts with others. Unlike either Marx or Hayek, we believe that the mode of production is only one of many determinants of social relations, although it is a very important one. We return to this point below.

Anthropologist Eric Wolf starts from the Marxian viewpoint, arguing that modes of production are critical to understanding social relations.[17] In contrast to Marx, however, he works from a theoretical model of each distinctive mode rather than an analysis of individual societies whose modes of production may

be only superficially distinct. Thus, rather than five or eight or thirty-seven different modes of production, Wolf categorizes all complex societies (beyond
hunters and gatherers) into three ideal types. These types highlight, in addition to the societies' authority and social relations, how the various parts connect up with one another—how they *articulate*—and direct change in real ecological settings. We discuss each of these three modes—kin-orders, tributary,
and capitalist—below.

The Kin-Ordered Mode of Production

Kin-ordered (or kinship-based) societies are based on both biological (parents-
to-children; sibling-to-cousin) and social (husband-to-wife) linkages within and
among specific groups of people. Within kin-ordered societies like these early
bands, both the production of goods and the reproduction of the social order
are governed primarily by familial relations. A kin-ordered society is often organized hierarchically, with leadership limited to specific descent lines even
though all members might be related either biologically or socially.[18] Wolf provides a useful description of kin relations in "the context of political economy":

> Kinship can . . . be understood as a way of committing social labor to the
> transformation of nature through appeals to filiation [parent-to-child rela-
> tions] and marriage, and to consanguinity [lineage] and affinity [descent
> groups]. Put simply, through kinship social labor is "locked up," or "em-
> bedded" in particular relations among people. This labor can be mobilized
> only through access to people, such access being defined symbolically. What
> is done unlocks social labor; how it is done involves symbolic definitions of
> kinsmen and affines.[19]

Generally speaking, kin-ordered societies are characterized by a *social* division
of labor in which specific tasks are assigned to men, women, and children, and
by a *lineal* division of labor in which other (often cultural-symbolic, such as
shaman or priest) tasks are limited to specific descent lines. Such kin-ordered
societies can be pastoral (nomadic) or settled (farmers). In their smallest forms,
they rarely produce more than they need for daily consumption, and may have
difficulty surviving when food becomes scarce.

According to Kees van der Pijl's analysis, early human groups developed
both their social organization and material activities within the environmental
constraints of the savannahs of East Africa. These kin-based groups were fairly
small but they already displayed a division of labor according to who hunted,
who gathered, who cooked, who maintained the household, who bore and
cared for children. Ultimately, such groups developed "foreign relations"
among themselves, exchanging goods as well as people (mostly women), the
latter presumably to diversify their gene pool, with other groups. As the groups
became larger, multiplied, and wandered farther afield, new internal social organizations developed in response to changing environmental circumstances.

Some groups were able to adapt—otherwise, humans would not have spread all over the world—but we can also assume that many did not survive.[20]

Such societies have often been regarded as "tribal" or "primitive," but kin-ordered relations are both complex and also essential to capitalism. Consider the modern household with its nuclear or extended family. In either, certain members, usually related by blood or marriage, engage in wage labor outside of the household while others perform housework and rear children. The wages become the "property" of all members of the household, making reproduction possible. (Contrast this to households in which each unrelated member works for wages and contributes only to those costs, such as rent and utilities, that cannot be easily individualized.) Kin-ordered relations may extend beyond the household, such as when nonresident biological and social relatives provide child care at no cost, or financial support to college students and elderly parents. Families in urban societies appear to be more atomized and less dependent on kin relations for support but, even in cities, we find families that pool housing, labor, and resources to maintain households.[21]

Kin-type relations reflect what economists and political scientists call "social capital."[22] As Robert Putnam defines it, "social capital refers to connections among individuals—social networks and the norms of reciprocity and trustworthiness that arise from them."[23] As we noted in chapter 1, people routinely do things for one another, not for money but as a result of family ties, social bonds (through institutions like churches, clubs, and schools), occupational and informational networks, and other linkages. A person in need can call on the assistance of others who may (but generally are not obligated to) provide assistance. Indeed, the old cliché "It's not *what* you know, it's *who* you know" describes perfectly the concept of social capital. Anyone who has worked in a large organization, be it government, corporation, or university, knows that things would never get done without such relations, even though they rarely show up in organizational charts. As such, social capital provides another large, albeit invisible, articulation of the kinship mode of production to capitalism.

We should not, however, leave the concept of social capital at this: recall that social individuals are embedded in various institutions and organizations within which they develop the relationships that generate social capital. In fact, social capital is available, for the most part, only within the framework of such collectivities. It is rare to be able to go up to a stranger on the street and ask anything more than a small favor ("could you direct me to the train station?"). Others argue that a necessary condition for accumulating and using social capital is "trust"; they believe that contract was developed because we do not know whom to trust once we move outside the groups and institutions in which we are normally embedded.[24]

The Tributary Mode of Production

Under the tributary mode of production, the means of production (usually land) is owned by a specific class (landlords), and production is undertaken by a different class (peasants). Goods can be sold in markets for profits, but the process here differs from capitalism in that acquisition of wealth also takes place through conquest (stealing from outsiders, a form of *primitive accumulation*; see below). Moreover, whereas in capitalism social relations are expressions of the economic system, in the tributary mode they also are defined by religion and tradition. Although there have been, historically, a variety of tributary forms—and some would argue they still exist today, even in the United States, in such practices as tenant farming and sweatshop labor—here we examine European feudalism because of its role as the ancestor of capitalism.[25]

Feudalism in Europe developed during what are often called the Dark Ages between the fall of (western) Rome in 410 C.E. (A.D.) and about 1000 C.E., and then declined, although it did not disappear entirely until well into the twentieth century.[26] Under feudalism, the hierarchy of social relations was overseen by the Catholic Church, with the pope in Rome at its apex and serfs or captive labor at the base (a differently organized feudal structure existed in Japan until the mid-nineteenth century).[27] The rule of sovereigns and nobles over particular territories was legitimated by the church, which demanded, in return, their loyalty to the pope and priests. These rulers were the owners of the agricultural lands they governed as well as the people who lived on them and, by extension, of whatever the people and land produced. Serfs and peasants held rights to cultivate and graze their livestock on specific tracts of land, but they were obligated to give part of their annual production to the lord of the land (landlord) as a form of rent. If the landlord didn't need the goods produced by his serfs, he could sell them in the market for money. Serfs also were required to work on the landlord's property or to do particular jobs for him without pay, a practice called *corvée* labor. Military service was one form of corvée labor, and some landlords rented out their peasants as mercenary soldiers to fight other landlords' wars. Note that, under feudalism, relationships among individuals were largely fixed and difficult to change: one's place in the "Great Chain of Being" was determined by God's plan, and not subject to alteration on the basis of individual desires or ambitions.

Under the tributary system, towns and cities occupied often anomalous roles. Port cities and long-distance trade had been destroyed throughout most of northern Europe during the seventh and eighth centuries. What trade remained took place at local and regional markets located in towns and cities, and at fairs. Markets also were located outside of the walls of a noble's castle, or near castles, cathedrals, and mosques, usually along a road or waterway. At these places, peasants could sell some of their produce and buy goods that could not be manufactured on the landlord's estate. Over time, skilled workers were attracted to these places to produce goods intended for the markets, and they took up residence within city walls or around the lord's castle.

During the high Middle Ages (roughly 1000 to 1300 C.E.), production by skilled workers was overseen by guilds, producer organizations that regulated the supply and prices of goods by limiting the numbers of skilled craftsmen. Some towns specialized in producing particular goods (like fine woolens or glass), and merchants transported and sold them in other towns and special markets, such as the Champagne fairs (discussed further in chapter 5), which convened for weeks at a time every year. Out of this system developed continent-wide networks of merchants and traders, such as the twelfth-century Hanseatic League, and independent city-states, such as Venice.

The power of the nobility lay in control of land and its feudal relationship to those who lived within those territories. The sovereign also was an owner of land, and he was expected to use his income, which included taxes such as tolls, to finance his own living and court expenses. But financing wars was another matter. The rulers of consolidating nation-states needed huge sums to establish sovereign autonomy and maintain their position vis-à-vis the nobility. Taxes provided some of this money, and loans supplied the rest. The financial systems devised to facilitate trade turned out to be equally useful for raising money for wars. Cities were also important for their growing roles as sources of finance, especially from ethnic groups, such as Jews, who were excluded from the skilled trades by guilds and other economic association.

Because usury—the lending of money at interest—was forbidden by the Catholic Church, non-Christians came to fill special financial roles. Due to their peculiar position and vulnerability, such groups tended to accumulate portable wealth in the form of money and gold that could be moved easily, and to develop financial networks with their kin in other cities. Using these networks, they were able to borrow and lend funds at long distances, and make such monies available to rulers who were always looking for ways to finance their wars. Such groups often enjoyed the protection of local lords or the king, protection that could be removed at a moment's noticed, especially when the inhabitants of a town rioted and looked for convenient scapegoats.

Capitalism emerged out of this tributary system, but scholars disagree about when it emerged and why. Markets existed for thousands of years before capitalism, but until land, labor, and, especially, money were commodified—that is, standardized, bought, and sold—opportunities for profit were limited. Commodification spread concurrently with the development of autonomous, sovereign nation-states ruled by a prince or king—in Thomas Hobbes's words, by "a mortal God." Two other important movements—which also inspired Hobbes—were the rise of science and rationalism as a way of understanding how things worked, and Protestantism along with the individualism it inspired. We discuss this aspect of social change in chapter 5.

The Capitalist Mode of Production

Whereas wealth had once been acquired and accumulated largely through war or forcible expropriation by a powerful few, capitalism made it possible for more people to accumulate wealth. As noted, the Jews of Europe and other transnational ethnic minorities, such as Armenians, played a central role in this process. Jews specialized in banking. They had been a privileged population in northern Europe during the Dark Ages, when the power of the church prevented Christians from engaging in banking and trade. As the power of the church declined, Jews became targets of envious Christians. Laws were passed forbidding them to own property.[28] When the bourgeoisie or middle classes expanded to encompass members of noble families as well as skilled craftsmen, merchants, and minorities, they demanded protection by and recognition from the sovereign. Sovereigns protected many segments of the new middle classes because they wanted both a counterweight to still-powerful nobles and reliable sources of status goods and loans to support military activities.

Ellen Meiksins Wood argues that it was the specific organization of English agriculture during the transition from feudalism that led to capitalism.[29] Her account is not entirely satisfactory, but it does explain why capitalism first appeared in England. According to Wood, property relations between landlord and tenant farmer, beginning in the fourteenth and fifteenth centuries, were no longer of the pure feudal type. Landlords wanted to get their rents in money, not goods, in order to accumulate wealth for investment and to pay their taxes. At the same time, better-off farmers wanted to rent more land on the basis of their individual needs and capacities, and their estimation of the land's productivity. Money rents were bid up by competition among farmers. To meet the rent, farmers had to make the land as productive as possible by "improving" it so as to increase crop yields. A farmer's profit then could be invested in other plots of land, concentrating land holdings among the most productive. Poor or unsuccessful farmers were outbid by wealthier ones and forced either to work for wages or migrate to the cities.[30] Ultimately, rents were limited by the productivity and availability of land and the cost of transportation to markets. Rich farmers, the rising gentry, and landlords sought other ways to invest their profits, and newly developing factories were an obvious place, launching capitalism.

But there is more to capitalism than its origins; organization is central. Capitalism is an arrangement based on several key concepts and practices. First, goods are produced through a *division of labor*, whereby individual parties, usually unknown to one another, specialize in making what they produce most efficiently. This leads to increase in the number of items that can be made in a given time.[31] Second, everything must have a *price* so that it can be bought and sold. Price is generally understood to be established by the interplay of supply and demand, although this is not a hard and fast rule, and anything that has not been transformed into a commodity—such as air—has no price in a market and is considered to be without value. Third, things to be sold (or alienated) in a market must be *private property*. A seller must possess free and clear title to an item in order to transfer it to someone else through exchange; otherwise, there is no assurance that the item has not been stolen or is not counterfeit or inauthentic in some other way.

In themselves, prices and markets are not unique to capitalism. What Wolf calls "merchant trade" involves a similar exchange of goods and services for money.[32] What is different about capitalism is a third element: it depends on *profit, accumulation,* and *reinvestment.* That is, the consumer pays not only the cost of producing a good or service, and getting it to market, but also an additional amount representing a premium beyond the cost of providing the good or service. This accumulated profit can be banked or reinvested to generate further returns through additional production or through speculation on stocks, bonds, and real estate.

We so naturally accept the notion of profit as a right of the producer and seller of goods that we rarely question it. It is usually claimed that profit is the only effective incentive for goods to be offered for sale, yet for much of human history, there was no such thing. Profit is possible because the means of production—factories, technology, word processors—are under the control of capitalists who, by law, are able to set the prices for goods and services and the wages they pay the laborers who produce them. Marxists call the difference between the cost of labor and the selling price of a good the *surplus value of labor.* (Neoclassical economists deny that such a thing exists; they argue that supply and demand determine the difference between production cost and retail price.[33]) Surplus value is appropriated by the capitalist by virtue of his ownership of the workers' time and labor through contract.

Capitalism is able to *articulate* with other modes of production and extract *surplus value* from them, too. As we saw in chapter 2, the unrecorded value of housework provides a massive unremunerated transfer that subsidizes production and profit. Capitalism also appropriates value through *primitive accumulation,* that is, the direct extraction or expropriation of natural resources and what is often called "common property."[34] States can grant individuals, groups, and corporations title to forests or mineral deposits or land, *even when other people have prior historical use claim to those resources.* As we observed in our discussion of the social and liberal individual in chapter 2, only authorized, written documentation of ownership of things is recognized as legal in modern societies; those who have no written title may find their property, into which they have put considerable labor, taken away without recourse. A forest used by people on a customary basis can be declared "wasteland" by the state and then sold or given to someone else without compensation to the former users. Although this might seem quite unjust, it is perfectly legal.[35]

Of course, making money is not simply contingent on a decision to become rich; one needs to find willing buyers of goods and services as well as a way to provide goods and services at a cost these buyers are willing to pay. In a perfectly competitive market, where there are many sellers of identical goods, it is difficult to realize profits. Each seller is motivated to cut prices below those of her competitor and, if she is desperate for cash to pay her workers (or her taxes), she might even cut prices below her break-even point. Indeed, it is quite possible—and common—to sell out one's stock in trade and still lose money. Consider the following example.

Let's assume that you go to your local farmers' market every week. During late summer and early fall, there are a half dozen stands offering peaches and nectarines for sale. How do you decide from whom to buy? You might, of course, compare prices, but if all of the fruit comes from the same type of tree there is unlikely to be more than a small difference from one stand to the next. Of course, some sellers might claim their fruit to be superior or from a different stock and charge a higher price (they offer samples to taste, as does everyone else). But if there is no difference in fruit or price, how do you decide? You might buy from a family member or a seller with whom you've developed a relationship; you might shop at the stand closest to you, although such reasons do not appear in standard market theory. If there is no reason other than price for you and other customers to choose one stand over another, each seller must charge the same price or go out of business. If even one were tempted to sell fruit at a lower price than the others—even at a loss—everyone else would have to do the same or risk being left with unsold fruit (which does not keep for very long). In the effort to move stock, sellers might well sell *all* of their fruit and still lose money.[36]

Similarly, in order to sell all their stock in a competitive market, the owners of factories and services must offer attractive prices to buyers. Price-cutting reduces profit margins, as do increases in wages, raw materials, and other production costs. This is described as the tendency in capitalism toward a "declining rate of profit." If the factory owner tries to keep her profits up by raising prices, customers will buy from other companies. She could try to reduce wages, but her employees will object and might go on strike. If goods of comparable quality and lower cost are imported from other countries (e.g., automobiles from Korea or India), she might have to automate (get rid of most of her employees), relocate production overseas, or go out of business. The now-jobless domestic workers will no longer be able to afford to buy any goods, domestic or imported. Under conditions of such "perfect competition," it is tempting to create oligopolies or monopolies, whereby one or a few capitalists produce all of a given good. Then, it is easy to raise prices because competition is limited or nonexistent. In fact, this situation exists in many industries today.

In competitive capitalist markets, therefore, it is important to develop consumer desire *and* to differentiate one's product from other, similar ones in order to limit downward pressure on prices and profits. This practice was developed during the last few decades of the nineteenth and early decades of the twentieth centuries, along with the growth of public literacy and print journalism.[37] Advertising became a linchpin of American capitalism, telling consumers what they lacked, what they needed, and most of all, what they wanted, whether it was a necessity or not.[38] But even such stimulated needs are not infinite. The average car can remain in service for ten or more years; the average refrigerator will last for fifteen years or more. Capitalism cannot depend for its growth on the demand for replacement cars and refrigerators (in the absence of adequate income and reliable electricity in developing countries, demand remains too sporadic there to make reliable profits).[39] How, then, to get the well-off to buy new appliances more frequently?

One way is to produce more elaborate appliances (designer colors, ice and water dispensers and computers in the refrigerator door); a second is to offer variants on the basic idea (wine refrigerators, freezers); a third is to develop entirely new appliances (microwave ovens, dishwashers). Another approach is to offer goods that quickly become obsolete (go out of style or out of date). In the 1950s, this niche was filled by automobiles, whose middle-class owners replaced them every three years. Today personal computers fill this niche. Each successive computer generation is faster, with more memory, more hard-drive space, and fancier CD players, cameras, scanners, and other capabilities. Each generation requires new software that is incompatible with older hardware or too large to fit on the old hard drive. Computers are typically replaced every three years. And, many new gadgets—cellular phones, personal digital assistants, MP3 players, iPhones—are linked to new systems of communication, new ways of keeping records, and new ways of consuming cultural products (all of which also must be purchased) that promise a happier, busier, and more rewarding life. Spiritual fulfillment is connected in consumer's minds with status goods that make people happy with their situation, legitimating the political and economic system that makes such happiness possible.[40]

At the same time, however, we should recognize that every human being is entitled to live a life free of hunger and deprivation and that this is not yet the case around the world. Capitalist markets have made available a volume of goods and services that were unimaginable one hundred years ago for anyone but the very wealthy. Many philosophers and intellectuals recognized that the advent of industrial capitalism made possible a more equitable and just distribution of goods—this was one of Karl Marx's key insights, but he was not alone in this belief. Why, then, have poverty and its correlates not been eliminated? What prevents the five billion poor of the world from gaining access to the goods so easily acquired by the other billion? The key point here is that, even with the expansion of production throughout the world, there are still too few employment opportunities for those five billion—indeed, it is their very poverty and willingness to work for low wages that keeps the price of goods low and allows the global middle class to live lives of luxury (at least by comparison). Today's high profits would not be possible if producers were merely providing basic necessities—undifferentiated commodities. This is one reason why the most highly developed markets are populated by so many poorly nourished consumers.[41]

The Origins of Today's Global Economic System

How did capitalism become what it is today? To answer this question we need to look back to the early part of the twentieth century and the production process now known as "Fordism." Henry Ford took the model of the mass production assembly line from other industries, mechanized and electrified it, employed unskilled and semiskilled workers to assemble autos, and paid them $5 a day, twice the going wage at the time. Workers could produce enough cars to lower their unit cost, while high wages allowed many workers to buy their own

Model Ts. During the early years of the company, Ford also provided housing and other social amenities to his workers, and even kept an eye on their moral behavior. "Company towns" were the norm in industry, in part because they made it possible for owners to exercise greater control over workers than they could if the workers lived independently.[42]

Fordism was adopted throughout American industry and elsewhere. During the 1920s, industrial countries prospered. But, as you might have guessed, demand for the items produced through Fordism was not insatiable.[43] By the end of that decade, industries in many countries were producing more than could be sold domestically or abroad. Demand declined, unemployment rose, stock markets crashed, countries put up barriers to international trade, and economies contracted. This horrible state of affairs was called the Great Depression, and it persisted until World War II was well under way.[44]

The economic lessons of depression and war were not lost on the leaders of the United States and the United Kingdom. Their plan for the postwar global economic system—the Bretton Woods agreements—sought, in effect, to internationalize the American form of capitalism through Keynesian demand management (government deficit spending during recessions and tax increases during booms) and consumer spending.[45] The cold war played a significant role in entrenching these arrangements throughout the "Free World."[46] Fordism underwrote the high standard of living that characterized prosperity in the United States, Europe, and Japan, as the growing desire for household goods was met through mass production in factories employing workers whose wages were high enough to enable them to buy houses and fill them with the things they produced on the assembly line.[47]

But capitalism is characterized by cycles of expanding production, competition, and market saturation, as new entrants into markets seek to reap windfall returns in sectors that are, initially, at least, highly profitable.[48] This is what happened to Fordism as a system toward the end of the 1960s.[49] The system entered an economic crisis as growth stagnated, and it encountered a political legitimation crisis as people began to question the system itself. One "normal" response to such crises is one of Schumpeter's gales of "creative destruction."[50] In order to be revived, capitalism depends on the destruction of uncompetitive firms and industries, unwanted goods, and infrastructure so that they can be replaced by new ones. Wars are one way to do this.[51] The emergence of new products and new means of production is another. A third is to reorganize relations of production and relocate production from high-wage, high-cost regions to low-wage, low-cost areas.[52] The planned obsolescence described earlier is another important strategy.

All of these and more were applied during the 1980s and 1990s. Beginning in the late 1970s, the United States launched a "new" cold war against the Soviet Union. The military buildup of the 1980s, begun by President Jimmy Carter, exploded under Ronald Reagan. This "imaginary war," as Mary Kaldor put it,[53] was never fought to the full, but vast resources were injected into the defense sector and its subsidiaries, totaling some two trillion dollars (in 1980 dollars).[54]

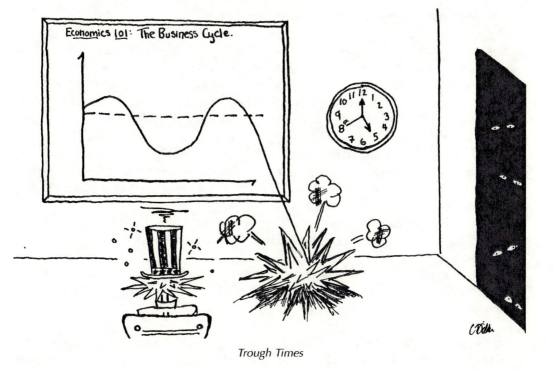

Trough Times

Second, the "information revolution," with its proliferation of electronic devices and infrastructure, came to fruition. It required new skills, new equipment, and new social relations of production. All helped to destroy Fordist practices and institutions. Older workers whose skills were no longer needed found themselves in what Marx called the "reserve army of the unemployed," competing for low-wage, low-skill jobs.

Third, factory owners began to move production "offshore" in the 1960s to jump foreign tariff barriers.[55] Outsourcing grew in the 1980s as capitalists shifted production to countries with low wages and fewer environmental and labor laws. They exported goods back to the United States, Europe, and Japan where the numbers of workers in agriculture and manufacturing has been declining steadily despite rising demand for their products.[56] Today a growing proportion of production takes place in relatively poor countries—developing countries (less-developed countries—LDCs) or the Global South—from which goods are exported to relatively rich countries—developed countries, or the Global North.[57] Job seekers in the Global South constitute another reserve army of unemployed, ensuring that the wages paid to those who do have jobs never rise too high. While those who work in factories, call centers, and outsourcing consulting firms are, at least, receiving a wage, and often can save enough of their earnings to buy nonsubsistence items,[58] they do not (as yet) constitute a primary market for these goods and services. The remaining billions of truly poor are of little or no interest to global capitalism.[59]

This does not mean, however, that those poor do not participate in capitalist markets. In economies where jobs and money are scarce, there are always niches where small volumes of high-demand items, such as individual cigarettes, can be sold. An enterprising individual who has a little money saved up can buy a few packs and sell individual smokes to those too poor to aspire to even this level of investing. The "profit" from a day's sales can support a family and finance the purchase of a few more packs of cigarettes to sell the next day. Such "gray markets" are widespread and appear to constitute a significant fraction of economic activity in many developing countries. As long as the cost of doing business is relatively high compared to the rate of profit, large capitalists ignore these petty opportunities, allowing the very poor to survive as petty entrepreneurs.[60]

The most important response to the crisis of the 1970s was the reorganization of capitalism under "neoliberalism."[61] Neoliberalism advocates a set of fiscal and monetary practices and principles designed to increase and preserve profit rates for capital investment. It has been followed by many nation-states, often under duress. We can summarize neoliberalism's practices and principles as follows:

- Investment should be based on a country's comparative advantage in the context of an international division of labor. Such advantages include low labor costs and taxation, limited social and environmental regulation, domestic political and economic stability, and well-developed infrastructure.
- Governments must not impose undue restrictions on investment or forbid investors' ability to send profits abroad (this is called "repatriation").
- Government spending must be constrained to maintain the value of the local currency. This means reductions in expenditures on health, education, and welfare and increases in spending that facilitate investment and production.
- Governments can impose only those restrictions on imports and exports permitted by international agreements, so as to maximize trade.

While these principles and practices seem reasonable, especially if they are intended to contribute to national and global growth, they have a number of often-ignored distributional consequences. The logic behind these principles and practices is that overall economic growth in a society generates jobs, higher tax revenues, resources, and consumption, which will "trickle down" to the poor and unemployed in the form of demand and payment for their services.[62] In practice, this may not happen for a number of reasons.

First, the principle of specialization according to comparative advantage in an international division of labor puts a premium on minimizing the cost of inputs, including labor, into the production process. The cost of labor in developing countries is quite low—even relative to the cost of living. This is a strong incentive for capital to move operations to developing countries and explains why production moves continually from low-wage to lower-wage countries.

But even a large low-wage workforce might not keep industries from migrating. Thus, the People's Republic of China possesses a large, low-cost, well-educated workforce, but some corporations are threatening to leave if the country's labor laws are strengthened.[63]

Second, even the trickle of wealth downward may be blocked by the state. Governments, international financial institutions, and foreign investors often demand that their loans be matched by local capital. To generate these funds, the state forces workers to save a portion of their wages by law or by suppressing nonsubsistence consumption. Such a strategy was pursued by both Japan and Korea during the cold war, and it persists in many countries that put heavy taxes on "luxury" items. Workers must therefore save and spend more in order to buy such goods. The state may also actively repress labor, forbidding the organization of unions and collective bargaining to keep wages from rising and to assure investors that the labor force is under control.

Third, when governments give maximum freedom to foreign investment and production, this sets up a "race to the bottom" among countries. Attempts by authorities to enforce environmental and other social regulations may be met by closing factories, leading some governments to lower fair labor standards and environmental protection standards, actively suppress movements to improve social conditions to attract investment,[64] and offer financial incentives like subsidies and tax holidays to keep corporations from leaving. Fourth, to keep taxes low, and ensure repayment of debts, international financial institutions and private banks often require governments to avoid "excessive" expenditures on social services and deficit spending that might make loan servicing difficult.

Finally, under the rules of the World Trade Organization (WTO), entry and exit taxes (tariffs) on imported and exported goods, the easiest taxes for developing countries to collect, are restricted in the name of free trade. In the past, tariffs were the revenue mainstays of today's developed countries. Even where state capacity allows the collection of income taxes, however, free trade increases international competitiveness and puts downward pressure on wages in all countries, thereby limiting tax revenues from that source.

The picture presented here is complicated by the transnational distribution of capital and labor. Workers, regardless of where they live, and developing countries in general face disadvantages relative to investors and rich countries. In a global economy, the division of labor applies both to countries and to people. Again, there is nothing new about this state of affairs; differential wages to skilled and unskilled workers has a long history. What is new is the rapidity of change in demands for particular types of specialized labor and the ability of firms to select the lowest-cost labor force from a global menu. Fifty years ago, a person living in an industrialized country could learn a trade or skill and be relatively certain of full employment until retirement. Today, there are no such skills or jobs. People must expect to change jobs, and even fields, five or more times during their lifetimes. Individual capabilities or skills that earn high incomes today may be outsourced, unwanted, or obsolete in a few years.[65] Furthermore, the work that is available is often short term and "flexible." People are hired on the basis of a business's immediate requirements, and often on contract rather than as full-time employees entitled to benefits and training.[66] Companies pay only the wages necessary to get a job done and, where benefits are not provided by the state, engage employees on terms that leave them without health, unemployment, and retirement insurance. Anyone unwilling to work under these conditions will, quite simply, not work at all, at least not for wages.

This is not a pretty picture, but it is already visible in many sectors of the economy, including higher education, where fully qualified teachers with degrees from prestigious institutions are unable to find full-time, tenure-track positions. To make ends meet, they commute from one institution to another, teaching one or two courses at each, at a small fraction of a full-time salary and without benefits.[67] Growing numbers of undergraduate students—the "echo of the baby boom"—were expected to require colleges and universities to add positions, but this has not occurred. Instead, both permanent and "nomadic" faculty are pressed by their employers to increase "productivity" by teaching more classes, each with more students, while their salaries stagnate or fall behind increases in the cost of living. Graduate programs provide prestige and cheap labor to universities, and also produce growing numbers of advanced-degree holders, most of whom join yet another reserve army of unemployed when they graduate.[68]

High unemployment is a political hot potato. After all, in democratic countries, people are also voters. If they understood why their economic prospects were so bleak, they might express their displeasure in the polling booth. Even the governments of authoritarian states must reckon with people's anger. Yet restoring domestic production of goods and services would make them more expensive. The lower cost of imported versus domestic goods not only is a boon to profits but also an implicit subsidy to consumers. Manufacturers lower their prices to big retailers like Wal-Mart and Target in return for a higher sales volume, and retailers pass on some (but not all) of their savings to consumers. Consequently, the consumer dollar "stretches further," and the relative decline in wages is not felt so strongly.[69]

Furthermore, with a few notable exceptions, it is a violation of WTO rules to impose trade barriers on imported items, while it is virtually impossible to block trade in services that can be provided through international communications networks. The treaties and agreements establishing international trade regimes like the WTO severely limit the freedom of governments to restrict trade, yet free trade does benefit developing countries. It permits producers to sell into rich, high-demand markets abroad as well as into domestic markets. In practice, however, capitalist markets are subject only to those kinds of rules and regulations that facilitate the flows of goods, services, and capital, while the domestic social and environmental costs of free trade and globalization are, for the most part, hardly addressed. Just as problematic for poor countries is the tendency of wealthy and powerful states to ignore free-trade rules when they are inconvenient.[70] The United States, Europe, and other industrialized countries restrict imports of agricultural goods from developing countries and offer domestic producers production and export subsidies, to the estimated tune of more than $250 billion annually. Not only does this depress international prices of commodities such as corn and sugar; these actions also undermine small (and often lower-cost) farming operations in developing countries.

Can predation by big corporations and industrialized countries be stopped or prevented? Amartya Sen and others have proposed the notion of "fair trade."[71] As Sen puts it, "There needs to be a watchdog institution which is concerned with inequality and fair trade, [which] asks why the USA and Europe are so restrictive to products from the third world."[72] Fair trade should not only redress the legal and institutional barriers put up by the rich but also see that more of the profits generated in industrialized countries be repatriated to primary producers. While the prospects for such a watchdog institution are low, rising numbers of organizations are importing goods from producers in developing countries directly. Groups like Equal Exchange (www.equalexchange.com/) for coffee and MarketPlace of India (www.marketplaceindia.org/MP36/) for textiles bypass the intermediary chains along which potential returns to producers are dissipated. Still, fair trade focuses on changing the distribution of income along the commodity chain, not on the particular organization of global capitalism that gives so much power to the rich and so little to the poor.

Where Are the People?

But where are the *people* in capitalism? Are they merely passive consumers, free to choose cereals, ties, and automobiles but compelled to accept low wages and poor working conditions, and denied a say in the kind of society in which they want to live? Are there strategies for restoring politics to market societies? Answering these questions requires a detour to consider the relationship of power to markets and politics and to discuss the role of people in those relationships.

The individual plays a dual role in capitalism—as both worker-producer and as consumer. As we noted at the beginning of this chapter, one has notional choice both in terms of what work one does and where one might do it, as well as in what can be bought and consumed. This is called "freedom." Yet, freedom in the market is limited to the freedom to choose from what is on offer, not necessarily what any person desires or needs. Moreover, people have few opportunities to influence the organization of markets.[73] It is common to hear policy makers and economists bemoan political meddling in markets. Their mantras fill the air(waves): "If things were left to the free market to decide, everything would turn out for the better." "Politics makes markets inefficient." "Markets are 'natural' (because of the human propensity to truck and barter—in the words of Adam Smith) but governments don't know how to invest." Such claims disregard the fact that today's markets are historically novel institutions and ignore the laws and institutions that make them not at all "free."[74] All markets operate under rules and regulations *designed and enforced by governments* that structure and organize exchange, specify what is permitted and what is forbidden, guarantee contracts and a particular regime of property rights, and provide the stability and trust required for people unknown to each other to exchange goods and money.[75] Without politics there would be exchange but probably not capitalism.

What this means is that markets and capitalism are constructed institutions. They can be changed. The nation-state changed localized medieval economies to integrated national economies. Globalization changed the organization and structure of national and international markets over the past several decades, and it is possible to change them again, in other ways. But such change requires an assertion of the power to *decide*, and that, in turn, requires more politics, not less. It also depends on becoming politically aware of how power maintains the fiction that capitalist markets are "natural." The claim that markets must remain outside of the sphere of politics rests on both discourse and practice, and these are part of the *reproduction* of social life. They are not fixed.

It is helpful to keep a few points in mind while thinking about such changes. Stopping globalization and global capitalism in their tracks is neither practical nor wise, but allowing globalization and global capitalism to continue along their current path is not a smart move either. Focused, collective action through politically aware social movements and organizations is essential. But the first step is political awareness. Where do things come from? How are they made? What is the history of their production—not only how they came to be produced, but how certain places are situated in the international division of labor? Who decides what is to be produced? How much—or how little—power do workers have? What is the effect of production on the environment? How are things and services sold? Why do people buy them? Why are so many people poor and lacking in basic necessities? What can be done about this state of affairs? Where do we begin? We return to these questions in the chapters that follow.

5

People and States

L'État, c'est moi!

—Louis XIV

"International relations" refers to how nation-states get along with one another. "World politics" reflects a more complicated perspective. Nation-states are still in the picture, but so are other corporate actors—firms and banks, labor unions and religious organizations, choral groups and theater companies, sports teams and terrorist cells—and individual persons from Hannah Montana to the pope. All are engaged in purposeful activities that constitute and shape our world. We'll begin this chapter by looking at states, the "big guns" in world politics. Then we'll enlarge our viewpoint to consider examples of "civil society," which we define as the complex of values, practices, and institutions that operate in and between the family and the state. Our objective is to look more closely at the variety of actors and activities that constitute world politics.

States before Nation-States

Most people agree that all of the earth (with the exception—and maybe not for much longer—of Antarctica) is now divided into nation-states. The subject of states is complicated. The verdict is not yet in about what is and is not a "real" state, and exactly how nation-states are different from other kinds of states. Scholars disagree about when nation-states arose, how that happened, and which other agents are important enough to include in our discussions when we talk about international relations.[1]

Most contemporary notions of the state are taken from the history of modern Europe, that is, Europe since 1500 C.E. A defining characteristic of all states is territory. In addition to where a state is located on the planet, territory includes what that land contains in material, strategic, cultural, and psychological assets and, of course, people. But when we look at politics and organization, the nation-state seems to be something new. Although in reality national boundaries continue to shift, especially as the result of war, we imagine nation-states as being relatively more fixed as compared to premodern states and empires, and also more exclusive. When Mary Ann Tétreault was little, she and her sister liked to stand in the middle of the Peace Bridge with one foot in the United States and the other in Canada, a rare opportunity to be in two places at one time. Less than one hundred years ago, the U.S.-Canadian border was not so clearly marked physically or in people's minds. During the 1920s, some houses built in Derby Line, Vermont, were constructed to straddle the border, a great convenience to householders and their guests, who could always find at least one room where they could drink alcohol legally despite Prohibition.[2]

Our genealogy of the modern states-system is one story of how it took shape.[3] Imagine the international system today and compare it to Europe after the fall of Rome in 410 C.E. A "Roman" emperor continued to reside in Constantinople, but political organization in western Europe fragmented into tiny kingdoms ruled by Germanic "barbarians." Even so, the basic organization of European society and economy did not become Germanic. It remained Roman. Absolute rulers enforced Roman law; society was mostly secular; and the continental economy was organized around trade based on the *dinarius* and other gold coins acceptable everywhere in the Mediterranean (and beyond).

The Muslim conquests that began in the mid-seventh century took this world by surprise. Muslim forces radiating outward from the Arabian Peninsula were halted at Constantinople in the east and near the border between what now are France and Spain in the west. Wars and resistance took a terrible toll, especially in northern Europe. The east remained cosmopolitan and wealthy, ruled by the emperor in Constantinople and protected by his powerful navy. Spain also retained its cosmopolitan character, but its cultural focus was the Muslim Fertile Crescent rather than Christian Rome or Constantinople.[4] In the rest of Europe, the fight to keep Islam from spreading north and east of Spain was spearheaded by warlords who parlayed their military conquests into claims to rule. During the centuries following the fall of Rome, the warlord dynasties and their Muslim foes looted and destroyed schools, church properties, and port cities with their shipping and banking infrastructure. Without port services or naval protection, trade ground to a halt in northern Europe. Literacy, which had been widespread, virtually disappeared, and Latin as a living language disappeared along with it. During these "Dark Ages"—from roughly 500 to 800 or 1000 C.E.—artifacts of Roman culture were preserved by Irish monks and also by clerics in Britain.[5]

Political fragmentation in the west offered opportunities to the Carolingians, a Frankish dynasty, and to the pope in Rome who, until this time, had been a mere bishop of a large city in an empire whose ruler lived in Constantinople, a much larger and richer city very far away. Popes and emperors had often disagreed, but when Byzantium no longer could protect Rome militarily, popes were freed to pursue their own religious and political destinies. As the effective head of a church that remained the only unifying institution between Spain and Constantinople, the pope found allies in the ambitious Carolingian rulers struggling to create a new governing order. The pope relied on the military power of the kings, especially Charlemagne, the most effective Carolingian who united, however briefly, most of the Christian West during the ninth century. The Carolingians wanted the pope to bless their role as upstart overthrowers of the old order, and Charlemagne allowed himself to be crowned emperor by the pope in 800 C.E. to be able to claim this religious legitimacy.

Charlemagne's empire supplied much-needed political scaffolding to Europe in the Middle Ages. The state on which it was founded gradually disintegrated, the result of inheritance laws requiring a deceased father's property to be divided among his sons. But the empire survived as the Holy Roman Empire, which embodied the cultural unity of Western Christendom.[6] Eventually, the position of Holy Roman Emperor became an elective one and not very effective in political terms—it was said that the Emperor ruled over something that was neither holy nor Roman nor an empire. In contrast, the pope continued to be an independent power in western Europe.

During this period, governance in Europe was highly localized. States were in effect the estates of ruling landlords/warlords. Through conquest, they enslaved and enserfed rural populations as the holders of the primary means of production, which was land. The sacking of port cities left inland towns with varying degrees of autonomy and different kinds of relations with local lords, thanks to their role as sites of commerce (see chapter 4). Effective political organization also was local, and the boundaries of these fragmented polities were contentious and fluid. Estates could be divided up after the death of a ruler: the sons of Charlemagne's heir, Louis the Pious, fought to see who would get which parts of their father's realm after he died.[7]

Medieval states also changed shape when their owners married or divorced. Eleanor of Aquitaine held title to a large territory in what is now France, which she brought as a dowry to her husband, King Louis VII of France. His concern about losing her property made him hesitate before divorcing her—rightfully so, because Eleanor married Henry II of England mere weeks after her marriage to Louis had been dissolved, transferring Aquitaine to the English king's control. Occasionally kingdoms were reorganized when the king of one country was invited to rule another. James VI of Scotland became James I of England *and* Scotland after the English queen Elizabeth I died without leaving a child or sibling to take her place. Emperors sold properties for ready cash well into the nineteenth century. Not only did Thomas Jefferson buy "Louisiana" from Napoleon in 1803, but U.S. secretary of state William Seward bought Alaska ("Seward's Ice-Box") from Czar Alexander II of Russia in 1868, during the presidency of Andrew Johnson.

Medieval and early modern European rulers dreamed of recreating a European empire to rival empires in Asia.[8] They fought almost constantly to preserve and extend their wealth and power. During the Hundred Years' War between England and France, thousands died in battle. Thousands more died as the result of "normal" rape and pillage by rampaging armies that lived off the countryside, supporting and amusing themselves with whatever they could find. "Free lances," knights for whom war was an opportunity to get rich and become famous, kidnapped people for ransom, sacked cities, and looted homes.[9] Population movements in war, as in trade, also spread disease. Writing about the Hundred Years' War, part of which coincided with an epidemic of bubonic plague, during which almost half of the population of Europe died, Barbara Tuchman says that it defined the "calamitous fourteenth century" for all that it consolidated the power of French and English kings among their peers.[10]

Very much like President Hamid Karzai in post-Taliban Afghanistan, European rulers had to struggle to subordinate locally entrenched warlords to their authority. In Europe, it took centuries to bring large (and often remote) baronies under control. Aspiring centralizers had to fight rivals and resisters among their peers and offer superior services to win and hold the allegiance of the wider population. One of the most valuable services supplied by kings was justice, or regularized procedures and institutions for resolving disputes and punishing criminals. Historian Joseph Strayer believes that the main magnet attracting loyal supporters to the nascent states of England and France was the development of formal legal institutions and the involvement of citizens in making them work.[11] Unlike China, where by that time courts were centralized and judges went from the imperial capital to the countryside to hear cases, medieval and early modern states in Europe had very little judicial—or any other kind of—capacity. Kings relied on local officials and assemblies to assess and collect taxes to support their wars.[12] Judges and juries helped to legitimate the decisions of the king's courts. Local residents could gauge the truthfulness of testimony against their own local knowledge, information that an outsider simply wouldn't have. Looking at tax policies and jury verdicts, we can surmise that the lack of medieval state capacity had positive value. Extensive local collaboration ensured that "state" policy would be seen as legitimate because it both accommodated local interests and acted as a check on kings.

Towns and cities were key elements of the late medieval order. Church and state officials lived mostly in restored port cities, trading centers, and large towns where local populations engaged in industry, commerce, and the production of culture. Artisan-crafted trade goods were fabricated and sold, along with domestic and imported luxuries like furs, jewels, and tapestries. Luxury goods showed everyone, especially rivals and peers, how rich and important their owners were. Medieval authority rested on performance and demeanor. Displays of wealth, such as beautiful jewels and impressive works of art, were marks of power.[13] Historian Janet Abu-Lughod tells us that even the Mongol warrior Tamerlane "assembled artisans and craftsmen who . . . produced goods for a luxurious court life" in his capital city, Samarkand.[14]

Rulers could make life easy or difficult for merchants and artisans. Traders traveling to the medieval Champagne fairs were protected by the counts of Champagne and Brie, who guaranteed safe conduct for merchants on their way to and from the fair. They also sponsored a local system of dispute resolution and contract enforcement that "created a nonnatural monopoly for the fairs, which assured that they would be preferred to those held elsewhere under less attractive conditions."[15] After French kings succeeded in taking over Champagne and Brie, the fair towns no longer could offer these services because their new rulers wouldn't pay for them. In fact, the French harassed Flemish merchants and restricted access to the fairs by Italian merchants, raising the cost of overland transport. Meanwhile, cheaper, waterborne commerce thrived, boosted by new technology that improved shipping from Genoa and Venice to North Sea ports in what are now Belgium and Holland. The Champagne fairs disappeared.

The Imperial Church

Before the Protestant Reformation, every European king had to contend with another powerful rival to his authority: the Roman Catholic Church. The Church was a virtual empire that included all of Christendom, the places throughout Europe where Roman Catholics lived. The symbiosis between the institutional church and kings forced rulers to share power and authority with the clergy. Unlike relations between church and state in the Byzantine East, relations between these two authorities in the west were contentious.[16] The "amphibious" church had bases on earth and "in heaven." Like the kings, the pope was an armed landlord, and so were estate-owning bishops and monasteries, which were little ecclesiastical kingdoms. The pope exercised authority over moral standards and the salvation of souls throughout his heaven-conferred empire, where he claimed the right to rule as God's "vicar," or representative on earth. Papal disapproval of lending at interest retarded the recovery of the economy in western Europe and explains why Jews, who were not subject to church law, were so valued as bankers and traders. Bishops were powerful in their own right. Some were entitled to vote in the selection of kings. Their cathedrals were at least as impressive as the palaces of local lords, and, like those palaces, cathedrals were filled with art attesting to the bishops' power. The cathedral in Mainz, Germany, for example, has more statues and reliefs of bishops and archbishops than of kings, lords, and nonclerical saints.

The church had particular leverage over kings through its imperial authority to offer or withhold the keys to eternal salvation. If a ruler displeased the church an interdict could be imposed on his territory under which no resident could be baptized, have a church wedding, or receive communion or last rites before death. An interdict put every believer in the community in danger of going to hell for eternity. The threat of interdiction encouraged kings to stay in line, but they chafed under clerical restraint and eventually used their earthly weapons to kidnap, threaten, and even kill troublesome priests—and popes. As the Middle Ages waned, some kings became "protestants"—protesters—and heads or sponsors of national churches. Hobbes thought this was the best way to prevent subversion from abroad because the Leviathan state could exclude foreign clerics. Perhaps the most famous royal protestant was Henry VIII of England, who retained the religious beliefs he had been taught as a child until the end of his life but broke away from the authority of the Catholic Church to escape papal interference with his plans to father a legitimate son to inherit his kingdom.[17]

Political scientists refer to this complicated, overlapping, and unstable configuration of territories and governance as a "heteronomous" system. This means not only that it was complicated, overlapping, and unstable but also that its elements were not equivalent. A little like Heisenberg's electrons, elements even changed character depending on an observer's perspective. Medieval agents were far from functionally identical and corporate identities multiplied the complications. A vassal family of powerful knights might marry a daughter to a king and have sons in the church. Even after priestly celibacy became a convention of the Catholic Church in the eleventh century, powerful clerics kept mistresses who bore children, some of whom became scholars, military leaders, artists, merchants—and popes. The identity of anybody or any place depended on particular spaces of appearance. A bishop could be more powerful than a king, as Lothar II, king of Lotharingia (855–868), found out when he tried to divorce his wife. The local archbishop objected, forcing Lothar to go to Rome to beg for a dispensation (exemption from the rule) from the pope. This ultimately fruitless trip brought on Lothar's untimely death.[18]

The situational quality of heteronomy is important in theory and in practice. Heteronomy makes it impossible to think of medieval "units of analysis" as interchangeable or to deploy them in relatively simple models like the balance-of-power theories we discussed in chapter 3. In practice, the multiple identities that heteronomy gave persons and territories made it difficult for anyone to domesticate them. Surveys, social security numbers, and birth certificates couldn't even be imagined—who would have issued them?

Becoming Modern

The transition to modernity—beginning roughly in the fourteenth century—introduced a differently rationalized hierarchy of large institutions like states and corporations. Paradoxically, modernity also brought greater equality to individuals. Under the orchestration of nation-states and entrepreneurs, land gradually became privatized, bounded, bought, sold, taxed, and regulated; resources were counted, exploited, and taxed; people were counted, regulated and taxed; and, in the process, personal identities were reorganized and regimented.[19] Nationality—who belongs to which state—was created under international treaties during the nineteenth and early twentieth centuries and enforced by passports and immigration controls.[20] People were required to adopt and use family names. Birth certificates were issued, along with the other paperwork identifying each of us and where we belong. Even "national forests" were regimented: surveyed, logged, and then replanted in straight rows of uniform trees. These and the many other organizing policies of centralizing states made it easier for governments to count and manage their human and natural resources. Governments (the ministers in charge of the state, along with the bureaucracies that actually do the work) became larger and better able to penetrate, observe, and control. This transformation occurred as nation-states and the capitalist economy developed symbiotically to create the modern world. As we discuss more fully in chapter 7, the state also was "made" through war.

As hierarchical states developed, equality within them increased. This occurred as unruly elements of identity were taken out of the public sphere and privatized, leaving a larger range of life choices up to individuals. States frequently regulated the market for such choices but they ceased making them directly. Consequently, economics and religion moved from the public to the private sphere. What to wear and where to live, choices we think of today as nobody's business but our own, also were privatized, giving modern people greater individual freedom than their medieval counterparts. But all good things come at a cost. The expansion of individual choice comes at the expense of ready resources for collective action.

Individualism

Modern persons define many of their own statuses and, with sufficient resources, social mobility is not only possible but expected. We call this "individualism," but the term is paradoxical. On the one hand, it reflects the fact that within the limits of their resources, people choose for themselves what to believe; whether and whom to marry; where, for whom, and how hard to work. Individualism is the bedrock of liberalism but, as we argued in the previous chapter, what can be chosen is limited by the availability of alternatives, and by individual resources, including power. Indeed, gauging differences in resources is how we make distinctions among persons. Modern individuals no longer are defined by their families, their towns, or the occupations they inherited from their parents, but by how much wealth, education, and income they have. Consequently, most modern persons are liberal *and* social individuals.

On the other hand, individualism comes at the expense of lifetime membership in stable communities of obligation. We need communities because the social individual depends on networks of mutual support, but liberal individuals have to construct and maintain these networks pretty much on their own. The conflict between liberalization and the needs of social individuals is encapsulated in the difference between the abandoned spouses and throwaway kids who populate daytime TV, and the hired man in Robert Frost's poem who called home "the place where, when you have to go there, they have to take you in."[21] Modern families can be as supportive as the idealized picture on *Leave It to Beaver* (or as unsupportive as its satirical analogues, *The Sopranos* and *The Simpsons*). Individuals, however, must make this happen without help from traditional institutions like female subordination and lifetime employment, two linchpins of the medieval order that also are unspoken assumptions about the lifestyles depicted in these TV series.

One puzzle is how such a radical new orientation emerged from the presumably closed medieval world. What we find is that this world was far from closed. Assumptions about medieval gender relations are stood on their head by evidence of powerful women and female-run communities, while social status generally was more fluid than we used to think. Women found ways to exercise authority individually, as property owners or "saints," and collectively in convents, parallel *poleis* housing educated and powerful women.[22] Knights were early secular individualists, younger sons and lower-class men whose ruthless talents in combat offered them ways to acquire money and rise in status. As shown by analyst Leo Braudy, the church domesticated knights materially, by channeling their activities away from Europe to the Crusades to capture Jerusalem, and ideologically, by promoting the heroic value system we call "chivalry." Both brought knights under religious, social, and political control.[23]

In contrast to the knights' marauder style, philosopher Isaiah Berlin suggests that social and political individualism are based on individual rights to privacy—rights to choose for oneself what to think and how to live. Berlin says that individualism arose from two intellectual movements: the rediscovery of classical civilization during the Renaissance and the assertions of morally responsible individuality that marked the Protestant Reformation.[24] The Enlightenment, which sought to replace superstition and tradition with science and reason, was the third major intellectual movement in European history that changed how people looked at themselves and imagined their rights.

C. B. Macpherson weaves the revolutionary ideas of the Reformation into a story of economic, political, and philosophical developments that brought changes in values and institutions to Europe and made individualism—what Berlin called "negative liberty"—a social and political practice, especially in England.[25] Negative liberty emphasizes the right of the individual to think and act for herself as long as her actions do not interfere with others' rights to do the same. Institutional expressions of negative liberty include markets and secularism. The institutions and values most responsible for defining and establishing the rules for modernity arise directly from the mutual construction of capitalism and the nation-state system.

Macpherson argues that Hobbes and another seventeenth-century philosopher, John Locke, along with worker-activists such as the Levellers, changed our values by introducing the novel idea of "possessive individualism." The hallmark of a society based on possessive individualism (a "market society") is the alienability of land and labor.[26] A market society is a legal regime for dividing land into sellable parcels and people's bodies and skills into sellable services. As a result, both become private property, making accumulation (the collection of wealth-producing assets by private individuals) and liberal—

"market"—society possible. Market societies allow the relatively advantaged to deploy their superior resources to command superior gains by disconnecting economic activity from particular persons and places, thereby "disembedding" them from customary social constraints. Social and political values like altruism and patriotism do not operate in the market, where self-interest is believed to produce the best possible result for all.[27]

Individualism naturally attracted people expecting to gain power and wealth from its acceptance. Worker movements like the Levellers also embraced individualism because it gave all human beings equal moral and political status. But the equality of possessive individualism comes with insecurity. On the one hand, if personal autonomy is a private property right, every free man owns himself and can decide whether to sell his labor and/or limited access to his body to a buyer who can pay wages. On the other hand, the buyer has no interest in any specific individual worker and is not required to be responsible for his welfare. Such "alienation of labor" is a basic requirement of capitalism. Without it, employers would have to house, feed, educate, and care for their workers. In a modern economy, workers must do these things for themselves.[28]

Although alienation of labor and commodification, which we discussed in previous chapters, detach the economy from the rest of social life, even highly privatized economies remain enmeshed in political and social structures. Businesses don't run schools for everyone's future employees or build roads to take everyone's goods to markets; banking systems and stock markets have to be regulated and supervised by the state to prevent market rigging and theft. If there were no laws against pollution, we'd all be choked by the poison gases, liquids, and solid wastes generated by people and corporations who would not want to pay to dispose of them properly, no matter how much they injured others. Indeed, when you think about how many local, state, and federal agencies produce systems and services to support industry and agriculture, you can see why the modern "private" economy is far more dependent on the services of the state than the traditional economies it replaced.[29]

Secularism and Sovereignty

A similar disembedding of religion from social life detaches religious authority and practice from political systems. The result is a secular society. Quasi-religious rituals (like saying the Pledge of Allegiance or singing "God Save the Queen") train citizens to venerate the state and its institutions,[30] while religion as such is protected by rights guarantees. In a secular state, citizens are not required to be religious at all, much less to be members of the ruler's religion of choice or to support religious organizations with their taxes. These principles are set out explicitly in Thomas Jefferson's arguments for Virginia's 1779 statute for religious freedom. Jefferson and James Madison argued for even stronger religious freedoms than the First Amendment guarantees in the U.S. Constitution, not because they themselves were unreligious but because they believed that state support of religion would corrupt both religion and human reason.[31]

Secularization is a foundation of the modern state system because of its intimate connection to sovereignty. Sovereignty for a state is equivalent to individualism for a person. Individualism as negative liberty, the idea that my rights end a millimeter from your nose, has its counterpart in negative sovereignty. Most definitions of sovereignty start where we did earlier in this chapter, with the proposition that a nation-state is a bounded territory and preserves its autonomous existence through its own efforts. A state governs itself by creating rules and institutions that give its agents a monopoly over the legitimate use of violence on its territory.[32]

This is a big change from the past, when mercenaries and free lances could be hired by anyone to challenge someone else's right to rule.[33] Sovereignty makes states responsible for protecting their populations from outside attacks and also from domestic criminality and unrest. Political scientist Robert Jackson says that negative sovereignty is only the beginning of the sovereign obligations of a mature state. He points also to "positive sovereignty," the ability to supply populations with goods and services, like roads, health care, education, and airports, necessary for modern life. The obligations of sovereignty are interdependent. State capacity to keep the peace and support a thriving economy depends in part on state capacity to protect citizens and provide for the general welfare.[34]

Negative sovereignty says that a state can do whatever it wants as long as it doesn't interfere with the internal affairs of another state. The rules and values that institute negative sovereignty are among the strongest constituting the nation-states system,[35] yet, in practice, there are limits to negative sovereignty. The U.S. national security strategies of 2002 and 2006, which we discuss further in chapter 7, challenge it directly by claiming the right to invade another country to topple a disliked regime or pursue people thought to be terrorists. As Cindy Weber shows, powerful states routinely ignored negative sovereignty when it was in their interests to intervene in the affairs of weaker states.[36] Before the announcement of the Bush Doctrine of preventive intervention, however, few did this openly. Indeed, despite the real flaws in negative sovereignty (such as its use as a screen for human rights violations),[37] serious repercussions would result from its disappearance. Among the most important is a likely increase in the frequency of war.

Positive sovereignty rests on the legitimacy (authority and social support) a state can claim as an effective defender of domestic rights and provider of goods and services for the general welfare. You will recall from chapter 1 that, in *Leviathan*, Hobbes imagines that the State of Nature ends when a state and its subjects agree to a social contract that gives the ruler the right to make and enforce the law. This is Hobbes's image of domestic legitimacy. Another view says that a legitimate state is the joint property of its citizens. The United States started out as a nation-state based on popular sovereignty. Its constitution begins with the words "We the people of the United States," not "The government of the United States" or even "The United States" to reflect that understanding.

In older nation-states, as people struggled to win more rights from their rulers, they gradually converted their status as subjects (inferiors) into citizens (members). The originally artificial notion of social contract became identified with constitutions and laws guaranteeing rights and entitlements to citizens by virtue of their membership in the political community.[38] Today we envision legitimacy as the state's reward for protecting civil liberties and acting as a disinterested referee among equally protected citizen-competitors.

Negative sovereignty and secularism were parallel developments incorporated into the rules of the game governing relations among European states beginning in the seventeenth century. Negative sovereignty was a strategy to prevent kings from excusing their invasion of other states by saying that they just wanted to "save" religious minorities from persecution. The Treaty of Augsburg in 1555 instituted the doctrine of *cujus regio, eius religio*—in effect, whoever governs a country gets to pick its official religion. This principle defines religion as a purely domestic concern between a king and his subjects. Failure to live up to it led to the bloody Thirty Years' War, resolved in the treaties of Westphalia (1648), which reconfirmed secularism and negative sovereignty as constitutive principles of states and the state system.[39]

After 1648, secularism developed as a principle of domestic politics, too. As religion became less likely to cause wars, rulers were less likely to see religious (and other) minorities as potential traitors. Religious majorities felt less compelled to convert religious minorities by force when they no longer were permitted to terrorize or kill them legally. A growing sense of security was both a cause and an effect of laws requiring legal toleration and norms encouraging prudent politeness. Both made it easier for people to live together peacefully (most of the time). Religious toleration did not guarantee complete political equality, especially when states had official religions and enforced laws in their favor. It did, however, encourage removal of religious dissent from the list of capital crimes and helped to shrink the scope of legal discrimination against religious minorities. Even so, some religious groups today—most notably Jews but also Roman Catholics, Muslims, Mormons, and others—continue to experience official and unofficial discrimination in various jurisdictions.

Secularism and the toleration it institutionalizes is called "cosmopolitanism" at home. As we noted earlier, Immanuel Kant recommends cosmopolitanism, or the extension of human rights to "strangers"—citizens of the world, if not of the particular nation they currently inhabit—as one of his strategies for keeping the peace.[40] Together, secularism and toleration offer individuals freedom to make personal life choices by discouraging the state (and the neighbors) from interfering. At the same time, they also increase the vulnerability of a society to corruption because they undermine the authority of coercive social structures, like the church, that lend legitimacy to the state's efforts to enforce universal beliefs and standards of behavior. This problem invites new ways to think about sin and virtue.

We tend to equate corruption with sin; so did people in earlier times, when greed was a "deadly" sin and a source of spiritual decay.[41] But when Renaissance thinkers rediscovered the heroic values of antiquity, some people began to think that greed might not be so bad after all. In their minds, greed changed from a "passion"—a sinful compulsion that should be resisted—to an "interest"—in this case, a rational desire for self-advancement. This change in meaning accompanied the acceptance of individualism and its emphasis on personal achievement (a kind of heroism) as a social value.

Excessive individualism could be oppressive, however. Royal "absolutists," like Louis XIV whose identification of the state with himself is the epigraph beginning this chapter, measured their individual achievement by seizing more territory, taming barons and bishops, and acquiring the capacity to control their

realms on power-over terms without the help of local intermediaries. Both Protestant and Catholic kings asserted a divine right to rule. They appealed to businessmen-clients for financial support, offering in exchange protections (privileges) and tax relief (immunities) that strengthened the new institutions associated with states and markets.[42] Religious dissidents protected by toleration often complained about overly powerful kings and their favored wealthy clients, but few argued that self-interest was bad. Many were businessmen themselves. Some believed that work was equivalent to a calling, and that making money in this world was a sign that they would be saved in the next.[43]

Personal achievement became a mark of virtue at the same time that power-seeking kings needed to be brought under control. This is how greed as self-interest became a political resource. Political theorists made distinctions between "rational interests" (which were acceptable) and "irrational passions" (which were not). A rational interest in profits might be used to counter an irrational passion for glory—make money, not war! (a sentiment Kant would recognize). By the eighteenth century, interests were seen as diffuse and multiple, able even to act as checks on one another, while commerce was touted as a more constructive mode of competition than warfare, both domestically and internationally.

This conception of checks and balances was consciously and deliberately imported into the structure of the state with the adoption of the U.S. Constitution in 1789. James Madison, writing in *Federalist 10*, identified competing interests as a brake on state power. He envisioned the legitimate state as an impartial referee among competing interests. Similarly, the First Amendment to the U.S. Constitution (ratified in 1791, along with nine others spelling out citizens' rights and liberties) forbade the establishment of a national religion and interference by the state in individual religious preferences and practice. While one could argue that it was the lack of state capacity in the new and diverse United States that made privatization logical and necessary, Madison's (and Jefferson's) belief in the ability of people with property to make good judgments in constitutionally protected spaces of appearance also helped ensure that basic decisions about religion, along with commerce, would be left to individuals.

International System or International Society?

What happens when we try to imagine relations among states as analogous to relations among individuals in society? We get something along the lines of "international society." This is a power-with concept that operates differently from power-over models. International society is not governed by "natural" laws but by arrangements that states determine collectively for themselves. The framework of international society is diplomacy and international law, the written and unwritten customs, conventions, treaties, and rules that states use in their dealings with one another. International law includes the institutions that states set up to enforce those rules, and the norms and values that give a regime its shape and coherence. Regimes are bundles of values, institutions, and conventions of behavior that most people working on a particular issue tend to follow. The Westphalian system is a regime and negative sovereignty is one of its norms, a value that states accept and support even if they don't live up to it all the time. An interesting example is the status of foreign embassies. Under the conventions of international law, an embassy is a little piece of the sovereign state it represents. Refugees try to get inside friendly embassies because governments are strongly inhibited from sending the national police to take them out of a foreign enclave and, under the principle of reciprocity, want the sovereign inviolability of their own embassies respected.

International law also connects the nation-states system with capitalism. Much of international law is codified in treaties regulating economic relations between states. NAFTA (the North American Free Trade Agreement) and the WTO (World Trade Organization) are modern examples. These bodies reflect a part of the vision of the Levellers in that they operate as though the various state participants (the technical term is "states parties") are equal. Every state party is supposed to obey the same rules. The norm of sovereignty says that all sovereign states have equal rights, are equally responsible for obeying international rules, and equally entitled to the benefits of doing so (there are practical problems with this assumption that we'll explore in chapter 9). Each agreement outlines conditions giving members access to one or more bodies authorized to resolve disputes under the rules, and describes situations in which rule violators are to lose their equal access to the trade regime defined by the treaty. Consistent rule-bound behavior is a qualification for membership. Such treaties are thereby self-enforcing because states parties must obey the rules to maintain their access to the trade regime. Loss of equal access to international markets is a high price to pay for an illegitimate resort to power-over.

"But that is not all!" as the Cat in the Hat used to say. When you look at them more closely, you can see that these agreements aren't just *saying* that all states are equal. They are *requiring* them to be equal, too. Member states must harmonize their trade laws to conform to international standards outlined in the agreements. If a state party subsidizes farmers who grow key crops, or industries that are its economic and political mainstays, it has to end these unfair protections or risk fines, suspension, or expulsion from the regime.

Fairness toward all is a good general principle, but problems arise when protections for workers are automatically defined as unfair under trade treaties. For example, under NAFTA, a state with environmental protection regulations that keep foreign and domestic investors from constructing polluting industries can be sued for damages by the foreign investor for infringing on her right to a profit (this is governed by NAFTA's infamous Chapter 11, a rule that we think should be changed—see chapter 9). Yet in spite of such drawbacks, membership in international trade regimes appeals to states at all levels of development. Nearly every state in the world wants to get into the WTO and, in spite of the horrors of Chapter 11, the governments of most countries in Central and South America spent years trying to get NAFTA expanded to include them as well.

The costs and benefits of membership may be unequal with regard to individual countries and different groups within each country, but the potential benefits encourage governments and populations to accept them. One example comes from Kuwait, a rich oil-exporting country in the Persian Gulf where a diverse parliamentary coalition composed of Islamists (religious fundamentalists), economic neoliberals (market fundamentalists—we'll talk about market fundamentalism in chapter 9), and aspiring democratizers (political liberals) all supported harmonizing Kuwait's laws with the provisions of the WTO. Kuwaiti Islamists, like the Puritans of early America, are businessmen who see the international economy as an avenue for religious renewal and economic freedom. Neoliberals, secularist and Islamist, want to get the state out of the economy, a big issue in a country where the state owns the largest industries and controls the vast majority of national income and wealth. WTO rules make it hard for the Kuwaiti state to resist privatizing entirely. Kuwaiti democratizers see the rules of the WTO, especially requirements that the state open its economy equally to all investors (including Kuwaitis) and conform to transparent accounting and trading rules designed to minimize corruption by eliminating the secrecy necessary for under-the-table deals, as the only way to get an authoritarian state under control (checks and balances again). Very different motivations led these often bitterly opposed parliamentary factions to the same conclusion—that conforming to WTO rules would be good for Kuwaitis.[44]

Altered States

"Globalization" is a catchall term that refers to a very large number of rapid changes whose overall effect is to connect people and resources more quickly and directly, making all of us more sensitive and vulnerable to events happening around the world.[45] Those who welcome globalization say that it adds to total wealth by expanding trade and investment, and contributes to peace by connecting individuals and groups across national borders in cooperative, mutually beneficial relationships.[46] Critics argue that capitalist globalization erodes the authority and integrity of the nation-state in world politics.[47] They fear that corporations and banks are undermining state capacity to serve populations. They see other offshoots of globalization, like mercenary military forces and international terrorism, as threats to individual welfare.[48] We'll discuss terrorism in chapter 7 and the economic and technical aspects of globalization further in chapter 9. Here we touch on some of the pathologies of contemporary states.

Positive sovereignty refers both to a state's authority throughout its territory and its capacity to enforce that authority. Before World War II, nation-states had to demonstrate capacity before their sovereignty was recognized by their peers. Afterward, decolonization gradually created new, formally independent nation-states that enjoyed negative sovereignty from the beginning, whether they had demonstrated adequate capacity or not.[49] This reflected the post–World War II value of sovereign equality but not always the reality because some of these new entities were quasi-states with little positive sovereignty. Their governments were unrepresentative, often a legacy of divide-and-rule tactics adopted by colonial powers. Their leaders took the state's resources for themselves and members of their group rather than providing them to the people as a whole, and sometimes local warlords contested that theft by getting the resources first and using them to challenge the regime. Warlord Charles Taylor, for example, seized control of diamond mines in his attempt to take over the government of Liberia, then held by another warlord, Samuel Doe.[50] Some states with weak institutions and rich resources were luckier because their leaders could claim legitimacy on other grounds. Tradition, provision of social benefits, and success on the battlefield also are useful in building state capacity and popular support. Examples include the oil-exporting monarchies of the Persian Gulf.[51]

A poorly institutionalized state harbors protected spaces where criminals and political entrepreneurs can operate in relative safety.[52] States that become unable to protect their borders, catch and punish criminals, or suppress rebellion are failed states. They are the favorite prey of warlords, who hope to take over as much of the dying state as they can. "Parastates" is the name journalist Misha Glenny, an observer of the demise of the former Yugoslavia, gives to the offspring of such failed states.[53] Seizing choice morsels of the parent body, leaders of parastates are often vicious heads of entourages that delight in inflicting violence, often with resources acquired from the dying/dead parent state. In the former Yugoslavia, for example, the Serb remnant inherited the bulk of the army and its weapons, giving the parastates of Serbia proper and the Serb enclave in Bosnia a military advantage over other fragments of the expiring country. Another example is Chechnya, still nominally part of the Russian Federation, where warlords acquired weapons from the disintegrating Soviet military when the Soviet Union collapsed. A third is Iraq, which cannot control its borders, provide public safety to the population, and has not had a competent government since the United States toppled Saddam in 2003.[54]

The inclusion of Yugoslavia and the Soviet Union in the ranks of failed states shows that this condition is not limited to Robert Jackson's postcolonial quasi-states. Any state can fail if its institutions decay or are smashed and it ceases to be able to serve and protect its people. Any state can crumble into parastates if leaders are ruthless enough and followers vicious enough to kill the people who stand in the way of their taking what they want. A failed state is a Hobbesian world; a parastate is even worse. Clea Koff asks:

> Why . . . [do] governments decide to murder their own people? . . . I think the answer is self-interest. Particular people in a government of a single ideology with effectively no political opponents have supported national institutions that maintain power for themselves. What muddied the waters were the "reasons" the decision makers gave for their political agendas. Take Kosovo: were the killings and expulsions in the 1990s really meant to avenge the Battle of 1389, as Serbian president Slobodan Milosevic was fond of stat-

ing? Or was it because mineral-rich parts of Kosovo can produce up to $5 billion in annual export income for Serbia? Or take Rwanda: did Hutus kill their neighbors *and* all their neighbors' children simply because they were Tutsi, as the government exhorted them to do? Or was it because the government promised Hutus their neighbors' farmland, land that otherwise could only have been inherited by those very children, and those children's children, ad infinitum?[55]

Even apparently stable states may experience pressures to divide.[56] A Scottish National Party (SNP) government in Scotland has renewed local interest in disuniting the United Kingdom. English citizens resent the disproportionate representation of Scots in the British parliament and the higher level of services Scottish citizens get from the British state. For their part, Scots like their state services but dislike British foreign policy in the Middle East. Since their 2007 parliamentary victory, SNP leaders have floated trial balloons about moving from "devolution," the home-rule policy that returned local power to the Scottish legislature, to dissolution, which would dissolve the United Kingdom into two (or more) completely independent states. It might not stop there, either. If the Soviet and Yugoslav experience is any indication, once a nation-state begins to unravel it is hard to predict where that process will end.

In fact, the former Yugoslavia is still dividing. The United States and Russia were at loggerheads about whether Kosovo, which left Serbia without the blessing of the UN in February 2008, should be independent. When the United States recognized Kosovo's unilateral declaration of independence, Russia refused to go along and noted that other separatist regions might equally well claim the right to independent sovereignty under this precedent. The Republika Srpska, the Serb enclave in the middle of Bosnia, is one example of a separatist region that threatens to follow suit. In 2008, first South Ossetia and then Abkhazia declared their independence from Georgia, with Russian but not U.S. support and consent, encouraging separatists in the Russian provinces of Chechnya and Ingushetia to regroup.

Moving westward, one among several other potential dissolutions could be undertaken in Belgium, where minority Walloons have long resented discrimination and ridicule from dominant Flemings. Walloons point to the surprising, rapid, and peaceful dissolution of Czechoslovakia in 1993 as a model of what they would like to do. And there are many more such cases; indeed, no country is immune to breakup. China relies on military force and religious manipulation to maintain its hold on Tibet, rightly fearing that if Tibet were to break away successfully, other marginalized regions, such as Xinjiang (aka, East Turkestan), might try to follow.

Postelection conflicts also show that the nation-state as a territory hosting an "imagined community" of citizens is perhaps more fiction than fact. One shocking example occurred following the December 2007 election in Kenya. Long thought to be the most politically successful sub-Saharan state in east Africa, as many as one thousand Kenyans were murdered and well over a million were made homeless in the violence following a disputed electoral count. And then there is the United States. Following the disputed 2004 election, maps circulating on the Internet projected a partly reorganized North America incorporating "blue" states into a "United States of Canada," and "red" states into "Jesusland." Most Americans reject the élite-led polarization that can destroy politics anywhere, but the unity of nation-states everywhere depends on the integrity of their leaders and the transparency of their elections.[57]

Are States an Endangered Species?

All states impose burdens on citizens, and many governments are corrupt, incompetent, or both. Critics of Anglo-American capitalism charge large and powerful states with choosing to support and protect corporations and banks at the expense of weak state institutions and vulnerable populations.[58] Some weak states rent out their sovereignty, hosting corporations seeking to escape taxation, supplying flags of convenience to ships too broken down to qualify as seaworthy to anyone who takes marine safety seriously, and accepting toxic wastes that no one else wants.[59] Could globalization be ending the era of the nation-state as the most powerful actor in world politics? To critics of capitalism who also are critics of states, this presents a dilemma: failed states are Hobbesian worlds in which no one wants to live, but states with capacity offer little improvement if their governments are oppressive at home and dangerous abroad. Other critics are more positive, saying that, whatever else globalization is doing, it is expanding civil society, helping individuals and groups operating at home and in the world to exercise checks on states and other concentrations of power. To them, civil society is an ensemble of participating agents affecting human destinies, part of "the international community" made up of states, firms, groups, and persons who embrace cosmopolitanism as a way of life.[60]

Institutions of domestic civil society—churches, firms, banks, and voluntary associations ranging from the Red Cross and the YWCA to Amnesty International and National Association of Broadcasters—are venues organized by citizens to assert and pursue their interests. As we noted earlier, business and religious groups have long been prominent in oppositional civil societies. Medieval businessmen were clients of kings, but this relationship was never trouble-free. You will recall that traders depended on rulers for safe passage to and from the Champagne fairs. When Champagne and Brie were absorbed into France, traders ceased to be protected and were actually harassed and harmed by the new rulers. Another example exists in artisans enriching the quality of life in Samarkand but who had been kidnapped and brought there by force rather than coming on their own. Kings routinely borrowed money from wealthy clients and, especially before government bonds became formalized through parliaments and investment regimes, they just as routinely defaulted on their loans.[61] Organizing to protect themselves against bad behavior by rulers was a perfectly reasonable response to the risks of doing business by traders and bankers in and with states.

Religious groups challenged states from a different framework of interests, mostly by objecting to encroachments on the authority of religious leaders but sometimes in response to the persecution of individuals. Their advantage was to be able to claim divine protection for their actions, just as kings claimed a divine right to rule. Religious leaders were more dangerous to rulers than business leaders because many were personalities in their own right. Some—think of John Calvin and Martin Luther—were more popular than many kings. They challenged the legitimacy of states through negative portrayals, like Saint Augustine's description of a corrupt Roman empire in *The City of God*, and by creating positive examples of enlightened rule, like the government Mohammad established in Medina that even attracted some of his former opponents. Continuing a tradition of "godly governance" going back to Moses, John Calvin set up a religious utopia in Geneva; many early settlers in North America crossed the Atlantic hoping to found communities that would approximate the kingdom of God on earth.

John Winthrop's career epitomizes the dual forces of religion and business as foundations of civil society. Winthrop led the group of settlers who came from England in 1630 to establish a trading company in Massachusetts. The charter of the Massachusetts Bay Company authorized its stockholders (called "freemen") to elect a governor and other company officials every year. The company was not allowed to make laws that did not conform to the laws of England, but otherwise there were few restrictions on its procedures.

> [T]he stockholders, taking advantage of the omission in the charter of any specified meeting place, carried the Company lock, stock, and barrel to Massachusetts Bay, where they turned the charter into the constitution of the colony and opened freemanship, without any requirement to purchase stock, to all free adult males belonging to a Congregational church.[62]

As historian Edmund Morgan observes, the charter created a republic, one whose governing principles were greatly at odds with those of the "mother country" the colonizing freemen had left behind. It required annual popular elections for what effectively were political leaders and, as amended, it made populist churches the cradles of citizenship. The risks of these assertions of independence were not lost on Winthrop, who served as governor of the new Massachusetts Bay Colony during most of its early history. He tried to convince freemen to make as few laws as possible at their quarterly meetings so that the king and his advisors might not notice that they were doing things that were "repugnant to the laws of England."[63] But the colonists demanded their democratic rights under the charter, insisting that the rule of law rather than the will of their governor should apply in Massachusetts. The freemen prevailed, especially during a three-year period when Winthrop was not the colony's governor. It is not surprising that the authorities back in England soon noticed the revolutionary nature of the Massachusetts experiment. Eventually, though not in Winthrop's lifetime, the king took the government of Massachusetts away from the freemen.

The Massachusetts Bay Colony highlights how religion and business served as dual foundations for civil society around the world. From the religious perspective, the colonists were idealists fighting for justice and righteousness. Idealism was the wellspring of their energy and determination to make new lives in the "New World." Unfortunately, the freemen also were stubborn and intolerant. They were hardheaded, insisting on making laws even though they knew it could get them in trouble with the king. They also were hardhearted toward any minority zealots willing to fight to the last breath against an equally zealous majority that was quick to punish doctrinal nonconformity. The majority banished dissenters like Roger Williams, who left to found his own colony of Rhode Island and Providence Plantations, and Anne Hutchinson, whose eviction led to her death at the hands of the native peoples being dispossessed by the colonists.

Yet the colony also was democratic and rule-bound. Its procedures were set out in a contract that not only specified "stockholder" rights but also community institutions—a governor and a "general court" composed of all the freemen meeting quarterly to make the laws for the company. (It was this right that the freemen refused to give up, even though by insisting on the letter of that right they jeopardized and eventually lost it.) The contract was a constitution and in its form and operation it can be seen as a direct precursor of the national compacts that limit the reach of governments in modern states. Unlike the Massachusetts Bay Company Charter, however, most constitutions today also offer some protection to dissenters and nonconformists. The contract as a product of political action constitutes the primary structure of regimes of toleration, making cosmopolitan life—plurality—possible.

Possible, but not guaranteed, which is why civil society is as important now as then, and why it extends beyond religious dissidents and corporations to other groups, including some organized across national boundaries. The Puritans' ideas about freedom and equality traveled from England to Massachusetts and Rhode Island and back to England, where they underpinned the first-ever modernizing revolution in the mid-seventeenth century.[64] Calvin's Geneva experiment in the 1500s attracted the attention of philosophers whose ideas contributed to two eighteenth-century revolutions, one in British North America and the other in France. As Alex Colás has observed, ideas of freedom and the often small but always enthusiastic groups that spread them were integral to the success of people seeking to establish representative governments.[65]

In chapter 3, we saw contemporary evidence that civil society in this sense is alive and well. Jiřina Siklová and Martin Luther King Jr. organized with like-minded partners to stand against authoritarian regimes and unjust legal systems. These and other activists are prominent in the global fight for human rights. Just as in the seventeenth century, civil society groups promoting human rights are organized across political boundaries. Human Rights Watch, Médecins sans frontières (MSF—Doctors without Borders), and Amnesty International are full of individuals committed to exposing rights violations and mobilizing international pressure to make them stop.[66] Along with nonstate corporate actors like the Catholic Church and ad hoc groups such as Let Free-

dom Ring, activists organized demonstrations against human rights violations by the Chinese government during the 1997 visit of Chinese president
Jiang Zemin to the United States and the 2008 tour of the Beijing Olympic
Torch. Human rights activists have saved millions indirectly through their
lobbying and publicity campaigns, and hundreds of thousands directly
through projects that, for groups like MSF, also provide the opportunity to observe conditions on the ground.

Analysts differ on the importance of human rights since the terrorist attacks
on the United States in September 2001. Michael Ignatieff asked in 2002, "Why
criticize Russia's war against Chechnya when Chechen jihadis are fighting
America in the mountains of Afghanistan"?[67] One year later, the U.S. military
asked a similar question—why criticize a terrorist group like the Mujahideen-e-
Khalq Organization (MKO) when it is attacking Iranians, residents of another
"axis of evil" power? Indeed, U.S. military leaders in Iraq signed a cease-fire
agreement with the MKO in April 2003 that allowed it to keep all its weapons,
including hundreds of tanks and thousands of light arms, as long as it did not
attack U.S. forces. The United States was publicly embarrassed and renounced
the agreement a few weeks later, but it continues to support the MKO, reportedly with financial backing and training of its activists.[68] Ignatieff's question is
reflected in how much human rights worldwide have been diminished since
then, including *by* the United States, which has been exposed as having tortured
prisoners of war,[69] and *in* the United States, where the government has violated
the law and constitution to spy illegally on Americans.[70]

If human rights activists are on the defensive around the world, how can civil
society challenge state power effectively? This can be answered by going back
to the source—religious and business interests. We examine contemporary religious activism in greater detail in chapter 9. Here we note how economic actors
are addressing human rights, nationally and internationally. The prominence of
businesspeople and business groups in civil society reflects their superior social
and economic resources. The record of these actors as promoters of human
rights is ambiguous, however, as is their effectiveness in promoting the economic development they themselves tout as their contribution to human society around the world. Indeed, statistics show that a majority of people living in
low-capacity states that rely primarily on "the market" for "development" have
experienced little, if any, of its promised benefits,[71] while we all live in societies
where the growing power of business has increased inequality and helped destroy traditional institutions.[72] Corporations, with governments' blessings, invest in impoverished areas, taking advantage of cheap labor to produce goods
for rich countries' markets. But as we showed in chapter 4, the migration of
manufacturing is just another way to describe the migration of jobs. Michael
Moore's 1989 documentary *Roger and Me* is an often horrifying snapshot of how
outsourcing automobile production from the United States to Mexico devastated one small U.S. city.

The dominance of business interests in civil society carries other risks. In the
United States, prodemocracy Republicans and Democrats in Congress call this

dominance both a cause and an effect of political and economic corruption, and they have struggled for years to limit business contributions to electoral campaigns. Even more troubling is the impact of business dominance on democracy itself. Analyst Kevin Phillips sees wealth becoming a substitute for the human resources that voters represent to politicians.[73] Especially when voter turnout is low, politicians can get what they need to be (re)elected by serving the interests of a few large donors rather than having to accommodate the many interests of the electorate as a whole. The result is crowding out—the wealthy few have direct access to decision makers who depend on their largesse, while the middle-income many can't get heard by the officials making decisions that affect their whole lives.[74]

Another question is whether civil society itself is democratic. To answer that we need to look inside civil society organizations and also at their behavior as part of larger political systems. Inside, we know that many such groups are not democratic at all. Quite a few churches and most businesses are like little kingdoms, bureaucratic hierarchies ruled by clerics and CEOs checked only by government and market forces. Civil society organizations also are exclusive— you had to belong to a Congregational church to vote in the Massachusetts Bay Colony, just as you must belong to the Sierra Club or the National Association of Broadcasters to vote in these groups. Exclusivity limits democracy outside, too. Civil society organizations work for the interests of their members, which means they often work against the interests of nonmembers. The U.S. Chamber of Commerce opposes unionization and other movements for workers' rights; the Ku Klux Klan opposes the rights of nonwhites, along with Catholics, Jews, and other groups the Klan calls anti-American. Insofar as civil society groups are parts of a larger system of checks and balances, one that is regulated by a higher authority (so that business owners can't shoot union organizers, and vice versa, and the Klan can't burn down people's houses or lynch people they disagree with), this self-centeredness is probably OK. But without an authority to make and enforce rules of engagement, "civil society" is just another term for "vigilantes."

Changes of State

The nation-state today is far stronger and commands more resources than its medieval predecessors. Even so, individuals and groups still manage to challenge state authority with some success. Human rights groups like Amnesty International and the Committee on Academic Freedom in the Middle East and North America bring state crimes into public view and mobilize international coalitions to apply pressure on offending governments and institutions.[75] Economic agents supply investment, trade, and jobs that improve the lives of many, and use their clout to gain advantageous positions in the undeveloped economies of weak states. Just like the Puritans, today's militant religious activists defy states in the name of God, often in causes many see as just.

A burgeoning industry gaining attention as a result of the Iraq war is military contracting. Preinvasion studies of these new mercenaries accepted the flawed neoclassical argument that mercenary forces are inherently cheaper than military organizations maintained by states (they aren't), although they did identify moral issues arising from creating an industry whose interests lie in perpetual war.[76] It is difficult to control private military forces in a world where only states are bound by international law. One example is the decision of four contractors working in Iraq to save time by driving through Falluja against military orders. That cost all four their lives and touched off a wave of violence that took two Marine battalions to subdue. Another example is the role of contractors in torturing prisoners at Abu Ghraib.[77] Even acts unrelated to their duties that would be regarded as crimes if they had been committed at home go mostly uninvestigated and unprosecuted when they are committed abroad.[78]

Mercenaries play all sides of a conflict in their search for profits, and much of what they do is criminal—they are neither subject to nor protected by the rules of war. Consequently, whether they take their skills into wars or criminal enterprises like the drug trade or human trafficking, mercenaries enjoy substantial impunity.[79] Perhaps the greatest danger from the reappearance of mercenaries in enterprises of violence in the world today is that it refutes the state's claim to be the only legitimate wielder of force. When states themselves go to the market to buy mercenary services and enter into treaties (make contracts) with freelance—potentially terrorist—organizations, they fritter away their legitimacy and undermine their capacity to keep order.

Contracting as a strategy for providing and delivering state services is visible in other areas, too, such as prisons, schools, and welfare services.[80] Contracting, and joint ventures between states and private organizations (public-private partnerships) are manifestations of the drive toward privatization that blossomed in the United Kingdom and the United States during the 1980s. It became an international project in the 1990s, when the Soviet Union and its bloc dissolved, opening the economies of the newly independent states of central and eastern Europe to foreign investment.[81] The growth of public-private partnerships occurred along with a pullback in regulation, especially in the United States. This new emphasis on privatization and deregulation allowed the formation of novel public-private projects and offshore financial instruments by corporations like Enron,[82] and whole industries such as "subprime" mortgage lending and the "packaging" of shaky mortgages into securities sold throughout the world.[83] Adding to the complexity and lack of transparency that are features of such arrangements,[84] the George W. Bush administration has extended domestic and international public-private partnerships to religious organizations, too.[85]

Most modern civil society actors are regulated by states, just as the Massachusetts Bay Company ultimately was regulated by the king of England. Yet the actions of John Winthrop and other freemen show that determined individuals and groups can challenge a powerful state directly and undermine its authority over the long term. Also, while it is true that the expansion of human rights in the New World through the American Revolution—and the U.S. Constitution—arose directly from actions taken by the freemen of the Massachusetts Bay Company, other actions by the colonists violated human rights. Colonists banished fellow freemen even though they knew that ejecting dissenters from the community would deprive the exiles of their property and expose them to mortal danger. They took the lands and lives of the native peoples they found in Massachusetts,[86] viewing them as outside of their communities of obligation and therefore as exploitable and expendable.

To argue that civil society in any era is either a benign or a malignant force is simplistic. Like states, civil society can be good or bad depending on what it does. The civil society debate is a symptom of a much larger change in how we view world politics. Although states use hybrid organizations for their own purposes,[87] the development of civil society represents a different vision of the distribution of power and authority than the one that states prefer. Unlike modern assumptions that place the state at the center of world politics, the postmodern thrust of the civil society debate counts nonstate allies and opponents of states as autonomous international agents. This debate and the events that produced it are signs that the heteronomy that made the medieval world interesting and difficult to control is not a thing of the past but a characteristic of the present and, perhaps even more so, of the future.

6

People and Borders

Borders are scratched across the hearts of men, by strangers with a calm, judicial pen, and when the borders bleed we watch with dread the lines of ink along the map turn red.

—Marya Mannes

Borders are lines that divide. They separate things from one another (especially countries) and keep things together (especially people). Sometimes borders are easy to cross. At other times, they are impossible to cross. This seems odd, for the borders that divide countries and people are largely imaginary.[1] Oh, sometimes they follow rivers or mountains, but there is nothing inherent in geography that says a border should be "here" and not "there." Borders are social constructions. Human beings draw them and, having done so, come to regard them as "natural" features of the landscape. Borders are imagined and could be marked anywhere, but they have real effects: border crossings, fences, barbed wire, guns, mines. "Your passport, please."

This chapter is about the lines that divide and contain us. We begin with a discussion of what borders do—that is, what social functions they perform. Next we examine how borders come to be, especially between countries. How is it that impermeable lines are drawn where formerly there were none? What keeps them there? After that, we consider how borders in politics contain and connect even as they keep apart what is recognized as legitimate political activity and what is not. In the fourth part of the chapter, we look at what might be called "in-between spaces": frontiers, borderlands, liminality, what the Greeks called *metaxu*. Finally, we ask whether borders should be regarded not as demarcating the safe from the dangerous but rather as lines that make both pluralism and diversity possible. In this sense, borders could be more about connections among people than a means of keeping them apart.

What Is a Border?

Borders are everywhere. They tell who is "in" and who is "out." They divide places, separate people, and sometimes appear where there were no borders before (occasionally, they disappear, too). Cyprus, for example, is divided by a "Green Line" that runs through the capital city of Nicosia. On one side of the line are Turkish Cypriots, on the other side Greek Cypriots. The border has been there for more than thirty years, ever since the island was invaded by Turkey's military forces, in 1974.[2] Before that line was drawn, Turkish and Greek Cypriots intermingled peacefully and lived next to one another; since then, they have been separated and often at odds.[3] Similar patterns can be found the world over: a line is drawn on the ground, often by force, and people on either side are kept apart.

Why are there so many borders? Who draws them? Why are they in the places where they are? Can they be changed? And what happens if they do change? At a very early age, children learn about difference and borders when they discover who belongs to their household and who does not; who is family and who is not; who can be trusted and who cannot. Borders are as much about order within as disorder without. As the child grows older, she discovers that borders are fundamental to an ordered and disciplined social life. They are central to the maintenance of social institutions and the consent we give to them. Revisiting Hobbes, the sovereign rules the order inside borders; no one rules the disorder outside them.

At one time or another, we become conscious of the invisible lines that divide some people from others, snaking through neighborhoods, schools, towns, religions, races, ethnicities, income groups, and classes. Crossing such lines can be socially difficult, if not physically impossible. Sometimes such crossings are deadly. Think of Shakespeare's *Romeo and Juliet*, of the war between the Capulets and Montagues, of the very thin line that sometimes divides virtually identical families from each other, or even the families themselves.

Those who cross such lines often do so at their own risk. The risk could be to life and limb, but more often it is to "belonging." If people outside the border seem to differ from those inside, then those inside must be the same (or, at least, appear similar to one another). Sameness extends beyond appearances; it also includes beliefs and practices. Indeed, beliefs and practices can be more important than appearances—the members of the two families in *Romeo and Juliet* are identical to each other except in terms of what Sigmund Freud called "the narcissism of minor differences."[4] Each believes that his house is the greater, even though the houses hardly differ at all. Romeo and Juliet cross the line, finding their differences so minor that they don't matter but, trying to defy convention, lose their lives.

Sameness becomes a refuge, a "source of help, relief, and comfort," as the dictionary puts it.[5] Sameness helps to produce an individual's identity, providing a pattern for behavior that names a person as belonging to one group and not another. The in-group is differentiated from all other groups, and the reenactment and reproduction of in-group patterns becomes instrumental to the maintenance of self, group, and difference. Group members are admonished if they deviate from these patterns and are punished if they do so consistently.[6]

Thus, if someone dares to cross a border defined as inviolate, yet returns without injury or change, the very act of crossing becomes a threat to group identity and cohesion. It demonstrates that crossing is possible, even at considerable real or imagined risk, and that beliefs and practices on the "other side" may not be so all-corrupting and dangerous that they cannot be tolerated or even welcomed. By the same token, however, a crossing and failure to return indicates the necessity of maintaining the border. Having "gone over" the line, that person has also gone over to those across the line, becoming the Other.[7]

Ultimately, the very existence of such imagined lines serves to keep some in and others out. Group members discipline themselves; they do not need someone to threaten them in order to stay in line. They act in prescribed and expected manners so as not to be named a threat to group identity and cohesiveness. Violators are punished, marginalized, or even ejected from the group. In earlier times, such a fate could be tantamount to a death sentence; today, it may have devastating psychological results. We seek solace and security in groups, it would seem, and to be a member of no group is to lose that sense of safety and belonging.[8]

Think about the borders in your life, about the beliefs and practices that separate your family or in-group from others. As a student, you might be regarded with disdain by "townies," and you might return the feelings. Does your college compete in sports with some other nearby school? Is the rivalry an intense one? Do you take care to not to wear the "wrong" colors on the day of the Big Game? What happens if you do? Now consider how those differences are magnified and reinforced between countries, in language, in customs, in appearances, in practices. Make a list of those differences and try to explain why they matter.

You will discover that they do not seem all that important, yet they seem to make all the difference.

A Short Genealogy of Borders

The primordial border may have divided kin groups from one another, a line inscribed in lineage and blood. Kin groups are communities and, although they might have shared a language and culture with other groups nearby, and traded and intermarried with them, kinship corresponded to territory, access to food and water, and survival. Many societies had elaborate systems for categorizing kin and nonkin, and complicated rules about who could marry whom. The effect was to maintain and reinforce distinctions in order to ensure group survival. In some societies even today, the marriage of a son or daughter into another kin group means his or her permanent departure from the natal community.[9] In countries where "honor killing" is still practiced, a woman who marries without her family's consent can be killed.[10]

As agriculture developed and spread, some parts of the world became crowded relative to available land. Residents sought to mark the boundaries of their communities of obligation more carefully. People inside these communities were entitled to food, protection, and respect denied to those outside. Yet the borders of kin-based communities were fluid, expanding when resources were plentiful or new members appeared who could offer valued services, then shrinking in times of shortages and stress.[11] Today, citizenship defines similar communities of obligation.

As cities, kingdoms, and empires emerged, borders came to signify rule and to distinguish among centers of power: on this side, my king; on that side, your king. Rulers took food, taxes, and labor from those who lived on their side of the border, and these extractions were used to maintain the rulers' power. Between the centers of power and the lands they governed were "borderlands," frontiers, zones where control was never complete and which often changed hands.[12] We shall return to the topic of borderlands later in this chapter.

Many of the borders between modern-day countries are as much a consequence of what we might call "historical accidents" as any type of primordial kinship practices described here and in chapter 5. Rulers sought to build alliances and expand their territories through marriages between royal families. In some cases, one king or queen ruled over widely separated bits and pieces of land, but all were subsumed under the same center of power.[13]

Such alliances were often unstable, and lines of succession were often in dispute. In Europe, the result was centuries of war leading to the further division of some territories and the unification of others. In central Europe there were still something like five hundred German states as late as the end of the seventeenth century. By contrast, by 1500, France had been welded into a single kingdom from more than a dozen formerly independent territories. Still, it was not until the final few decades of the twentieth century that most of the world's borders were firmly fixed, and, even now, some remain in dispute, and a few have yet to be drawn.[14]

Oddly, however, borders did not become significant barriers to passage until the twentieth century. Before then, it was relatively easy to cross them without much in the way of official restrictions or requirements. The passport did not come into general use until the turn of the twentieth century, and many countries were indifferent to migration across borders for many years after that.[15] There are several reasons for the change to a more vigorous policing of borders.

First, until late in the nineteenth century, most countries were overwhelmingly rural, and people routinely moved across notional borders in the course of their everyday activities—herding, farming, taking goods to market towns. Beginning with the shift to capitalist agriculture, stimulated by international trade, and proceeding through the growth of manufacturing and subsequent industrialization, rising demand for food overseas and in increasingly accessible domestic markets favored larger, specialized farms. The poor found themselves pushed off the land. Some made their way into cities where their lack of skills, tools, and other economic resources condemned them to an existence as an underemployed *lumpenproletariat*. Cities offered opportunities for the ambitious and talented to rise, but their social organization was often rigid, denying the upwardly mobile the status they believed should be theirs. Thus, cities also were places where the disaffected among the lower and middling classes mounted uprisings and revolutions. Rulers became concerned about who was living in the cities they governed, where they came from, what they did, and the ideas they held.[16]

Second, state involvement in the management of the national economy, the source of state power, grew as states became more and more involved in providing expensive infrastructure like railroads and, by the end of the nineteenth century, social services and support for dependent groups like the disabled and the elderly. States found that they needed even more information about who lived where, how much money and wealth they had and thus their ability to pay taxes, and the kind of support they needed to stabilize society and ensure their allegiance to the state. Governments became concerned about the demographics of the people living within their jurisdictions, and this led to further measures to control flows into and out of countries.[17]

Third, mass migration, especially to the New World, expanded dramatically during the nineteenth century.[18] Millions of people left Europe due to famine, oppression, and war. This altered the demographics of sending and receiving countries and introduced new languages, practices, and ideas, especially into receiving countries. By the 1920s, most states had installed rigorous immigration controls that limited the number of new arrivals and required that they meet certain standards regarding their health, wealth, and intelligence.[19] States began demanding passports, visas, and all the other paraphernalia of border crossing. After World War II, with its displacement of millions throughout Europe and Asia, movements across borders at first increased and then slackened as the borders of both new and old states crystallized under the pressures of the cold war. But this, too, was a relatively short-lived phenomenon.

By the last decade of the twentieth century, the obsession with national borders had been overtaken by their growing permeability under the pressures of globalization. It began to seem as though goods, capital, environmental pollution, diseases, refugees and migrants, drugs, guns, culture, and ideas could all cross borders without much restriction. The European Union and other regional entities, such as the Gulf Cooperation Council, became more open internally, although this often meant that their restrictions on outsiders increased. Nationalist claims to exclusive rights over territories and people were seen by many as a bane of human civilization; their harmful effects were evident in the civil and social wars in ex-Yugoslavia, Central Asia, the Middle East, and Africa. Some pronounced "the end of the nation-state,"[20] although the evidence supporting this claim was claimed by others to be rather thin.[21]

The Borders Outside

At the same time that national borders seem to be losing their power to contain and exclude, new borders are being drawn everywhere. These, however, are not lines on the ground; rather, they are lines in the mind. Anthropologist Benedict Anderson wrote a book about nationalism with the title *Imagined Communities*.[22] During the last decade of the twentieth century, such communities proliferated, based not only on "nations" but also on other dimensions of solidarity like race, gender, and sexuality. Scholars named this unexpected phenomenon "identity politics."[23] Identity-based groups drew borders between themselves and others. Sometimes these borders differentiated on the basis of ethnicity and at other times on the basis of lifestyle and cultural practices.[24] We will return to this topic below.

Following the attacks on New York and Washington on September 11, 2001, national borders returned with a vengeance. Today there is much more scrutiny than before of who is in and who is out, who is trying to enter, where she comes from, and what she might wish to do. The American state, like others, seeks to reinforce its borders without obstructing economic flows, but finds itself stymied by an equally imperative desire to control the movement of people and money that might be connected to terrorist activities. The results are rather surprising.[25]

In one sense, the United States no longer has real borders, not because lines on the ground are not policed and protected, but because America's presence, and its interests, are so pervasive in so many parts of the world. Despite the bursting of the mortgage bubble and the economic downturn that began in 2007,[26] America's economy remains the largest in the world.[27] U.S. corporations have subsidiaries and strategic allies in all parts of the globe. According to Chalmers Johnson, the U.S. Defense Department admits that it has "some 725" bases outside of the United States around the world.[28] U.S. culture, products, and influence have colonized many places, even those where the presence of American corporations and citizens is invisible or absent.[29]

Borders serve, more and more, to separate *classes* of people rather than *nationalities*. The wealthy encounter few problems crossing borders; they and their money are welcome everywhere. Criminals with funds are also able to cross borders without too much trouble; for the right price, they usually can acquire the necessary identity documents. Only those without money or power find that borders constitute a significant barrier to movement, making them far likelier to be subject to search and arrest by the states whose borders they have crossed than their richer conationals.[30]

The poor also discover that there are as many, if not more, borders within the societies in which they live. Economic stratification makes the well-off and the poor strangers to each other. Even though they may live in the same social space, poor people are denied access to many places within that space. Such denial is effected in many different ways. Sometimes there are physical barriers, such as the gates and fences encircling growing numbers of communities and rising along national borders. Guards, police, and cameras keep an eye on who is present where, and those deemed to be "out of place" can find themselves hustled back whence they came. Restrictions also can be imposed through appearance, dress, manners, practices, and possessions—such as cars. Such borders may not be visible but people "know" where they can go and where they cannot, what they can do and what is forbidden.[31]

The Borders Inside

Borders not only keep people apart; they also keep people together. First, as we saw, borders contain nations within the spaces we call "nation-states." Of course, the uniformity of nation-states is fictitious. There are very few whose populations include only one nationality.[32] Even in states like Austria, where one ethnicity is overwhelmingly dominant, socially obvious borders are drawn among groups according to class, language, and religion.[33] Second, there are often very distinct borders between what is accepted as political and "public" and what is nonpolitical and "private." This type of internal border helps both state and society to maintain order and stability. Third, there are borders within which we are socialized as children and adults, lines that both connect and divide in everyday life, such as those drawn between bodies and genders.

Internal Borders

Prior to the creation of today's nation-states, much of the world was divided into empires or protostates made up of inherited properties. Each had at its core a dynasty that supplied the head of state and chose the allies and advisors who made up the ruling class. Other interests allied themselves with the rulers and constituted one or more elites.[34] Inhabitants of cities, towns, and other territories were subordinated in varying degrees to the rulers of these territories. Nationalism proved able to generate cohesion even among some residents of multinational empires,[35] but this meant little to individuals who aspired to their own seats of power, to groups like native populations in imperialized regions who suffered severe discrimination, or to populations resistant to cultural assimilation, often for religious reasons. In the last half of the twentieth century, most of the colonies of European powers were granted independence as autonomous nation-states. Near the end of the century the last large empire in Europe, the Soviet Union, dissolved; the binational state of Czechoslovakia separated peacefully into two independent states; and Yugoslavia, a multinational state plagued both by power seekers and antagonistic religious minorities, dissolved into secessionist daughter states and warring parastates.[36]

Despite the "ethnic cleansing" marking the redrawing of state boundaries in Europe, few nation-states, old or new, are ethnically homogenous. Those national borders (re)drawn after the two world wars and the end of the cold war were products of imperial history, located according to criteria that had no necessary relationship to where people actually lived or to whom they might be related. Some tribal and ethnic groups were combined into one country; others found themselves residing in and even in control of more than one. In Africa especially, the borders of postcolonial states came to be sacrosanct under decolonization agreements.[37] Today, according to international law, state borders cannot be changed except through domestic ratification and international recognition.[38] It is not difficult to see that war often breaks out because these two conditions are so difficult to meet.[39]

As we noted in chapter 5, among the legacies of imperialism is that, in many new states, one ethnic group was granted or acquired power at independence, after which it ruled the state as its own nation. Which group was left in charge was a result of the administrative policies of the imperial power. The result was that people from other groups were left at a great disadvantage, not only because they were shut out of political power but also because those who controlled the machinery of government also controlled the machinery of the economy. They were the ones who could create property rights and themselves acquire title to the best land and resources. They could issue work and business permits and make rules imposing restrictions on who else could receive them. They could allow activities that favored some groups, and forbid those that favored others. If the differences between groups became great enough and the borders hard enough, violence and civil war could break out.[40]

Consider the case of Rwanda, a small country in Central Africa that was once a colony of Belgium. When the Belgians arrived in Central Africa, they found the region's residents engaged in two occupations: farming and herding. The Belgians believed there were physical as well as historical differences between farmers and herders. The Tutsi were taller, handsomer, and lighter skinned, claimed the Belgians, who also thought that the Tutsi, originating in the Horn of Africa, possessed European blood. The Hutu were imagined as shorter, less attractive, and darker. In fact, the distinction between the two groups in terms of appearance and origin was not a hard and fast one, and had a great deal to do with class and occupation. Many Rwandan families had both Tutsi and Hutu members.[41]

The Belgians favored the Tutsi and exaggerated differences between the two groups by giving more resources and greater opportunities to the Tutsi elite. Because the Tutsi were a small minority, they depended on the Belgians to keep them in their high position, a situation that was just fine with Belgium. But shortly before independence, the Belgians orchestrated a "revolution" that transferred power to the Hutu, who greatly outnumbered the Tutsi and resented them for their greater wealth and privilege. The result was a state and government that, over the following three decades, became more and more authoritarian, and a politics marked by recurrent pogroms and rebellions. The worst episode of violence occurred over a three-month period in 1994, triggered by unknown persons who shot down the plane carrying the Rwandan president, Juvenal Habyarimana, as it prepared to land in Kigali, the capital of Rwanda, on a flight from Burundi, a neighboring state with similar ethnic tensions.[42]

He was returning from a peace conference in Tanzania meant to address growing tensions between Hutu and Tutsi. After Habyarimana's death, eight hundred thousand Tutsi and Hutu were killed in a campaign of genocide masterminded by a large remnant of the Hutu-controlled state.[43] Because of the ethnic differentiation between Hutu and Tutsi and the violence that arose from it, the social borders between the two groups became more "real" than the national borders separating Rwanda from its neighbors. People were forced to keep to their own group because crossing over meant risking injury and even death. Hutu Rwandans asked well-placed friends to conceal their Tutsi relations; others betrayed family members and friends to demonstrate their loyalty to Parmahutu, the genocidal parastate.[44] Similar social borders have hardened in other places as a result of violence among different groups. Examples include Sri Lanka, Kashmir, Israel/Palestine, Kenya, and what was once Yugoslavia.

Borders between Public and Private

The second way borders keep people together within countries is quite different, and depends on the often-fluid distinction between "public" and "private." Conventionally, the public sphere is considered to be the realm of politics and the political, while the private sphere is restricted to familial and market matters (sometimes a border is drawn between family and market, too). In liberal societies the state is in the public realm, and it is not supposed to meddle in the affairs of the private realm. For the most part, however, the distinction is not nearly so clear or obvious as generally supposed—the border between the two is highly contingent.[45] This will be discussed further.

The public-private distinction became important in a different way with the rise of the European nation-state and capitalism.[46] Prior to the development of capitalism, states were heavily involved in regulating the economy and social life. The private was considered to be the realm of human activity in which the state had no legitimate interest and its intervention was to be kept to a minimum. Before the eighteenth century, landed and business interests took measures to encourage the sovereign to stay out of family and business affairs so as to protect their property and persons (including various types of kinship relations, as seen in English films and novels about the eighteenth and nineteenth centuries). In return, these groups and classes paid taxes, most of which were locally set and collected, while supporting the sovereign in various ways, which ranged from sending armed men to fight his wars to lending him money to finance them.

With the rise of the bourgeoisie in Europe, a struggle developed over control of wealth, property, and the economy.[47] Who would protect the new middle class against expropriation by their rulers? The capitalist market and private property were the answer: by "disembedding" the economic from the political, limits were put on the state's tributary rights. As time passed this distinction was "naturalized," so that, by the nineteenth century, in a misinterpretation of Adam Smith, the market could be imagined as a primordial human institution ruled by an "invisible hand."[48] Moreover, as the state became more involved in governing the economy, and as law and relations among states and their citizens became critical to states' interests, the bourgeoisie also demanded regularized representation in the government.[49] While such a right might be granted, it was usually highly limited. Under some regimes, representation existed on paper but mattered not at all. Whether representation began in the Middle Ages or in modern times, it was not extended to include everyone until well into the twentieth century.[50]

Despite the extensive state support and regulation necessary to make capitalism work, markets were depicted as working automatically, kept civilized through norms, manners, and rules that everyone knew and everyone observed.[51] In today's liberal societies the border between public and private serves a very political function. It prevents people from becoming too politically active and populist by rendering "private" those matters affecting society that elites prefer to decide by themselves. If everyone were entitled to participate fully in making political decisions about the market—or, for that matter, the conditions of everyday life—capitalism as we know it would be impossible because each of us would demand that our individual interests be served.[52]

This did not (and does not) mean that intervention by the state is not extensive in the *political economy*—that is, the rules that structure markets. Like the British monarch surveying the activities of the Massachusetts Bay Company, America's founding fathers—there were founding mothers, too, but we rarely hear of them—recognized the threat posed by too much popular participation in decision making. They were virtually all men of property who desired to protect their possessions from expropriation by either the state or the people. In the first instance, they made sure that the laws of the new United States were friendly to property owners and protected their possessions, including slaves. Even though they all agreed that the role of the state should be relatively limited, these elites did clash repeatedly over how much the state should be involved in governing the economy.[53] In the second instance, they carefully drew borders around the public sphere and limited popular participation to selected segments of the people.

Theorists and commentators believed that liberalism was not possible in a system in which human beings were property and had no control of their labor. Thus the quarrel over slavery in the United States, even more than the earlier clash over whether or not to have a central bank, became so furious that it took a brutal civil war to resolve it.[54] Over time, the right to vote was extended to minorities and women, albeit with significant limitations. The "government of the people, for the people, and by the people," as Abraham Lincoln so eloquently put it, has always attached limits to the "of," the "for," and the "by." The abolition of slavery democratized politics by freeing the slaves and making them citizens, but the implementation of the post–Civil War "settlement" granting personhood to corporations closed politics back down again by shifting important decisions about the economy out of politics and into "administration." The emergence of the American regulatory state during the late nineteenth and early twentieth centuries was directed toward this very end: emerging out of the Progressive movement, regulation focused on limiting the power of corporations, even as elites opposed those Populists who wanted to break capital through greater state intervention into the economy.[55]

This has never meant, of course, that the border between the public and private realms has been impermeable. On many matters, people involved in the public sphere have found reasons to interfere with and regulate the private, not only with respect to economics but also by restricting certain forms of sexual relations between consenting adults and exercising various forms of control over the bodies of both women and men. From the private sphere, some citizens have found it in their interest not only to become active in affairs of state but also to use the state to enrich and empower themselves through insider deals—as was the case, for example, in the collapse of Enron. The enrichment of private U.S. corporations in Iraq, such as Halliburton, Blackwater, and Custer Battles, the upsurge in corporate crimes as a result of inadequate state regulation of market activities, and the bailout of failing financial institutions by the Federal Reserve in 2008 all illustrate how the private can use the public for its own benefit.[56]

What are the practical consequences of this border between public and private, and how does it serve both to connect and to divide? All societies are organized around "imagined" principles and norms. These are rules of belief and practice that serve to define the "virtuous" life within the society. If people subscribe to these principles and norms and agree that they are fundamental to social life, and if people behave accordingly, people support the status quo organization of the society. This is the case *even if those rules give advantage to some and not others.*[57] The trick is to get people to accept the rules as "natural" and immutable, as facts that cannot be changed.

The principle that some things are private and others are public seems invio-
lable in economics, even though it is challenged constantly with regard to personal status issues like marriage and reproductive rights. Yet the location of the
border between politics and the economy is accepted in Anglo-American societies as natural, unchangeable, and fundamental to the maintenance and success of society. Whereas conflicting interests on personal status issues like the
regulation of marriage and reproduction loom large in national debates, conflicts among economic (and property) interests are treated as largely illegitimate
(and, when raised, are often characterized as "class warfare"). This is because
to acknowledge them could undermine the society itself.

So the border between public and private unites society along one axis while
dividing it along another. Borders can be curious things.

Borders between Bodies

At a very early age, children learn who is in and who is out, what is in and what
is out, whom to connect with and whom to avoid. Our bodies are borderlines:
boys and girls, men and women, fathers and mothers, friends and strangers;
color, religion, morals, values, beliefs. All of these categories and differences are
internalized at such a very early age that they seem "natural." Each individual,
each body, has a role. Those who transgress their assigned roles are regarded as
"unnatural," as aliens (in the sense of not belonging), or even as sinners (in the
sense of moral estrangement).

Why do such borders develop, and what keeps them in place? It would be relatively easy to explain them as biological—as some do—and say that humans by
nature are territorial and categorizing animals. Claiming that such behavior is
natural is tantamount to saying it cannot be changed: if we are that way "by design," we might as well learn to live with it. But the historical evidence suggests
that what appears to be fixed among humans is almost never so. Even where
sameness is a norm, as in collectivized societies and among pairs of identical
twins, people differ from one another in many ways. In fact, something that
seems as distinct as gender is much more fluid than commonly believed.[58]

While it is impossible to explain exactly how social distinctions and hierarchies were first put into place, we know they are not rigid because we have so
much evidence of how they have changed over time.[59] The development of
agriculture probably had enormous consequences for group organization. Permanent settlements and established households emerged. The allocation of use
rights to land created geographic borders. Customs and rules were formulated
that made distinctions of all kinds. Hedges were planted, ditches dug, and
fields patrolled. Hierarchies were created within villages. Succession and inheritance made men interested in being able to identify their children. Only by
exercising control over a woman could a man be sure that her children were his.
How or when this pattern began to develop we do not know, but it seems to
have been the source of patriarchy as a specific type of social relation through
which older men dominate women and younger men.[60]

At first, such domination existed only within families and kin groups; later, it became the model for authority over the village, the city, and the state.[61] At some time, somewhere (perhaps in many places), armed men seized the reins of power and began to put into place rules that differentiated not only between male and female but also among families, language groups, physical types, and other characteristics. Those differences served to enhance the power and authority of some and disempower others. Under such circumstances—always contingent and contextual—borders were drawn and redrawn. Although their origins might be forgotten, they seemed natural because they had "always" been there. Boundaries became more rigid with the invention of writing, which inscribed rules and rituals and, as we can see with the Bible and other "scriptures," created permanent artifacts that served as sources of tradition and authority that were highly resistant to challenge.[62]

The category of race, for example, so deeply embedded in American politics and political discourse, has no biological basis. All human beings can interbreed, the touchstone of genetic similarity. Different physical characteristics among human groups have less to do with genetics and more to do with patterns of migration and isolation whose long-term results were to scatter genes across many groups or sequester them among a few.[63] But although race is a biological fiction, it is a political convenience. Centuries of Euro-American "science" justified assertions of superiority by some groups who looked at others as less than human.[64] Even after the biological bases of racism had been demolished, racial distinctions remained. To recognize that persons from other groups deserve equal treatment, not only under the law but also in everyday practice, threatens hierarchies and norms founded on distinctions between rich and powerful and poor and weak.[65] Yet the distinctions that separated people by color, religion, lineage, and language united as well as divided. Thus, in the United States before the Civil War, the poorest, most ignorant white was deemed superior to the wealthiest, most educated black, simply by virtue of race. That very small grant of recognition to poor whites by the rich and powerful cemented a social coalition that even today has not disappeared entirely.[66]

Borders are, in other words, a product of power. This is evident in relations among countries. When those on the other side of the border are named "enemy," social hierarchies are created, legitimated, and reinforced, even if the border has no material significance with regard to the people who live on each side.[67] Similar principles are applied at every level of human social organization (think of sports competitions between cities or schools), extending even into the family. Borders separate us and keep us together at the same time.

In-between Borders

Because borders are not natural they are not immune to change, regardless of how timeless they might appear. Indeed, the very distinctions that borders are meant to establish and reinforce are also sources and sites of contradiction. Borders are produced and maintained by power, but they are always blurring and dissolving because of how power tries to maintain them and how the less powerful try to evade them. A useful way to think about this paradox is through the concept of borderland.[68] At its most literal, a borderland or frontier is the space straddling a border where distinctions between the two "sides" are difficult to make. For example, many residents of national borderlands are bilingual and reflect social and cultural characteristics of the societies on both sides. The politics and economies of the two sides tend to be integrated in many ways in a borderland, and people routinely move back and forth across the line on the ground. Borderlands are multicultural; they are sites where borders are constantly being constructed and just as constantly being destroyed.[69]

The American Southwest is an archetypal example of such a borderland. It comprises areas that less than two centuries ago were part of Mexico, extending from Texas to California and several hundred miles into what is now the United States (there is a corresponding, but much smaller, zone of Americanization on the Mexican side of the border). Within that region, both English and Spanish are commonly spoken. Many U.S. Latinos of Mexican origin live in this borderland, where in some ways, "American" culture is the foreign one.[70] The United States has long been a destination for Mexican migrants, both legal and illegal. Mexico is a poor country, and the border is a long way from the center of political and economic power in Mexico City. Work was always available in the United States, as were long-established communities of Spanish and Mexican origin stranded north of the border after the American territorial conquests in the nineteenth century.

U.S. policies like the *bracero* program, which welcomed temporary workers from Mexico during and after World War II, along with the creation of the *maquiladora* zone along the border in the 1960s, served to make crossing it easier and more attractive.[71] As a result, the U.S.-Mexican borderland has extended more and more deeply into both countries, with people, enclaves, and outposts found thousands of miles from the juridical line that separates the two countries.[72] With numbers comes recognition, as with wealth comes power.[73] The border is dissolving.

Yet, there is a continuous effort to reconstruct the border. The United States is motivated by the fear of some of its citizens that their power and prerogatives are under threat from immigration. Calls to halt immigration are usually couched in terms of jobs, welfare, and the economy, but they are equally motivated by threats to long-established hierarchies and social divisions. The U.S. government has repeatedly strengthened patrols at the U.S.-Mexico border—since September 11, 2001, it has done so at all international borders—in response to these constituent demands. The Bush administration and the U.S. Congress have authorized construction of hundreds of miles of real and virtual fences and walls along the U.S.-Mexican border.[74] The result may be a diminution in nonlegal border crossings but there seem to be few other effects overall. The very organization of economic and political life in the United States continues to encourage both border crossings and expansion of the borderland.

On the Mexican side, regulatory efforts are directed toward policing the borderland as a geographic region, and the nation-state as a site that is acutely permeable. Historically, that state's strategy has been to regulate property ownership so that foreigners are barred from owning economically desirable coastal property and land adjoining the U.S. border. Mexicans who became naturalized U.S. citizens found themselves treated like foreigners because Mexico did not permit dual nationality. In March 1998, the laws were modified to divide citizenship from nationality. For a period of five years following the change, Mexicans holding U.S. citizenship could apply for Mexican nationality, which exempted them from property-ownership restrictions and allowed them to exercise basic citizenship entitlements, such as voting and even running for political office. The law was later modified again to permit Mexicans to hold dual citizenship with no restrictions.[75] Migrants to *el Norte* remit billions of dollars every year that help to support the Mexican economy, and countless others regularly cross the border (although for those without the appropriate documents, this has become more and more difficult). The president of Mexico, Felipe Calderón Hinojosa, has lobbied for greater protection and rights for Mexicans in the United States,[76] although many white citizens of the United States seem to think this wholly unreasonable. (Movements of people and relationships between the European Union and North Africa have a similar character.)

Under the pressures of economic and cultural change, borders become porous, even fluid, and borderlands emerge. Borderlands and frontiers are not limited to the areas along international borders but also include various aspects of social life and practices. Indeed, one could say that in historical terms, fluidity and change are the norm rather than the exception. Stable social systems tend to be stagnant; fluid social systems tend to be dynamic.

What types of changes are we talking about, and what might they involve? When pressures are intense and the rate of change is great, virtually all institutions, from the family to the state, can incorporate "borderlands." Old or conventional ways of doing things become dysfunctional; social arrangements are disrupted or destroyed; adaptation to new conditions becomes necessary. Consider, for example, how globalization has affected the family. Rather rigid borders have been drawn between the private realm of the family and the public realm outside. As with other borders, these serve to contain the family as well as to keep out certain types of external influences.

But things change, and stuff happens. The economic and cultural circumstances that make a particular family type normative in society do not stay the same. We noted that as it became more and more difficult for middle-class American families to survive on a single income (something that had never been possible for the poor and never a concern to the wealthy), wives and mothers entered the labor force in larger numbers than ever before. Social movements contributed to cultural changes that broadened popular acceptance of working women and households whose adult members did not conform to the traditional social norm. Today, a family might consist of two women or two men with or without children, or three or more adults with or without children, or single parents, or unmarried couples—or any number of other arrangements. Although legal struggles over status, entitlements, and protections continue, borders have been breached.

This does not mean that new types of family are regarded with equanimity by those in positions of political and economic power.[77] Remember that borders contain and keep out. When borders are breached, new ideas, practices, and expectations come in along with the other intruders. If they were to spread, they could upset old orders. The hierarchy of power in a society depends on keeping socially destabilizing ideas and practices contained. The borderlands in which change manifests itself become a threat to that power. Hence, the backlash against alternative forms of family constitutes an effort to reimpose the old borders and discipline those who would try to cross them.

When borders become fluid and dissolve, just as when new forms of family emerge or different languages are spoken in everyday life, authorities worry that society will change or collapse. Enemies are sought in the quest to reinforce borders and reestablish order.[78] Yet, human life is a chronicle of change. What's so bad about that?

7

People and War

The prospect of war is exciting. Many young men, schooled in the notion that war is the ultimate definition of manhood . . . willingly join the great enterprise. The admiration of the crowd, the high-blown rhetoric, the chance to achieve the glory of the previous generation, the ideal of nobility beckon us forward. And people, ironically, enjoy righteous indignation and an object upon which to unleash their anger. War usually starts with collective euphoria.

—Chris Hedges

If the prospect of war is exciting, then the problem of war may be unsolvable. As we have seen, scholarly and policy literatures are full of theories describing why wars happen, but often these theories disagree. In this chapter we look at war systematically. In general, we believe that war is overdetermined—wars have so many causes that picking one or even several risks leaving out the explanation that fits a particular conflict best. No one theory can fit all cases of a phenomenon that, as we show in this chapter, changes so often and so fundamentally. We have emphasized throughout this book that particular wars must be confronted on their own terms and in their own times if we are to understand why and how they came about. We are especially skeptical of theories about war that do not incorporate ways to assess the responsibility of policy makers. This is because, even though we believe that wars are overdetermined, we also believe they are neither accidental nor inevitable.

We do believe, however, that some theories, often in combination, are better than others at explaining war. General propositions can be devised that explain why wars are more likely to occur in some situations than others, and even why some leaders are more likely to resort to war than rely on diplomacy. Finally, we believe that theories of war should be widely discussed and debated to help us understand violent conflict, limit it, and perhaps even prevent it in the future.

What Is War?

"Violent conflict" is a synonym for "war," but the definition we develop here excludes some forms of group violence and includes a concept that frequently is not seen as war despite its association with "regimes of punishment." When we speak of war, we are talking about the deliberate application of organized violence by one or more states. "Deliberate" and "organized" mean that this activity is planned, rehearsed, and directed. "Violence" means to inflict harm, and it may be acute or structural. "Acute violence" refers to agents applying direct physical means (guns, bombs, knives, fists, machetes, fire, etc.) to hurt, damage, and destroy people and property. This is the conventional view of war as fighting. The requirement that states or state agents direct and apply this violence distinguishes war from other violent acts that might be similarly destructive, such as riots; be similarly organized, such as gang conflicts; or kill lots of people, such as the Oklahoma City bombing or the 9/11 attacks. Nothing on that list qualifies as war under our definition, because none is a state project.[1]

Wars also are fought by manipulating structures. Examples of "structural violence" include regimes such as boycotts (refusals to buy) and embargoes (refusals to sell), both of which are features of "economic sanctions."[2] We extend this understanding to include "structural adjustment" policies, such as IMF demands that debtor nations give a higher priority to foreign lenders than to domestic needs. Structural adjustment may not be acknowledged as violence by the agents who impose it, yet it is experienced by targeted leaders and populations as "war by other means." As a result, it is little or no different in effect from the embargoes and boycotts more conventionally seen as acts of war.

Means and Ends of War

Since 1648, the date of the treaties of Westphalia inaugurating the modern international system, the conventions of great power warfare have changed significantly. As a result, how we explain the causes and outcomes of war must change as well. One change is actually a return to the past.

> From prehistoric tribal feuds through the wars of antiquity and the Middle Ages, [the] threat [of extinction] was directed at all members of the enemy people, not just its soldiers. While the cabinet wars of the eighteenth and nineteenth centuries restricted violence to the direct participants on the battlefield, the scorched-earth policies of twentieth-century total war once more universalized the threat. Limited warfare, conducted by a professional military apparatus and carrying no real or imagined peril to the populace at large, was thus a phenomenon that lasted a mere two centuries.[3]

Here historian Wolfgang Schivelbusch traces a complex trajectory.

Before the eighteenth century, most wars in Europe were "total." Everyone on the other side was a potential target. The destruction of entire communities and the expropriation of valuable resources has been a—if not the—primary objective of warfare throughout most of recorded history—total war is the norm. In Homer's story, elaborated by Euripides, the Trojan War ended with the destruction of the city, the slaughter of its surviving male inhabitants, and the capture of Trojan women to take back to Greece as slaves. Similar tales are recounted in the Hebrew Bible and Thucydides' history of the conflict between Athens and Sparta.[4] Civilians and their property were targets in other wars, such as Genghis Khan's sweep through Asia into eastern Europe, the Hundred Years' War, and the seventeenth-century religious wars, whose conclusion inaugurated the nation-states system.

"Limited war," what Schivelbusch calls "cabinet war," is the exception. Limited wars are competitions for status and authority between rulers and states that are won or lost based on the relative effectiveness of professional armies. Limited war is what Kant had in mind when he said war was a contest among kings and what Clausewitz was thinking of when he said that war is the continuation of politics by other means.[5] If diplomacy failed to get a ruler what he wanted, he could deploy his forces like chess pieces to continue his pursuit of political objectives such as a boundary adjustment or his preferred outcome of a contested dynastic succession.

A limited war applies limited means to achieve limited ends. Its prominence in eighteenth-century Europe allowed Kant to envision war as a moral enterprise in which ethical rulers could draw lines between acceptable and unacceptable tactics. The image of war as a rational pursuit governed by codes of conduct sped the development of the "rules of war" that make up a significant body of contemporary international law.[6] An international system "adjusted" by limited war reflects the belief that the principals have fundamental interests in common, such as their personal survival, the survival of their populations and lands, and the persistence of the relationships among themselves that constitute the international society of their time.

Interstate conflicts during the era of cabinet warfare resembled competitions between knights in medieval tournaments rather than the contests among rulers, invaders, and would-be rulers characterizing ancient, medieval, and most contemporary wars. Philosopher Anatol Rapoport notes that military forces might not actually fight a cabinet war. "The object of the campaign frequently was to reach a situation (by proper maneuvering) in which it could become clear that one's own side had a strategic or tactical advantage." At that point, the side likely to lose could capitulate with honor and everyone could go home.[7]

Unlimited wars also were fought during the era of cabinet warfare, but they were rarely fought in Europe. Total wars were waged by Europeans against indigenous populations in Africa, Asia, and the New World to take over land, enslave or exterminate peoples, and expropriate possessions. Inside Europe itself, the transition from cabinet war back to unlimited or total war also was more ragged than Schivelbusch's thumbnail sketch indicates.

Napoleon mobilized a huge citizen army and harnessed the French economy to support his drive to establish an empire. Until his defeat, Napoleon and his enthusiastic citizen-soldiers swept through Europe like a latter-day Genghis Khan, winning easy victories over armies schooled to fight cabinet wars. The American Revolution also demonstrated the power of nationalism applied to warfare. Rebellious colonial leaders saw their struggle (quite realistically) as a life-or-death fight. Much to the surprise of the British, the colonies' ragtag and part-time citizen forces defeated an army of professional officers, "impressed" (involuntary) naval forces, and ground troops composed of peasants rented from landlords/warlords like the Landgrave of Hesse-Cassel (where the term "Hessian" as a synonym for "mercenary" comes from).[8] Toward the end of the nineteenth century, the citizens of Paris organized to continue fighting the Prussian army after Napoleon III had surrendered at Sedan in September 1870.[9] This second phase of the Franco-Prussian War lasted for less than five months, but it marked a radical democratization of military forces in European societies, and convinced the German high command directing World War I that citizens should not automatically be regarded as noncombatants.[10] Along with the importation of industrial technology into war fighting, which made fine discrimination among targets difficult, the democratization of war further blurred the distinction between civilians and military forces.

War and Technology

During the twentieth century, industrial technology operated by unskilled and semiskilled citizen-soldiers (and soldiers drawn from colonial populations) dominated the battlefield. "Maneuvering" in the style of cabinet warfare was difficult for massive armies and large weapons operating along extensive fronts, making major-power wars far more deadly than before. Too, as the notion of war changed from contests between rulers to struggles between nations, national pride and the desire for clear dominance over the defeated side returned war aims to demands for the unconditional surrender of the enemy.

Given these changes in ends and means, limited war became untenable. One of the oddest twentieth-century conflicts in terms of what was left of the distinction between limited and unlimited war was the American phase (1965–1972) of the Vietnam War (1930–1975). With some notable exceptions (like the treatment of U.S. prisoners of war by the North Vietnamese and the U.S. "Christmas bombing" of Hanoi in 1972), both sides usually followed international conventions in setting rules of engagement between U.S. military forces and the military forces of North Vietnam. At the same time, the territories and the civilian populations of Laos, Cambodia, and South Vietnam (the nominal U.S. ally) were brutally ravaged.[11]

Technology made the democratization of warfare possible. The implications of this transition are revealed in a short book by historian Noel Perrin describing the two-hundred-year Japanese ban on guns imposed by the Tokugawa military elite.[12] Japanese elites were repelled as they saw guns transform warfare from a specialized art to unskilled mayhem that undercut the status and value of daimyo (lord) and samurai (knight) in state and society. A similar ideal of war as an art infused the image of cabinet war. But no nation, including Japan, could afford to treat war as an art when national survival was at stake. Although a gunless Japan managed to win a war against an armed Korea, when Commodore Perry made his second visit to Japan in 1854 with seven U.S. warships, Japanese elites demanding military modernization ousted the Tokugawa and, soon after, ended the power of the feudal warrior classes.

The impact of technology on warfare became clearer with the advent of larger guns, automatic weapons, chemical weapons, and aerial bombing. Most soldiers needed only easily acquired skills to be able to use this technology. Armies could field citizen-soldiers with confidence, and their "blunt instrument" reach brought combat conditions to every living thing in a path far greater than what could be measured by sword, spear, or the distance a horse could run at top speed. Coupled with large-scale mobilizations of populations and resources and routine applications of sanctions and other forms of structural violence, the total wars of today are far more murderous and destructive than total wars before the cabinet-war era.[13]

Industrial technology continues to effect systemwide changes in conventions of warfare. One is the application of industrial machines and techniques to mass-produce death and destruction. During WWI, set-piece battles on the western front, eastern campaigns like Gallipoli, and submarine warfare demonstrated the power of automatic weapons, artillery, and torpedoes to kill tens of thousands of persons efficiently. The mass production of death expanded radically with the routine air delivery of bombs to cities during WWII. Aerial bombardment killed millions of persons and laid waste to vast expanses of territory.[14] Industrial technology was applied to genocide, the deliberate attempt to eliminate a specific group of human beings.[15] Some suggest that industrial technology was not necessary for Rwandan Hutus to slaughter eight hundred thousand Tutsis and Hutu moderates in only one hundred days in 1994. Yet technology in the form of hate radio played a very important role in the Rwandan genocide, mobilizing killers, broadcasting lists of targets, and directing truckloads of *genocidaires* to places where Tutsis had sought refuge. Mary Ann Tétreault and her colleague Harry Haines argue that the skillful use of electronic media by states marks a fourth technology-driven transition in conventions of warfare in the modern period, marking a shift from modern to "postmodern" war, which we discuss below.[16]

War and warfare change over time, but these examples show no sharp break dividing war into eras. Even so, we can make fairly clear distinctions among different types of war. For example, a variant of limited war continues today in Afghanistan and Iraq, a function of the power differential between the United States and the countries it (and the Soviet Union) attacked during and after the cold war. To a superpower such wars are limited, but for its adversaries they are total, "asymmetric" wars recalling the imperial invasions of earlier times. Other contemporary wars, including "civil" conflicts (wars between contenders living in the same nation-state) and genocide campaigns aimed at eliminating an entire group of people may be symmetrically or asymmetrically "total" in that the aim of at least one side is to destroy enemy leaders, their resource base, and the independent existence of the enemy population.[17]

The return of total war explains why civilians are military targets. They are killed in large numbers "accidentally," part of the "collateral damage"[18] inflicted in the process of killing enemy troops and destroying enemy infrastructure. They are killed in even larger numbers on purpose: to eliminate support for fighting forces; to erase evidence of war crimes like theft, torture, and rape; to demoralize troops and governments; to demonstrate the power of terrorists; and, in genocidal conflicts, to eradicate members of a target group.[19] Direct violence often is augmented by structural violence aimed at reducing an opponent's capacity to wage war or resist occupation. Because of its systemic nature, structural violence targets an entire society. Finally, most of today's wars are industrialized to some degree, especially those involving major powers. Major powers mobilize armies that operate machine technologies like railroads; tanks and automatic weapons; bombs; aircraft; chemical, biological, and space weapons; and sophisticated systems of surveillance and command and control. Modern war thus adds blunt-instrument, industrial efficiency to the premodern objective of destroying one's enemy.

Wounded Warriors

The glamour of high-tech war machines and the perspective from which we view them—the killers', not the victims'—divert us from seeing soldiers as casualties. Most people don't like to think of dead and wounded young men and women. In the current war in Iraq, this natural uneasiness supported the Bush administration's strategy of directing popular attention away from U.S. casualties through press policies forbidding coverage of bodies being delivered to Dover Air Force Base and discouraging stories about the postconflict lives of the wounded. The U.S. military refused to record the number of Afghan and Iraqi casualties at all—"I don't do body counts," said U.S. Defense Secretary Donald Rumsfeld,[20] a reflection on the Vietnam War, when U.S. and Vietnamese wounded and dead, enumerated in weekly body counts, were constant reminders of the human costs of war that served as focal points of antiwar rhetoric. The U.S. government also ignores the refugee issue, and has rejected countless applications for residence visas by Iraqi refugees, including people who worked as translators or fixers for the U.S. war effort.[21] By refusing to acknowledge the dead, wounded, and displaced, the Bush administration masked the human cost of its war of choice.

But that human cost doesn't go away. Dead and wounded soldiers have families whose primary breadwinners are disabled or destroyed as the result of war. Theda Skoçpol has found that the first "welfare" program in the United States (and one of the first welfare programs anywhere) was a system of pensions for Civil War veterans and their families.[22] The number of fighters in that

war was very large, nearly 4 million, and produced correspondingly large numbers of military casualties: 560,000 dead and 412,000 wounded. The figures for WWI are even more harrowing: a total of 8 million dead, 22 million wounded, and 2 million missing, from all sides.[23] Military casualty totals for WWII vary radically depending on the source, as do estimates of civilian casualties. We are probably safe to assume that between 25 and 30 million military personnel and a somewhat larger number of civilians were killed.

The dead and the visibly wounded are not the only casualties of war. For many, having to kill is a more difficult prospect than having to die. Watching others die violently may be even more affecting, whether one is responsible for those deaths or not, and perhaps especially when the deaths appear to have been caused by leader carelessness or betrayal.[24] Soldiers have a term for the effect of battlefield violence on individuals: they have a "thousand-yard stare." Emotional reactions to combat severe enough to be disabling were common during WWI, but military organizations, civilian societies, and even doctors didn't want to admit that what ailed these men was a natural emotional reaction to the horrors of war. They preferred to think of it as a physical ailment—which they called "shell shock"—or a character defect—cowardice or shirking.[25] Some fighters discover that they actually enjoy hurting or killing people,[26] a taste that if not suppressed or controlled can be expressed as criminal behavior, addiction, or suicide. P. W. Singer notes that unemployed military personnel who enjoyed their former jobs or simply cannot fit back into civilian life are prime recruits for the new private firms selling military services.[27] Perhaps the most common long-term emotional effect of war fighting is a different kind of addiction, to the adrenaline that stimulates effective fighting and escape from danger. War memoirs are full of the difficulties of adjusting to the boredom of civilian life.[28]

War and "War"

In recent years, "war" has become a synonym for other kinds of campaigns. The "war" on cancer, declared by U.S. president Richard Nixon, is an obvious example of a nonwar "war." (We'll continue to distinguish between such campaigns and war as we defined it at the beginning of this chapter by putting quotation marks around the nonwar "wars.") Some, such as the U.S.-led "war" on drugs, occupy the frontier separating "war" from war. Military equipment and advisors are sent to attack farmers and drug lords and sometimes the political enemies of host regimes. The mix of policing (aimed at criminal activities) and civil conflict (between political opponents) makes such conflicts hard to classify. The 9/11 terrorist attacks on New York and Washington confused the issue even more. Despite the attackers' "declaration of war," the attacks themselves were criminal acts performed by civilians. Al-Qaeda is neither a state nor an aspiring state, and its actions are not warfare: they are crimes. The U.S. government responded by declaring a "war" on terrorism, but it fights it primarily by policing—examples include passenger inspection at airports, massive surveillance and espionage activities, new regulations for international economic transactions, and close cooperation with other police organizations.[29] The United States also initiated wars in Afghanistan and Iraq, nations it accused of harboring and aiding terrorists.

Both "war" and war are useful to leaders. The "war" on terrorism waged by the United States has increased the power of the executive branch to a degree that would have been unthinkable before September 11. Domestically, under the "theory of the unified executive,"[30] it justified reorganizing government departments to give the president greater control over personnel and policy at the expense of workers' rights and checks and balances exercised by Congress. Civil-liberties guarantees were curtailed or ended for citizens and aliens, reducing personal autonomy and protection from state violence and challenging the autonomy of courts. Budget priorities were reorganized to favor expenditures on military and quasi-military activities, national monopolies directed by the executive branch, at the expense of programs like education and health care, operated by states and localities. The overseas "war" on terrorism also incorporates war components that expand government authority and centralize state power under executive control, and undermine targeted foreign governments ("regime change").

War increases the power of states and their leaders, and historically it has been integral to nation-state building. Charles Tilly describes early nation-states as rackets run by warlords offering protection in return for loans and taxes.[31] Successful war making expanded state power by bringing new territories with all their resources under state control. War making left warlord kings, who had raised effective armies, with the means to subdue internal rivals and crush political opposition. Military expenses could be paid from booty and then from taxes, efficiently collected by states with effective intelligence and surveillance agencies. Most critically for the shape of the modern world order, strong states commanding vast resources could offer special protection to key economic elites who, in return, supported the governing elites by paying "protection rent."[32] This is a share of the excess profits a business makes when the state awards it a monopoly or attacks its competitors.

This alliance between kings and entrepreneurs explains why nation-states and capitalism evolved together as mutually supporting systems and also why the modern world system experiences recurring "hegemonic" wars. These large-scale interstate conflicts establish the dominance of a core state over the "international system" of nation-states. The winner not only is strategically dominant but also gets to impose economic regimes that favor its national interests and the interests of key elite supporters of its regime on the rest of the world. Hegemony thereby extends the length of time winners can claim the fruits of victory.[33] Postmodern war is analogous to hegemonic war. It funnels state resources to the core constituencies of the state's leaders, strengthening their hold on power by attracting votes from enthusiastic consumers of war-as-spectacle.[34] There are so many reasons for wanting to get to or stay at the top of the international hierarchy of power that we can see why nations and leaders might risk total war to do so.

Waltz and His "Images" of War

In an influential 1958 book, political scientist Kenneth Waltz divides theories of war into three "images," or categories. The first image finds the cause of war in human nature; the second image locates it in particular regimes or kinds of regimes; and the third image sees war as the inevitable result of system structure.[35] Waltz himself believes that international system structure, which he describes in Hobbesian terms as "anarchy," is the primary engine driving states to war. He dismisses as "reductionist" theories derived from other images—such as the democratic peace thesis (a second-image theory); psychological theories, such as the notion that wars arise from the deliberate choices of particular individuals or from popular pressure on the state to attack an enemy, and theological theories asserting that humankind has a propensity toward evil (all first-image theories).[36]

But systemic theories like those based on balance-of-power models also have problems. How the balance of power is envisioned—as a power-over mechanism that operates by itself, as a mitigated system that incorporates "international society," as the policy of a leading state, or as a convenient way to interpret a mixed bag of events and decisions (in other words, as an artifact)[37]—shapes predictions and explanations. Niall Ferguson's realist examination of the causes of WWI combines a first-image analysis of the role of Edward Grey on the British side with a third-image analysis of systemic pressures on the German side. Together, these analyses lead him to conclude that WWI was "unnecessary"—and yet it happened. Ferguson says this was because Germany felt compelled by the Franco-Russian alliance and its inability to keep up with British naval expansion to launch a war against France and Russia.[38] Germany's leaders feared they were falling behind strategically and saw attacking in 1914 as a "now or never" proposition. But the decision of Britain to send its army to France was discretionary. Britain did not need a war with Germany to protect its naval supremacy, and it could have delayed making any military response until it was too late to send the British Expeditionary Force (BEF) to France.

Indeed, Ferguson says that Britain's decision to send the BEF is what made the war a "world war" rather than one limited to continental Europe. Although a smaller war confined to the continent might have "adjusted" quite a few borders, Ferguson believes it was unlikely to have produced revolution in Russia, the sudden creation of a large number of new—weak—nation-states from the carcasses of the Austrian-Hungarian and Ottoman empires, and a second world war two decades later. Ferguson's analysis challenges the Waltz third-image model by making third-image factors contingent on first-image causes. Other theorists explain the failure of events to unfold the way systemic models predict as the result of errors of perception by policy makers; some, like Robert Jervis, incorporate the likelihood of making such mistakes directly into their theories.[39]

As Ferguson's complex analysis shows, perhaps the greatest problem with any theory of war is the attempt to explain it as having only one kind of cause. Even though war is evident in what we know about virtually every human culture,[40] it is as much of an oversimplification to explain war as having a single cause as it is to say there is only one cause for marriage, another social practice that is evident in all cultures and throughout recorded history. Systems theorists can say that war is the result of competition for scarce resources by rival human groups, just as they can say that marriage is the result of biological competition to reproduce the species. But how this happens and what form it takes in any era is a function of values, structures, and the particular agents involved. As a result, more complex theories are needed to explain war than any one "image" can generate.

Ethics and War

In most conventional IR theories, ethics are either entirely absent (balance-of-power theories); are mentioned but discounted (the first moral principle of statesmanship is to preserve the lives and property of citizens no matter what it takes); or construe the behavior of the theorist's country as morally superior—war is someone else's fault, and all we are doing is defending ourselves (the subtext of the democratic peace thesis). Theories that do attempt to address ethical and moral concerns are marginalized, relegated to lawyers, clergy, women, and others charged with being too "soft" to face "reality." This logic of ethics is laid out by Hobbes, who says, "To this war of every man against every man, this also is consequent; that nothing can be unjust. The notions of right and wrong, justice and injustice, have there no place. Where there is no common power, there is no law; where no law, no injustice."[41]

There are two key elements in the Hobbesian position. One is that in a total war (a "war of every man against every man") all means are ethical. The other points to the reason why this is so: in the absence of law, there is no "right and wrong." Hobbes says that this is why a strong state is necessary for domestic peace: only a strong state can legitimately apply the force that ensures the security of all. His position has been generalized by realists such as Hans Morgenthau to hold for the international system—in the war of all states against all states, there is neither right and wrong nor a way to prevent war. The duty of the statesman is to ensure the security of the nation, and duty requires that he be prepared to defend it by whatever means he must. While Morgenthau dreamed of an international regime capable of protecting people against war, he was not optimistic that such a regime would come about any time soon.[42]

The twenty-first-century Hobbesians popularly known as neoconservatives returned to power during the George W. Bush administration. Their position corresponds to what scholars call "hegemonic stability theory." It argues that a hegemonic power is necessary if the world is to be stable and orderly. Putting this theory into practice in accordance with U.S. interests is the basic idea behind George W. Bush's national security strategy, which claims for the United States the right to initiate wars or otherwise topple regimes that threaten its vision of its preferred world order, one based on political and economic marketization.[43] The U.S. invasions of Afghanistan (2001) and Iraq (2003) were guided by this strategy,[44] as is the ongoing "war" on terror. The strategy also informs attempts to effect "regime change" in places such as Iran, Syria, Cuba, and Venezuela, where, so far, it has been unsuccessful, and it guided the administration's support of rebels in Haiti who brought down the government of Jean Bertrand Aristide in February 2004.

"Softer" proponents of hegemonic stability theory, such as Robert Gilpin, Robert Keohane, and Joseph Nye, see hegemony more benignly.[45] Keohane calls the neoconservative position "the crude basic force model,"[46] and attacks it by saying that the most successful hegemons were not dominating but rather nurturing, motherly states that provided economic and security services to weaker partners. Like Gilpin, Keohane sees self-interest, not force, as the primary motive for cooperating in a stable hegemonic regime, making his another power-with model. In his 1984 book, *After Hegemony*, Keohane argued that U.S. allies should continue to support the U.S.-led international system even though U.S. power seemed to be in decline. This was because the subordinate states continued to benefit from security and economic services underwritten by the United States. This view is known as "neorealism."

A very different vision of world order comes from "idealists." At their extreme, realism and idealism as theoretical and ideological points of view constitute two "ideal types," schematic models of how the world operates. Some of the differences between realism and idealism lie in the units and levels of analysis that each one uses. Realists see states in conflict as their units of analysis and the system of international anarchy as their level of analysis. All other actors are conceived as subordinate to states, the "power-maximizing" units whose competition creates the international system. Idealists see the world as composed of many units, not only states but also individuals, firms, churches, and a whole range of public and private organizations.[47] These actors are envisioned as operating within relationships constructed and maintained by their own efforts. In consequence, although idealists' level of analysis is the individual, their units of analysis are medieval in their variety. Idealists also see choice as variable, motivated not just by the desire to have more power but also by moral and practical concerns. Like politics in the Middle Ages, idealist models of politics are hard to boil down into a few basic propositions.

Idealists also operate from wider frames of inclusion than realists. Realists follow philosopher Friedrich Nietzsche in their idea that "the world is horrible and fundamentally unintelligible; the bad thing was to pretend that it has an intelligible rational structure *or* anything to make us optimistic about political progress."[48] As a result, they have a narrow view of who is entitled to the state's protection—its citizens or subjects—and what they ought to pay for it—total loyalty and whatever material resources the state demands. Idealists operate from what Kant called a "cosmopolitan" perspective. They see all human beings as entitled to dignity and respect, and view politics as decision making based on human reason. Idealists condemn group loyalties such as nationalism, religion, ethnic identity, and economic interest as inherently emotional and divisive. To them, only reason allows us to arrive at a politics that is "active, reformist and optimistic, rather than given to contemplating the horrors, or waiting for the call of Being." In other words, idealists believe that reasonable people can collaborate to create a world order based on human rights rather than group rights, one that includes strategies for containing "global aggression and [promoting] universal respect for human dignity."[49]

Martha Nussbaum shows how Kant's image of cosmopolitanism grew out of the ethical and political views of ancient Roman thinkers, including Marcus Aurelius, who ruled the Roman empire from 161 to 180 C.E.[50] Known as one of the "five good emperors," Marcus showed that cosmopolitan ideals were compatible with effective governance, thereby refuting the claims of realists that a humane politics based on the articulation of common purposes and committed to peaceful relations could never succeed. Marcus and those who share his views hold that aggression is wrong and that force should be used only in self-defense. This Stoic position in Western thought shaped concepts of human rights, the development of international law, rules of war, and repeated attempts to create international institutions that might be sufficiently shielded from the emotional demands triggered by group loyalties to pursue the common purposes of human beings.

Kant contributed to this tradition throughout his writings. In *Perpetual Peace* he offers a short list of practical rules to help reasonable leaders avoid violent conflict. One encourages transparency by renouncing secret treaties; another promotes mutual respect among nations by forbidding states to interfere in the constitution and government of other states, assassinate their leaders, foment domestic unrest, encourage treason, or break agreements with them. Another rule encourages respect for citizens by forbidding territories and populations from being treated like the personal property of rulers. Two rules attack systemic pressures for war, calling on states to abolish standing armies and to refrain from borrowing money to support aggression against another state. We could summarize these rules as advocating honesty, openness, mutual respect, responsibility, and cooperation.

As we noted in chapter 1, Kant argues that to have an international system based on rules like these requires that the parties to them have representative governments incorporating a separation between legislative and executive branches—checks and balances. This is why Kant is regarded as an early proponent of the democratic peace thesis. But Kant's vision of the international system is more complicated than that. It also requires what he calls "a federation of free states," international institutions in which sovereign states come together in a diplomatic forum to determine how to achieve the common good: "peace can neither be inaugurated nor secured without a general agreement between the nations."[51] This is a formula for discussion and negotiation. It describes neither a world state that could become a global despotism, nor a world of perpetually warring states. In other words, perpetual peace is a project, not a destination. Kant's essay suggests ways to move that project along.

Kant has many descendants. Prominent among them are feminist theorists like J. Ann Tickner and V. Spike Peterson, who point out that the Hobbesian perspective that dominates contemporary security policy actually creates global and national insecurity: recurrent "total" wars, genocide, pollution and resource depletion, climate change, and a world economy in which inequality is growing by leaps and bounds while resistance to the degradation and suffering it causes becomes deadlier every day.[52] If reasonable people can agree that these are problems, can we engage in Kantian dialogue to resolve them? Perhaps, but first we'll also have to deal with the fact that many people profit from war, and some also enjoy it.

Postmodern War

The impact of technology on the causes and conduct of war reaches a new peak in "postmodern war." Chris Gray defines postmodern war as a product of technology and culture leading to a "limited definition of rationality and science as an institution to replace valor."[53] Mary Ann Tétreault and Harry Haines see that definition as too limited. They agree that postmodern war is a product of warfighting technology, including pure robotics and "cyborg" (bionic) technologies that allow human beings to do such things as "see" in the dark and stay awake for days at a time. Electronic technology is key to postmodern war. It promotes the illusion that policy makers are invulnerable while, in practice, it allows many fighters to remain at safe distances from combat operations. Prosecutors of war can focus destruction on the buildings, vehicles, and even individual persons who are their actual targets; this gives the prosecutors a sense that what they are doing is morally correct because injury to the "innocent" is minimized. Meanwhile, for the war's "consumers" at home, news broadcasts from the front echo what for some is a lifetime of experience playing war games via computer and "reality" simulation.[54]

Tétreault and Haines see postmodern war as part of a high-tech culture but, unlike Gray, they believe it comes not only from technology but also from new understandings of how to produce personal and historical memory through the use of electronic and other media.[55] "Historical memory" is what "everybody knows" about past events, not only a particular version of what happened but also how to link that common knowledge to contemporary events. An example is how arms inspections in Iraq ended in 1998. "Everybody knows" that Saddam kicked the arms inspectors out, but that isn't what happened. In reality, the inspectors were withdrawn by the United Nations when chief arms inspector Richard Butler complained that Saddam was not cooperating with them.[56] By revising this story in October 2002, at the precise time that UN arms inspections were resumed, the spinners reinvented a past suitable for creating expectations that the arms inspections would fail.

Historical memory is deeply implicated in postmodern war, which resembles cabinet war in that its defining quality is *performance*. Its target audience includes populations as well as leaders. Being able to manipulate experience and memory is critical to its political success because postmodern wars are wars of choice—they are not necessary for national survival. Unlike cabinet war, however, postmodern war is not a duel. It is a team sport in which both promoters (political leaders) and "fans" (voters) must be protected from direct exposure to violence. Like modern war, postmodern war is an expression of nationalism, the source of the "team spirit" that supports rising defense budgets and the (re)election of armchair-warrior leaders by armchair-warrior voters.

Governments and media work together to stage postmodern wars. This is relatively easy because governments are primary sources of authoritative information. A government's status as the dispenser of information makes it easy for that government to deceive when it decides to dispense *dis*information—otherwise known as lies. The period leading up to the invasion of Iraq in 2003 is riddled with examples of government-generated disinformation presented as neutral, authoritative truth.[57] The "Downing Street Memo," is a memorandum written in July 2002 reporting what went on at a secret meeting of British prime minister Tony Blair with senior foreign policy and security officials. It reveals not only the lies already told by U.S. president George Bush when he denied that he planned to go to war with Iraq, but also reveals the lies expected from Blair and Blair's willingness to tell them.

> C (Britain's chief of intelligence) reported on his recent talks in Washington. There was a perceptible shift in attitude. Military action was now seen as inevitable. Bush wanted to remove Saddam, through military action, justified by the conjunction of terrorism and WMD. But the intelligence and facts were being fixed around the policy. . . . Prime Minister said that it would make a big difference politically and legally if Saddam refused to allow in the UN inspectors. Regime change and WMD were linked in the sense that it was the regime that was producing the WMD. . . . If the political context were right, people would support regime change.[58]

The memo was published in Britain on May 1, 2005, before the May 5 election that returned Tony Blair and his Labour Party to office. Its revelation was tarred as an election ploy, and Labour lost 57 seats, although it seems a stretch to say that the loss was due entirely to the memo.

The memo had almost no effect in the United States because it was not covered as a major story. It was mentioned in the *New York Times* on May 2, 2005, but in a story about the British election.[59] Even a column by the new public editor reporting on reader anger at the lack of coverage was buried inside the paper.[60] The memo itself did not appear in a U.S. news outlet until Mark Danner's essay about it appeared in the *New York Review of Books* the following month.[61] Proadministration pundits commenting on the growing stack of books about the deception leading up to the war dismiss them as the work of conspiracy theorists. They feel secure knowing that the administration is skilled at transforming major stories into what Danner calls "frozen scandals" hiding "queasy secrets." And yet the problem, of course, is that they are not secrets at all: one of the most painful principles of our age is that scandals are doomed to be revealed—and to remain stinking there before us, unexcised, unpunished, unfinished.[62]

Because postmodern wars are fought by choice, leaders must market them relentlessly to sustain the illusion that they are necessary and therefore worth their high cost in blood and money. Commercial media are natural partners of governments in this enterprise. Mass marketers of news are as interested as political leaders in minimizing context and simplifying stories because that attracts the consumers, particularly in the demographic group most cherished by advertisers: young men. Competition for readers, listeners, and viewers also encourages standardization, stories based on stereotypes that appeal to the prejudices and expectations of people in the target markets.[63] Cost pressures dictate doing this as cheaply as possible, such as by eliminating expensive background pieces, along with facts incompatible with story "genres" and style conventions that make reported events intelligible and palatable to naive consumers.

Examining coverage of antiwar protestors during the American war in Vietnam, for example, Daniel Hallin found that the few stories centering on out-of-the-mainstream groups and ideas (i.e., protesters and antiwar messages) tended to marginalize the actors and belittle the policies they advocated.[64] This treatment reinforced the out-of-the-mainstream status of dissenters and their identity as "bad guys." The depiction of bad guys is stylized in other ways. Terry Thompson discovered floating signifiers—symbols detached from their real-world settings—in CBS television news coverage of Eastern Europe during the 1980s. These stories featured pre–WWII footage of marching Nazi troops as "illustrations" of contemporary life fifty years later (and in different countries).[65]

Visual presentations are more effective at creating historical memory than print or audio messages. "Pictures" stick in people's minds. Because the same pictures are seen by millions of persons, they validate themselves by increasing the number of "witnesses" to the stories and events they portray. Television is more powerful than film in this regard because more people are exposed to it, and they view it in settings where they rarely engage critically with what they are seeing.[66] The power of television to create historical memory that conflicts with history was revealed in polls taken in the fall of 2003. Persons who relied on commercial television for news about the third Gulf War (GWIII)[67] harbored significantly more misconceptions and outright errors of fact about the conflict and its causes than those who relied on newspapers and noncommercial radio and television.[68]

Another trend is especially disturbing to those interested in resolving international conflicts peacefully because it promotes the enjoyment of war as an entertainment product. The widespread consumption of video war games blurs boundaries dividing virtual from actual events. As representations of battlefield violence in the news comes closer in appearance to the parallel universes generated by video games, war news is both more absorbing and less shocking.[69] Viewers of the popular general Norman Schwarzkopf's nightly TV reports during the second Gulf War (GWII) could justify their consumption as fulfilling the responsibility of citizens to stay informed while they enjoyed the thrill of participating in a video game they had a real-world stake in winning. Representations allowed viewers to occupy the positions of actors dropping bombs on "targets" indicated by crosshairs imposed over vague images of "facilities" and "installations," or to watch "tracer" images of "their" Patriots knocking out "enemy" Scuds. These images delivered excitement, validation, and political support as coalition forces prepared to move on the ground.

The parallels between civilian video and television consumption and modes of wartime news coverage developed further during GWIII when embedded journalists individually accredited to military units became the analogue to civilian reality TV. Confined to their small units, embedded journalists could "see" and report only on narrow yet highly emotional events, offering a perspective that drew viewers into vicarious participation on the front lines.[70] Even more than GWII pool reporting and Schwarzkopf briefings, embedded reporters limited viewers' perceptions of the war by shrinking its context. The multiple news stories fragmented understanding of the policy frame of the conflict, reducing it to genre representations of combat units, each with its obligatory complement of embattled all-American "kids" up against a faceless and terrifying enemy.

As the war continued, however, embedding also allowed military members to make their own case about the war and its impact on individuals and military organizations. Much to his surprise, Michael Massing, a critic of the Iraq war, was allowed to embed to assess the effects of the surge of troops sent to Baghdad in 2007 to stem rising levels of violence, and of the "Sunni awakening" to retake towns from al-Qaeda activists. He talked about "unscripted moments," events and conversations he had not expected to encounter as an embed.

> As I'd expected, my embed had provided little opportunity to hear the Iraqi point of view. Rather, it offered a look at the war through the eyes of the US military. . . . On the one hand, it had left me with little doubt about the very real gains the surge had brought about, and about the effectiveness of the Petraeus-led counterinsurgency strategy. The situation in Dora had obviously improved, and the combination of aggressive raids, large-scale detentions, and mixing with the community (together with the Sunni Awakening) had had a big hand in achieving that.
>
> At the same time, I'd gotten a look at the crushing effect the war is having on the troops. The breakdown in the Army has advanced so far that in a mere thirteen hours, I could see the rising dissatisfaction, anger, and rebellion within it. The message from the soldiers themselves was that keeping so large a force in the field over the long term seemed unsustainable.[71]

News and efforts to shape it continue to mark the consumption of information about the U.S. wars in Iraq and Afghanistan, while the struggle to shape historical memory of these wars has penetrated the movie lots and TV studios where popular culture is produced.[72] Among the most disturbing examples is the FOX series *24*, which depicts torture not only as acceptable but also, and more crucially, as effective in generating information crucial to saving "innocent" lives. Torture had been shown on *24* during its first three seasons but became "a main thread of the plot" following revelations that U.S. personnel were torturing prisoners at Abu Ghraib, so much so that TV critic Adam Smith wondered whether "its current interest in torture could be seen as a way of questioning the limits of just war."[73] Whether the normalization of torture was intended by the producers or not, an October 2006 poll commissioned by the BBC showed that "opposition to torture in the United States is less robust than in Europe. The percentage of Americans favoring the practice in certain cases (36%) is one of the highest among the 25 countries polled."[74]

Torture exposes the fantasy world of postmodern war. Throughout history, torture has been organized as a spectacle, one used to elicit false confessions that justify the harsh policies of authoritarian regimes.[75] Elaine Scarry argues that the coupling of torture and interrogation constitutes a ritual of violence, a domain in which the basic propositions describing domination and subjection are inscribed.

> Torture consists of a primary physical act, the infliction of pain, and a primary verbal act, the interrogation. The first rarely occurs without the second. . . . The connection between the physical act and the verbal act, between body and voice, is often misstated or misunderstood. Although the information sought in an interrogation is almost never credited with being a *just* motive for torture, it is repeatedly credited with being the motive for torture regimes.[76]

The infliction of pain and humiliation at Abu Ghraib, Guantánamo Bay, and other sites where U.S. prisoners are held, is such a spectacle, one whose audience was theoretically limited to the prison, the "intelligence community," and top levels of the Bush administration.[77] Yet what was taking place at these sites was known before the Abu Ghraib photos became public,[78] while after its exposure, the public outcry quickly died away and even the trials of the low-level scapegoats have not merited the level of press coverage given to summer shark attacks or Paris Hilton's woes. Torture is a crime under U.S. and international law. That it became the official policy of the U.S. government in 2002,[79] and was tolerated by more than a third of the U.S. population as late as 2006, shows the influence of postmodern war on the construction of policy and how far postmodern policy makers are from Kant's vision of transparent and honorable republican governments.

Curbing Knights and Knaves

"The prospect of war is exciting." Yet the reality of war is something else again, especially as the toll in death, destruction, corruption, and cost weighs like a hangover after a wild party. Realist leaders hope to avoid war by building up a preponderance of power so that no one will dare to attack them, but that strategy triggers the security dilemma.[80] Whenever any country beefs up its armaments, other countries see it as preparing to attack and arm themselves in response. Even hegemons are not immune to unpleasant consequences when they add to their arsenals. As an Iranian scholar of our acquaintance once put it:

> The greatest irony of nuclear weapons is that security for country X requires insecurity for country Y. Naturally, and as a corollary, as country X continues to [improve] its nuclear (and other) weapons instead of abiding by international agreements to work towards disarmament, and as it claims that as a Great Nation it is not bound by international law or the UN Charter [but

rather] has the "moral clarity" to wage wars of aggression with impunity, country Y will inevitably conclude that its security requires obtaining equal or better weapons. This isn't a matter of envy on the part of country Y; it is a matter of survival.[81]

The charms of war, so appealing to people who clothe their drive for power as a story of the forces of good battling the forces of evil, do not attract people who recognize the common humanity shared by fighters on both sides. One of the most evocative stories of a personal transition from realism to idealism is recounted by Vera Brittain, a young woman just beginning her university studies as WWI descended on Europe.[82] Vera, like her brother and his friends, was caught up in the excitement of the war, and she left Oxford to become a volunteer nurse caring for wounded troops. First in London hospitals and then on Malta and in France, Vera encountered thousands of mangled and dying soldiers. While she was overseas, she also nursed badly wounded German prisoners of war and found herself shocked that she could think of them—the enemy—as sharing a common humanity with her own wounded and dead countrymen.

During the war Vera's fiancé and two close friends were killed and, as the war was drawing to a close, her only brother died in Italy. Throughout the book she published fifteen years after the end of the war, she rails bitterly at her loss of these and other things, like her youthful enthusiasm and her sympathy with those in her country who had not experienced the war directly, as she had. Vera returned to Oxford, graduated, and embarked on a public life as a speaker and writer. Although at first it made her feel disloyal to the memories of the dead, she found new interests and formed new friendships. Eventually, she married and had children, finding a life she had once believed that the war had foreclosed to her forever.

As Vera's career flourished, she began to use her position as a public figure to work for peace, speaking all over England about the virtues and shortcomings of the League of Nations and, through novels and reporting, writing contemporary history as stories of individual lives caught up in world-shattering events. In her memoirs she tells about traveling in Central and Eastern Europe shortly before her marriage. She was repeatedly struck by how people living in the countries she visited were as bitter as she was about all they had lost in the war, yet, unlike her, found their feelings hardening in response to nationalistic appeals naming outsiders as the source of their pain. Her way of reaching some of these emotionally isolated people was to share her own experiences. She told one of the directors of the Krupp corporation, a man with a war wound who had made his hostility to his visitors obvious, that she had nursed German soldiers during the war.

> "German soldiers!" he exclaimed. "You mean—prisoners?" "Yes," I replied, "At Étaples." . . . This experimental information had been the mere impulse of shamed nervous tension, but had it been most carefully calculated, it could not have proved more effective. . . . [T]he alarming director became positively communicative, and pointed out to us the square where the Essen

riots had broken out, and the tree-shaded park which had once been used for testing munitions. . . . Later, he took us through the spacious workrooms that had once been used for the manufacture of field artillery, and showed us how swords were now, literally, being turned into ploughshares in their modern guise of typewriters and surgical instruments.[83]

Even then, in 1925, Vera sensed the seeds of another war in Europe germinating in the misery and hostility of the people she interviewed. As that impending war drew closer during the 1930s, she became a committed pacifist. She remained so throughout WWII despite hostile criticism from friends and strangers alike. When that war was over, Vera and her associates founded the Campaign for Nuclear Disarmament, and she continued her peace activism until she died in 1970.

Vera Brittain's pursuit of her vision of Stoic cosmopolitanism was noteworthy for how much of her life and energy it consumed. Yet Vera's quest for intellectual openness and flexible institutions sturdy enough to support negotiation and cooperation is not unique. In response to the horrors of modern and postmodern war, thousands, even millions of others have worked and continue to work to establish and preserve islands of common ground on which people and nations can stand together and work out differences among themselves without going to war.

It is too simple—even naive—to say that human beings ever can abolish war. The need to defend populations and habitats from predators is likely to persist as long as there are people willing to stop at nothing to achieve their goals. Yet, at the same time, the prospect of war as a response to fear and ignorance, as something to pacify citizens, as something to distract them from the failures of their leaders, or as merely a source of excitement and entertainment is, as Kant believed, a problem resolvable through reason. In his first inaugural address, Franklin Roosevelt appealed to reason when he said, "The only thing we have to fear is fear itself." James Sheehan argues that the experience of two world wars opened Western European leaders and populations to a politics that transformed the continent from a killing field to a community of prosperous, cosmopolitan states.[84] Chris Hedges appeals to the common ground human beings share as mortal, and moral, beings. He ends his book on war this way: "[Love] does not mean we will avoid war or death. It does not mean that we as distinct individuals will survive. But love, in its mystery, has its own power. It alone gives us meaning that endures."[85]

8

@

People and Justice

The law, in its majestic equality, forbids the rich as well as the poor
to sleep under bridges, to beg in the streets, and to steal bread.

—Anatole France

Why are there so many poor and hungry people in the world? Why are
so many people killed because of their religion, race, or ethnicity?
Why do powerful countries invade weak ones? Why do women continue to suffer from patriarchal oppression? In short, why is there so much *injustice* in the world? Is global justice possible? What would it involve? What
would be required to achieve it?

Most of us know injustice when we see it, yet, what, exactly, is justice? Justice
might have as many definitions as there are people in the world, but how might
we define it? In this chapter, we examine the concept of justice in the world,
how it is understood, and some of the ways in which it is (or is not) practiced.
Justice, or its absence, is closely linked to three topics we have already discussed at some length: power, the state, and markets. Injustice is an age-old
problem, of course, but its particular manifestations in contemporary life are
not simply a consequence of some inherent flaw in human nature. As we discussed in chapters 6 and 7, injustice also is linked to structures and regimes that
discriminate against particular people and groups. In a world in which some
modicum of justice is both feasible and desirable, the causes of injustice must
lie in our institutions and the practices they foster. Certainly, people do commit
unjust acts against other people, and should bear responsibility for the consequences of those acts. Nevertheless, if we understand ourselves as "social individuals" whose awareness and behavior are strongly motivated and directed
by norms and principles, it becomes clear that injustice is more than merely the
malicious acts of bad individuals.[1]

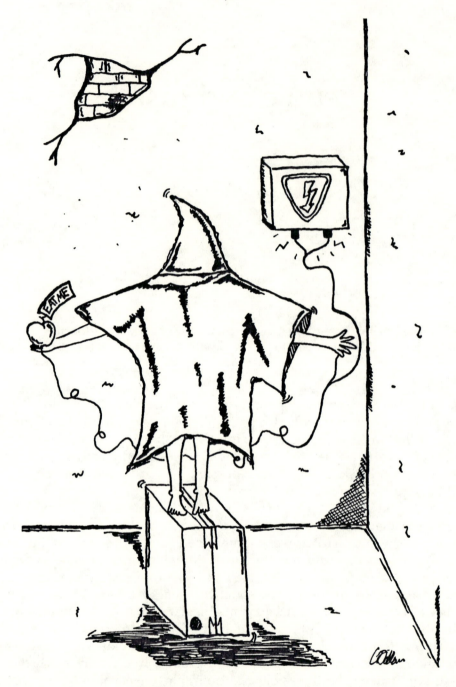

Theorists of justice and injustice fall into several distinct camps. One is most concerned with the problem of *distributive justice*, that is, how are income, goods, opportunities, and wealth parceled out among members of a society, and what can be done to make this division fairer? A second school focuses on *rights* and *recognition*, that is, how does the legal and cultural status of a group contribute to the injustices it suffers, and what might be done to overcome these conditions? A third group addresses *structural sources* of injustice, the social and institutional norms and practices that perpetuate injustice even as people fight for redress. These are not mutually exclusive approaches: there is considerable overlap among them. Much of the literature on justice—both distributive and social—addresses abstract situations and focuses on human rights, mostly for the individual. A growing literature argues that particular groups must be accorded collective rights in order to achieve both social and economic justice. Here, we develop the notion of "respect" to go along with rights and recognition. That is that, if we acknowledge that respect for others is foundational to justice, we must also acknowledge the consequences of our everyday behaviors and consent in reproducing conditions of injustice.

Defining Justice

At its most basic, justice can be defined as getting what one deserves—the root of the phrase "just deserts." The idea here is that we all engage in activities for which we seek some kind of reward or remuneration; our due is what we deserve for what we have done. Thus, we expect to be fairly paid for our work, fairly recognized for our status, fairly rewarded for our achievements, fairly treated whoever we might be. Those who commit crimes and are tried and convicted, thereby receive their just deserts—"criminal justice" implies exactly this. But we know that justice is not always meted out fairly. Some receive more than their due, while others manage to avoid paying for their crimes.[2] The distribution of rewards and punishments is often unfair. Why?

Although we tend to regard luck as playing a role in the distribution of goods and bads, chance does no more than exacerbate already existing tendencies and conditions. Those who are well-off or have "connections" receive their due (and more!) when others do not. Criminals represented by highly skilled—and expensive—lawyers are more likely to walk free than those relying on the overworked employees of legal aid or, worse, on third-rate lawyers who depend on court appointments for subsistence. Significant accomplishments go unnoticed in the absence of a good publicist or extensive networks—how well-known was Iranian human rights lawyer Shireen Ebadi before she received the Nobel Peace Prize in 2004? We know of what justice consists; what we don't know is why it seems so difficult to achieve.

It is difficult to devise general rules of justice that everyone will agree are fair. After all, what if expanded social services enjoyed by all were to result in less private wealth or limited access to those public services? There are three basic ways to think about this problem. First, we could simply decide that resources and wealth should be reallocated to decrease the gap between rich and poor. Second, we could try to formulate a set of rules that would grant to every individual equal rights and access to opportunities and institutions. Finally, we could intervene actively in an attempt to enhance the access and opportunities of those who have been disadvantaged by the existing rules governing society.

Justice as Distribution

In the early 1970s, during a famine in East Bengal, Peter Singer published a famous article entitled "Famine, Affluence, and Morality."[3] In the article, Singer criticized the relative lack of provisions for the relief of the hungry by inhabitants of rich countries and their governments. Singer's primary argument was that "if it is in our power to prevent something bad from happening, without thereby sacrificing anything of comparable moral importance, we ought, morally, to do it." His reasoning was based on what we can call "marginal utilitarianism." Singer believed that we should minimize the amount of pain in the world, and famine and starvation certainly cause a great deal of pain. Furthermore, the solution to starvation was (and is) straightforward: famine relief in the form of food shipments from rich countries to poor ones. Therefore, every individual ought to be sending money for famine relief, and should do so until his situation becomes equal to that of the people receiving the relief, as long as doing so does not impose a greater moral sacrifice. In other words, it would not be moral to starve your children in order to feed others, but it would be immoral to live in luxury while others were starving.

At the extreme, Singer seemed to imply that the greatest level of global justice could be achieved only by the near-equal distribution of the world's wealth. There are some obvious problems with Singer's proposal, some practical and others philosophical. In the article, Singer ridiculed the amount of aid that was actually being provided by the United States and Europe. He believed that charities provided competent means of getting relief to where it was needed but, in practice, and in the absence of coordination, some sufferers would receive a great deal of assistance while others would get little or none.[4] In general, however, Singer disapproved of the notion of "charity" because, he argued, people and groups compete with each other in the hope of receiving credit for "moral" behavior, a point with which other analysts agree.[5] Even governments send aid to appear morally correct and also to benefit their own economies. But, as Singer emphasized, moral acts should not be contingent on any kind of return, material or other.

Regardless of these practical considerations, Singer's proposal raises a troubling question: what do we owe morally to those who are neither family nor members of any of our communities of obligation, such as fellow citizens? We help kin without question because the ties of blood are strong; we help fellow citizens because we live in the same society and we are tied together through common history, rituals, and institutions. Must we help those whom we don't know and with whom we don't share attributes such as religion, language, or culture? According to Singer, yes. To illustrate this point, he drew a comparison between a child in danger of drowning nearby and people in danger of starving far away. You would not fail to jump into the water to save the child even if the child were a stranger and the rescue came at the cost of ruining your new suit or dress. Singer argued that the second case was similar; if people unknown to you are dying far away and you can do something to save them, you are morally obligated to do so.

Not everyone agrees with this reasoning. A year or so after Singer's article was published, Garrett Hardin issued a riposte. Hardin was a biologist best known for his 1968 article in *Science*, "The Tragedy of the Commons," which argued that shared resources were inevitably abused. The title of Hardin's rebuttal to Singer was "Life Boat Ethics: The Case against Helping the Poor."[6] Like Singer's, Hardin's argument was utilitarian, but he drew the relevant lines (or borders) differently, claiming that we have no obligations to those who live outside of our country.

Hardin was particularly concerned about global population growth and its impact on humanity's prospects for survival; this reasoning is Malthusian.[7] Imagine, wrote Hardin, that you and some number of people are adrift at sea in a lifeboat with sufficient food and water to last until you are rescued. In the water around you are a large number of people who can swim but will drown if they are not saved. Imagine further, he continued, that the lifeboat represents your country and the people in the water represent the poor of the world in need of help. You could, of course, save those in the water, but at what cost? The lifeboat is already full. If too many additional people climb into the boat, it will founder and everyone will be tossed into the water to drown. You could save a very few, but then you would have less food and water for each person and it might not last until you were rescued. And how would you decide whom to save? You can't very well interview people as they are going under!

Completing the metaphor, Hardin argued that the residents of wealthy countries, secure in their national lifeboats, could not afford to feed the world's billions of poor and hungry, swimming in the sea. First, the rich simply do not have enough food. Second, helping the poor would only encourage them to have more children, creating an ever-growing demand for food. Eventually, as Thomas Malthus argued in 1778, population growth would outstrip agricultural growth, and everyone would starve.[8] Better to let the poor fend for themselves by halting immigration into the rich countries, and by providing aid only to one's needy and deserving conationals. According to Hardin, we have no moral or other obligations to anyone who is not a bona fide, legal citizen or resident of our country. He insisted that the only acceptable approach to distributive justice was what is fair and acceptable to us and our descendants; we cannot rectify the injustices of the past or injustices in other countries. Indeed, wrote Hardin:

> We Americans of non-Indian ancestry can look upon ourselves as the descendants of thieves who are guilty morally, if not legally, of stealing this land from its Indian owners. Should we then give back the land to the now living American descendants of those Indians? However morally or logically sound this proposal may be, I, for one, am unwilling to live by it and I know no one else who is. Besides, the logical consequence would be absurd.

> Suppose that, intoxicated with a sense of pure justice, we should decide to turn our land over to the Indians. Since all our other wealth has also been derived from the land, wouldn't we be morally obliged to give that back to the Indians too?[9]

His answer was, self-evidently, "No!"

But Hardin's conclusion is not quite so self-evident as he claimed. Consider that a significant portion of the United States' wealth came from the surplus value produced by slave labor prior to the Civil War. Over the intervening century and a half, that wealth has been reinvested many times and, through both economic growth and compound interest, now constitutes an enormous sum. (One dollar invested in 1860 at an annual interest rate of 4 percent would today have compounded to more than $80. Even with inflation, this is a substantial increase.) It does not seem wholly unreasonable to imagine that the descendants of U.S. slaves ought to receive some sort of reparations (similar, perhaps, to what West Germany paid to Israel as reparations for the Holocaust), even though it could never fully compensate for the injustices of slavery. Or consider the issue of Palestinian properties confiscated since 1948 without compensation by Israel. These made major contributions to the prosperity of Israel, while millions of Palestinians live in deep poverty. Why shouldn't Israel provide reparations to them, and why shouldn't Jewish refugees from Arab states be compensated for the loss of their properties, too?

Singer and Hardin illustrate the poles of the debate over justice as distribution, and one can imagine all kinds of positions in between. But what is critical about this debate is its singular focus on material goods. To repeat one of our earlier questions: is it fair that some people have so much and others have so little? Neither of these two authors is especially interested in explaining how things got to be so unjust or asking whether we have any responsibility for the actions of our ancestors or our governments. Other philosophers of justice acknowledge our inability to do anything about the past, but believe that simple redistribution is not the answer to injustice, either. They seek sets of social rules according to which justice can be achieved and which, to some degree, will function more effectively than Singer's morality and Hardin's self-interest.

Justice as Fairness

The late John Rawls, considered by some to be the most eminent twentieth-century theorist of justice, believed that "justice is fairness."[10] Rawls recognized that societies are organized in ways that tend to institutionalize injustices, but he also thought it is possible to determine and follow fundamental principles that would increase the level of fairness in a society. Once its members recognized the centrality of such principles in seeking and achieving just outcomes, they would willingly accept those principles and the outcomes, however unfair the results might seem to them. Rawls devised a thought experiment that, he argued, makes it possible to establish the necessary conditions for justice. He called the experiment "decision making from the original position, behind a veil of ignorance."

Imagine, if you will, a situation in which no one knows anything about his own situation: his wealth, education, lineage, skin color, nationality, and so on—and we use "his" in this case because Rawls ignored gender as a category of analysis; his people were all men. This is the "original position." The "veil of ignorance" guarantees that all decisions about distribution will be made "disinterestedly," that is, that people will make decisions based on what is right rather than on what would be best for themselves. The decision to be made is about the riches of a society or the world. How should they be divided up, and what are the rules that will ensure that the division is fair?

Rawls concluded that such a group of people would most likely decide to divide the wealth into equal shares. How each might use his share, what each individual's condition might be in the future, and the constitution of other rules were of no importance in establishing the initial rule. Individuals are not equal in intelligence and capabilities, but they should not be penalized for what are accidents of birth. Over time, of course, some people might find ways of turning their share of riches into fabulous wealth, while others might see their initial endowment disappear. But outcomes were not of concern to Rawls; procedures were.

Clearly, the real world is not like this, and people's views of what is and is not fair are heavily influenced by their personal "original positions." We are each born into families, some poor, some wealthy, and our individual life chances and opportunities are shaped even earlier, by our genetic endowment, events during our fetal existence, and our families' life situation. After birth, and as we grow older, we become aware of our own and others' endowments and learn that they are unequal. Some can use their endowments to increase this inequality even further. The result might be unfair, but if they have done nothing illegal to obtain or increase their wealth, is it unjust? Moreover, why should anyone agree to rules that might diminish her share of the wealth? In contrast, someone who is poor in comparison to others is likely to see things very differently. Fairness, it would seem, is in the eye of the beholder.

But that trivial conclusion was not the point of Rawls's thought experiment. His goal in devising this scenario was to derive principles of justice about which everyone could agree, regardless of their initial position. Rawls concluded that two principles follow from such a deductive exercise: first, an equality of basic rights, and second, what he called the "difference principle," which regards any inequality as unjust unless its removal makes worse the situations of the worst-off members of society.[11] Here we can see an echo of Singer in Rawls's argument.

There are numerous complications to Rawls's arguments that need not concern us here, but the fundamental point is that his reasoning was purely theoretical. Rawls may have hoped that recognition of these rules of fairness would stimulate discussion and even become the basis for justice in society, but he offered no program to make them so. Fairness as conceived by Rawls was not, moreover, the same as equality. An equal division of resources might not, in fact, be fair, because some might make greater sacrifices than others (think of inequalities in the household division of labor or the greater risks and responsibilities carried by soldiers as compared to civilians during wartime). At best, one might seek to equalize opportunities and be willing to leave the rest in the hands of individuals.

Rawls's arguments, published almost forty years ago, have generated a vast literature, both supportive and critical.[12] What is most important, perhaps, about the original position and the veil of ignorance is that Rawls limited their application to liberal societies, that is, those that are both democratic and capitalist. He believed that it is only in such countries that the individual is central to the beliefs and practices that lead to both justice and injustice. Only in liberal societies, he argued, could the individual even begin to conceive of himself in the original position, behind the veil of ignorance, a situation devoid of power, hierarchy, and history. We know, however, that even in liberal societies the original position is a fiction. It is not so much that the theorist himself failed to fulfill the requirements of the thought experiment, as that he does not take into account the lack of connection *between* the thought experiment and action. As experience shows, even liberal societies have been unable to envision rules reflecting the original position, because liberal elites are unwilling to assume the veil of ignorance.

Justice as Rights

Another approach to justice that relates tangentially to Rawls's original position and to liberalism argues for the provision or availability of "human rights" to all individuals.[13] Conventionally, such rights are divided into different categories: civil, political, social, economic, and cultural. *Civil* rights are linked to citizenship and include freedom from discrimination. *Political* rights, such as the right to vote or run for office, enable full participation in the institutionalized political processes of a country. *Social* rights allow an individual to participate in society to the greatest extent possible and include the right to an education. *Economic* rights provide access to those activities and goods that ensure livelihood. Finally, *cultural* rights permit groups to identify themselves as distinct, in some fashion, from the society in which they live. Theoretically, a society in which all these rights were available to every individual and group would be a society in which everyone is treated fairly and has access to goods, services, and opportunities that redress inequalities among them.

Human rights occupy a rather problematic position in the search for justice, however. Explicit political and civil rights have their origins in events such as the seventeenth-century revolutions in England and the eighteenth-century revolutions in the United States and France, but the recognition of economic and social rights is more recent, both cause and effect of the rise and evolution of the welfare state. The sources of all these rights are the focus of continuing debate. Originally, political and civil rights were regarded as "natural law," which is how they are presented in the American Declaration of Independence and Constitution. Political rights, described by Isaiah Berlin as "positive liberty" (or "freedom to"), include rights of free association, free press, and access to the public square.[14] Civil rights, which Berlin calls "negative liberty" (or "freedom from"), have to do mostly with the freedom of the individual from control by outsiders, not only the sovereign with his capacity to violate the body through such practices as incarceration and torture, but also neighbors and the church, which is why freedom to choose a religion (or no religion) and the right to choose a spouse, a domicile, and a job belong here. John Stuart Mill was particularly incensed in his essay *On Liberty* on the effect of such socially imposed constraints. These freedoms relate to one's right to a private life.

The individual in a liberal society cannot function autonomously if she is overly constrained by rules and laws, but she also cannot function if her rights are not protected by rules and laws. Thus, at the extreme, these two sets of rights are in conflict. Full expression of positive liberty erases negative liberty for everyone else; full expression of negative liberty erases the public sphere for all. As with all rights, there are conflicts that must be addressed and settled by each and every society. To take just one example, consider the practice of male and female circumcision. Male circumcision has been found to cut the risk of contracting HIV; female circumcision, widely condemned throughout the West, eliminates sexual pleasure and usually leads to severe physical impairment.[15] These are long-standing cultural practices among certain religions, marking the individual's bond to the society and constituting a rite of passage. Yet, circumcision can also be seen as a form of child abuse and a violation of the individual rights and bodily integrity of children.[16]

The other sets of rights—social, economic, cultural—arise from the observation that civil and political rights are of little use or benefit to those who are poor, hungry, homeless, and unemployed, and to those who belong to groups that are the focus of organized discrimination and even violence. In liberal societies, people are supposed to be able to satisfy their need for food, a home, and employment through individual initiative without the assistance of others. The United States, for example, does not recognize social, economic, and cultural rights as rights, arguing that state and society have no responsibility to provide them. We shall return to this issue later. Groups in liberal societies presumably are granted no exceptional privileges on the basis of ascribed characteristics such as race, ethnicity, or gender, even though we know that some ethnic and religious groups in civil society enjoy exceptional privileges for other reasons, such as social class or political connections.[17]

Indeed, can we say that any human rights are really "natural"? Recall that in Hobbes's State of Nature, men were completely free of limits but also lacked all security. They were not, to be sure, threatened with torture by some ruling king, but they lived under constant threat of violence and death from other men. Indeed, the rights of individuals could not exist without a sovereign who is above the law to enforce the law. Hence the paradox of such rights: while they are constraints imposed on the state, they are also granted and protected by the state. Yet although natural rights theory calls these rights "inalienable," in practice, what the state giveth the state can taketh away. The capacity of the state to revoke rights is clearly evident in both the actions of the U.S. executive with regard to incarceration and torture of individuals captured in Afghanistan and elsewhere, and legislation passed by the U.S. Congress, such as the U.S.A. Patriot Act (the "**U**niting and **S**trengthening **A**merica by **P**roviding **A**ppropriate **T**ools **R**equired to **I**ntercept and **O**bstruct **T**errorism Act of 2001"), which, among other things, erases the right to privacy and severely constrains the right to travel.

In order to address this apparent contradiction, efforts have been made to locate rights beyond the reach of states. Human rights are embedded in international conventions and agreements, such as the Universal Declaration of Human Rights (UDHR),[18] the International Covenant on Civil and Political Rights (ICCPR),[19] and the International Covenant on Economic, Social and Cultural Rights (ICESCR).[20] The United States has signed the UDHR but, as a declaration by the UN General Assembly, it is not a treaty and not binding, although it does set out norms and aspirations that have influenced the writing and passage of subsequent binding treaties. Thus, it is unfortunate that, even though the United States did sign the two international covenants, it has ratified only the ICCPR and is highly unlikely to ratify the ICESCR. And, while the various rights agreements have been ratified by countries whose actual practices leave much to be desired, international treaties and resolutions such as the UDHR nonetheless represent important constitutive elements in a human rights regime whose status transcends the individual states that are parties to them. Yet implementation remains in the hands of individual states, and the international mechanisms for evaluating state performance are run by states that rarely criticize themselves.[21] More disinterested assessments of actual practice come from nongovernmental organizations such as Amnesty International and Human Rights Watch, which also condemn these practices when necessary.[22]

Even countries active in the promotion of human rights find it difficult to balance various rights against one another. The provision, in particular, of economic and social rights requires either a high rate of economic growth and widespread prosperity that "trickles down" to all, regardless of status and position, or a substantial degree of redistribution certain to be fiercely resisted by the wealthy. Inasmuch as capitalism's efficient operation depends on a certain degree of inequality in a society, there are real structural impediments to providing greater access to resources—think of offering open admissions to Harvard, for example. Moreover, resistance to raising taxes suggests that there are limits to what the public is willing to pay in order to provide social and economic rights. Even social programs directed at the poor come under criticism by the middle and upper classes, as contemporary Venezuelan, Bolivian, and American politics illustrate, leaving many governments with little interest in fighting this battle. To put all of this another way, while the fulfillment of all five sets of human rights would theoretically result in a reduction in injustice around the world, merely acknowledging such rights without recognizing the tensions among them has little effect on the problem of injustice.

None of this is meant to suggest that human rights are irrelevant; they play a critical role in the struggle for justice, and their pursuit, as much as their enforcement, is central to eliminating injustice around the world. Yet the troubling relationship between human rights and the state is visible in many places. Among the most important is the liberal state's reluctance to enforce civil and political rights where the market is concerned, such as in the sometimes violent suppression of popular protests against WTO rules and practices.[23] This suggests that justice must be based on more than principled statements. Moreover, the individualized nature of life in liberal societies, where the bonds of kinship and interdependence have been weakened (see chapter 2), exacerbates for many those social and economic conditions that are so central to the problem of injustice. Consequently, it would seem that, if the onus for redressing these conditions falls on the individual, she should be able to acquire the tools and capabilities to do so.

Justice as Opportunity

Redistribution is politically treacherous; rights are difficult to enforce fully; and the original position requires a strong moral commitment to justice. Moreover, members of liberal societies tend to argue that no one can or should guarantee equality of outcomes. They say that the best that can be done is to try to ensure that no one is blocked from efforts to overcome the disadvantages she might have been born with. Amartya Sen is probably the most articulate proponent of this position, making his arguments in the language of freedom.[24] As he puts it,

> The constitutive role of freedom relates to the importance of substantive freedom in enriching human life. The substantive freedoms include elementary capabilities like being able to avoid such deprivations as starvation, undernourishment, escapable morbidity and premature mortality, as well as the freedoms that are associated with being literate and numerate, enjoying political participation and uncensored speech and so on.[25]

In other words, Sen equates freedom with fulfillment of Berlin's positive rights. He argues further that freedoms that include civil and political rights cannot be achieved if the substantive freedoms guaranteeing social and economic rights are lacking. At the same time, he also recognizes the obstacles to simply providing substantive freedoms, and the many failures that have accompanied "development" projects intended to do precisely this.[26]

Sen focuses instead on what he calls "capabilities," that is, "expansion of the 'capabilities' of persons to lead the kind of lives they value—and have reason to value."[27] Capabilities differ according to an individual's situation and needs, but we can think of them as an autonomous capacity to act in ways that enhance her quality of life, a term that means not simply "ways that add to her income" but ways to achieve the combination of factors, both material and intellectual, that enable a person to live a full and fulfilling life. Elaborating on Sen's list, these include low infant mortality, access to family planning, adequate food and housing, employment at a living wage, technical skills like reading acquired through education, full participation in political and community activities, protection from violence, and so on. Sen's concept of "development as freedom" is highly utilitarian, but it does not seek to maximize aggregate utility. The distribution of capabilities among individuals is more important to Sen than the greatest happiness for the largest number.

Yet Sen is critical of the basic principles of distributive justice that rest largely on the possession of income and wealth. Although he acknowledges the virtue of economic growth as essential to achieving development, he does not believe that growth alone is sufficient. Examining the People's Republic of China and, in particular, the state of Kerala in southern India, Sen points out that the development of capabilities found in Kerala (and China) did not take place in other parts of India. Kerala, it should be noted, has one of the lowest average per capita incomes in India. What, then, accounts for the difference, and why does Sen offer the case of a "poor" society as a "good" example?

We have to acknowledge that neither India nor China is an exemplary provider of rights and that, although both economies are growing at prodigious rates, both also suffer from a growing gap between rich and poor. But whatever their shortcomings, Kerala and China have been strongly committed to social development through the provision of education (especially for women), employment, health care, food, housing, and land reform. Interestingly, perhaps, both also were governed by communist parties during the period in which these capabilities were most substantially developed. In China, in particular, claims Sen, this laid the foundation for the subsequent introduction of markets and the high economic growth rates of the past two decades.[28] While Kerala remains quite poor, and many of the social services once provided by the state have disappeared, it still remains one of the most socially developed states in the Indian Union, and its level of urban communal violence is among the lowest in the country.[29]

Sen argues that, although his program for development requires a high degree of state involvement, it is nevertheless a liberal one, committed to individual freedom. It also is a capitalist program, dependent on private investment and growth to support and guarantee full access to capabilities. Sen makes no arguments about outcomes and whether they should be equalized; people should be free to do with their capabilities whatever they wish. Individuals simply must have the capacity to recognize and seize opportunities when they appear, and the rest will be, as they say, history.

Not everyone who values Sen's approach to justice, development, and freedom is quite so sanguine about outcomes, however. John Isbister points out that "unequal outcomes in time create unequal opportunities."[30] As he explains the problem,

> This reasoning [about justice] leads to the possibility that equality of opportunity actually *requires* equal outcomes. This possibility exists because we live our lives over a period of years, our generations overlap, and our societies continue over time. My opportunities are determined in large measure by the resources—including economic, educational, technological, and moral resources—given to me by my parents and by my society. If my parents and my society are vastly different in their access to these resources from yours, you and I will be unequal at the starting blocks. Until each person has an equal opportunity to develop his or her talents—something that cannot exist while the distribution of outcomes in the world remains unequal—we cannot be equal at the starting line.[31]

Addressing this contradiction clearly requires some means of restoring equality of opportunity. That means, at the least, a larger allocation of resources to providing public goods, such as education and welfare. Even with that, the social capital comprising the various networks and contacts associated with privilege and family history would still remain with the individual. Libertarians and economists such as Milton Friedman argue that shifting the provision of goods from the private to the public sphere amounts to an infringement on people's freedom, since what they have acquired fairly is being taken away unfairly. Isbister does not subscribe to this argument, quoting Philippe Van Parijs, who says that "real freedom is not only a matter of having the right to do what one might want to do, but also a matter of having the means for doing it."[32] Thus, while Isbister supports Sen's basic approach, he also favors a progressive tax policy to reduce the income ratio between richest and poorest to roughly eight to one.[33] He would also impose a steep inheritance tax on estates in order to minimize inequality at the beginning of life.[34]

There is an additional complication here that is worth considering, one that goes beyond both Rawls's veil of ignorance and Isbister's case against generational advantage. Justice as opportunity internalizes the idea that, if provided with the appropriate tools, anyone can be successful on his or her own terms. Yet, it is clear that many people with substantial capabilities do not succeed in their efforts to excel in particular areas; by some estimates, seven to eight out of every ten new businesses in the United States fail within their first ten years of operation.[35] Similarly, many very bright and well-trained individuals find themselves rejected by medical, legal, or graduate schools, through no particular fault of their own. We assume that those who fail are individually responsible for their failure, and that such an outcome is fair and just, even as those who fail may feel they have been discriminated against. Both are too simple as explanations. They disregard, once again, the *social* nature of success and failure as well as fairness and injustice, and the fact that rights are often in tension and conflict.[36]

Recall our discussion of the social individual in chapter 2. There, we saw that the individual is very much a "product" of the many social relations across time and space that she has with other people, with things, and with institutions. We can call these relations a "social network." Social networks are built up through the many activities that we undertake, in school, work, and play. They constitute what political scientists call "social capital," in the sense that we invest energy and commitment into developing such relationships and realize various forms of "return" on them. Building a strong relationship with professors can be important if you will need letters of recommendation for graduate or professional school, or for a job application. Having good relations with your boss will help you advance through the company. The people your parents know from school might be valuable connections for you as you search for work, and so on.

It should not have escaped your notice that the social capital inherent in networks of this sort correlates strongly with status and wealth. The poor may have as many relationships as the rich; the difference is that rich people's networks have greater scope and capacity, and more members with resources that can be used to influence others. That, in turn, builds up more social capital and gives the rich a further advantage. Moreover, social capital can be turned into financial capital through these networks—think of that first job someone gets through a friend of the family. None of these relations can be measured easily (as opposed, say, to years of education or scores on achievement tests), yet they can be as important to success as other opportunities offered to a person or any capabilities that person might possess. So how could we fold such advantages into the notion of "justice as opportunity"? And how might we redress the inequalities that arise because some people have impoverished social networks compared to others?

The short answer is: "We can't." The long answer is: "Perhaps we can, but not without time and tolerance." Affirmative action represents one approach to redressing social inequalities, but it is badly flawed. We are used to hearing that affirmative action gives minorities and women an unfair advantage over equally or better-qualified white men.[37] But this argument implies unfair advantages to groups, which is incorrect: affirmative action selects out specific *individuals* who are deemed to be representative of the most qualified members of a particular group and gives them an advantage over other specific individuals in other social groups. This assumes that, all else being equal, were that person born into a social context with opportunities comparable to the majority selected, he or she would have performed at the same level. Note this is pretty routine practice among the already privileged in all walks of life—that job you got through a family friend did not go to someone else. It does not, however, mean that the positions of other members of the group are improved by comparison with members of other, more-advantaged groups. A successful individual might have a high income and live in a great neighborhood, but this doesn't do anything for anyone else in her natal social group. The average income of the group will rise if hers is included, but there is no personal benefit from her inclusion for those at the bottom of the distribution.[38]

The argument for affirmative action rests, therefore, on the assumption that providing meritorious individuals from disadvantaged groups with access to institutions rich in networks and potential social capital will improve the situation of the disadvantaged groups as a whole. The reasoning is that as larger numbers of disadvantaged individuals improve their positions—through opportunity—a sort of "trickle down" to others in that group will follow. Yet, there is now a growing understanding that middle-class African Americans can coexist comfortably with and in remarkable isolation from a growing population of poor African Americans. The successful middle class might raise the average, but it does not improve the lot of the worst off. Justice is not served.[39]

Moreover, to what are people entitled? Those who are born rich may squander much of their wealth. We might critique or ridicule them, but we consider them entitled to do so. Those who are born poor but with much promise may never succeed simply for lack of support and access. Is it fair that the hand we are dealt at birth has so much effect on our lives and capabilities? And when we have to make choices about comparably qualified candidates for, say, admission to medical school, on what basis do we decide? Is it better to support those who have come from a relatively impoverished home in the hope that their eventual success will generate broad social benefits? Or should we select those who meet specific technical criteria such as minimum grade point averages and test scores? Which candidate is most entitled to admission?

This was the issue in the case of Allen Bakke, who was denied admission to the medical school at the University of California, Davis, in 1973 and 1974, even though his scores were higher than those of a number of minority candidates who were admitted under an affirmative action program. The supreme court of California ruled that he had been discriminated against and should be admitted. Eventually, the case made its way to the U.S. Supreme Court, which also found in Bakke's favor.[40] Since that time, similar cases have been brought; in more recent ones, the Supreme Court has been more equivocal about affirmative action programs,[41] but the fact is that the courts should not be left to rule on these matters; they are issues for political debate and ought to be decided in the public square.[42]

Is there a better way? One possibility might be to develop an institutional infrastructure specifically for those groups that are disadvantaged because of poverty, race, ethnicity, or all three. Special projects and funds could provide large endowments (rather than specific program or project funds) to institutions serving disadvantaged groups. Imagine, for example, if schools and colleges serving minority and disadvantaged students in the United States had access to resources such as those available to prep schools or Harvard! Unfortunately, the resources to fund such endowments would have to come from somewhere—presumably taxes—undoubtedly evoking bitter opposition and loud cries of "injustice!"

Justice as Recognition, Respect, and Dignity

Yet another approach to the problem of injustice can be found in the concept of "recognition." Nancy Fraser, in particular, has been a strong advocate of recognition, although in recent years she has also argued that it is of little use without some degree of distributive justice.[43] Fraser is especially concerned about social justice, that is, some kind of equalization in terms of both distribution of resources *and* respect from others. Connected to the discussion about social capital and networks, social justice would amount to the incorporation of disadvantaged groups into the social relations of the dominant group. This is not assimilation, but what Fraser and others call *recognition*. With respect to discrimination against women, she writes,

> From the recognition perspective . . . gender is a status differentiation. A major feature of gender injustice is androcentrism: the authoritative construction of norms that privilege traits associated with masculinity and the pervasive devaluation and disparagement of things coded as "feminine," paradigmatically—but not only—women. When these androcentric norms are institutionalized, women suffer gender-specific status injuries, including sexual assault and domestic violence; objectifying and demeaning stereotypical depictions in the media; harassment and disparagement in everyday life; and exclusion or marginalization in public spheres and deliberative bodies. These harms are injustices of misrecognition. They are relatively independent of political economy and are not merely "superstructural." Thus, they cannot be remedied by redistribution alone but require additional independent remedies of recognition.

She goes on to argue,

> Treating recognition as a matter of justice has a second advantage as well. It conceives misrecognition as a status injury whose locus is social relations, not individual psychology. To be misrecognized, on this view, is not simply to be thought ill of, looked down on, or devalued in others' conscious attitudes or mental beliefs. It is rather to be denied the status of a full partner in social interaction and prevented from participating as a peer in social life as a consequence of institutionalized patterns of cultural value that constitute one as comparatively unworthy of respect or esteem. This approach avoids difficulties that arise when misrecognition is understood psychologically.

Because redistribution will not afford redress of the injustice associated with misrecognition, which itself cannot address the injustice associated with redistribution, Fraser argues for a "two-dimensional" approach to justice. At the heart of her approach is what she calls "parity of participation." As she explains it,

> According to this norm, justice requires social arrangements that permit all (adult) members of society to interact with one another as peers. For participatory parity to be possible, I claim, at least two conditions must be satisfied. First, the distribution of material resources must be such as to ensure participants' independence and "voice." Second, the institutionalized cultural patterns of interpretation and evaluation must express equal respect for all participants and ensure equal opportunity for achieving social esteem.

In other words, without access to the resources necessary for a valued life, the individual has neither time nor opportunity to interact in society. And without the respect and legal basis for participation, redistribution is not likely to make much difference in terms of social justice.

While Fraser is on to something here, she has also fallen into the old "ought-is" trap: she is arguing for a social change in consciousness and practice without specifying clearly how that might be accomplished. What's more problematic is the tautological nature of this two-dimensional framework: each alone cannot accomplish justice in the absence of the other, yet neither seems likely to come about unless the other happens first (well, perhaps redistribution could precede recognition, although recognition would certainly cost less). Political philosophers rarely are responsible for seeing through their proposals and projects; their job is to conceptualize the conditions under which a particular objective might be achieved. Where, then, is the lever that could "move the world"?

Communitarianism versus Cosmopolitanism

Let us return, for a moment, to the contrasting approaches of Peter Singer and Garrett Hardin. Singer, you will recall, argues that every human being is deserving of help, whether a conational or not, and that each of us should help others until we are no better off than they are. Hardin argues that we have obligations only to our families and conationals and should not help others lest we cause our "lifeboat" to founder. Singer's approach is an extreme version of *cosmopolitanism* (or, perhaps, what Karl Marx called "species being"). It is extreme because it accords equal respect and dignity to *all* human beings as individuals, whereas Kant distinguishes between obligations to one's community and hospitality to the stranger (see chapters 1 and 7).[44] As a political philosophy, cosmopolitanism involves a good deal more than matters of justice;[45] as it applies to justice, there are several ways in which it can be articulated.[46] One approach we find to be of particular interest is that offered by Onora O'Neill, who writes about the *obligations* associated with justice even to those who are "distant strangers."[47] We will return to her argument shortly.

Communitarianism draws lines outside of which we have no moral obligations and need not be concerned about justice; it is similar to Hardin's views in that those lines are generally the borders of *nation-states*. Hence, communitarianism is an approach that is consonant with contemporary world order, and its proponents have little concern for people who live and die in faraway lands. While there are differing approaches to communitarianism, we can say that, in general, the limits to justice may ignore even proximity and suffering.[48] Thus, an individual who is among us, but not of us, has few or none of the rights or privileges granted to members of the community. Strictly speaking, according to this view, we are not even obligated to take in someone who has grounds for fearing persecution, torture, or death if she is returned to her homeland.

International law mandates that such individuals be granted asylum if they can prove their fear is justified. But those who might leave their home countries for what are judged to be purely economic reasons have no grounds for requesting asylum, and it is the host state that decides whether any petitioner is a political or economic refugee. As a result, in communitarian systems injustice is often committed on any number of fronts: there are the conditions that create the injustice in the first place; there are the conditions under which those who seek to escape unjust conditions must live; and there are the conditions that make a supposedly moral distinction between "political" and "economic" injustice, with the latter deemed to be morally unimportant. Evidently, communitarianism not only accepts but even encourages injustice.[49]

Let us return, then, to the obligations of justice. O'Neill counterpoises these obligations to a "rights-based" approach that relies, in effect, on individuals claiming rights and demanding that others—whether fellow citizens, state authorities, or international agencies—fulfill them. More to the point is that the rights discussed earlier in this chapter are discussed in the abstract: people deserve them but there is no ensuring, even in the best-off societies, that they will be met. Obligations, by contrast, are imposed on or accepted by each individual, whose duty is to see that they are fulfilled. And, as O'Neill puts it,

> There are reasons enough to show that obligations provide the more coherent and more comprehensive starting point for thinking about ethical requirements, including the requirements of justice. Although the rhetoric of rights has a heady power, and that of obligations and duties few immediate attractions, it helps to view the perspective of obligations as fundamental if the political and ethical implications of normative claims are to be taken seriously.

Even if we are not sure to whom we owe obligations, she argues, "we at least begin with a practical task."[50]

O'Neill does not go quite so far as Singer in her definition of the extent of our obligations, and she is willing to consider a mix of strategies and tactics beyond simply giving until we have no more to give without causing ourselves moral or physical injury. But what is important about her approach is that it requires *agency*: we must act in order to be just and achieve justice, and we must do so regardless of states, governments, and even conationals. Better yet, we should do so with others, as a collective political project. As Arlo Guthrie once said (in a somewhat different context), "If you want to end war and stuff you got to sing loud."[51] If we want to have justice, not only do we have to sing loud but also sing together—that is, we must *act* together.

How Far Do Our Obligations Extend?

Much of this chapter has been concerned with justice in an abstract context, as something that we all desire but about which we disagree. Although the conflict between communitarian and cosmopolitan approaches to justice might seem the most antagonistic, the real guts of the problem are to be found in *structures* that we tend to regard as "natural" but that are not, and that reproduce again and again the very social relations that are the source of injustice in the first place.[52] We discussed structures and naturalization earlier in this book when we considered people and economy (chapter 4). Here, we examine the injustices perpetuated by particular structures, not all of them economic, that lead to the acceptance of injustice as "natural."

Consider the notion of reparations to the American descendants of slaves discussed earlier in this chapter. This is an idea that has been around since the first rumors that "forty acres and a mule" would be given to the newly freed slaves at the end of the U.S. Civil War. In recent years, the proposal has surfaced as a means of rectifying the long-standing socioeconomic gap between the majority of African Americans and the majority of whites.[53] While it is difficult to estimate the appropriate value of reparations, somewhere between $1 trillion and $10 trillion is a reasonable estimation of the fair value of the wages earned but never paid to black slaves.[54]

Whether this sum is absurdly large or insultingly small is not important; the critical question is whether such a payment is not only fair but also obligatory. Many people, when confronted with this question, respond that they bear no responsibility for what happened centuries ago and therefore they owe nothing to the descendants of slaves. (Besides, who would get the money, how would you know who is legally entitled, and how could we possibly pay for it?) Another, somewhat smaller group of people respond, "That was then. Slavery was legal, and the slaves were freed. We cannot change the past." A few legalistically inclined observers claim that slavery has caused no injury to anyone now alive and, therefore, that no one is owed any compensation.[55]

Recall Garret Hardin's argument about the theft of land from Native Americans, quoted earlier. Disregarding for a moment Hardin's cynicism, does his argument of innocence point to his conclusion regarding justice? He wrote,

> Clearly, the concept of pure justice produces an infinite regression to absurdity. Centuries ago, wise men invented statutes of limitations to justify the rejection of such pure justice, in the interest of preventing continual disorder. The law zealously defends property rights, but only relatively recent property rights. Drawing a line after an arbitrary time has elapsed may be unjust, but the alternatives are worse.
>
> We are all the descendants of thieves, and the world's resources are inequitably distributed. But we must begin the journey to tomorrow from the point where we are today. We cannot remake the past. We cannot safely divide the wealth equitably among all peoples so long as people reproduce at different rates. To do so would guarantee that our grandchildren and everyone else's grandchildren, would have only a ruined world to inhabit.[56]

But Hardin is evading the point. No one is arguing for infinite redress; only for something proportional to the original injustice. What Hardin and others attempt in making arguments such as "we are all descendants of thieves" is to naturalize both theft and injustice as inherent to human nature and society. It is a way not only to avoid responsibility for unjust actions themselves, but also to deny legitimacy to the moral call for redressing them. Yet, as even Hardin acknowledges, our current prosperity is due in no small part to the original capital in land, labor, and resources provided by both Native Americans and slaves.

The same argument can be extended to virtually all rich countries whose wealth is not only the result of prudent investment, technological innovation, and brilliant entrepreneurship, but also a product of colonialism, exploitation, and theft. The "fact" that, in the absence of such historical crimes and injustices, the world today could be a much poorer and, perhaps, even more unjust place is hardly a basis on which to justify the acts of our ancestors. Where we are able to rectify such injustices, we are obligated to do so in the name of cosmopolitan justice.

Carol Robb makes an interesting argument about the notion of "debt" to preceding generations that belies Hardin's claims that we have no obligations to those whom we might have dispossessed or treated unjustly. She argues that we are obligated to "make payment on the social mortgage," which is "the debt all must pay back to a society in recognition that one inherits wealth in the form of goods or knowledge or technology from those who have gone before or who walk with us now."[57] Robb claims, in essence, that there is no such thing as a purely "private" return on investment or property and that all human activities, whether social, political, or economic, are built on foundations laid down by others.[58] Even at 1 percent, the interest on current social wealth would amount to a goodly sum that could go a considerable way toward redressing historical injustices.

How far must we go to fulfill such obligations? And how might we go about it? O'Neill does not provide more than general guidelines, and there is no sign that she concurs with Singer's dictum. She does, however, offer the following:

> Kantian economic justice does not point simply to increasing average income or wealth, let alone achieving economic uniformities of any sort. Like other aspects of justice, it is a matter of limiting relative power and powerlessness, so securing the external freedom within which people can seek to obtain the means to lead their lives. . . . If justice is fundamentally a matter of securing external freedom for all, reforms which build a more just transnational economic order might have to regulate and police international markets, transactions and relations so that the conditions that make [sure that] some local markets and transactions and domestic social relations relatively secure even for the weak [are available] . . . more widely.[59]

Accordingly, we are obligated to work toward the kinds of institutional changes that will facilitate and foster the conditions under which all people can pursue a valued life.

Justice for the People!

In our discussion of the many approaches to the problem of injustice, there is one point that we have, so far, failed to discuss: the relationship between global politics and justice for people. After all, if the sources of injustice are to be found in the actions of states, the operations of markets, and the structures of societies, what can a focus on individual justice accomplish? This question points back to an earlier discussion about the nature of social change and how it takes place. Some argue that what is most important is a change of perspective: once enough people start to demand justice, states and corporations will have no choice but to comply. Others believe that technology is more important: if biotechnology can increase world production of food, fewer people will go hungry and injustice will decrease. A few still place their hopes in class struggle and the changes that would accompany revolution against capitalism and the state.

We regard these arguments, taken separately, as something like the old parable of the blind men and the elephant. Each man touched a different part of the elephant and imagined it to be a different kind of animal from the ones the others reported sensing. Justice demands that we believe all our fellow human beings to be worthy of dignity and respect; that we act in ways that facilitate and foster dignity and respect among human beings; and that we provide the material necessities that enable people to live dignified lives worthy of respect. Indeed, we are obligated to do these things and also to help to construct a discourse that will propagate justice and embed it in institutions at every level of life. In chapter 10, we will return to this obligation and the political action necessary to meet it.

9

People and Globalization

> I'd like to teach the world to sing in perfect harmony.
>
> —Roger Cook and Roger Greenaway

We've talked a lot about globalization, and now it's time to look more closely at what "globalization" means. Its most basic definition—this version is taken from economist Joseph Stiglitz—is "the closer integration of the countries and peoples of the world which has been brought about by the enormous reduction of costs of transportation and communication, and the breaking down of artificial barriers to the flows of goods, services, capital, knowledge, and (to a lesser extent) people across borders."[1] Political scientist James Mittelman says that globalization is "[d]riven by changing modes of competition [such that it] compresses the time and space aspects of social relations. [It] is a market-induced, not a policy-led, process,"[2] but, as we discuss in this chapter, there are many engines of globalization in addition to the market, and globalization occurred long before "the market" as we know it existed.

Globalization takes many pathways. It brings people and places closer to one another at a faster and faster rate, forcing both to adjust to the continual change demanded by its disruption of social space. Strangers come to new lands to exploit resources that formerly were out of reach; people change jobs, locations, and identities repeatedly in a single lifetime. Some argue that this makes the global economy more stable and efficient than national economies, but others note that it increases individual insecurity and we can see from the economic downturn spreading outward from the U.S. subprime lending fiasco that it increases national insecurity as well.[3] As we saw in chapter 7, economic competition is an element of modern and postmodern warfare. In consequence, both globalization and the resistance it evokes can be intense and violent.

Globalization Then and Now

These qualities of globalization were evident in the late nineteenth century, the only period of hyperrapid incorporation into global capitalism closely similar to what is happening today. Then as now, globalization grew out of new transport, communication, and command-and-control technologies. Karl Marx and Frederich Engels describe the rapidly globalizing nineteenth-century world as one where "all that is solid melts into air."[4] Karl Polanyi traces the role of nineteenth-century globalization in creating what today we call "the Third World," where local cultures were shattered by a combination of market mechanisms and crushing tax burdens imposed by imperial powers:

> The catastrophe of the native community is a direct result of the rapid and violent disruption of the basic institutions of the victim (whether force is used in the process or not does not seem altogether relevant). These institutions are disrupted by the very fact that a market economy is foisted upon an entirely differently organized community; labor and land are made into commodities, which, again, is only a short formula for the liquidation of every and any cultural institution in an organic society.[5]

Trade, finance, and investment are the biggest engines of globalization; local structures and cultures are its victims. Among its results are the centralization of governance, cultural convergence, the loss of local autonomy, and the redistribution of wealth and income within and between nation-states.[6]

Despite the prominence of capitalism in both phases of modern globalization, we should not think of this process as either totally modern or merely economic. Older forms of "contact" affect people's lives and life chances, too. Trade and markets have always connected peoples, as studies of the transmission of infectious diseases like plague and influenza show.[7] War, conquest, colonization, and enslavement are globalizing processes that, like trade and investment, initiate or speed up the redistribution of power and wealth among persons and countries.[8] Natural disasters like floods, droughts, and earthquakes also trigger population migration and wealth redistribution, sometimes with a little help from human beings in positions to take advantage of the misfortunes of others.[9] One example familiar to Americans is the great famine in Ireland (1845–1850). When potato blight wiped out the food crop that most Irish peasants depended on, landowners reaped a bonanza. Food prices soared across Europe, and landlords exported grain that the domestic population could not afford to buy. More than one million peasants starved to death, and as many migrated to the New World in search of a better life. The pattern of starvation and migration was repeated during the great El Niño famines of the late nineteenth century.[10]

The movement of people, goods, and money depends on the movement of information. Superior information increases the ability to command and control events at a distance, not only in trade and diplomacy, but also in war fighting. During the eighteenth and early nineteenth centuries, locally based British East India Company (BEIC) employees policed the boundaries between their trading enclaves and the hinterlands surrounding them pretty much as they chose.[11] Company military forces expanded BEIC territory along this "turbulent frontier," justifying each added increment as necessary to ensure the security of what they had taken before. Although the British government, which had chartered the company, was ultimately responsible for its actions, it had little to say about how the BEIC conducted military operations.[12] The inadequacy of British command and control of the BEIC was exposed when British-trained Indian troops rebelled against the company in 1857–1858. Spurred by egregious violations of their religious sensibilities, Hindus and Muslims rose up in the bloody Sepoy Mutiny, which spread rapidly to disaffected groups in major cities like Delhi.[13] After two years of fighting and thousands of deaths, London took direct control of India.

Today's technology allows political leaders to supervise military activities closely, even if they are taking place thousands of miles away. The command authority for U.S. troops fighting in Iraq and Afghanistan is located at MacDill Air Force Base in Tampa, Florida, conveniently close to Washington yet no more isolated from the battlefields than Saigon-based general William Westmoreland had been during the Vietnam War. Paradoxically, the increase in state command-and-control capability comes with the proliferation and mass marketing of communications technology in the private sector—"command and control" does not guarantee "control" outside of "command." The commercial availability of telecommunications and air travel democratizes globalization and challenges the ability of states to restrain the movements of ideas, people, and goods undertaken privately. The same infrastructure that allows states to command and control armies half a world away allowed terrorist organizers equally far from action fronts to devise and coordinate a set of suicide attacks on two large U.S. cities using planes owned by commercial airlines. "Control" is tenuous even in the realm of "command." Military members serving at Abu Ghraib prison sent photos of prisoners being tortured to friends and colleagues over the Internet. The photos were "commodities" within the prison walls—one member of Abu Ghraib's office of military intelligence even put the now-famous image of naked detainees arranged in a pyramid on his computer desktop.[14]

This movement of virtual "goods" such as images, designs, symbols, and money from their cultures of origin to somewhere else is integral to globalization, but the dispersion of virtual goods also precedes modern times. Textile and pottery designs migrated widely among "primitive" people. A particularly good collection for observing the impact of cross-cultural contact on textile design is held by the Museum of the American Indian, recently transplanted from New York to Washington, D.C., which has many textiles from widely separated places that feature similar motifs and patterns. Another example is the blue and white Delft tableware patterns manufactured and sold by Dutch potteries. They were derived from Japanese pottery designs, both influenced by the earlier diffusion of the Blue Willow design from China, itself a product of the demand for high-quality Chinese porcelain from new Muslim elites in Europe and west

Asia and only later sold in Chinese markets.[15] What is different about the dispersion of virtual goods today is how quickly this happens. Textile designs in the pre-Columbian Americas traveled "on foot" and in small boats; Blue Willow pottery designs circulated throughout Asia and Europe on pack animals and ships. The Internet offers a much faster way for images to get around. But at the same time, design transmission is constrained by copyright laws that give rights to first claimants of those rights.

Social critics from the twentieth-century Frankfurt School argued that the same mass production techniques that gave us the Model T Ford (and its successors) now are routinely applied to the manufacture of cultural artifacts.[16] But, as with pottery and textiles in the past, the films, music, and television programs produced by large media companies do more than standardize citizen-consumers. As the popularity of YouTube shows, they also offer ways for individuals to express their own values and aesthetics in symbols that are intelligible cross-culturally.[17] Even complicated ideas like human rights, and their antithesis, suicide bombing, take similar meanings in the minds of persons from widely disparate cultures.[18] Although commercial values and pop culture are spread by modern communication technologies, they travel with additions, contentions, and reinterpretations, thereby constituting a far larger repertoire of values and cultures than whatever might have come in the original package.

Structures

Structures of globalization are complex regimes incorporating technology, organization, and sets of norms, values, and rules that are codified and enforced by international and national bodies. During the first round of El Niño famines in India, for example, Edward Robert Bulwer Lytton, Britain's viceroy of India, used military technology to keep distressed populations from stealing food; British law to prevent private charities from giving food to the starving; the rail system to collect and export "surplus" food from India to earn foreign exchange for his pet project, a war in Afghanistan; and his power to tax to trigger foreclosures on drought-stricken land, enabling wealthy Indians and Britons to purchase it at rock-bottom prices. Lytton blamed the millions of deaths that resulted from the famine on "natural causes," but it is clear that man-made structures and his own decisions as a powerful agent contributed heavily to these terrible consequences.[19]

This mixture of structures also highlights the distinction we made in chapter 7 between "acute" violence—physically destroying, maiming, and hurting people—and structural violence, which we defined as institutions and practices imposing systematic injustice on target groups. Imperialism is a transnational system of structural violence built on rules and practices that confer advantageous access to resources on the imperial power, its agents, and its citizens, and corresponding disadvantages on local communities and their agents and citizens. Yet as we have argued throughout this volume, "the system" alone does not determine outcomes. Lytton as an agent prevented food aid from being distributed by the state or by private parties while other agents—compassionate English citizens like Richard Grenville, the Duke of Buckingham, journalist William Digby, and the most famous nurse in the world, Florence Nightingale—struggled to open India to famine relief supplied through their official and social networks. The impact of structure on agency also is clear. Agents with charitable impulses were structurally blocked not only by rules but even more by Lytton as an agent and interpreter of these rules, and by another agent with vast structural resources, the British prime minister Benjamin Disraeli.[20] Without structures like railroads, the telegraph, an industrialized British military, and the British government in London, the harm that Lytton and Disraeli could have inflicted on Indians during the famine would have been far less, but if other agents had been in charge of these same structures, the famine might never have occurred.[21]

The most prominent structure facilitating globalization in the nineteenth century and today is "the market," vast, interconnected, national and transnational systems of rules and practices that govern capitalist relations of production and exchange. The "incorporation" (absorption) of territories and populations into global capitalist networks takes place on many different fronts. Barriers to trade and investment set by protective local and national legal regimes are broken by treaties and laws, and by transportation and communication technologies that allow buyers and sellers to penetrate former backwaters. Transport technologies are critical to creating and maintaining integrated markets. Until railroads were built, most goods traded over long distances went by ship or barge, still the cheapest mode of transport even though higher oil prices forced a reorganization of production that incorporates distance from major markets, just as the very first econometric model, constructed in 1826, predicted.[22] Before railroads, products from microeconomies in interior regions were isolated from towns and cities located on rivers and seacoasts, trapped by the high cost of getting goods from one place to another via human and animal transport over land. The result was many small subsistence markets, some market towns and fairs, and a few cosmopolitan centers such as we described in chapter 5.[23]

One prominent exception was the land route to Asia, over which camels carried packs of precious objects from East to West. "Precious" explains this trade. Silk, jewels, and spices could be transported long distances over land because of the high prices per unit of weight that sellers received for them, enough to buy food, water, and lodging for the men and beasts operating the trade route and still make a healthy profit. What determined whether a land route was economic was the cost of protection money that had to be paid to the warlords who controlled the territories the traders crossed. As long as most of Asia remained politically fragmented, there were too many warlords to make the land route profitable.

Genghis Khan's conquests and subsequent political consolidation allowed the land route to compete with the two sea routes between Europe and Asia. The availability of the land route also greatly increased the volume of Europe's trade with China—and with cities in between, such as Samarkand, which otherwise would not have been the crossroads of commerce and centers of culture that they became during this time.[24] Modern rulers of nation-states sought to integrate the economies in territories they controlled. Among the first steps to opening the interiors of consolidated realms was to improve transportation. This allowed rulers to subdue and pacify remote regions and, by stimulating trade, to increase the state's income.[25] Road systems and canals linked to navigable rivers made travel cheaper and faster. China's economy was organized around market towns located on waterways that drew agricultural produce from hinterland villages into larger networks of trade.[26] State-regulated monetary systems boosted internal trade, while taxation and the "invention" of the national debt mobilized financial support to pay for larger and more active governments.[27] People were required to pay taxes in money and not "in kind"— corn or chickens or whatever else they produced. To get money for taxes peasants had to sell goods, their labor, and sometimes also their land, deepening the spread of market relations. For many peasants, market relations represented a great improvement over feudal dues in the form of forced labor and military service, and servile (unfree) status,[28] helping to explain the fervor with which groups like the Levellers embraced possessive individualism.

Railroads increased the integration of national markets and extended the reach of traders and investors into interior regions abroad. The role of railroads as tools of imperialism and marketization is especially clear in sub-Saharan Africa, where most colonial-era rail lines ran only from ports to regions in the interior rich in raw materials rather than from city to city, ensuring that the socially fragmented territories of postcolonial states would have few physical supports for creating national economies.[29] Building railroads in developing areas provided a market for European steel companies after rail networks were substantially completed in their home countries.[30] It speeded up capital accumulation by the investors who financed these rail lines and sometimes by the investors' home governments, which felt compelled to take over the economies of countries unable to repay the cost of railroads and other goods and services they had received (whether they wanted them or not).[31] Railroads were just as important to the progress of nineteenth-century globalization as the construction of highways and airports for motor vehicle and air travel are to globalization today.

Not coincidentally, multinational oil companies were leading agents of globalization during much of the twentieth century. From the beginning of the oil industry, supplying fuel to consumer markets required cross-border transactions.[32] Struggles between imperial powers often masked and were fueled by conflicts over who would control oil-producing regions. A classical example of cascading damage from these conflicts is the formation and subsequent history of the nation-state of Iraq. It was assembled by the victors of World War I from large segments of what had been three districts of the defeated Ottoman Empire: Baghdad, with its majority of Sunni Muslim Arabs; Basra, where the majority of the population is Shi'i Muslim Arab; and Mosul, where Iraqi oil was first discovered on territory occupied mostly by Sunni Muslim Kurds. The construction of this "multinational" state was masterminded by the British government, the "mandate power" in Iraq, to guarantee British authority over Iraqi oil. In 1990, the goal of limiting Iraq's oil-market power was one of several reasons offered by the U.S.-led coalition for its decision to liberate Kuwait in 1990 and 1991, and protecting Western access to Iraqi oil was a major objective of the U.S.-British invasion of Iraq in 2003.[33]

Oil and globalization go hand in hand because of the importance of transportation to global networks. Automobiles started off as toys for the very rich, became conveniences for the well-to-do, and finally found their way into working-class life. As we described in chapter 2, cars became necessary adjuncts to a new lifestyle financed by the post-WWII "GI Bill of Rights." Car ownership allowed urban workers to live outside urban cores, changing housing patterns and stimulating real estate markets. Mobility helped to "rationalize" labor markets; workers could travel longer distances to jobs that paid higher wages or offered better working conditions. Favorable regulation enabled trucks to replace trains as long-distance carriers of products and, following airline deregulation, lower fare prices made air transport of goods and people an economical alternative to other modes. People "voted with their feet"—or wheels and wings—leaving home and country to study abroad, enjoy vacations in exotic places, or join the military to see the world.

Railroads moved supplies and troops to war zones during the U.S. Civil War and WWI. Air transport became a far-reaching and destructive element in the technology of violence early in its history. Aircraft carry troops and supplies to far-off fields of battle and deliver death directly by bombing and strafing enemy targets. Even motor vehicles are incorporated into warfare. Perhaps the most famous early story of the deployment of cars in battle tells of the September 1914 transport by Paris taxicabs of six thousand French reservists to the front during the first battle of the Marne. Motor vehicles are integral to war fighting. Tanks were used by Italy in its conquest of Libya during the 1920s. Armed (and armored) versions of what started out as trucks and road-building equipment, military "humvees," made the transition back to consumer markets in the form of extra-large SUVs. Roads themselves are part of the technology of violence. The Kuwaitis built a road to carry military supplies to Iraq during its 1980–1988 war with Iran. The same road was used by Iraq to invade Kuwait two years after that war was over. In February 1991, the road attracted fleeing Iraqi soldiers in stolen cars trying to escape coalition forces liberating Kuwait. Fighter plane crews incinerated cars and their passengers with murderous efficiency on what the press dubbed "the highway of death."

Cheap oil lubricates the globalization of the economy. It rationalizes an international division of labor that makes it profitable to catch fish in the north Atlantic, process them in Southeast Asia, and send them back to be sold in retail markets in the United States. A simple T-shirt made in China from Texas-grown cotton and then sold virtually anywhere in the world has a globalization-produced afterlife in the used-clothing markets of Africa.[34] Globalization continues when oil prices rise, but its structures and modalities change.[35]

Globalization and Neighborhoods

Technology drives "bottom-up" globalization, speeding processes whose agents are people making choices about their own lives. Space programs started out as part of the cold-war competition between the Soviet Union and the United States, and large corporations still choke radio, TV, and the Internet with advertisements for their products. Yet individuals manage to transform the products of both activities into ideas and symbols with meaning for themselves. Images of the earth as seen from space were captured by cameras carried by satellites. These images evoked a new understanding of the planet as a unity, one that is finite, beautiful, and, in the vastness of space, small and vulnerable. The image of a fragile unitary earth was not what U.S. policy makers had intended to generate from the space program; it occurred spontaneously and was reinforced by the products of mass culture. World music, international films, and televised sports also encouraged human beings to see themselves as participants in a global culture belonging to that precious blue planet, fostering appreciation of systemic linkages that produce problems transcending state boundaries and jurisdictions. Technology analyst Clark Miller writes:

> Underpinning the construction of ideas about the ozone layer and the climate system is a dramatic change in people's conceptual frameworks. Until the 1970s, scientists and lay observers alike [thought of the] atmosphere in predominantly local terms. In 1941, for example, the first US government assessment of human-climate interactions defined climate as follows: "the climate of a place is merely a build-up of all the weather from day to day." . . . This . . . supports the notion that Boston and Miami have different climates. [In contrast] . . . the definition of climate adopted by the 1992 UN Framework Convention on Climate Change . . . is an integrated, global system comprising "the totality of the atmosphere, hydrosphere, biosphere, and geosphere and their interactions." From this perspective, climate is not specific to an individual locale but rather encompasses the planet as a whole.[36]

We think of globalization as something new because, thanks to commerce, it is more accessible today than before. Money, even more than family background or nationality, offers agency to billions of people. Small outlays at an Internet café can buy access to a worldwide virtual audience for anyone's ideas or complaints. But democratizing globalization doesn't guarantee understanding or appreciation of human difference any more than elections guarantee governments committed to citizens' rights. People turning on their television sets are not always charmed when they are confronted by images of the alien features, immoral sexual behavior, and disgusting cuisines of others who, twenty years ago, they might not have known even existed. Invasions of private, communal, and sacred spaces by students, tourists, and soldiers, and the economic changes imposed by trade regimes that formerly sheltered people still might be unaware of, are contradictory effects of globalization that contribute to rising resentment.

It is true that globalization is an engine of integration—the conventional image is "the global village." Forces as diverse as images of the earth as seen from space, the worldwide consumption of Coca-Cola, McDonald's, and Levi's, and the dependence of nearly everyone in the world on products and services all or parts of which are produced somewhere else, give us the impression that the world is becoming smaller and people are becoming more like one another. This illusion of similarity is fostered by the structure of media industries. Media analyst Naomi Sakr traces the business and personal links connecting the interests of media moguls like Bill Gates, Rupert Murdoch, and Silvio Berlusconi—people you've probably heard of—to others like Prince Alwaleed bin Galal, Leo Kirch, and the late Rafiq Hariri, whom you might not know about at all.[37] She argues that the global village metaphor might describe relationships among the oligopolistic elites who control multiple media conglomerates, but its deceptive coziness hides the political connections that shape news and information coverage to suit the interests of governments that regulate media in national markets. Although "CNN look-alikes" abound on satellite services, the product delivered to viewers varies according to the dictates of power holders in corporate boardrooms and national capitals.[38] Even CNN produces one program for viewers overseas and another for home consumption.

This is because distinctions of all sizes and kinds can become sharp and painful to viewers with little autonomy and few resources. Media producers react by shaping products to conform to both political pressures and consumer demand. Divergences in news content from country to country are particularly evident during wars,[39] but overseas coverage of the Summer 2008 Olympics were full of complaints from broadcasters about restrictions on the press imposed by the Chinese government. Governments—and consumers—everywhere like to see their country and themselves portrayed in a favorable light. We should not be surprised that governments do whatever it takes to get favorable coverage, while consumers choose media sources and products that suit their self-images and preferences.

The Amorality of Globalization

"Globalization" also describes the proliferation of private and relatively unpoliced networks for raising and transferring funds and mobilizing armies; such networks are also used for moving and selling both relatively benign products like Coca-Cola and deadly ones, like guns, heroin, and cocaine. Globalization speeds up traffic in persons, the theft of ideas and identities, and the proliferation of sophisticated weapons and weapons systems formerly monopolized by states. States must adjust to a world in which they no longer are the sole proprietors of the means to inflict great violence. Although they continue to insist that they remain the only *legitimate* wielders of violence, states' legitimacy as well as their capacity are challenged directly by terrorists at home and abroad.

Political analyst Olivier Roy argues that globalization is integral to the creation of contemporary terrorists and their networks.[40] It produces "deracination," a term that refers to the results of transplanting people from familiar surroundings to strange new environments.[41] Deracination detaches such persons from the social structures that used to protect and connect them to family and friends, supply their needs and desires, and constrain their behavior; it places them in new structures that endanger their lives and shape their choices and behaviors differently. Deracination is the first stage in commodification, a process that transforms people into products. Deracination works by separating young persons from protective settings and making them into strangers dependent on entrepreneurs who profit from transforming their bodies and minds into commodities. Sex workers and terrorists are similar products of different kinds of transnational commodification networks. Sex tourists take advantage of deracination to gain cheap and ready access to the bodies of children and youth, and terrorist organizations use it to gain access to bodies and minds they can deploy in their strategic conflicts. Globalization provides the efficient and democratized transportation networks that serve both of these dark-side markets.

The commercial quality of globalization allows actors to move resources and themselves quickly, cheaply, and easily from one jurisdiction to another. Carolyn Nordstrom tells how movie producers race with large amounts of sophisticated equipment to war zones, perfect places for finding young refugees to use—and use up—as victims in violent pornographic films.[42] Afghan war zones have been a destination for religious idealists since the late 1970s; post-Saddam Iraq became a new magnet for young persons who went there to fight the "Crusaders" and ended up as terrorists. During the fighting in Falluja in November 2004, religious Kuwaiti youth would "drive to Falluja" to defend fellow Muslims from the infidel Americans.[43] Indeed, contemporary terrorist movements get their strength from the ease with which individuals can cross national boundaries and find allies whose interests coincide at least in part with their own. One example is the symbiotic relationship between the Taliban government in Afghanistan and the al-Qaeda network. The Taliban provided sanctuary and recruits for al-Qaeda. In return, al-Qaeda provided money and other assistance to a government whose policies had earned it the status of an international pariah and cut it off from normal channels of aid and assistance.[44]

Al-Qaeda and other mass movements incorporating terrorist elements are usually led by members of educated and/or privileged social classes. The late Yasir Arafat, leader of the Palestine Liberation Organization, was originally an engineer; the second in command of al-Qaeda, the Egyptian Ayman al-Zawahiri, is a physician. Two other al-Qaeda stalwarts, the Saudi Osama bin Laden and the Kuwaiti Sulaiman bu Ghaith, were able to avoid imprisonment because family status led to their being exiled instead of arrested and tried (and possibly executed) for their crimes. The bin Laden family's great wealth and political connections in the United States and Saudi Arabia, and the financial contributions that mullahs such as Sulaiman could attract through appeals to the faithful and then transfer abroad under the guise of charity, supported their day-to-day operations.[45] These resources and the geographic mobility supplied by globalized transit networks increase the capacity of terrorist organizations to act.

Just as globalization is a perfect environment for terrorism it also is hospitable to the growth and spread of organized crime. As we discussed in chapter 6, borders are not the only strategies for dividing different regimes. Frontiers are often quite large, areas whose borders are ambiguous, and where sovereignty is fragmented enough to correspond to Hobbes's State of Nature. The nineteenth-century U.S. frontier harbored outlaws, refugees, and entrepreneurs of all kinds. After the Civil War, racial hatred was conflated with criminality in much of the "old west,"[46] justifying brutal ritual murder and other violence. The same pattern is visible across the warring regions of Africa, and in so-called failed states like Yugoslavia and parts of the old Soviet Union, like Chechnya and Ingushetia, that resist becoming part of the new Russia. Occupied territories are frontier areas, too, because neither the occupier nor the victim state can ensure security, and either or both sides arm frontier factions to serve as their proxies. Frontiers are violent places precisely because state power is nonexistent, unevenly applied, and/or credibly challenged by armed groups with substantial popular support.

Turbulent frontiers are ideal areas of operation for illegal enterprises. Poor or absent policing, crippled courts, citizen accomplices, along with their myriad dependents make catching criminals on the frontier difficult even if their activities are detected. In his study of the Camorra crime network centered on Naples, Italy, Roberto Saviano begins his story with Italian and Chinese sweatshops operating with an illegal-immigrant workforce at the port of Naples where the sweatshops turn out counterfeit designer items for the global market under the noses of fatally underresourced Italian police. He ends it with a glimpse of the extensive money-laundering "investments" of Camorra clans in the tourism industry in Aberdeen, Scotland.[47] The ability to cross national borders transforms capos and thugs into "management," just as it transforms copies into highly profitable "Versace" and "Armani" products.

Misha Glenny traces the growth of transnational crime through the activities of criminals based in parastates in Eastern Europe and the former Soviet Union, and those connected to highly fragmented industries such as international oil. Glenny identifies the influence of the frontier on organized crime by stressing impunity as a main reason why criminal syndicates thrive and spread.

> "I can't pick up the person [shaking] you [down], Artyom Mihailovich. . . . For one thing, nobody's issued a directive telling me to. And secondly, unless he were caught red-handed, then we'll have to carry out a long and tedious investigation, which would probably lead absolutely nowhere." . . . "When he shoots you or kidnaps you," one of Rushaylo's subordinates chipped in helpfully, "then we'll go after him!"[48]

Russian hydrocarbon firms such the gas giant Gazprom are suspected of carrying out money laundering, among other criminal activities run by affiliates and partners. Here the state—two states, actually, Russia and Ukraine—were partners in Gazprom's projects, protecting it, profiting by them, and conferring immunity from prosecution on anyone involved in this $300 million scam who might be caught red-handed by accident.

> [T]his company ETG had a turnover of $2 billion per annum—with no proper oversight of these accounts, all manner of funds could be channeled through the company that were not necessarily the product of the Ukranian gas trade. . . . For this perverse business operation to succeed, ETG . . . required the absolute support of the Gazprom and NAK leaderships. But it also required protection from both the Russian and Ukranian states.[49]

State-criminal partnerships also conceal the hand of the state in repression of dissidents, such as in Egypt, where the government hires thugs to beat up demonstrators and channel them into the arms of the uniformed police so they can be assaulted again, and arrested and detained for disorderly conduct.[50] State-criminal partnerships are used to finance operations that governments are forbidden by law to carry out, a common rationale for CIA involvement in the international drug trade.[51] Sometimes these activities escape state control, such as happened in Turkey when the government impressed village youth into "village guards" to fight Kurdish activists.

> Since 1984 the Turkish armed forces have been engaged in a brutal and costly war against the Kurdistan Workers' Party (PKK), a militant Kurdish opposition group. As noted above, since the outbreak of the war, over 37,000 people have been killed, most of them Kurds. In addition, approximately 3,000 Kurdish villages have been destroyed in the southeastern provinces as part of the Turkish military's strategy of attempting to eliminate support for the PKK by attacking entire areas inhabited by suspected PKK sympathizers. . . . If villagers provide food or logistical support to the PKK, they risk attack by the Turkish military. If they decide instead to join the government-aligned "village guards," they will be subject to attack by PKK forces. . . . Some villagers willingly join the village guards out of economic need or political commitment, but many are pressured to enter the system.[52]

Some village guards enjoyed their power over their neighbors, and resisted demobilization when a new Turkish government inaugurated wide-scale human rights reforms early in this century. Armed and living in a frontier region bordering Kurdish-occupied areas of Iraq and Iran, they turned to gun- and drug-running to support themselves, engaging in the frontier lawlessness that is a hallmark of the current round of globalization and becoming targets of the Turkish police.

Along with all the negatives, globalization has positive outcomes, too. It is credited with being the primary engine of growth for "new social movements." These relatively unstructured networks come together when an "opportunity structure"—a series of events, the appearance of a charismatic leader, a sudden influx of resources—allows people to take action with a reasonable hope for success.[53] As we discussed in chapter 5, many international movements resemble national counterparts working for human rights and environmental protection. Others fit descriptions suggested by analysts David Ronfeldt and John Arquilla, who see them as agents of "netwar," social struggle carried out by flexible, nonhierarchical coalitions of sometimes widely dispersed activists. Netwar activists come together for a particular purpose at a particular time and then disperse when that task has been completed.[54] An alternative view of networked revolutionary social movements is offered by Michael Hardt and Antonio Negri.[55] To them, netwar is "bio-power," a term coined by French philosopher Michel Foucault to describe a kind of cyborg politics combining human agents and modern technology. In the Hardt and Negri view, bio-power allows oppressed people to mobilize on their own behalf against "Empire," a worldwide combination of state and capitalist institutions—both networks and Empire also being agents and products of globalization.

The networks described by Hardt and Negri are available to every interconnected element of globalization: not just to Citibank but also to informal banks and agents that allow guest workers abroad to send money home cheaply and quickly to families residing in remote rural areas,[56] and to terrorists, thieves, and drug lords; not just to the rich and famous but also—and especially—to the ordinary and anonymous, whose very lack of distinction allows them to move through network channels unnoticed and still mostly unchecked. This point highlights both the key role of agents acting within structures, and how small differences in structures open new possibilities for action to agents who are alert.

The amorality of networks as such and their dependence on the actions and ethics of agents is illustrated in an example that compares India and Pakistan, two countries with a common heritage and a common border. *New York Times* columnist Tom Friedman describes Indians and Pakistanis as people who share "blood, brains and civilizational heritage" but the differences he finds show how little individual measures like "blood," or IQ, or "heritage" matter when structures interfere with persons being able to realize their full potentials. In India, "50 years of . . . democracy and secular education, and 15 years of economic liberalization," produced a nation in which religious violence is localized and, increasingly, anomalous.[57] But political scientist Ashutosh Varshney concludes that these different outcomes are explained less by different trade regimes than by differences in local civil societies.[58] Varshney presents a more nuanced picture of India than Friedman. Varshney's India is composed of regions. Some enjoy a functioning civil society that alerts the community to the possibility of violence and works purposefully to head it off—usually with some success. But others lack civil society structures, and these are the places where intergroup violence is far more common. People who live there have low levels of literacy, and there are few voluntary associations that cross religious lines.

Friedman argues that religion is a main reason for Pakistan's problems: "Across the border in Pakistan . . . 50 years of failed democracy, military coups and imposed religiosity have produced 30,000 madrassahs—Islamic schools, which have replaced a collapsed public school system and churn out Pakistani youth who know only the Koran and hostility toward non-Muslims." But Varshney shows that authoritarian politics prevents the kind of citizen activism he finds in some parts of India from developing elsewhere. Storefront religious "education" and youth unemployment provide a fertile ground for terrorist organizers in socially impoverished areas of Hindu India, just as they do in most of Muslim Pakistan. As Varshney and development analyst Amartya Sen emphasize, the real explanation for differences in communal violence between parts of India and nearly all of Pakistan lies in the differences between economically healthy democratic communities whose populations have autonomous political and economic choices, and impoverished, authoritarian communities whose populations have very little autonomy or hope.[59]

Market Fundamentalism

Fundamentalist social movements that thrive in today's globalized environment are not always motivated by religion in a theological sense. Economic "prophets" also seek to propagate their doctrines and make them real by forcing changes in social practice. This is why Nobel laureate economist Joseph Stiglitz and billionaire investor George Soros call the ideas of these economic prophets "market fundamentalism."[60] Like religious fundamentalisms, market fundamentalism asserts the inerrancy (literal truth) of selectively drawn texts.[61] In his list of the sacred texts of market fundamentalists, Stiglitz includes Adam Smith's *The Wealth of Nations*, the writings of twentieth-century economists like W. A. Lewis and Simon Kuznets, and the speeches of British prime minister Margaret Thatcher and U.S. president Ronald Reagan. The market fundamentalist "religion" is sometimes called the Washington Consensus because of the dominance of Americans in the development and propagation of this ideology and the location of its primary institutions and leaders in Washington, D.C.

> The Washington Consensus policies . . . were based on a simplistic model of the market economy, the competitive equilibrium model, in which Adam Smith's invisible hand works . . . perfectly. Because in this model there is no need for government—that is, free, unfettered, "liberal" markets work perfectly—the Washington Consensus policies are sometimes referred to as "neo-liberal," based on "market fundamentalism," a resuscitation of the laissez-faire policies that were popular in some circles in the nineteenth century.[62]

Liberalization is a primary tenet of market fundamentalism. We described this in earlier chapters as the removal of government participation, regulation, and oversight from financial markets, capital markets, and trade relations. Faith in liberalization is based on a single mention by Adam Smith in his classic book of an "invisible hand" guiding markets.[63] Fundamentalists interpret the term as an analogue of providence (divine direction) and evidence that markets are inherently self-regulating, leading them to promote a state of affairs they also describe (as Stiglitz does in the quote above) as laissez-faire—freedom of contract.

The terms "liberal" and "laissez-faire" are not equivalent, however, and they impose contradictory demands on governments. Liberalization requires that governments refrain from regulation and market participants refrain from collusion that could interfere with market mechanisms. Governments should let the invisible hand do its work. A laissez-faire system assumes that private interests, from labor to capital, buyers, and sellers, can legitimately organize to pursue their own interests. Unions can strike as legitimately as business can divide markets or form oligopolies, and consumers can organize boycotts.[64] Fundamentalists and nonfundamentalists both oppose some kinds of laissez-faire behaviors, such as making and selling goods that are harmful to consumers, although they disagree on how that should be stopped. But usually their interests diverge. Fundamentalists want to restrict labor organizing and collective action by consumers, while nonfundamentalists want environmental protection and an end to business concentration.

Privatization is another tenet of market fundamentalism. This refers to the conversion of state-owned and/or -managed producers of goods and services to private ownership and management. Belief in the inherent superiority of private enterprise as opposed to socially owned production grows out of a belief that markets are inherently efficient and always spring up to meet every human need.[65] Pressures for privatization reflect investors' desires to take over lucrative state-owned industries such as oil production, and necessary public services like drinking water delivery.[66] These promise large returns to their new owners from relatively small financial investments. A similar ethic underpinned privatization in the former Soviet Union, where often-criminal interests snapped up the best investments at fire-sale prices.[67]

Market fundamentalists are better than religious fundamentalists at getting governments to adopt and enforce rules to transform their visions into reality because of the magnitude of their money and power. They occupy the commanding heights of structures that reach beyond nationality and religion to encompass most of the earth. The term "Washington Consensus" reflects agreement among U.S. policy makers whose positions on liberalization and privatization are well-known, and those who are in charge of international financial institutions such as the International Monetary Fund, the World Bank, the World Trade Organization, and NAFTA. It even includes informal institutions like the G-5/G-7/G-8, a variable but always small group of leaders of the most economically powerful governments who meet regularly to "fine-tune" the global economy to suit their interests.[68] Through the "self-enforcing" mechanisms at their disposal, these organizations can force financially distressed governments to cut education and health services, and open markets to cut-price goods from abroad. The organizations are impervious to outcomes that include forcing thousands into destitution and undermining those governments' authority and ability to provide basic services.[69] Among the many examples that could be cited is Rwanda, which was forced to adopt open market and structural adjustment policies that impoverished its rural population and provided a platform for government officials to instigate a massive genocide against an ethnic minority.[70]

At their best, however, markets can be a force for economic democratization insofar as what they define as good behavior is both fair and the same for everyone. The WTO ruled against the United States in 2003 for subsidizing some manufactured exports and authorized U.S. trading partners to impose tariffs to make up for the losses these subsidies imposed. If the WTO were to mandate the end of agricultural subsidies by the United States, Japan, and Western Europe, developing nations could sell their products abroad at competitive prices and make the money they need to increase living standards for their populations. But the WTO, NAFTA, and other global economic regimes are not sufficiently egalitarian to have these beneficial effects, while market fundamentalism allows multinational lenders to demand that debtor nations grow commodities instead of food crops to earn income they can use for debt service. In 2008, global food shortages stemming from a combination of drastic weather conditions and cash-crop agriculture put populations at risk of starvation, and contributed to the collapse of the Doha Round of trade talks in Geneva in July.[71] If liberalization is to be preserved or extended, international trade organizations will have to expand interest representation beyond business to include labor and consumers, change their rules to include environmental protection, and reform their own practices to make them more transparent and democratic.

The need for a change in NAFTA's infamous Chapter 11 is just one example. Writing in the *New York Times*, Joseph Stiglitz discusses the consequences of Chapter 11 on democracy and social justice in North America.[72] Under Chapter 11, as we noted earlier, a foreign investor is entitled to sue for damages if he believes he is harmed by local regulations. This is a problem, for several reasons. First, it gives special rights to foreigners that are not enjoyed by national investors. Second, these rights are enforced in an unfair way. The foreign investor does not have to take his case to a national court, which decides cases of national and local law in a public forum, but instead can go before special NAFTA tribunals that hear international trade cases in secret. Third, the party that is liable is the national government. This contravenes a basic tenet of federalism (all three NAFTA signatories are federal systems), which is that states and localities have the authority and right to regulate in their own jurisdictions. NAFTA gives incentives for national governments to supersede local regulations by justifying state quashing of local environmental and labor laws, along with local land-use regulations, as necessary to reduce the costs incurred as the result of industry challenges—and the costs could be very high: by May 2005, foreign investors were awarded $35 billion in claims, with an additional $28 billion in claims pending.[73] Finally, the NAFTA system includes an additional inequality: localities have no right to sue in an international tribunal if they are harmed by the actions of foreign firms. This lets foreign firms operate under "moral hazard," a situation in which any gains from risky or careless behavior go to the agent, while any losses are borne by someone else. A foreign firm can block regulation intended to limit damages from its operations but is not itself liable for damages. As Stiglitz notes, U.S. businesses have tried to get a deal like this domestically but usually have been rebuffed by Congress or the courts. NAFTA gives them a free pass as long as they operate in Mexico or Canada. It gives similar free passes to Mexican and Canadian investors operating in the United States.

The failure of reigning global economic institutions to incorporate protections for workers and the environment closes off the most favorable forum for developing international regulations in areas far more difficult to control than trade. As we noted earlier, the main source of leverage that international economic regimes like NAFTA and the WTO have at their disposal is self-enforcement. Would-be members have to change their domestic regimes to conform to international standards. Countries with widely differing cultures and economies struggle to bring their institutions in line with WTO standards because they know they can lose significant economic benefits if they remain outside the system. We noted in chapter 5 that economic opening can lead to political liberalization. If existing trade regimes were to extend their standards to other aspects of the global economy, they could strengthen workers' rights—free trade could also be fair trade—support democratization, and even protect the environment.[74]

Globalization and Interdependence

In a very basic sense, globalization, or the movement of human beings and their cultures across the planet, has been taking place for a very long time. Yet it also is true that, under capitalism, globalization is taking place far more rapidly and through the spread of structures that increase human interdependence by many orders of magnitude. In their 1977 study, Robert Keohane and Joseph Nye describe international interdependence as occurring along two dimensions.[75] The first they called "sensitivity," which refers to the rapidity and magnitude of responses in one country to events occurring somewhere else. The events that stimulated them to write their book were the energy crisis and oil revolution of the early 1970s, whose effects were rapidly translated into higher energy prices, economic recession, and rising foreign debt obligations around the world. In this example, sensitivity is measured by how efficiently the market operates as a transmission belt for economic signals—how quickly the hurt travels.

The other dimension of interdependence is "vulnerability." This is the ability of a country to defend itself against the domestic effects of outside events, and the speed with which this defense can be mobilized. Responses to vulnerability constitute "adjustment"—how states and populations change their behavior to diminish the pain and costs of sensitivity and perhaps to reduce sensitivity itself. The results of adjustment demonstrate differences in state capacity far better than the standard measures of stuff that some political scientists calculate when they look for power under lampposts (see chapter 3). In the context of vulnerability, state capacity would include being able to reconfigure the national political economy to adjust not just rapidly but also advantageously to external shocks. That ability rests on resources, but resources broadly defined—a list that includes flexibility, innovation, and resilience. These characteristics belong to human beings as well as to economies. People too show differences in their capacity to adjust to unanticipated change. Those who are active and alert may benefit from interdependence-caused upheavals, finding new opportunities when old structures are rocked on their foundations. Like globalization, the interdependence that it both cultivates and reveals is amoral—neither good nor bad in itself but available to be used for good or bad by agents as large as states and firms, and as small as persons, viruses, and even genes.

That having been said, interdependence also presents grave problems because it reduces the autonomy of states and makes their populations vulnerable to the actions of persons outside the state's authority to regulate. Consequently, in addition to inflicting pain, interdependence intensifies competition as states, firms, and people struggle to displace the costs of adjustment onto agents other than themselves. That trading partners did not receive equal benefits from trade was obvious to the rulers of early European nation-states, who chose mercantilism as their preferred policy. The philosophy behind mercantilism is that a state would be stronger if it exported more than it imported, thereby accumulating gold and other forms of commodity money allowing it to buy whatever it might need. As you can imagine, mercantilism restricted trade. Strong states imposed regulations to ensure that they would come out on top of whatever trade did take place. The series of British laws known as the Navigation Acts are an example of regulations that impose such a regime of punishment; they were drawn up to cripple trade with Britain's then-rival Holland and to wring the greatest profit for the mother country from British colonies in North America. The colonists responded with energetic smuggling and, eventually, armed rebellion.

Neoclassical theories beloved by market fundamentalists say that trade benefits both parties if each one offers what it can produce most efficiently.[76] Yet "terms of trade"—how much of the things other countries produce that an exporting country can buy with what it earns on its overseas sales—tend both to be unstable and to favor the higher-value-added products that come primarily from developed countries. This means that even when trade regimes operate without mercantilist interference in the form of tariffs on imports or subsidies and other price supports for domestic products, inequalities persist and even grow. During the last rapid period of globalization, which ran from about 1850 to 1914 (with a little coda from about 1920 to 1930), domestic expansion kept the peace in Europe until the depression of the nineteenth century, which began in the early 1870s and lasted for more than twenty years. As domestic markets shrank, Europeans sought to expand their colonial possessions and wring even more from the ones they already had. At that time Africa was the least exploited world region, a place where amateur explorers sought the source of the Nile and some even preached the Gospel. Although Europeans held parts of western and south Africa, in the mid-1870s, 80 percent of the land in sub-Saharan Africa remained in the hands of local people.[77]

The need to replace falling profits with what could be squeezed from colonies and trade dependencies, like the ones Germany had created in neighboring Slavic regions, led to fierce competition for new colonies in that "empty" 80 percent of Africa. Europeans also sought cash by imposing regimes of punishment on borrowers slow to repay their foreign debts. Egypt had borrowed heavily to invest in cotton production during the U.S. Civil War, only to be hit by plummeting prices when cotton from the U.S. South returned to the world market after the war was over. Another desperate borrower was the steadily disintegrating Ottoman Empire, unable to put down independence movements in its Balkan possessions or protect its domestic economy from European traders. Yet the wealth torn from new African colonies and the large amounts of money siphoned from debtor nations were not enough to halt the growing economic and political rivalry among the European powers, a rivalry that persisted through two world wars.

The economic regimes adopted after WWII tried to rein in globalization, substituting for open trade and investment arrangements that limited both. But economic globalization could not be halted. It was extended through the operations of multilateral financial regimes like the IMF and the World Bank, cold war politics, the growing reach of multinational industries, and the evolution of an integrated economy in much of Western Europe. Even before the late-twentieth-century fall of the Soviet Union and the opening of Eastern Europe to trade and investment from the West, technological development and the deepening of capitalism had intensified interdependence. Countermovements, many presenting themselves as protectors of traditional values and exploited or humiliated populations, also were visible in the politics of nations from the United States to Afghanistan. These movements have since strengthened.

The question in many minds is whether the current round of globalization can be sustained through the development of representative international institutions and regulatory regimes, or it will instead collapse in depression and war as earlier globalizing regimes did. The outlook seems significantly grimmer as world financial and goods markets collapse in a slow-motion reaction to fraudulent mortgage lending and securitization after an economic recovery that did not penetrate much below the highest 20 percent of income earners.

One World, Ready or Not

Trade, investment, and even war are in some sense voluntary activities that can be regulated by borders. Other activities go on regardless of borders, even though their harmful effects can be reduced by policing. Practices that leave chemical residues from pesticides and herbicides and bacterial contamination on foods endanger consumers around the world even though establishment and enforcement of standards of best practice could reduce the damage arising from globalized industrial agriculture. Hepatitis A infections have become increasingly common in the United States where, by 2000, fully half of the reported cases were traced to vegetables irrigated or washed in sewage-contaminated water. Foreign imports are frequently blamed for hepatitis A outbreaks, such as the one in the Pittsburgh area in 2003 that killed four persons and made more than six hundred others ill. But the problem is not only in foreign countries: reportedly half of the contamination in food products sold in the United States is homegrown.[78] There are no international standards for testing foods destined for foreign markets, and many national agencies, such as the Food and Drug Administration in the United States, conduct inadequate analyses of samples of imported and domestically originating foods. Testing standards vary widely, and some results are not available until the food has already entered the distribution system. Unlike most other developed countries, U.S. agencies have no system for tracing the origin of contaminated foods. During the salmonella outbreak that swept the United States in the summer of 2008, it took more than two months to determine the sources.[79]

Changes in local practice raise the risks for failing to develop international standards for testing new foods and new food production techniques. The spread of bovine spongiform encephalitis, known popularly as "mad cow disease" (MCD), brought this issue into prominence. The disease was first encountered in Britain in 1985, probably as the result of changes in animal feeding. Scientists believe that MCD originated with a genetic mutation whose effects were spread by the contamination of animal feed with brain and nerve tissue from afflicted animals.[80] Starting in the 1960s, vegetarian animals like cows were fed protein obtained from otherwise unmarketable body parts of slaughtered animals, including other cows. People were no more aware that the beef they were eating came from cows that had dined on animal remains than they were that the "meat by-products" listed on packages of sausage and other processed meat they dined on referred to the same thing.

The British government insisted that MCD would not affect people, a position they were able to support for some time because it takes years for humans to present with symptoms. In 1996, ten cases of the human form of MCD (officially known as variant Creutzfeldt-Jakob disease) were diagnosed, leaving the British government with no alternative but to admit that there was a connection between eating beef from "mad" cows and coming down with the disease. Experts estimate that between the time MCD was first discovered and the time when the British government acted to halt the spread of infection, more than one million infected cows had been consumed in Britain, and an unknown number of others had been shipped abroad.[81] As more people became infected, some governments tightened their regulation of beef production, but industry pressures in major beef-producing countries like the United States and Canada ensured that, as in Britain before news of infected people hit the front pages, little was done. In contrast, Japan was among the first countries to require that even the parts of a slaughtered animal be tracked and tested.[82] Beef-importing country governments can be as cavalier about MCD as exporting countries, however. In 2008, angry Koreans demonstrated against their new president's unwelcome decision to resume beef imports from the United States.[83]

A different globalized disease threat from the food supply links the development of new viral diseases like SARS (severe acute respiratory syndrome) and epidemics of varieties of avian (bird) influenza (another viral disease) to unsanitary methods of raising animals for food and inadequate sanitation in their slaughter and preparation. Avian flu is a hazard for people because a few individuals do catch it, encouraging the virus to mutate in ways that contribute to its wider infectiousness in other human beings. Agricultural practices that failed to halt the spread of avian flu is thought to have triggered the great influenza epidemic of 1918–1919, which began near the end of WWI and killed at least twenty million persons; viral mutation also is associated with other notable influenza epidemics, such as the one in 1957–1958.[84] Diseases like SARS and influenza spread easily from person to person, making international travel a disease vector. This is how SARS spread so quickly to Europe and North America from Asia in the spring of 2003.

A different problem related to globalized food production has been identified by the U.S. National Research Council of the National Academy of Sciences. In a 2004 report, it pointed out that many measures currently used to prevent the escape of genetically engineered plants and animals into the wild are unproven and even ineffective. Genetic engineering is used not only to grow plants and animals with specific qualities, like resistance to a certain disease, but also to produce desirable products like pharmaceuticals. The report notes specific concerns with the escape of engineered genes placed into plants and animals used for food. In a manner similar to how viruses mutate when they move from one kind of host to another, engineered genes could spread from transgenic plants to wild ones. "Genes giving crops resistance to herbicides or insects might spread to weeds, making the weeds harder to eradicate. Pollen flow from corn engineered to produce a drug could allow the drug to get into corn destined for the food supply." Corn in Mexico already has been contaminated by manufactured genes spread from the United States. Here again, national regulation lags behind, leading to a need for international regulation and enforcement to avoid situations that could endanger everyone in the world.[85]

Global climate change represents what is perhaps the greatest danger to human and other life on the planet that cannot be contained by borders or confined to frontiers. The consensus among scholars worldwide is that global climate change is the result of rapidly rising levels of carbon dioxide in the atmosphere, much of it from human activity.[86] Climate scientists ask whether we are still living in the Holocene era that began about twelve thousand years ago when the glaciers retreated following the last ice age, or have moved into an entirely new era, the Anthropocene, an age where human activity changes the fundamental

fabric of our planet.[87] In 2008, the Stratigraphy Commission of the Geological Society of London, the "college of cardinals in the adjudication of the geological
time-scale," decided that we have moved. As reported by Mike Davis,

> They adduce robust evidence that the Holocene epoch—the interglacial span
> of unusually stable climate that has allowed the rapid evolution of agricul-
> ture and urban civilization—has ended and that the Earth has entered "a
> stratigraphic interval without close parallel in the last several million years."
> In addition to the buildup of greenhouse gases, the stratigraphers cite hu-
> man landscape transformation which "now exceeds [annual] natural sedi-
> ment production by an order of magnitude," the ominous acidification of the
> oceans, and the relentless destruction of biota.
>
> This new age, they explain, is defined both by the heating trend . . . and by
> the radical instability expected of future environments. In somber prose,
> they warn that "the combination of extinctions, global species migrations
> and the widespread replacement of natural vegetation with agricultural
> monocultures is producing a distinctive contemporary biostratigraphic sig-
> nal. These effects are permanent, as future evolution will take place from
> surviving (and frequently anthropogenically relocated) stocks." Evolution it-
> self, in other words, has been forced into a new trajectory. [88]

Top scientists have been warning policy makers about the potential danger of
the trajectory traced by relentless, globalized growth since the late 1980s. Few
paid attention, preferring to take their cues from industry lobbyists. In the
United States, these lobbyists even penetrated the White House where they and
the George W. Bush administration cooperated to discredit scientists' conclusions about climate change and prevent actions that would support competition against the corporate oligopoly controlling energy markets.[89] James
Hansen, the director of NASA's Goddard Space Center and a professor at Columbia University, indicts both.

> [It is] exactly twenty years after my 23 June 1988 testimony to Congress,
> which alerted the public that global warming was underway. There are strik-
> ing similarities between then and now, but one big difference.
>
> Again a wide gap has developed between what is understood about
> global warming by the relevant scientific community and what is known by
> policymakers and the public. Now, as then, frank assessment of scientific
> data yields conclusions that are shocking to the body politic. Now, as then, I
> can assert that these conclusions have a certainty exceeding 99 percent.
>
> The difference is that now we have used up all slack in the schedule for ac-
> tions needed to defuse the global warming time bomb. . . .
>
> Special interests have blocked transition to our renewable energy future.
> Instead of moving heavily into renewable energies, fossil companies choose
> to spread doubt about global warming, as tobacco companies discredited the
> smoking–cancer link. Methods are sophisticated, including disguised fund-
> ing to shape school textbook discussions.
>
> CEOs of fossil energy companies know what they are doing and are aware
> of long-term consequences of continued business as usual. In my opinion,

these CEOs should be tried for high crimes against humanity and nature. If their campaigns continue and "succeed" in confusing the public, I anticipate testifying against relevant CEOs in future public trials.[90]

The largest countries present the most severe problems. The United States refused to recognize that there is a problem until very recently and still is unwilling to shift from subsidizing fossil-fuel industries to other energy sources.[91]

No sweat

India and China, large, rapidly industrializing countries, argue with others that the already industrialized countries were not constrained in their development but now want to slow development in potential competitors by making it impossible for them to exploit relatively cheap coal.[92] Europeans have progressed furthest and are already reaping economic gains from investment in new energy and energy-using industries.[93] Yet as James Hansen notes, there is very little time left for a concerted effort to reduce carbon dioxide levels. In the words of environmental writer Bill McKibben, we may already be living on Earth II.[94]

Containment is an oxymoron in a globalized world. All countries are affected by rising sea levels, climatological upheavals, rising food and fuel prices, and the fallout from wars anywhere. Even so, collapse and war are not inevitable. Technology, as we have emphasized throughout this book, has expanded steadily and in a direction that allows more people to become directly engaged in influencing international structures and events. Elections can produce governments that are responsive to citizens' needs and desires, and agents in addition to governments can exert independent influence in an interdependent world. Indeed, they were indispensable to diplomacy, institution-building, and conflict resolution during the nineteenth-century wave of globalization.[95]

We think that a mobilized and vibrant civil society is a necessary condition for system transformation in the direction of plurality, democracy, and cooperation in a globalized world. But we understand that system transformation could change the relationship between people and states in undemocratic ways, toward the normalization of social fragmentation—deracination—and political and economic dominance by tightly organized, secretive, and exploitive elites. This would put us on the road to global war.

This is why agents are so important. Structures, including economic cycles, have their own logic. But structures are malleable. Alert agents who understand structural constraints, processes, and opportunities can take effective action if they choose. What is needed is accurate information, a space of appearance, and a commitment to citizen activism. In the last chapter, we suggest some ways for agents to take advantage of opportunities to alter structures to preserve life and the life world.

10

People Matter

The discovery of society is, indeed, the anchor of freedom.

—Karl Polanyi

And, so, we arrive at our last chapter. Throughout this book, we have tried to offer a framework for thinking about global politics in terms of the people who comprise the world. We have argued—persuasively, we hope—that it is the social individual who is at the heart of global politics and, indeed, is both its architect and building block. We have offered stories and explanations about how individuals act in response to the conditions they find and how they attempt to change those conditions. We have tried to frame the possibilities of agency in relation to what sometimes appear as overwhelmingly complex structures and processes. And we have tried to combine a certain amount of idealism with what we believe is an accurate realism. In this chapter, we turn from description, explanation, and analysis to action, and discuss how *you* can be an agent in global politics.

We begin with what might be called the "human enterprise." The political world is united and divided, integrated and fragmented, but all of it is organized around complex relations and interactions among people. While it is conventional to think about such relations and interactions as somehow contained within states, drawing national boundaries is only one aspect of the human enterprise, and to focus on that obscures more than it reveals. The human enterprise is social *and* cultural *and* economic, but, most of all, it is political, and in the broadest sense. Politics shapes every one of its myriad forms.

But politics is not simple. Throughout this book, we have tried to emphasize that politics is about the power to make decisions and choices with and for people. Power is not one-dimensional, and yet, although it is possible to accumulate some tools of power (such as weapons), the most important manifestations of power and politics cannot be stockpiled. This is because power enlists people in reproducing that which *is*, while it also enlists people in striving for what *could be*. Politics, in other words, is rooted in acting together with others, conscious of what power can help to make possible.

Countering this vision is a recent history during which those "in power" have struggled to minimize or eliminate what Sheldon Wolin has called "the political," that is, action that threatens to destabilize the social order that puts them at the top.[1] In Hannah Arendt's formulation, they are struggling to prevent the emergence of something really new and therefore—by definition—uncontrollable.[2] Critical decisions and choices are left to "experts"—economists, scientists, and analysts—who proffer "rational" proposals that leave little to be decided except, perhaps, how much should be spent.[3] The result is a machine inside which individuals perform specific functions but have little say about whether it ought to be switched on or off, or what it ought to be doing if it is switched on.

Is it possible to develop a "theory of global politics" out of all of this, a framework that is descriptive, analytical, and action-oriented? Can we find ways to describe the world as it is without conveying the message that this is how things must always be? We think so. That is why the social individual is at the center of our theory rather than the state or the multinational corporation. Remember that the social individual lives and acts within a complex web of social relations and institutions, some of which appear "natural" and others of which do not. Our task, therefore, is not to do away with states or corporations or international organizations or NGOs. Instead, we should re-form our research problem into one of understanding how these institutions emerged through the activities of social individuals.

The Human Enterprise

The *American Heritage Dictionary of the English Language* offers the following definition of "enterprise": "1. An undertaking, especially of some scope, complication and risk; readiness to venture; boldness; initiative; 2. A business; industrious effort, especially when directed toward making money."[4] Fans of *Star Trek* and its many spin-offs will recognize that the first definition—"to boldly go where no one has gone before"—is a basic characteristic not simply of individuals but even more of humanity's many and diverse societies.[5] The second definition might seem more apt as a description of the economic dimension of globalization, and the objectives of those who drive and benefit from it: "making money." Together, the two definitions offer some useful insights into what we are calling "the human enterprise."

Coming down from the trees to the savannah and relying on wits rather than speed or camouflage were pretty bold undertakings when humans first appeared in Africa many millennia ago. Whether this shift in habitat and habits was due to climate change, neural evolution, or something else, it resulted in what might be thought of as the first glimmerings of politics. Members of human groups had to act socially to avoid predation and starvation, and they had to make decisions in order to survive and reproduce. Out of such prototypical "political" organizations emerged the tribes, cities, kingdoms, empires, and states of recorded human history.[6] How many different forms of social and political organization were tried? How was it possible to get large numbers of people to go along? And what determined the kind of world we see around us today?

No one knows with certainty the answers to these or any other questions about how our world came about. It seems logical to argue that the activities of Sir Edward Grey, described in chapter 1, had an effect on the way Britain fought in WWI. But can we be sure that, in the absence of Grey, the war would have been avoided or taken a different turn? It is just as easy to assume that something else would have triggered German insecurity, or that the outcome of the war would have been more or less the same, even if England had not come to the aid of Belgium or if it had come into the war at a much later date. We might imagine a different British history, one in which some king or another dodged a knife or sword, with the result that Edward Grey became a chimney sweep rather than a foreign minister. The question is whether and how this might matter.

If we believe that "great men" (and, occasionally, a "great woman") make history because they control the levers that can move mountains, then the human enterprise looks very much like the product of a very few people out of the billions who have lived on earth.[7] Yet if this were true, political change would look different. It would be slower, because "great men (and women)" want to preserve their own power by the way they control those levers that can move mountains. It might be faster if greatness were simply the result of talent or position and anyone with energy and connections could seize the day and make the world her oyster. But as it is—complicated, contested, and constantly changing in many different directions—the human enterprise is probably more like an iceberg than an ice cube—from where you stand you can see the tip, but, underneath, there is a lot more substance. Yet the iceberg metaphor still doesn't capture the quality of the submerged 90 percent of the human enterprise. A single molecule of water trapped in an iceberg can only hope and wait until external conditions change and it is freed. A person may be constrained, but she is not trapped. She can use her wits to free herself.

Even so, as we have made clear throughout this book, social individuals are not the autonomous atoms of classical liberalism. From its inception, and notwithstanding Hobbes's mythic State of Nature, the success of the human enterprise has depended on sociality rather than autonomy, interdependence rather than independence, natality rather than stasis. Sociality in the sense of cooperation and coordination through time and space makes possible the complex societies in which we live today, including the organized violence and systemic injustices that we are able to visit on one another. Natality, a term coined by philosopher Hannah Arendt, refers to new beginnings, the opening up of social organization when people invent and begin something new.[8] What is key here is what we might call the *differential complexity* of those societies—not social relations as such or the institutions that comprise them, but the extent to which human ingenuity and complex organization have made it possible for some people and societies to dominate others.

We have no illusions about this: domination is something that is not likely to end during our lifetimes or yours, and perhaps not even during the lifetime of the human species. We do not see this as a matter of human nature, as Hobbes and many others have claimed, but as a consequence of the social structures and organizations within which we live. What, then, is possible? How can natality work for us? What might we do to transform things as they are into things that are more to our liking? If we cannot do away completely with injustice, poverty, hunger, and violence, can we at least make them less pervasive and, especially, less harmful? Questions such as these push us to ask, "What is the purpose of the human enterprise, anyway?" If we could define a purpose, perhaps we could begin to think about what we might do.

Unfortunately, there is no easy answer to that question, either. Those who are deeply religious or spiritual have no trouble finding a purpose in life although, for many of them, that purpose seems to be to get through their existence as quickly as possible and move on to a better one somewhere else. For those whose understanding of life begins and ends right here on earth, an answer to the question of life's purpose is fundamentally different. In the absence of God (or gods) or some notion of a universal teleology (a utopia or nirvana where we will go at the end of our material existence), we are left on our own to devise a purpose.[9]

Both religious and nonreligious people have hierarchies of values, sets of ideals and goals that are not quite so cosmic as *the* purpose of life but still move us as individuals and communities to cherish and invest in them because we see them as good and worthy of struggle. Over the past two hundred years or so, one such purpose has been conceived primarily in terms of nation-states, via nationalism, in the struggle to achieve national independence and recognition. Nationalism seems stronger than ever, even though there is a growing sense that the future of all of humanity is, more or less, yoked together.[10]

How about the pursuit of happiness and improvement? The Enlightenment introduced the secular concept of progress into the human lexicon and, since then, progress has become a goal of many societies. Looking from one perspective, progress is moving right along. Many of the world's people are better off than most people were a century ago: they live longer, eat more, own more, and have more comfortable lives. For them, progress has been a material benefit as well as an idea. For others, however, not that much has changed, and, tragically, we can identify many places and situations where people are worse off today than they were a hundred years ago.[11]

This leads to the question of how far progress can progress. To the point that no one is hungry and everyone has access to clean and plentiful water? To the point that everyone has a bicycle? A car? To the point that everyone lives as well as the average North American or European? Even these sketchy images of progress reveal tensions between human desire and what is called the earth's carrying capacity. Progress for the already developed world by itself may be too much for the earth to sustain. If everyone were to enjoy the same lifestyle and standard of living as North Americans and Europeans, the consequences could be disastrous.[12] So, perhaps the purpose of the human enterprise cannot be progress if that means high levels of material consumption.

An alternative objective might be to ensure that every person can live a full and satisfying life in which neither poverty nor injustice forecloses opportunities for her to reach for her heart's desires. This is what Amartya Sen argues, and it does not seem to be an unreasonable program.[13] More to the point, it is eminently achievable with a relatively modest global expenditure of a few hundred billion dollars per year for food and clean water, health care, and education. This is not a large sum compared to the trillion or more spent on military forces by all countries. But even this modest objective is unlikely to be undertaken through the existing states system. Countries and leaders with money to spend refuse to spend much of it on things that do not serve their interests, and those without money have had only marginal success persuading the others to use their wealth for the benefit of the less fortunate.[14] Yet even if economic "have-nots" were to control other tools of influence, it is not clear that this would be a positive development. Imagine a group of poor countries holding rich ones hostage with the threat of nuclear attack: what might be the outcome of that?

The difficulty of accomplishing such projects obscures another, more important question: who is to decide what the program will be? For that matter, by what right would someone, or some group of people, countries, or businesses, make such a decision for everyone else? Deciding together, after all, is what politics is all about and, it must be said, this is what the human enterprise ought to make a priority. Politics has done much, in concert with culture and economics, to shape that enterprise, its diversity, and its conflicts. No one should expect or seek a unity of purpose, because anyone's purpose would, in all likelihood, clash with the purposes of billions of others. As we suggest in the next section, however, at least one of the major projects under way in the world does seek to impose such unity, not surprisingly, through the *elimination* of politics.

Power and Politics

In chapter 3 we discussed power at some length. There, you will recall, we tried to illustrate that power is not merely force or stuff, although that is what most people talk about when they speak of power. Power is fundamentally the ability to get things done, to influence and persuade, to convince people that a particular project is worth doing and that they ought to join in. Think about that for a moment. As analysts from Arendt to Foucault emphasize, power is not a thing, and it cannot be accumulated or stockpiled. Rather, it is better understood as a relation, that is, something that requires two or more

people to create. While many people on both the Right and the Left feel un-
comfortable thinking about power, because they believe it is useful only to
abuse or oppress others, in fact, power is essential to the human enterprise. It
is not power-over, but power-with plus power-to and power-as-if that make
the human enterprise and its riot of projects, good and bad, constructive and
destructive, possible. And, because power is so central to those projects,
power must also be, of necessity, about politics.

Think about some of the examples and cases offered in earlier chapters of this
book. Hitler conceived of a project—a repulsive one, to be sure—that relied not
only on force but also on relational power. The German people did have a sense
of themselves as a nation, although their concept of nationhood was incomplete
and flawed. At the same time, even the small, preunification German statelets
had little experience with politics, although some, especially Prussia, had a long
experience of force. Hitler's appeals to the German *Volk* struck one of the nerves
connecting Germans to one another and, drawing on the "productive network
that runs through the whole social body,"[15] mobilized them in support of the
Nazi regime. Whether the people had any awareness in 1933 of where the Third
Reich would go in 1939 (to war) and 1941 (to the Holocaust) is difficult to say,
notwithstanding Daniel Goldhagen's arguments.[16] But once bound into a "social body," individuals and groups found it exceptionally difficult to escape the
demands of a regime built from both peer pressure and state sanctions—force—
as was the case in Nazi Germany.

Regimes of power based on peer pressure and state sanctions are actually
quite common. They are revealed by the routinized beliefs and social practices
in which we all engage, often unreflectively. No matter how aware we might be
of having been socialized into accepting any number of beliefs and practices as
"natural," and no matter how hard we might resist them, it is difficult to escape
them entirely. Consider gender and patriarchy. Our society is steeped in gender
roles whose "naturalized" forms are reinforced through advertising, political
campaigns and controversies, and even social movements. Each generation of
women and men feels enormous implicit and explicit pressure to conform to
the era's gender stereotypes, and both construct and consume gendered "family romances" as political narratives.[17]

But naturalization is a continuing process. During the 1990s, the prospect of
gay rights was a surefire way to mobilize the Christian Right base and get Republican candidates elected in the United States. Despite the results of the 2004
U.S. presidential election, and the revival of such attempts in California in 2008,
however, the "usual suspects" did not get an unambiguous result from their introduction of constitutional amendments to prohibit gay marriage on ballots in
swing states. Quiet naturalization of gay relationships is proceeding, and two
American states have legalized same-sex marriage. More people "coming out"
to parents and friends, and the incorporation of gay characters into popular-
culture artifacts like *Queer Eye for the Straight Guy*, have made gays seem less
scary. What social conservatives thought was their power to reinforce the status

quo and make homosexuality seem alien, even deadly, to the social body, is dissolving as spaces of appearance become more inclusive.[18]

There are other examples of positive and progressive trends in politics. Think, for example, of the International Campaign to Ban Landmines (ICBL), a project that was initiated in Canada and grew into a global social movement consisting of more than fourteen hundred groups in ninety countries.[19] At the outset of the project, no one believed that it would be possible to get governments to sign on to an international convention prohibiting the use of antipersonnel mines. Yet, between 1992 and 1997, a convention was formulated, signed, and ratified into international law, all within a relatively short time, as these things go. (The United States and Finland are the only rich countries that have not signed the agreement.) Diana, Princess of Wales, is remembered even by people who aren't very interested in royalty for using her celebrity to naturalize this fight, and the ICBL and its coordinator, Jodi Williams, received the Nobel Peace Prize in 1997. More recently, the ICBL has participated in a new coalition, to ban cluster munitions, which contain small bomblets, some of which fail to explode on impact and later injure innocent civilians who stumble upon them. Over one hundred countries have signed a convention banning such weapons.[20]

Here, we see how *power-to* is productive, creating both knowledge and discourse. Williams and her colleagues, famous and not, managed to tap into a kind of global awareness, an "episteme," if you will, of people dedicated to a broad range of causes—"human rights, humanitarian, children, peace, disability, veterans, medical, humanitarian mine action, development, arms control, religious, environmental and women's groups"[21]—all of whose members shared an idea of what was necessary to eliminate one source of random and meaningless violence against innocent civilians. Working together, these individuals and groups were able to educate, lobby, and pressure legislators, policy makers, and bureaucrats to support the treaty.[22] In the process, they also created a community that spilled over national boundaries, one composed of a wide diversity of people, ideas, and loyalties, yet is united by the shared exercise of the power of an emerging global "social body."

Politics Disappears

Unfortunately, as the case of Nazi Germany illustrates, negative forms of power persist. They are exercised through repression and, even more effectively, through attempts to do away entirely with politics. This is a mostly subtle process, one that constrains alternatives by suppressing opposition, substituting expertise for political choice, and changing rules to move authority outside of politics. Take, for example, economic policy, in which decisions are based on the application of economic models and principles to "aggregates," but ignores the outcomes for real individuals whose jobs are "rationalized" away and whose investments are "restructured" into failure and loss.[23] Such expert recommendations acquire an illusory sheen of science as experts tell us that their models and principles, if applied properly, always provide "correct" answers. We don't think the answers are necessarily correct; we even question the questions.

One question that is sometimes asked of economists is: "How much should we spend on guns as opposed to butter?"[24] This question presumes that there is an absolute trade-off between the size of a country's military forces and the amount that can be spent on consumer goods, welfare services, and so on. Of course, any sum of money spent on a gun cannot be used to purchase butter directly, but the makers of guns, who are paid handsomely for their products, find themselves with much higher incomes with which to buy everything from butter to yachts. Meanwhile, the makers of "butter"—in the sense of providers of education, health care, roads, scientific research, and other social goods—may have less income, and many might lose their jobs, while basic services are cut back and the living standard of the people declines. It's not only what we buy and how much we spend but also who profits from what we buy that is the story here.

The guns-versus-butter trade-off tends to be framed as a stark choice between "security" and "consumption." The concrete meaning of both terms is left unarticulated other than in extraordinary cases. For example, in the ongoing debate over the goals of Iran's nuclear research and development program, and what other countries might "do" about it, the security of Israel, Europe, Persian Gulf states, and American military forces is routinely invoked as being at risk from hypothetical Iranian missiles carrying as-yet-undeveloped nuclear warheads. What is left largely unmentioned is the role the latter countries have played in making Iran insecure, or the fact that threats to attack Iran's nuclear facilities also have the objective of maintaining the flow of oil to the West and, especially, American consumers. In this instance, a major and potentially less-expensive restructuring of the U.S. energy supply system might well accomplish the same goals—that is, denuclearization of Iran—without death and destruction.[25]

Even "consumption" could bear some deconstruction.[26] Scientific research, education, and health care could just as appropriately be defined as capital outlays and investments in greater productivity in the future. By suppressing the guns-versus-butter debate, or casting it in a format that excludes thinking beyond the artificial boundaries constructed by imagining policy as a zero-sum game,[27] the enemies of democracy remove these important issues from politics. The World Bank and International Monetary Fund routinely impose structural adjustment programs (SAPs) on countries that seek financial support for major projects or help in rolling over their international debts. As we discussed in previous chapters, SAPs impose specific spending restrictions on governments, especially when it comes to social welfare, health, and education programs, while encouraging expenditures on items such as infrastructure, more efficient revenue collection programs, tourist facilities, and tax rebates for foreign investors.[28] Experts guarantee that these policies will lead to economic growth, but they ignore the costs of increasing the misery index of the population as a whole, and the expectable outcome on income distribution— a few local people will get richer, but the vast majority will get poorer. The people, in any case, have no say about the provisions of SAPs or whether their governments should adopt them. These kinds of prescriptive measures are not restricted to poor, developing countries; similar medicines are sometimes hawked in wealthy countries.[29]

When people and politicians argue that decisions must be made on a "scientific basis" and not be left to the dictates of politics, what are they really saying? We suspect that it's not that they would accept a scientist's judgment about what ought to be done, but rather that they would like an expert to support what they want.[30] What such claimants seek are authoritative propositions that eliminate the possibility of political debate. After all, we tend not to argue if a biologist says, "It is absolutely certain that shortly after you ingest large quantities of sodium cyanide, you will die!" But each of us still can choose to ingest cyanide, however fatal it might be—and the biologist can offer no advice with respect to that decision.

Two examples illustrate this point. The first was the George W. Bush administration's decision to invade Iraq and depose Saddam Hussein. Prior to launching this adventure, conflicting advice was offered on whether it was justified, especially in terms of international security (there's that term again!). The initial argument, at least, rested on the claim that Iraq possessed weapons of mass destruction (WMDs) that could be used to attack its neighbors, American allies, and U.S. troops. Although the evidence of WMDs was highly equivocal, and UN inspections found little to warrant the White House's claims about them, the available information was presented in a way that suggested very strongly that these weapons did, indeed, exist.[31] In his presentation to the UN Security Council in February 2003—which Colin Powell later said he regretted[32]—the then U.S. secretary of state told the gathered audience, "My colleagues, every statement I make today is backed up by sources, solid sources. These are not assertions. What we're giving you are facts and conclusions based on solid intelligence."[33] Presumably, "experts" in the CIA and other intelligence agencies had vetted the information and found it sufficiently compelling to guarantee its validity.

Of course, we now know that the evidence was not only flawed: it wasn't even there.[34] Apart from a few diehards who still insist that WMDs will be found or were moved to Syria and Iran before the Americans could find them, it is clear that Saddam Hussein had shut down Iraq's nuclear weapons program during the 1990s and was being coy about his WMD programs in order to maintain the confidence of his generals and to deter his potential enemies in the region.[35] In fact, even before the American invasion, the evidence was relatively strong that few, if any, WMDs would be discovered. Why, then, was the Bush administration so insistent that "provocation" had to be met with force? As a good deal of reporting since then has shown, the desire to end all political debate was a primary goal, and it certainly succeeded in the U.S. Congress and among most American elites and media.[36] Repeated claims about Iran's nuclear research program have a similar character.[37]

Climate change, or global warming, is our second example. There is strong and growing scientific evidence that climate change is taking place largely as the result of high volumes of greenhouse gas emissions into the earth's atmosphere from cars, trucks, planes, factories, power plants and agriculture.[38] Scientists are not of one voice on how much warming will take place, which countries will be most affected, or how rapidly. There is, nonetheless, a broad consensus that global climate change already is occurring as measured by average air and water temperatures, and large changes in weather patterns that correspond to computer simulations run since the 1980s when concern about anthropogenic (human-caused) climate change reached a critical mass among scientists.[39] In fact, the changes are taking place more quickly than had been projected, in part because scientists did not incorporate equations describing subsystems in their models, such as likely results of snow melting in the Arctic on the generation of methane (another greenhouse gas).[40] A few scientists dispute the causes of the changes we are witnessing and the data on which they are based; almost none argue that human-caused climate change is immaterial, but most of these people argue that natural causes are more to blame than human behavior.[41]

Since the late 1990s, the United States has been only weakly committed to doing anything about climate change, even though it signed and ratified the UN Framework Convention on Climate Change. Action would be costly and, more to the point, would require significant changes in government policy, industrial practices, and citizen behavior. The Clinton administration did little; the George W. Bush administration has done even less, rejecting every international proposal to reduce greenhouse gas emissions—although, at the 2008 G-8 Summit in Hokkaido, Japan, the United States finally did propose a relatively toothless commitment. This rejectionism is based on assertions that climate modeling is an uncertain science and doing anything about greenhouse gas emissions would injure now-dominant segments of the American economy.

For a long time, the White House, its allies in Congress, and a few oil companies argued that "more research is needed" before a change in policy would be warranted, pointing to a handful of scientists who disputed the work of the Intergovernmental Panel on Climate Change (IPCC).[42] Meanwhile, polar ice sheets are melting at accelerating rates and climate patterns appear to be changing. Plants and animals are finding new ecological niches and some are becoming extinct. Scientists have become very alarmed about the closing window for policy changes that would have an impact on the rate of climate change.[43] This shows the fundamental flaw of relying on experts to justify policies made behind closed doors. You can pick your experts to ensure the answers you want to hear.[44]

Interestingly, the general refusal of the American government to develop and implement policies and practices that address climate change has not been paralleled by states and cities, many of which have begun to develop their own programs. One of the first to do this was Burlington, Vermont.[45] From an economic perspective, this does not make much sense: the additional costs associated with reducing local or statewide greenhouse gas emissions involves a combination of regulations and taxes, which makes these localities "uncompetitive" compared to jurisdictions that do not act. Yet, notwithstanding this "collective action problem,"[46] some 815 cities have joined the ICLEI Local Governments for Sustainability,[47] while 700 mayors have signed the U.S. Mayors Climate Protection Agreement.[48] In 2006, the California Legislature passed, and Governor Arnold Schwarzenegger signed, AB 32, the California Global Warming Solutions Act, which seeks to reduce the state's greenhouse gas emissions to 1990 levels by 2020, while an executive act issued by the governor sets a target for 2050 that is 80 percent below 1990 levels.[49] To be sure, these examples are only commitments for most localities, but they do illustrate how scientific data can be used to support political goals or oppose them.

Another realm of expertise routinely mined for the answers one wants is neoclassical economics. Over the past few decades, the "logic of the market" has invaded the realm of politics to the extent that decisions about many issues no longer are open to broad debate. How many times have you heard that "the market is more efficient and effective than government"? Or that public services should be turned over to the private sector, which can provide the same benefits for less money and still make a profit? Or that the decision about whether or not to implement a particular policy should depend on the ratio of benefits to costs? Statements such as these are saying, in effect, "Let the (capitalist) market do it."[50]

Of course, the market may be good at providing things, such as cereal, computers, and cars. It might provide services such as street cleaning and garbage collection at lower rates than city government can, although this conclusion is contested—there are still many experts on each side.[51] One way to assess the likelihood that one side or the other comes closest to the facts is to ask how the same services can be provided by a profit-making organization for less than it would cost for a nonprofit to provide them? And that question has answers. Some suggest reducing the cost of city services through contracting, which means that city workers lose jobs paying good wages and providing health insurance and other benefits. Most replacement workers—such as the hourly workers hired by a contractor to pick up the garbage—earn lower wages and receive no benefits.[52] Another way is to reduce the services themselves. In our example, that means fewer garbage pickups. The idea that an inherently higher-cost operation can supply anything more cheaply than a lower-cost operation should make anyone suspicious and, indeed, in our example, lower wages and fewer pickups translate into higher profits but not necessarily better service. The real story here is who pays for these—taxpayers? Workers? Householders? We never ask.

Some services cannot be left to the market at all because markets simply fail to provide them—no one sees any profit potential. Research on drugs for illnesses that afflict very few people—so-called orphan drugs—is rarely supported by private firms because, even if their scientists are successful and find something effective, the companies won't make much money on sales to so few people. Thus, despite the need, these drugs are not supplied without socially provided intervention and support, such as publicly funded research and subsidies to drug companies.[53] Such intervention also makes sense in markets that otherwise provide too much capacity—think of fiber-optic cable and telecom services generally—leading to plummeting prices, bankruptcy, investor losses, unemployment, and a waste of the resources used to build redundant plants and equipment (this is why public regulation of monopolies like utility companies is so important).

The ethics of relying solely on economic criteria as the basis for choosing public policies also should be considered. If an expert says that lowering air pollution levels will cost $10 million but save only ten lives, does that mean we shouldn't bother?[54] (Some people—besides insurance actuaries, whose job it is to decide how much a lost life is worth—actually do think this way.[55]) Self-interest also is an ethically suspect basis for making public policy. What if the president's budget advisor argues that a particular social service for the poor will cost $10 billion a year, but a $10 billion tax cut for the rich will garner more votes (because the poor tend not to vote, and the rich tend to contribute heavily to political campaigns): does that mean that the votes of the rich are worth more than the welfare of the poor, or that it is acceptable to subvert the electoral process to suit the interests of a particular candidate or party?

Again, and even in the case of the election example, politics as we commonly understand it often disappears from the policy equation. Politics is not merely deciding how much money will be spent, where it will go, and who will pay, especially if those decisions are little more than signing off on some "expert's" recommendation. Politics is debating about what kind of society we would like to live in and how we should go about trying to make it happen. Should we spend our money on weapons or welfare? Should we lower taxes or improve public schools and ensure that all our citizens have health care? Should we give foreign aid to a country to make its youth available to fight our wars, or should we finance opportunities for education that would allow them to grow into adults able to support themselves and their families? Those kinds of debates rarely happen, because the forms of power circulating through the social body lead people to accept the status quo as "natural" and as difficult, if not impossible, to change. We elect leaders on the basis of what they promise, but often we discover afterward that they have little intention of fulfilling those promises—think of George Bush who ran in 2000 promising to regulate carbon dioxide emissions and reneged on this promise once he was safely in the White House. Whatever their promises, many leaders reinforce negative power to keep citizens out of the decision-making process. Decisions are made, but politics plays a very small part.

What Can Be Done?

At this point in many texts on global politics, you probably would be treated to a long list of things that ought to be done: reduce military spending, fund family planning, provide education (especially for women), foster sustainable development, protect biodiversity and human rights, democratize, eliminate agricultural subsidies, and on and on. We too believe these are useful and even necessary steps, but, as the old nursery rhyme says, "If wishes were horses, then beggars would ride." Making a list is not acting, especially if there is little inclination to act by those who benefit from the status quo. You also might be told that voting, communicating with legislators, joining public interest organizations, and putting pressure on officials is the way to get governments to change their policies. We strongly urge that you do these things. It really does matter who gets elected, and a policy maker who has not already decided on a course of action may be open to ideas from constituents. Sometimes, as in the example of the movement to support corporate divestment from South Africa during the 1980s,[56] or more recent efforts to push for university divestment from the Sudan (see below), mass campaigns for a course of action actually work. More often, however, they do not—the "political" system resists because embedded interests are so strong.

Furthermore, relying on citizens to do the job of policy makers and governments is bound to fail to meet crucial social needs. Compassionate individuals have limited material resources, and few have the time to volunteer to help the poor, the oppressed, the environment, and so on, directly. Most people are interested in making a living, being comfortable and happy, and getting on with their lives. Their interest in changing the world is limited, for some because they see no reason to change it and for others because to make even some of the improvements we and others suggest seems like an impossible dream.

This points to another difficulty. Many things that ought to be changed are linked together so that treating them individually might make things worse. For example, enlarging the area of arable land to increase food supplies might require water for irrigation to be supplied from deep aquifers. More food could be produced, but drawing down the water table in one place can cause wells and springs to go dry elsewhere. If the water we exploit is fossil water, deposited in tiny amounts over thousands of years, that solution is not only the source of new problems but also has a limited life span if consumption exceeds replenishment. Similarly, building a dam to generate environmentally clean hydroelectric power erases downstream communities and their means of earning a living after their lands are flooded.[57] It also reduces the amount of water available to people downstream. Or, as we have seen recently, raising grain crops to manufacture "biofuels" as a way to reduce our reliance on costly, imported oil has had the apparent effect of raising food prices worldwide and causing great hardship among the very poor. Each party in these examples can make legitimate claims. There is no inherently "right" solution to such "conflicts of interest."

We believe that the primary reason problems like these tend to be decided by "experts" lies in the general belief that people do not matter where the "big things" are concerned. When IMF advisors go to a poor country on a mission to fix national finances, they don't go there to make people miserable. Yet because their fix-it focus is under the lamppost, in areas where progress is easy to measure—imports and exports, budget deficits, foreign reserves, grain production, social expenditures, and so on—that's often what they do. People as such never appear on the books, except as sources of tax revenues and sinks for social service expenditures. "Welfare" is a central concern, of course, but it is welfare in the aggregate—growth. People—the social individuals of real life—are irrelevant.

Michel Foucault, whose views of power we discuss throughout this book, calls this approach to problem solving "governmentality." Governmentality is not about politics; rather, it is about management, about ensuring and maintaining the "right disposition of things" in the territory that is being governed or ruled. As Foucault puts it, governmentality is "the ensemble formed by institutions, procedures, analyses and reflections, the calculations and tactics that allow the exercise of this very specific albeit complex form of power, which has as its target populations, as its principal form of knowledge, political economy, and as its essential technical means apparatuses of security."[58] This means that people are treated as statistics in a very large spreadsheet, as numbers rather than as social individuals.

Governmentality is effected through "bio-politics," another term from Foucault that we've encountered before. According to Mitchell Dean, bio-politics "is concerned with matters of life and death, with birth and propagation, with health and illness, both physical and mental, and with the processes that sustain or retard the optimisation of the life of a population." Dean writes,

> Bio-politics must then also concern the social, cultural, environmental, economic and geographic conditions under which humans live, procreate, become ill, maintain health or become healthy, and die. From this perspective bio-politics is concerned with the family, with housing, living and working conditions, with what we call "lifestyle," with public health issues, patterns of migration, levels of economic growth and the standards of living. It is concerned with the bio-sphere in which humans dwell.[59]

Even here, and with the best of intentions, people are imagined as groups to be dealt with rather than as agents able and entitled to participate in charting their own destinies.

What Are We to Do?

Lenin once asked, "Shto delat?—What is to be done?"[60] We want to introduce some reflexivity into Lenin's famous question, and ask "what are we to do?" When we answer this question, our first impulse is to focus on affecting policy.

We assume that public opinion as well as scientific and other forms of knowledge are tools of persuasion and change. But as Deborah Stone points out, "public policy" is not about politics. It is about accomplishing particular ends in a rational—read "market-oriented" or "administrative" or "governmental"—manner. For policy makers enmeshed in an ethic of biopolitical management, social goals are already known. All that matters is how to achieve them most efficiently, at the lowest cost and with the least resistance. Stone looks to Plutarch to highlight this distinction: "They are wrong who think that politics is like an ocean voyage or a military campaign, something to be done with some end in view, or something which levels off as soon as that end is reached. It is not a public chore, to be got over with; it is a way of life."[61]

What *we* regard as politics is not the exercise of power-over. We do not even subscribe to the definition found in most texts on social problems, which says that politics is about distribution, or who gets what share of the pie.[62] We think that politics is about *constitution*, about how, and to what ends, power is to be used. As we saw earlier in this book, power has multiple facets. It can be used not only to persuade or coerce but also to construct and produce. In practicing politics, we seek to do more than bribe or reward others for supporting our project. We want to create communities of obligation at all stages made up of committed persons so that the realized outcome will reflect all of our needs, recognize everyone's status, and generate productive outcomes that are just and beneficial for both people and nature.

Politics is about engagement with the principles and conditions of life, and the explicit processes whereby people make decisions collectively and act on them. Politics does not have to involve "global" strategies with grand objectives; indeed, it is such grand approaches that, as often as not, produce unintended consequences and failure.[63] It is less important to think big than to act, to decide with others of like mind (or those who can be persuaded), to become political as a way of life rather than to treat politics as a spectator sport with yourself in the audience rather than on the stage.

Foucault argues that power is constitutive of contemporary social relations. The (post)modern subject—each of us—is a product of power, power that is diffused in "capillary" fashion throughout human civilizations and societies. Foucault also pointed out that power is productive:

> If power were never anything but repressive, if it never did anything but say no, do you really think one would be brought to obey it? What makes power hold good, what makes it accepted, is simply the fact that it doesn't only weigh on us as a force that says no, but that it traverses and produces things, it induces pleasure, forms knowledge, produces discourse. It needs to be considered as a productive network that runs through the whole social body, much more than as a negative instance whose function is repression.[64]

Although Foucault was nowhere very explicit about how power, in his understanding, could be directed against the "productive network" of governmentality, we have seen throughout this book and in our own lives that power can "traverse and produce things." This does not involve rearranging parts of the web so as to create different arrangements of governmentality (reform), or destroying it so as to create a chaos out of which a new system might arise (revolution). Rather, it is about generating, through politics, new or different webs of power.

To put it another way, power "produces" us, the subject, and it also produces ruptures in the web of governmentality. Most ruptures are small discontinuities that are hardly noticeable at first. Think of the housewives who went back into the job market despite the pressures from 1950s family ideology, or the decision of gay women and men to come out to their parents and friends so that the world could see them as persons, not monsters. Like a spider's web, the human social web also can tolerate many such small ruptures. These are of no real concern to a spider until her web falls apart, after which she spins a new one. What happens as such ruptures accumulate in the webs of governmentality is an open question. Usually "the system" changes but, as Hannah Arendt's discussion of natality recounts, it changes in unpredictable ways. Although the web-of-governmentality metaphor is only approximate, it still suggests something about politics, power, and action. Power must be applied and practice altered within the micropolitical spaces of contemporary life, in the realm that, in Arendt's words, "rises directly out of acting together."[65]

As we have shown throughout this book, Arendt has much to say about politics, power, and action that is germane here. In *The Human Condition*, she notes,

> What first undermines and then kills political communities is loss of power and final impotence; and power cannot be stored up and kept in reserve for emergencies, like the instruments of violence, but exists only in its actualization. . . . Power is actualized only where word and deed have not parted company, where words are not empty and deeds not brutal, where words are not used to veil intentions but to disclose realities, and deeds are not used to violate and destroy but to establish relations and create new realities.[66]

Where can such politics take place? In the "space of appearance," according to Arendt, which "comes into being wherever men [*sic*] are together in the manner of speech and action, and [it] therefore predates and precedes all formal constitution of the public realm and the various forms of government, that is, the various forms in which the public realm can be organized."[67] For Arendt, politics could take place only through the *polis*, the self-conscious political body first constituted in ancient Greece and inherent in any human community that seeks to realize its potential for speech and action.

> The *polis*, properly speaking, is not the city-state in its physical location; it is the organization of the people as it arises out of acting and speaking together, and its true space lies between people living together for this purpose, no matter where they happen to be. . . . [A]ction and speech create a space between the participants which can find its proper location almost any time and anywhere.[68]

This particular conception of the *polis* is an interesting one, for it suggests that although space is fundamentally important, place is not an essential concomitant to politics and action. We shall return to this point later but first want to consider how politics conducted in spaces of appearance can create something new, an alternative that does not reproduce the relations of power that constitute governmentality and its subjects.

From inside spaces of appearance, democracy becomes radically different from the diluted representational form we normally see it as taking. We contribute our own voices to creating the power to act, perhaps the most important step in resisting governmentality and recognizing how limiting it is. We also realize the indeterminacy of action. Anyone who has been fortunate enough to live in Iowa during a presidential election year knows how much the final decision of a caucus depends on who comes, what she says, and how she says it. The outcome of politics is not the cut-and-dried affair it appears to be from in front of the television set. Yet how can we know what democratic politics is if we have never participated in it? How can we comprehend what is missing from our "democratic" systems if we have not experienced democratic politics? And how can we challenge the marketization of politics if we think only about the monetary cost of decision making and not about the disposition of power?

Governmentality is about management, but politics and action as we envision them here are not. Management seeks to suppress diversity and dissent. Politics as speech is inevitably contentious. It brings conflicting interests into the foreground, letting everyone know what those interests are and how each interest might be affected by politics as action. It challenges governmentality, one of whose preoccupations is to remove accountability and responsibility from decision making. Speech and action challenge exactly those principles, practices, and policies that seek to "manage" both populations and nature even as they undermine and destroy them. Politics and action offer a different way of thinking about and acting for people and nature. Governmentality is about order; politics and praxis are not.

Escape from the Spherical Cow

The flowering of social movements over the past four decades, although not without problems and contradictions,[69] suggests that new spaces for political life are constructed continuously. The creation of these political spaces results from the productive use of power generated by relationships of action and commitment among social individuals. It is by now a cliché to claim that human institutions are "social constructions," although this claim still is regarded by some as tantamount to a threat to rationality and by others as the sheer denial of "reality."[70] Such defensiveness is most likely to come from those whose vocation approximates protection of authority. It grossly misunderstands the concept of social construction but, nevertheless, reflects awareness of the implications of Arendt's—and Thomas Jefferson's—ideas about democratic politics acquiring widespread currency.

The concept of "political space" is a fairly old one,[71] although it has been given many meanings. In the interstate realm, political space is treated as "full" yet anarchic, lacking rules and therefore requiring the imposition of "order" by great powers or hegemons. The nation-state, of course, is the archetypal political space in our time. Even within "international regimes," institutionalized politics has been, for the most part, restricted to practices considered legitimate on the territory of each political actor—and therefore implicitly located in a place rather than existing as a space. When "politics" is defined as encompassing only practices permitted by the structures that organize and constrain political space (rules, beliefs, laws, acts, agencies, etc., created and disciplined through dominating power) in particular places (nation-states), other forms of political practice are marginalized and may even be suppressed by force.

Social movements that challenge institutionalized practices—especially those like labor and women's movements during the late nineteenth and early twentieth centuries,[72] the environmental movement, peace movements during wars, and indigenous rights and antiglobalization movements—are by definition without a legitimizing framework and, for that reason, are castigated by opponents as unrepresentative, illegal, and even traitorous.[73] Over time, some become legitimate (e.g., labor unions) or are co-opted into institutionalized politics (e.g., the German Greens). Some of the issues and organizations that emerge from them are institutionalized through bureaucratized nongovernmental organizations, thereby becoming integral to governmentality.[74] So far, we seem to be saying that the best ideas of novel movements just turn into "normal" politics.

But that is not all. Engendering these unauthorized political spaces and movements shines a bright light on the inadequacies of institutionalized politics. Social movements are not the product of rational calculations of self-interest, and this is their great strength. If they were "rational," they could be anticipated, obstructed, and co-opted by the defenders of the market-based "faith." But because they are based on principled commitment to action that is inherently independent of a unitary construction of self-interest, their logic is opaque to the practitioners of institutionalized politics. As a result of the collective action of social individuals, united not by contract but by commitment, such movements have objectives but no cost-benefit calculus. The satisfaction they offer cannot be reduced to those countable things we might find under a lamppost.

Given legal and social constraints on the production of political spaces, how do social individuals create and move into them, and how do they generate support and legitimacy for their projects? How are social individuals constrained, limited, or marginalized by political projects and spaces already in existence? What enables some but not others to open political space and launch their political projects?

In established contexts governed by patterned rules, relations, and behaviors, social individuals seeking agency bring two kinds of resources to bear on their project; let us call them "social" and "material." Social resources include intellectual arguments, social capital, and structural knowledge, often called "local knowledge," which embraces the personalities, institutions, rules, and distribution of resources in a particular political space. Material resources include authority, wealth, and offers of benefit. "Getting things done" requires being able to field both types of resources according to the "rules" for action. Having decided upon an objective or a project, social individuals operating in a space of appearance devise a strategy. As we implied earlier, such plans are rarely worked out completely because they have to be responsive to changing conditions, including the ideas and goals of new entrants into spaces of appearance where action is taking place.

Such a strategy uses the two forms of resources (social and material) to mobilize supporters through intellectual argumentation and the dissemination of benefits and promises. Most analyses of social action, especially economistic ones, focus on material resources because their effects are easier to observe and measure. Even so, as Arendt emphasizes, intellectual resources in the form of "speech" are at least as important. Yet ultimately, as Norman Long points out,

> Effective agency . . . requires organizing capacities; it is not simply the result of possessing certain persuasive powers or forms of charisma. . . . *[A]gency (and power) depend crucially upon the emergence of a network of actors who become partially, though hardly ever completely, enrolled in the "project" of some other person or persons.* . . . It becomes essential, therefore, for social actors to win the struggles that take place over the attribution of specific social meanings to particular events, actions and ideas.[75]

As the discussion in chapters 2 and 3 emphasized, we are especially concerned here with the ways in which power-over "produces" isolated individuals— objects of governmentality—and discourages or even crushes people and groups that threaten to become agents and engage in politics. We are equally concerned about the ways in which persons might use power productively to emancipate themselves as social subjects.

Most of the international relations and international political economy (IPE) literature concentrates on the structural power wielded by and inherent in the dominating institutions that cluster underneath the lamppost. Conventional questioners look only where the light is brightest and regard the penumbra as uninteresting, unimportant, and even a little scary. As one moves away from the lamppost, the light decreases, and so, it appears, does power. This may be why discussions of international politics always contrast "states" with "other" actors, ask whether those others possess any juridical power, and dismiss them when it becomes clear that they do not.[76]

But productive power—what Mary Ann Tétreault and Robin Teske argue is a "function of the distribution and strategic location of capacities"[77]—has an entirely different character. It is, first of all, relational. Social bonds connecting individuals play a major role in their constitution: productive power appreciates how emotions and bonds marginalized by juridical power and dismissed by liberalism are actually constitutive of human life. Second, productive power operates in the microspaces of everyday life, not through domination but rather through the *respect* that individuals give to one another and the *empathy* and *love* they have for one another. Finally, productive power is useful: the individual can apply it to resist and undermine structures of domination.

It is in this context that we can ask, "Who acts?" For inhabitants of the world of IR and IPE that question is a relatively simple one. Their ready answer obscures not only the complexity of the unit to which action is ascribed (to them this already is limited to the state or the individual) but also the very meaning of the term "action." The denizens of IR and IPE often note that, strictly speaking, corporate organizations such as the state do not "act" in the generally understood meaning of the term which, at its simplest, is based on an image of a rational actor choosing among alternative paths to reach a single objective.[78] Nonetheless, it also is evident that corporate behavior is not the sum of the individual behaviors of those who make up the corporate organization. Historically, we have elided (papered over) this difficulty by "assuming the spherical cow,"[79] that is, by pretending and behaving as though we could interpret actions by a corporate body the same way that we interpret the actions of individuals.

What we lose as a result of clinging to that spherical cow is both an appreciation of the complexity of individual action and any conception of nonindividual social action. Here is where the notion of "social agency" becomes central. We envision social agency as a product of the histories and social relations of each person who acts, alone and together. This is not a contradiction in terms because, just as no one is an isolated individual, no one acts in isolation from others. The social contexts of each person are products of complicated histories and relations with other persons and, of course, with structures. Such relationships remain important throughout the individual's life, even though they shift and change as a person lives longer and gains more experience.

The location of each social individual in global politics is the result of such unique social histories. They unfold among social relationships that differ according to culture and position, making possibilities for agency that, although they are similar, are never identical. (Think of marriage. If you were to marry J, you would have a life that would be similar in some ways and yet different in others from the life you'd have if you were to marry N.) Another element in shaping agency is more broadly systemic, arising from the dynamism of global politics and political economy, which makes some types of change virtually ubiquitous but, at the same time, differently expressed and having different impacts depending on the cultures and peoples responding to them.[80] Only by mapping out the life choices and trajectories of particular social individuals in a range of different social contexts can we begin to comprehend the complexity both of global politics and those conditions experienced by the social individuals we select. What a people-centered analysis would look like in practice is less than evident (and is a project in progress), but here is an example that draws on Mary Ann Tétreault's research and experience.

Kuwait is a small country bordering the Persian Gulf. It is a major oil exporter and, consequently, a rich country. Its government is a monarchy, but one that, for its region, is uniquely blessed with a liberal constitution and a parliament with substantial constitutional authority. The emir (prince—the ruler) has closed the parliament twice. When the parliament is not in session, he is allowed to rule by decree, but popular pressure forced him to reopen it and subject himself once more to the rule of law. Kuwait also is a hierarchical society where women are subjected to men and young people of both sexes are subjected to their elders. Yet it was a small group of twenty-somethings, women and men, who, in the spring of 2006, mobilized first their friends and then the country to bring the government down, thereby forcing the emir to call for new elections.

The emir was caught off guard in May, when a long-running struggle to redraw election districts suddenly attracted thousands of vociferous supporters to a broadly based movement spearheaded by young Kuwaitis. The electoral system, based on twenty-five small election districts each electing two members to the parliament, had been imposed unilaterally twenty-five years earlier by the late emir, Jabir al-Ahmad, to give tribal voters more representation and also to make it easier to affect election results. Opponents of the new system complained periodically, but words were not enough to produce change.

During the spring 2006 push to reduce the number of constituencies, young Kuwaitis stepped forward to organize a series of demonstrations in favor of a five-district plan. The core group of activists numbered about a dozen young women and men, including Khalid al-Fadhala, Fatima al-Hayat, Dana al-Mutawwa' and Jasim al-Qamis. They organized the first "We want five" demonstration on impulse, sending text messages to friends to gather outside the Sayf Palace on May 5, when a cabinet meeting was scheduled.

Everyone was surprised by how successful the event was—including the organizers. Text messages were sent out and forwarded to friends of friends. In the end, about two hundred young Kuwaitis wearing orange T-shirts and waving orange flags showed up in front of the palace. The ministers were startled at the sight as they drove through the gates to their meeting and again as they came out. "The prime minister waved to us," one activist reported. "And we heard in *diwaniyyas* [salons held in private homes] that they kept asking why was everyone wearing orange." News about the demonstration spread rapidly, to favorable reviews. The warm reception encouraged the activists to hold another rally the following week, where more than five hundred gathered to hear their speeches. The rapid increase in population of the space of appearance created by the organizers led to their decision to hold another demonstration a week later.

The demonstration began on May 14, with "flag night," said one organizer. "If you pass by and if you are with us, you can plant a Kuwaiti flag in the grass in front of the parliament building [on the median]. We were there all night. It was huge. Maybe 1,000 people and even MPs came out that night, seven or eight, after the 29 [members of parliament supporting the five-district plan] had a meeting. . . . Volunteers slept on the grass." The organizers cut strips of orange cloth from large bolts of fabric and handed them to the demonstrators so they could identify themselves as part of what was already being called the "Orange movement." The next morning, the demonstrators entered the National Assembly to place orange leaflets on the desks of cabinet ministers and MPs, and then took seats in the gallery. "[Our] message to the ministers and MPs [was] that we the people are basically upset and demand a change," said another organizer. "We mentioned our founding fathers. They acquired this country for us and you treat it cheaply. We distributed the leaflets on their desks and from up in the gallery all you could see was orange." But for all its color, the proposal backed by the Orange movement did not attract a parliamentary majority.

As soon as a roll call on a competing proposal indicated that it would be supported by the cabinet, whose members are part of the National Assembly *ex officio* ("from their office," that is, by virtue of their positions as heads of ministries), the twenty-nine parliamentarians who did support the five districts walked out, eliminating the quorum necessary to conduct business. "Two MPs left, [Ahmad al-]Saadoun and another, and then all 29 rose and left," reported a third organizer. "It was not organized. It just happened. The people in the gallery went crazy. The parliamentary session was postponed until the next day. We decided to gather the next morning to do it again."

When demonstrators converged on the National Assembly building the following morning, it was surrounded by police and special forces dressed in riot gear. Several MPs came outside to stand with the protesters but, in spite of parliamentary immunity, they, along with the others, were pushed back from the gate by the special forces. One of the organizers was struck with a baton and knocked to the ground, angering the MPs who refused the Speaker's entreaties to come inside and vote. One called a public meeting at the parliament that evening, which happened to be the first anniversary of the passage of the women's rights law. Perhaps four thousand persons gathered that night. More speeches were made—some of them, according to the Orange organizers, extraordinarily impassioned. The next day, the emir dissolved the parliament and called for new elections.

Over those four tumultuous days, orange insignia went from being the logos of the youth movement to markers of support for the five-district plan. After the campaign started, and in response to public reaction, orange paraphernalia were sported and distributed by a wide range of parliamentary candidates seeking to get on the train before it left the station. Following the election, which returned the Orange supporters, the five-district plan was passed. But we should not forget natality. The emir dismissed the 2006 parliament in 2008 and when the next election was run under the new, five-district, ten-seat system, a parliament much more reactionary than its predecessors was elected.

The experience of the Orange movement illustrates the power of politics and the need to sustain political action even after landmark victories. The Orange movement created an opening for change but activists expected what essentially was an administered solution—the five-district plan was devised and implemented by experts—to be able to deliver the change they desired. In reality, the advantages of the five-district plan could be exploited by anybody. The large tribes and conservative organized Islamists used them most effectively. The Orange activists worked hard and they came very close to getting the first woman elected to the parliament. Aseel al-Awadhi came in eleventh in her district, nearly defeating an Islamist incumbent who took the tenth seat. After the results were published, many voters came to Aseel to tell her that they never thought a woman would attract so many votes, and that next time they would vote for her, too. This is not enough to base a campaign on, but it is enough to encourage activists to continue and expand their efforts for the next time.

What can we learn from this and similar stories? Few political leaders or state agencies are entirely comfortable with independent groups. As we see from the Kuwaiti example, movements tend to be more radical, less manageable, more impulsive, and less systematic than bureaucrats and technocrats. Independent groups are not impressed by social expectations, although the Orange activists were scrupulous about cleaning up after demonstrations, having learned from the movement for women's rights that leaving a mess gives opponents a free pass to attack them. They are not impressed by legal niceties or regulatory procedures, especially when they see themselves as citizens with rights. They do not pay adequate attention to the advice of experts.

They are *too political*.

"Too political" is code for the creation of a space of appearances in which people can engage in politics and practice. People experience what is possible in these spaces, and they learn that action is a form of productive power. They find that politics is not only the pursuit of shared interests, as social movement theorists generally describe it,[81] or the mobilization of resources, as social movement theorists believe it should be.[82] They understand it as the application of power to produce. *People choose. People decide.* This is an experience that institutionalized political processes—campaigning, voting, lobbying, e-mailing representatives—rarely offer. It is one that illuminates the possibilities of politics in its raw, elemental form.[83] Thus, it is disruptive and aggravating—but it is also productive. It is not a "solution" to a problem but a means of engaging with what exists and moving toward what should and could be.

Engagement can start with even smaller tears in the web of governmentality. So much of what we think of as normal is just what "everybody says." The most powerful tool of propaganda is to repeat without ceasing what people are supposed to believe, and the most effective weapon against it is to say something different. This is why Arendt says that "speech" and "action" are equivalent. In politics, they are. As Eric Wolf puts it,

> The construction and maintenance of a body of ideological communications is . . . a social process and cannot be explained merely as the formal working out of an internal cultural logic. The development of an overall . . . "design for living" is not so much the victory of a collective cognitive logic or aesthetic impulse as the development of redundancy—the continuous repetition, in diverse instrumental domains, of the same basic propositions regarding the nature of constructed reality.[84]

Being "too political" means challenging those "same basic propositions" wherever we find them to be mean, unfair, and false. It means speaking out, asking different questions—not just "What is the most efficient way to do this or that?" but "Why are we doing this or that, and what are we not doing because we are doing these other things?" It means stepping forward to say "I don't agree," and even "I'm not sure." Dissent is another name for diversity among ideas. At its most fundamental, dissent offers the possibility that what "everybody knows" might not be correct. To say that the way things are is not the way they have to be, or ought to be, is to create a space of appearance where politics can happen.

Being "too political" ruptures the web of governmentality but, like tears in the spider's web, most are small ruptures and are not very conspicuous. No one in Washington or Saõ Paulo, in Delhi or Beijing, cares very much about small groups causing small ruptures nearby.[85] They don't care very much about what people are saying to planning boards or in town meetings or student governments or local officials. They have important problems to worry about, thank you. No one loses sleep worrying that such small tears in the fabric of governmentality threaten the stability of the republic or the kingdom or the union. At most, they might be a nuisance for municipal and civic sensibilities. (But who, in the capitals of the world's great nation-states, cares about that?) They are hardly a threat to the established order.

But as the Orange movement shows, perhaps they are.

After all, if governmentality is about management, politics as we envision it here is not. Indeed, politics challenges the very basis of governmentality. It challenges exactly those principles, practices, and policies that seek to "manage" problems by managing populations in a way that keeps people out of the process. Speech and action offer a different way to build a life, one that grows out of association, coming together to engage in a common enterprise. Speech and action create politics, spaces of appearance in which people have the power to make the world. People matter!

Notes

Chapter 1: Global Politics Because People Matter

1. Thomas Hobbes, *Leviathan*. This work was first published in 1651. It is available in many editions, but be careful—most of them include only the first two "parts." The last two parts, where Hobbes discusses religion, are too interesting to miss, so be sure when you choose your edition that you get the whole story.

2. Christine Di Stefano, "Masculinity as Ideology in Political Theory: Hobbesian Man Considered," *Women's Studies International Forum* 6 (1983): 638.

3. Neta Crawford, "The Passion of World Politics: Propositions on Emotions and Emotional Relationships," *International Security* 24, no. 4 (Spring 2000): 115–56.

4. Hobbes, *Leviathan*, Book XIII.

5. Patricia Springborg, "Politics, Primordialism, and Orientalism," *American Political Science Review* 80, no. 1 (March 1986): 188; Jürgen Habermas, *The Structural Transformation of the Public Sphere: An Inquiry into a Category of Bourgeois Society*, trans. Thomas Burger and Frederick Lawrence (1962; Cambridge, Mass.: MIT Press, 1991), 7; Ernst H. Kantorowicz, *The King's Two Bodies: A Study in Mediaeval Political Theology* (1957; Princeton, N.J.: Princeton University Press, 1997), 13.

6. Kenneth N. Waltz, *Man, the State and War: A Theoretical Analysis* (1954; New York: Columbia University Press, 1959), 159–60. This view is elaborated in Waltz's *Theory of International Politics* (Reading, Mass.: Addison-Wesley, 1979).

7. Anthony Giddens, *The Nation-State and Violence, Volume Two of a Contemporary Critique of Historical Materialism* (Berkeley: University of California Press, 1987), 11.

8. Giddens, *The Nation-State and Violence*, 13.

9. Philip Greven, *Spare the Child: The Religious Roots of Punishment and the Psychological Impact of Physical Abuse* (New York: Vintage, 1990).

10. Waltz, *Theory of International Politics*.

11. A relatively recent example of this approach can be found in Jared Diamond, *Guns, Germs, and Steel: The Fates of Human Societies* (New York: Norton, 1997).

12. Some of these theories are discussed and "deconstructed" in Edward W. Said, *Orientalism* (New York: Vintage, 1979).

13. Clifford Geertz, *Negara: The Theatre State in Nineteenth-Century Bali* (Princeton, N.J.: Princeton University Press, 1980).

14. J. M. Blaut, *The Colonizer's Model of the World: Geographical Diffusionism and Eurocentric History* (New York: Guilford, 1993).

15. Said, *Orientalism*.

16. Scholars who subscribe to this viewpoint include Spencer R. Weart, *Never at War: Why Democracies Will Not Fight One Another* (New Haven, Conn.: Yale University Press, 1998); and Bruce Russett and John R. Oneal, *Triangulating Peace: Democracy, Interdependence, and International Organizations* (New York: Norton, 2001). For a statement by the president, see William Jefferson Clinton, "Confronting the Challenges of a Broader World," in U.S. Department of State, Bureau of Public Affairs, *Dispatch* 4, no. 39 (1993): 3.

17. Joanne Gowa, *Ballots and Bullets: The Elusive Democratic Peace* (Princeton, N.J.: Princeton University Press, 1999).

18. Ido Oren, "The Subjectivity of the 'Democratic' Peace," *International Security* 22, no. 2 (Fall 1995): 147–84. Oren found a similar project, to (re)construct images of the Soviet Union during the cold war. See *Our Enemies and US: America's Rivalries and the Making of Political Science* (Ithaca, N.Y.: Cornell University Press, 2003), chap. 4.

19. Niall Ferguson, *The Pity of War: Explaining World War I* (New York: Basic Books, 1999).

20. Ferguson, *The Pity of War*, 81. Ferguson cites Zara S. Steiner as another historian who takes this position.

21. Ahmad Rashid, *Taliban* (New Haven, Conn.: Yale Nota Bene, 2001), chap. 10; Steve Coll, *Ghost Wars: The Secret History of the CIA, Afghanistan, and Bin Laden, from the Soviet Invasion to September 10, 2001* (New York: Penguin, 2004). The Stinger missile story is covered in detail in Alan J. Kuperman, "The Stinger Missile and U.S. Intervention in Afghanistan," *Political Science Quarterly* 114, no. 2 (1999): 219–63.

22. The ideology governing the operations of these international financial institutions is called "the Washington Consensus" after the city where both are headquartered—and the country most involved in mobilizing the consensus. Most structural adjustment policies require debtor nations to open their economies to investment and products from overseas, thereby devastating local business and creating massive unemployment. This is discussed further in chapters 4 and 9.

23. Peter Uvin, *Aiding Violence: The Development Enterprise in Rwanda* (West Hartford, Conn.: Kumarian, 1998).

24. M. Rodwan Abouharb and David L. Cingranelli, "The Human Rights Effects of World Bank Structural Adjustment, 1981–2000," *International Studies Quarterly* 50, no. 2 (June 2006): 233–62.

25. Ferguson, *The Pity of War*, 59.

26. Jane J. Mansbridge, *Beyond Adversary Democracy* (Chicago: University of Chicago Press, 1983).

27. A similar argument can be made about the failure of the press and the Congress to scrutinize the Bush administration's decision to go to war in Iraq. See for example, Michael Massing, "Now They Tell Us," *New York Review*, February 26, 2004, at www.nybooks.com/articles/16922 (accessed August 25, 2007); and "Unfit to Print?" *New York Review*, June 24, 2004, at www.nybooks.com/articles/17210 (accessed August 25, 2007). Seymour M. Hersh, *Chain of Command: The Road from 9/11 to Abu Ghraib* (New York: HarperCollins, 2004), chap. 5; George Packer, *The Assassins' Gate: America in Iraq* (New York: Farrar, Straus and Giroux, 2005), 46–65; Ron Suskind, *The One Percent Doctrine: Deep Inside America's Pursuit of Its Enemies since 9/11* (New York: Simon and Schuster, 2006), chap. 1.

28. Daniel Jonah Goldhagen, *Hitler's Willing Executioners: Ordinary Germans and the Holocaust* (New York: Knopf, 1996).

29. See the detailed overview of this literature in Ron Rosenbaum, *Explaining Hitler* (New York: Harper Perennial, 1999).

30. Benedict Anderson argues that shared experiences across classes and other identities is the basis of national identity. See *Imagined Communities: Reflections on the Origin and Spread of Nationalism*, rev. ed. (London: Verso, 1991).

31. Eric R. Wolf, *Envisioning Power: Ideologies of Dominance and Crisis* (Berkeley: University of California Press, 1999).

32. Wolf, *Envisioning Power*, 211.

33. John F. Kennedy, News Conference April 21, 1961, in *The Public Papers of Presidents of U.S.* (1962): 312.

34. The original stab-in-the-back legend comes from the story of Siegfried, told in the poem "Nibelungenlied." Siegfried was stabbed by Hagen in the only place he was vulnerable, his back. When Germany surrendered in World War I, it still had troops in the field, leaving the impression that it had not been defeated but rather betrayed by subversive forces on the home front—it was stabbed in the back. In Jeffrey P. Kimball, "The Stab-in-the-Back Legend and the Vietnam War," *Armed Forces and Society* 14, no. 3 (Spring 1988): 433–58, we see how right-wing elements in the United States used this concept to shift the blame for the loss of Vietnam to subversive forces in the United States. According to commentators like conservative Andrew Sullivan, who writes for *Atlantic Monthly*, the Bush administration was preparing a stab-in-the-back charge to deflect blame for its Iraq misadventure onto Democrats and other opponents of this war. See his "Weimar Watch I," at andrewsullivan.theatlantic.com/the_daily_dish/2007/08/weimar-watch-i.html (accessed August 25, 2007). Liberals also have noted the orchestration of blame away from the administration. See, for example, Jeremy Brecher and Brendan Smith, "The 'Stab in the Back' Trap," *Common Dreams*, April 26, 2007, at www.commondreams.org/archive/2007/04/26/766/ (accessed August 25, 2007).

35. Ian Kershaw, *Hitler: 1889–1936, Hubris* (New York: Norton, 1998), chaps. 4–5. The popular culture of and important movement in right-wing German politics during this period, the Freikorps, is detailed in Klaus Theweleit, *Male Fantasies*, 2 vols., trans. Stephen Conway, Erica Carter, and Chris Turner, vol. 1, *Women, Floods, Bodies, History* (1977; Minneapolis: University of Minnesota Press, 1987); vol. 2, *Male Bodies: Psychoanalyzing the White Terror* (1978; Minneapolis: University of Minnesota Press, 1989).

36. Kershaw, *Hitler*, chap. 7.

37. Rosenbaum, *Explaining Hitler*, chap. 3.

38. Elaine Scarry, *The Body in Pain: The Making and Unmaking of the World* (New York: Oxford University Press, 1985). See also Mark Danner, *Torture and Truth: America, Abu Ghraib, and the War on Terror* (New York: New York Review Books, 2004); and Adam Shatz, "The Torture of Algiers," *New York Review*, November 21, 2002, at www.nybooks.com/articles/15824 (accessed August 25, 2007). Peter Ehrenhaus and A. Susan Owen see lynching as another variant of such rituals enacted out of a combination of dominance and fear. See "Race Lynching and Christian Evangelicalism: Performances of Faith," *Text and Performance Quarterly* 24, no. 3/4 (October 2005): 276–301.

39. Michel Foucault, *Discipline and Punish: The Birth of the Prison*, trans. Alan Sheridan (New York: Vintage, 1995).

40. Greven, *Spare the Child*, 19–20.

41. For example, see Peter Gay, *The Enlightenment: The Rise of Modern Paganism*, new ed. (New York: Norton, 1995).

42. Anthony Giddens, *The Nation-State and Violence, Volume Two of a Contemporary Critique of Historical Materialism* (Berkeley: University of California Press, 1987).

43. Vivienne Jabri, *Discourses on Violence: Conflict Analysis Reconsidered* (Manchester, U.K.: Manchester University Press, 1996).

44. See, for example, Anthony Lewis, "Making Torture Legal," *New York Review*, July 15, 2004, at www.nybooks.com/articles/article-preview?article_id=17230 (accessed August 25, 2007).

45. Scarry, *The Body in Pain*, 29.

46. Jane Mayer, *The Dark Side: The Inside Story of How the War on Terror Turned Into a War on American Ideals* (New York: Doubleday, 2008).

47. Sereno Dwight, quoted in Greven, *Spare the Child*, 21.

48. Stanley Cohen, *States of Denial Knowing about Atrocities and Suffering* (Cambridge, U.K.: Polity, 2000). That Bob Woodward calls his third book about the Bush presidency *State of Denial* signifies his own and others' reluctance to confront evidence of the deceit of the Bush II administration. Bob Woodward, *State of Denial: Bush at War, Part III* (New York: Simon and Schuster, 2006).

49. See the appendix on "newspeak" in George Orwell's 1948 novel *1984*.

50. Cohen, *States of Denial*, 294. Similar mechanisms of denial greeted the two studies estimating the death toll among Iraqis resulting from the U.S.-U.K. invasion and occupation of Iraq that appeared in the British journal *The Lancet*. See (listen to) Ira Glass, "What's in a Number? 2006 Edition," *This American Life*, Chicago Public Radio, broadcast November 3, 2006, listen at www .thislife.org/Radio_Episode.aspx?episode=320.

51. Cohen, *States of Denial*, 293–94, emphasis in the original.

52. Kees van der Pijl, *Nomads, Empires, States: Modes of Foreign Relations and Political Economy*, vol.1 (London: Pluto, 2007).

53. Nikki R. Keddie with Richard Yann, *Roots of Revolution: An Interpretive History of Modern Iran* (New Haven, Conn.: Yale University Press, 1981); Haideh Moghissi, *Populism and Feminism in Iran: Women's Struggle in a Male Defined Revolutionary Movement* (New York: St. Martin's, 1995).

54. This is how David Halberstam described the people who brought the United States the Vietnam War. See *The Best and the Brightest* (1972; New York: Ballentine Books, 1993).

Chapter 2: People, Households, and the World

1. Nicholas Abercrombie, Stephen Hill, and Bryan S. Turner, *Sovereign Individuals of Capitalism* (London: Allen and Unwin, 1986); C. B. Macpherson, *The Political Theory of Possessive Individualism: Hobbes to Locke* (London: Oxford University Press, 1964). Here we are making a distinction between classical liberals, who focused on the freedom of the individual and the freedom of markets, including markets for ideas, and contemporary uses of the term in the United States.

2. See Christopher Hill, *Reformation to Industrial Revolution* (Harmondsworth, Middlesex: Pelican, 1967); Lawrence Stone, *The Causes of the English Revolution, 1529–1642* (London: Routledge, 1994).

3. Thomas Hobbes, *Leviathan* (New York: Collier, 1962; Oakeshott ed.), chap. 13, p. 101; see also John Locke, *Two Treatises of Government* (1690; Cambridge: Cambridge University Press, 1988, ed. Peter Laslett), chaps. 2 and 7, and Jean-Jacques Rousseau, *A Dissertation on the Origin and Foundation of the Inequality of Mankind* (1754), part I.

4. Hobbes, *Leviathan*, chap. 13, p. 101; see also Mark A. Heller, "The Use & Abuse of Hobbes: The State of Nature in International Relations," *Polity* 13, no. 1 (Autumn 1980): 21–32.

5. Up to this point, wars in Europe often involved family networks subject to the laws of the "Christian commonwealth." Only with the emergence of the sovereign nation-state in the 1800s did a form of anarchy really come into being. See Hedley Bull, *The Anarchical Society: A Study of Order in World Politics* (New York: Columbia University Press, 1977).

6. The first chair in international relations was established at the University of Aberystwythe, Wales, in 1919; the first "real" IR book is often considered to be Edward Hallett Carr, *The Twenty Years' Crisis, 1919–1939* (1939; London: Macmillan, 1946). But see also Torbjørn L. Knutsen, "Origins and Originality: The 19th Century Rise of International Relations as an Academic Discipline" (paper delivered at the 46th annual convention of the International Studies Association, Honolulu, Hawaii, March 4, 2005).

7. Bull, *The Anarchical Society*.

8. Locke, *Two Treatises*; Jean-Jacques Rousseau, *The Social Contract: An Eighteenth-Century Translation*, ed. Charles Frankel (New York: Hafner, 1947).

9. This particular trope can be seen in William Golding's *Lord of the Flies*, at least as it is commonly taught in American high schools.

10. An interesting discussion of the possible origins of language can be found in David Dobbs, "The Gregarious Brain," *New York Times*, July 8, 2007, at www.nytimes.com/2007/07/08/magazine/08sociability-t.html (accessed September 21, 2007).

11. See the discussion in Macpherson, *Possessive Individualism*, 221–29.

12. "Badges? We ain't got no badges! We don't need no badges! I don't have to show you any steenkin' badges!" *Treasure of the Sierra Madre* (1948).

13. J. A. L. Singh and Robert M. Zingg, *Wolf-Children and Feral Man* (Hamden, Conn.: Archon Books, 1966); John Bowlby, *A Secure Base: Parent-Child Attachment and Healthy Human Development* (New York: Basic Books, 1988).

14. Immanuel Wallerstein and Joan Smith, "Household as an Institution of the World Economy," in *Creating and Transforming Households: The Constraints of the World-Economy*, ed. Joan Smith and Immanuel Wallerstein (Cambridge: Cambridge University Press, 1992), 7.

15. Eric Wolf, *Europe and the People without History* (Berkeley: University of California Press, 1982), 90–94.

16. Gayle Rubin, "The Traffic in Women: Notes on the Political Economy of Sex," in *Toward an Anthropology of Women*, ed. Rayna R. Reiter (New York: Monthly Review, 1975), 157–210.

17. Laura Gowing, "Secret Births and Infanticide in Seventeenth-Century England," *Past and Present* 156 (August 1997): 87–115; Carole Pateman, "'God Hath Ordained to Man a Helper': Hobbes, Patriarchy and Conjugal Right," in *Feminist Interpretations and Political Theory*, ed. Mary Lyndon Shanley and Carole Pateman (University Park: Pennsylvania State University Press, 1991), 53–74; Amy Dru Stanley, *From Bondage to Contract: Wage Labor, Marriage, and the Market in the Age of Slave Emancipation* (New York: Cambridge University Press, 1998).

18. This was fully in keeping with America's "containment" of the Soviet Union during the cold war—to ensure that neither June nor the Soviets ever got out of hand and caused trouble. For an entertaining look at what might happen if the American nuclear family ever escaped from containment, see the film *Pleasantville* (1998).

19. Katharine Q. Seelye, "They Stand by Their Men, Loudly," *New York Times*, August 26, 2007, at www.nytimes.com/2007/08/26/weekinreview/26seelye.html (accessed September 21, 2007).

20. Jodi Kantor, "In 2008 Race, Little Ones Go on the Trail with Daddy," *New York Times*, August 26, 2007, at www.nytimes.com/2007/08/26/us/politics/26kids.html (accessed September 21, 2007). Mitt Romney also sent his five sons onto the campaign trail, arguing that "one of the ways my sons are showing support for our nation is helping to get me elected," rather than serving in Iraq. This statement did not reflect so well on him. See Michael Luo, "Question of Sons' Choices Dogs Romney Campaign," *New York Times*, August 15, 2007, at www.nytimes.com/2007/08/15/us/politics/15romney.html (accessed September 21, 2007).

21. Two articles by Katherine Boo in *The New Yorker* illuminate this process very clearly (which is also discussed in chapter 4). See Katherine Boo, "The Churn: Creative Destruction in a Border Town," *New Yorker*, March 29, 2004, at www.newamerica.net/publications/articles/2004/the_churn (accessed September 24, 2007); Katherine Boo, "The Best Job in Town," *New Yorker*, July 4, 2004, at www.newamerica.net/publications/articles/2004/the_best_job_in_town (accessed September 24, 2007).

22. Vance Packard, *The Hidden Persuaders* (New York: D. McKay, 1957); Richard Wightman Fox and T. J. Jackson Lears, eds., *The Culture of Consumption: Critical Essays in American History, 1880–1980* (New York: Pantheon Books, 1983); Charles F. McGovern, *Sold American—Consumption and Citizenship, 1890–1945* (Chapel Hill: University of North Carolina Press, 2006).

23. See, for example, Prabhu L. Pingali, "From Subsistence Systems to Commercial Agriculture: The Need for a New Development Paradigm," *American Journal of Agricultural Economics* 79, no. 2 (May 1997): 628–34.

24. Andres Duany, Elizabeth Plater-Zyberk, and Jeff Speck, *Suburban Nation: The Rise of Sprawl and the Decline of the American Dream* (New York: Northpoint Press, 2000); Jane Holtz Kay, *Asphalt Nation* (Berkeley: University of California Press, 1998).

25. William Irwin, Mark T. Conard, and Aeon J. Skoble, eds., *The Simpsons and Philosophy: The D'oh! of Homer* (Chicago: Open Court, 2001); Mark Poster, *Critical Theory of the Family* (New York: Seabury, 1978).

26. William H. Chafe, *The American Woman: Her Changing Social, Economic, and Political Roles, 1920–1970* (New York: Oxford University Press, 1972).

27. Arlene S. Skolnick, *Embattled Paradise: The American Family in an Age of Uncertainty* (New York: Basic, 1992).

28. Timothy Sosnovy, "The Soviet Housing Situation Today," *Soviet Studies* 11, no. 1 (July 1959): 1–21; Bryon MacWilliams, "Communism at Uncomfortably Close Quarters," *Chronicle of Higher Education*, April 26, 2002, at chronicle.com/weekly/v48/i33/33a05601.htm (accessed September 25, 2007).

29. Remember that the Great Depression had come to a final end only as a result of World War II, and remained a live fear in the minds of those who had come of age before 1940.

30. Fred W. McDarrah, Gloria S. McDarrah, and Timothy S. McDarrah, *Anarchy, Protest, and Rebellion: And the Counterculture That Changed America* (New York: Thunder Mouth's, 2003); Richard M. Fried, *Nightmare in Red: The McCarthy Era in Perspective* (New York: Oxford University Press, 1991); John Shelton Reed, *Whistling Dixie: Dispatches from the South* (New York: Harvest Books, 1992).

31. Margaret Gibelman, "So How Far Have We Come? Pestilent and Persistent Gender Gap in Pay," *Social Work* 48, no. 1 (January 2003): 22–32.

32. Robert B. Reich, *The Future of Success* (New York: Knopf, 2000); Boo, "The Churn," "Best Job in Town."

33. *Migration and the Labour Market in Asia: Recent Trends and Policies* (Paris: Organisation for Economic Co-operation and Development, 2002); Caitlin Flanagan, "How Serfdom Saved the Women's Movement," *Atlantic Monthly* 293, no. 2 (March 2004): 109–28.

34. Susan Faludi, *Backlash: The Undeclared War against American Women* (New York: Crown, 1991); Doris Buss and Didi Herman, *Globalizing Family Values—The Christian Right in International Politics* (Minneapolis: University of Minnesota Press, 2003).

35. See, for example, Leo P. Ribuffo, *The Old Christian Right—The Protestant Far Right from the Great Depression to the Cold War* (Philadelphia: Temple University Press, 1983); Susan F. Harding, *The Book of Jerry Falwell—Fundamentalist Language and Politics* (Princeton, N.J.: Princeton University Press, 2000).

36. Thomas Frank, *What's the Matter with Kansas* (New York: Metropolitan Books, 2004); Carolyn Gallaher, *On the Fault Line: Race, Class, and the American Patriot Movement* (Lanham, Md.: Rowman & Littlefield, 2003).

37. Nancy Fraser, "After the Family Wage: Gender Equity and the Welfare State," *Political Theory* 22, no. 4 (November 1994): 591–618.

38. That is: 1.5 billion households × 6 hours/day × 365 days/year × \$7.50/hour = \$24.6 trillion.

39. Eric R. Wolf, *Europe and the People without History* (Berkeley: University of California Press, 1982).

40. Flanagan, "How Serfdom Saved the Women's Movement."

41. To put this more clearly: 70 hours of housework and childcare a week at an average of \$12/hour in the United States has an economic value of \$840. A salaried professional woman might be paid \$1,500 to \$2,000 per week—which will probably be taxed at a marginal rate of at least 30 percent and, perhaps more, when other costs are figured in—compared to a male who might receive \$2,000 to \$2,500 per week. Her take-home pay is then on the order of \$1,050 to \$1,400. The employer does not have to pay the \$840 per week for the value of the housework and also saves \$500 by paying the woman less than a comparably qualified man.

42. Eyal Press, "Family-Leave Values," *New York Times*, July 29, 2007, at www.nytimes.com/2007/07/29/magazine/29discrimination-t.html (accessed September 21, 2007).

43. Flanagan, "How Serfdom Saved the Women's Movement"; Arlie Hochschild, with Anne Machung, *The Second Shift: Working Parents and the Revolution at Home* (New York: Avon, 1990).

44. John Agnew, "Representing Space: Space, Scale and Culture in Social Science," in *Place/Culture/Representation*, ed. James Duncan and David Ley (London: Routledge, 1993), 262.

45. Nick Paumgarten, "There and Back Again," *The New Yorker*, April 16, 2007, 58, 60, 62, 64–68, 70.

46. Amartya Sen, *Development as Freedom* (New York: Anchor, 1999), 8.

47. The full quote is "Men make their own history, but they do not make it as they please; they do not make it under self-selected circumstances, but under circumstances existing already, given and transmitted from the past." Karl Marx, *The 18th Brumaire of Louis Bonaparte* (1852).

48. Tensions between the worlds of the liberal and the social individual are described by environmentalist Bill McKibben in *Deep Economy: The Wealth of Communities and the Durable Future* (New York: Times Books, 2007).

49. Alfred Hirschman, *The Passions and the Interests: Political Arguments for Capitalism before Its Triumphs* (Princeton, N.J.: Princeton University Press, 1997).

50. Or, as Henry Kissinger once said, "Power is the great aphrodisiac." Quoted in the *New York Times,* January 19, 1971. A potential partner's income prospects are also an aphrodisiac. See Barbara Ehrenreich, *Hearts of Men: American Dreams and the Flight from Commitment* (New York: Doubleday Anchor, 1984).

51. Benjamin R. Barber, *Consumed: How Markets Corrupt Children, Infantilize Adults, and Swallow Citizens Whole* (New York: Norton, 2007).

52. This is often framed in terms of the "collective action problem," or the parable of the stag hunt, inferred from the brief discussion by Jean-Jacques Rousseau in *A Discourse on Inequality.* Imagine a group of men pursuing a deer. If they catch it, all will eat; if not, everyone will go hungry. Suddenly, a rabbit crosses in front of one of the men, who knows for certain that he can catch the rabbit and eat. But, if he chases the rabbit, the deer will escape and the rest of the group will go hungry. In this instance, self-interest commands "defection" from the group, and so the others do not eat. See *A Discourse on Inequality,* part 2 (1754), at www.constitution.org/jjr/ineq_04.htm (accessed September 21, 2007) and Brian Skyrms, "The Stag Hunt," *Proceedings and Addresses of the American Philosophical Association* 75, no. 2 (November 2001): 31–41.

53. But, see Ellen Meiksins Wood, *The Origin of Capitalism: A Longer View* (New York: Verso, 2002).

54. Adam Smith, *The Wealth of Nations.* Originally published in 1776.

55. Karl Polanyi, *The Great Transformation* (New York: Farrar and Rinehart, 1944), chap. 5.

56. Francis Fukuyama, *Trust: Social Virtues and the Creation of Prosperity* (New York: Free Press, 1995); also Ehrenreich, *Hearts of Men.*

57. Fred L. Block, *The Origins of International Economic Disorder: A Study of United States International Monetary Policy from World War II to the Present* (Berkeley: University of California Press, 1977).

58. Karl Marx, *Capital,* vol. 1, part 1, chap. 4; Thomas Frank and Matt Wieland, eds., *Commodify Your Dissent* (New York: Norton, 1997); Barber, *Consumed.*

59. Lisa Jardine, *Worldly Goods: A New History of the Renaissance* (New York: Norton, 1998).

60. See, for example, Janelle Morris, "The Modern De Beers and the Significant Changes to the Diamond Pipeline over the Past Decade—A Literature Review," prepared by the author in partial fulfillment of the requirements for the award of The Gemmological Association of Australia's Diploma in Diamond Technology for 2003, at www.australiangemmologist.com.au/modern_de-beers.pdf (accessed September 25, 2007).

61. Yet another example of defection from the stag hunt.

62. The flooding of the market with diamonds became a major problem in the 1990s, a direct outcome of African wars, as warlords would sell "conflict diamonds" to raise money for more weapons. See, for example, William Reno, *Warlord Politics and African States* (Boulder, Colo.: Rienner, 1998). Of course, diamonds remain a store of wealth only as long as their price is high. Over time, the value of a particular piece of jewelry may increase because of its artistic value, but most of the diamond jewelry one sees advertised in the media is mass-produced and overpriced, and has little long-term value. But this is the reason for the sly and cynical joke at the end of the film *Blood Diamond,* in which, recalling the final scene of *Raiders of the Lost Ark,* the much-prized object of so much death and violence is locked up in a vault full of safe-deposit boxes where, we are led to assume, diamonds are stored so they will not flood the market and cause prices to fall.

63. Justin Burton, "Lab-grown Diamonds Sparkle Blood-Free," *San Francisco Chronicle,* September 10, 2008, A1, at www.sfgate.com/cgi-bin/article.cgi?f=/c/a/2008/09/10/MNSV12KA8K .DTL&hw=diamonds&sn=002&sc=507 (accessed September 13, 2008); Janet Maslin, "Diamonds: A Girl's Best Path to Selflessness?" *New York Times,* September 5, 2008, at www.nytimes.com/2008/09/05/books/05book.html? (accessed September 13, 2008).

64. The stag hunt, again; for the definitive statement of this dilemma, see Mancur Olson, *The Logic of Collective Action* (Cambridge, Mass.: Harvard University Press, 1965). For a critique, see Lars Udehn, *The Limits of Public Choice: A Sociological Critique of the Economic Theory* (London: Routledge, 1996).

65. Gary Younge, "US Imposes Controls on a New Security Threat—Birdwatchers," *The Guardian* (London), July 7, 2005, at www.guardian.co.uk/usa/story/0,12271,1522968,00.html (accessed September 21, 2007).

66. Robert J. Brym, "Hip-Hop from Dissent to Commodity: A Note on Consumer Culture," *Society in Question: Sociological Readings for the 21st Century*, 3rd ed. (Toronto: Harcourt Canada, 2001), at www.brymsociologycompass.nelson.com/Hip_Hop_Article.pdf (accessed September 25, 2007); Claire Dwyer and Peter Jackson, "Commodifying Difference: Selling EASTern Fashion," *Environment and Planning D: Society and Space* 21, no. 3 (2003): 269–91, at www.envplan.com/epd/fulltext/d21/d349.pdf (accessed September 25, 2007).

67. Sidney Tarrow, *Power in Movement: Social Movements and Contentious Politics*, 2nd ed. (Cambridge, U.K.: Cambridge University Press, 1998).

68. Olson, *Logic of Collective Action*.

69. Milton Friedman and Rose Friedman, *Free to Choose* (New York: Harcourt Brace Jovanovich, 1980). See also Ronnie D. Lipschutz, with James K. Rowe, *Globalization, Governmentality and Global Politics: Regulation for the Rest of Us?* (London: Routledge, 2005).

70. The term is attributed to Max Weber, who wrote of *"stahlhartes Gehäuse"* resulting from bureaucracy and rationalization in *The Protestant Ethic and the Spirit of Capitalism*. This was rendered as "iron cage" by his translator, Talcott Parsons (New York: Charles Scribner's Sons, 1958). Apparently, a literal translation of the German is "a steel encasement," which is not nearly so poetic.

71. In some ways, the Internet has facilitated communication among individuals with shared political interests (e.g., MoveOn.org), but it has also greased the wheels of commerce (e.g., eBay).

72. Olson, *Logic of Collective Action*.

Chapter 3: People and Power

1. Kenneth Waltz, *Theory of International Relations* (Reading, Mass.: Addison-Wesley, 1979); Robert Dahl, "The Concept of Power," *Behavioral Science* 2 (1957): 201–18.

2. Michael Barnett and Raymond Duvall, *Power and Global Governance* (Cambridge: Cambridge University Press, 2004).

3. See, for example, Hannah Arendt, *The Human Condition: A Study of the Central Dilemmas Facing Modern Man* (Garden City, N.Y.: Doubleday, 1959); and Hannah Arendt, *On Revolution* (New York: Compass Books, 1965).

4. Robin L. Teske, "The Butterfly Effect," in *Conscious Acts and the Politics of Social Change*, ed. Robin L. Teske and Mary Ann Tétreault (Columbia: University of South Carolina Press, 2000), 107–23.

5. Arendt, *The Human Condition*, 177–78.

6. Antonio Gramsci, *Selections from the Prison Notebooks* (New York: International Publishers, 1971); Walter L. Adamson, *Hegemony and Revolution: Antonio Gramsci's Political and Cultural Theory* (Chapel Hill: University of North Carolina Press, 1983).

7. C. Vann Woodward, *Reunion and Reaction: The Compromise of 1877 and the End of Reconstruction* (Boston: Little, Brown, 1966); David W. Blight, *Race and Reunion: The Civil War in American Memory* (Cambridge, Mass.: Belknap, 2001).

8. Ruth Whiteside, "Justice Joseph Bradley and the Reconstruction Amendments" (PhD diss., Rice University, May 1981), chap. 6.

9. Clare Dyer, "Confidential Tobacco Documents Enter Public Domain," *British Medical Journal* 316 (April 18, 1998): 1185, at bmj.bmjjournals.com/cgi/content/full/316/7139/1185/c (accessed December 2007).

10. Other examples are given in Douglas Starr, *Blood: An Epic History of Medicine and Commerce* (New York: Knopf, 1998), which deals with wrongful injury lawsuits brought against companies and organizations that collected and knowingly distributed blood products contaminated with HIV. *New York Times* reporters found similar successful resistance by the U.S. beef industry to regulations preventing sick animals from being used for food. See Christopher Drew, Elizabeth Becker, and Sandra Blakeslee, "Despite Warnings, Industry Resisted Safeguards," *New York Times,* December 28, 2003, 19. An especially worrisome example was the refusal of federal regulators to remove the arthritis drug Vioxx from the market in spite of evidence that it contributed to heart attacks. "By the time it was withdrawn, an estimated 80 million people worldwide had taken Vioxx (rofecoxib). A memo posted by the U.S. Food and Drug Administration (FDA) on its website on 2 November 2004 suggests that Vioxx may have contributed to almost 28,000 heart attacks in the US between 1999 and 2003." See Anna Gosline, "Vioxx Heart Risks Apparent for Years," *New Scientist* 12, no. 16, (November 5, 2004), at www.newscientist.com/article/dn6627-vioxx-heart-risks-apparent-for-years.html (accessed December 2007).

11. Although Bosnia had separated from Yugoslavia and been recognized as an independent country, UN members spoke and behaved as though they believed it was still part of Yugoslavia, and therefore Yugoslavia's to do with as it wished.

12. Howard Ball, *Prosecuting War Crimes and Genocide: The Twentieth-Century Experience* (Lawrence: University Press of Kansas, 1999). For more information on the ICC, see www.iccnow.org/.

13. Cynthia Weber, *Simulating Sovereignty: Intervention, the State and Symbolic Exchange* (Cambridge: Cambridge University Press, 1995).

14. Václav Havel, "Kosovo and the End of the Nation-State," *New York Review of Books,* June 10, 1999, 4, 6.

15. Evidence of the use of torture by the United States since 2001 has grown exponentially since the revelation of abuses of detainees by low-ranking U.S. military personnel in May 2004. By 2008, it was clear that torture had been authorized at the highest levels of the U.S. government. For some recent analysis, see Jack Goldsmith, *The Terror Presidency: Law and Judgment Inside the Bush Administration* (New York: Norton, 2007); and Charlie Savage, *Takeover: The Return of the Imperial Presidency and the Subversion of American Democracy* (Boston: Little, Brown, 2007).

16. Jamie Mayerfeld, "The Democratic Legacy of the International Criminal Court," *Fletcher Forum of World Affairs* 28, no. 2 (Summer 2004): 147–56, at fletcher.tufts.edu/forum/archives/pdfs/28-2pdfs/mayerfelda.pdf.

17. For an analysis of the importance of the Pinochet case to the development of international law see Naomi Rhot-Arriaza, *The Pinochet Effect: Transnational Justice in the Age of Human Rights* (Philadelphia: University of Pennsylvania Press, 2005).

18. Adamson, *Hegemony and Revolution.*

19. Václav Benda et al., "Parallel Polis; or an Independent Society in Central and Eastern Europe: An Inquiry," *Social Research* 55 (1988): 211–26.

20. Jiřina Siklová, "Women and the Charta 77 Movement in Czechoslovakia," in Teske and Tétreault, *Conscious Acts,* 270.

21. Louis Fisher, "The 'Sole Organ' Doctrine," The Law Library of Congress, August 2006 (2006-03236), at www.fas.org/sgp/eprint/fisher.pdf (accessed September 26, 2007).

22. "Nixon's Views on Presidential Power: Excerpts from an Interview with David Frost," broadcast May 19, 1977, at www.landmarkcases.org/nixon/nixonview.html.

23. Charlie Savage, "Bush Challenges Hundreds of Laws," *Boston Globe,* April 30, 2006, at www.boston.com/news/nation/articles/2006/04/30/bush_challenges_hundreds_of_laws/ (accessed August 13, 2007).

24. Savage, *Takeover.* The conservative Goldsmith also sees this as a danger.

25. Ronnie D. Lipschutz, *The Constitution of Imperium* (Boulder, Colo.: Paradigm, 2008).

26. Diane M. Duffy, "Finding Power in a Hegemonic Environment: Lessons on Surviving and Thriving from Five Women's Organizations in Poland," in *Partial Truths and the Politics of Community,* ed. Mary Ann Tétreault and Robin L. Teske (Columbia: University of South Carolina Press, 2003), 238–62.

27. Two of our students observed repressive practices at universities in Egypt during study-abroad semesters in fall 2007 and spring 2008 as part of a larger project studying repression and dissent in the Middle East. The slightly veiled repression of Muslim Brotherhood political activity is discussed in one of the papers from the project, Jillian Schwedler, Katherine Meyer, and Mary Ann Tétreault, "Hidden Forms of Repression and Dissent" (presented at the Second World Conference on Middle East Studies, Amman, July 9–15, 2006).

28. That the capture of the "occupied territories" was accidental is the thesis of Michael B. Oren, *Six Days of War: June 1967 and the Making of the Modern Middle East* (New York: Oxford University Press, 2002).

29. Amos Elon, "War without End," *New York Review of Books,* July 15, 2004, 26–29.

30. Balance-of-power models are discussed in Inis Claude, *Power and International Relations* (New York: Random House, 1962); and Karl Polanyi, *The Great Transformation* (New York: Farrar and Rinehart, 1944), esp. 259–62.

31. Robert Gilpin, *War and Change in World Politics* (New York: Cambridge University Press, 1981).

32. Niall Ferguson, *The Pity of War: Explaining World War I* (New York: Basic Books, 1999); George Frost Kennan, *The Fateful Alliance: France, Russia, and the Coming of the First World War* (New York: Pantheon Books, 1984). Ferguson goes on to argue that, despite having more stuff, Germany's opponents almost lost the war, another reason to take balance-of-power theory with a grain of salt.

33. Although he attributes the initiation of WWI to the actions of the Austrian Empire as the tail that wagged the German dog (also panting for war), Alan Kramer sees the mass killing and cultural destruction that characterized the conflict from its beginnings on the western as well as the eastern front as enough to induce Britain to send the BEF "to come to the assistance of France to prevent a quick German victory and German hegemony on the Continent." Alan Kramer, *Dynamics of Destruction: Culture and Mass Killing in the First World War* (Oxford: Oxford University Press, 2007), 80.

34. Hedley Bull, Andrew Hurrell, and Stanley Hoffmann, *The Anarchical Society*, 3rd. ed. (New York: Columbia University Press, 2002).

35. Such conversations and their results are reported in Jean Edward Smith, *George Bush's War* (New York: Henry Holt, 1992).

36. Niall Ferguson, *The War of the World: Twentieth-Century Conflict and the Descent of the West* (New York: Penguin, 2006), 93–102.

37. Ferguson, *The Pity of War*, chap. 3.

38. Larry Berman, *No Peace, No Honor: Nixon, Kissinger, and Betrayal in Vietnam* (New York: Free Press, 2001).

39. Lawrence E. Walsh, *Final Report of the Independent Counsel for Iran/Contra Matters*, vol. 1, *Investigations and Prosecutions*, Washington, D.C.: U.S. Court of Appeals for the District of Columbia, August 4, 1993, at www.fas.org/irp/offdocs/walsh/ (accessed December 2007).

40. Norman Angell, *The Great Illusion: A Study of the Relation of Military Power in Nations to Their Economic and Social Advantage* (1910; repr., New York: Garland, 1972); Edward Hallett Carr, *The Twenty Years' Crisis, 1919–1939* (1939; repr., New York: Perennial, 1964).

41. Joseph A. Schumpeter, *Business Cycles: A Theoretical, Historical, and Statistical Analysis of the Capitalist Process* (New York: McGraw-Hill, 1939); also *Imperialism and Social Classes*, trans. Heinz Norden (New York: Kelley, 1951).

42. Paul Kennedy, "The Tradition of Appeasement in British Foreign Policy, 1865–1939," in *Strategy and Diplomacy, 1870–1939* (London: George Allen and Unwin, 1983), 13–40.

43. The United States participated in the negotiation of the Versailles Treaty, which marked the formal resolution of World War I. However, the Senate refused to ratify the treaty, and the United States did not participate effectively as a strategic partner in the peace.

44. John Maynard Keynes, *The Economic Consequences of the Peace* (New York: Penguin Reprint, 1995).

45. Kramer, *Dynamics of Destruction.*

46. Kramer, *Dynamics of Destruction.*

47. Steve Coll, "The Atomic Emporium," *New Yorker,* August 7, 2006, at www.newyorker.com/archive/2006/08/07/060807fa_fact_coll?printable=true (accessed December 2007).

48. Jason A. Beckett, "Interim Legality: A Mistaken Assumption? An Analysis of Depleted Uranium Munitions under Contemporary International Humanitarian Law," *Chinese Journal of International Law* 3, no. 1 (2004): 87–134; also Katherine Stapp, "Experts Warn of Radioactive Battlefields in Iraq," Inter Press News Service Agency, September 13, 2003, at www.veteransforcommonsense.org/?page=article&id=1094 (accessed December 2007).

49. GlobalSecurity.org, "World Wide Military Expenditures," at www.globalsecurity.org/military/world/spending.htm (accessed December 2007).

50. George Soros, *George Soros on Globalization* (New York: PublicAffairs Press, 2002); Joseph E. Stiglitz, *Globalization and Its Discontents* (New York: Norton, 2002).

51. Associated Press, "U.S. Booed at Climate Conference," *Chicago Sun-Times,* December 15, 2007, at www.suntimes.com/news/world/699125,climate121507.article (accessed December 2007).

52. Andrew E. Kramer and Thom Shanker, "Russia Suspends Arms Agreement Over U.S. Shield," *New York Times,* July 15, 2007, at www.nytimes.com/2007/07/15/world/europe/15russia.html?_r=1&oref=slogin (accessed December 2007); also Thom Shanker, "Russian Pullback on Arms Treaty Obscures Progress, Official Says," *New York Times,* July 16, 2007, at www.nytimes.com/2007/07/16/world/europe/16treaty.html?ref=world (accessed December 2007).

53. Alan J. Kuperman, "The Stinger Missile and U.S. Intervention in Afghanistan, *Political Science Quarterly* 114, no. 2 (1999): esp. 249–53.

54. James William Gibson, *The Perfect War: The War We Couldn't Lose and How We Did* (New York: Vintage, 1988).

55. Taylor Branch, *Parting the Waters: America in the King Years, 1954–63* (New York: Daedalus Books, 1988); Diane McWhorter, *Carry Me Home: Birmingham Alabama, the Climactic Battle of the Civil Rights Revolution* (New York: Simon and Schuster, 2001).

56. Darius Rejali, *Torture and Democracy* (Princeton, N.J.: Princeton University Press, 2007), 39–43.

57. Schwedler et al., "Hidden Forms of Repression and Dissent."

58. Eva Fogelman, *Conscience and Courage: Rescuers of Jews during the Holocaust* (New York: Anchor Books, 1994).

59. Evgenia Ginzburg, *Into the Whirlwind,* trans. Paul Stevenson and Namya Harair (London: Harvill, 1999); and *Within the Whirlwind,* trans. Ian Boland (New York: Harcourt Brace Jovanovich, 1981).

60. Ginzburg, *Within the Whirlwind,* 354.

61. Charles Tilly, "War Making and State Making as Organized Crime," in *Bringing the State Back In,* ed. Peter Evans, Dietrich Rueschemeyer, and Theda Skoçpol (New York: Cambridge University Press, 1985), 169–91.

62. Michael Walzer, *The Revolution of the Saints* (Cambridge, Mass.: Harvard University Press, 1965).

63. Jane J. Mansbridge, *Beyond Adversary Democracy* (Chicago: University of Chicago Press, 1983).

64. Kevin Phillips, *Wealth and Democracy: A Political History of the American Rich* (New York: Broadway Books, 2002).

65. Hamid Zangeneh, e-mail communication to Mary Ann Tétreault, July 22, 2002.

66. Alejandro Colás, *International Civil Society* (Cambridge, U.K.: Polity, 2002); also Darrow Schecter, *Sovereign States or Political Communities? Civil Society and Contemporary Politics* (Manchester: Manchester University Press, 2000); and Teske and Tétreault, *Conscious Acts.*

67. John M. Cotter, "Sounds of Hate: White Power Rock and Roll and the Neo-Nazi Skinhead Subculture," *Terrorism and Political Violence* 11, no. 2 (Summer 1999): 111–40.

Chapter 4: People and Economy

1. Cited in ABC30.com, "Stocks Rebound on Rate Cut," January 22, 2008, at abclocal.go
.com/kfsn/story?section=news/national_world&id=5907601 (accessed February 6, 2008).

2. "Stocks Rebound on Rate Cut."

3. Warren E. Buffett, "Chairman's Letter to the Shareholders of Berkshire Hathaway Inc,"
February 28, 2002, at www.berkshirehathaway.com/2001ar/2001letter.html (accessed February 6,
2008).

4. John Agnew, "Representing Space: Space, Scale and Culture in Social Science," in *Place/
Culture/Representation,* ed. James Duncan and David Ley (London: Routledge, 1993), 262.

5. Roy Nash, "Bourdieu on Education and Social and Cultural Reproduction," *British Journal
of Sociology of Education* 11, no. 4 (1990): 431–47.

6. It is estimated that at least one billion people live on a dollar or less per day, and another billion or so on two dollars or less per day. These data can be found in the statistical tables in both the
annual *Human Development Report* published by the UN Development Programme (www.undp
.org/) and the *World Development Report* published by the World Bank (www.worldbank.org/).

7. Michael Chibnik, "The Value of Subsistence Production," *Journal of Anthropological Research*
34, no. 4 (Winter 1978): 561–76; John F. Morton, "The Impact of Climate Change on Smallholder
and Subsistence Agriculture," *Proceedings of the National Academy of Sciences* 104, no. 50 (December 11, 2007), at www.pnas.org/cgi/reprint/104/50/19680 (accessed March 4, 2008).

8. Kees van der Pijl, *Nomads, Empires, States—Modes of Foreign Relations and Political Economy,*
vol. 1 (London: Pluto Press, 2007), esp. chap. 1.

9. René Girard, *Violence and the Sacred,* trans. Patrick Gregory (Baltimore: Johns Hopkins University Press, 1977); van der Pijl, *Nomads, Empires, States.*

10. Eric R. Wolf, *Envisioning Power: Ideologies of Dominance and Crisis* (Berkeley: University of
California Press, 1999).

11. Wolf, *Envisioning Power.*

12. Many would argue that "spiritualism" is also central to capitalism. See, for example, Max
Weber, *The Protestant Ethic and the Spirit of Capitalism,* trans. Talcott Parsons (New York: Scribner,
1958).

13. John Urry, "The System of 'Automobility,'" *Theory, Culture, Society* 21, no. 4/5 (2004): 25–39.

14. Peter Drahos with John Braithwaite, *Information Feudalism* (New York: Norton, 2003).

15. Charles Maier, *Among Empires—American Ascendancy and Its Predecessors* (Cambridge,
Mass.: Harvard University Press, 2006), chap. 6.

16. Jürgen Habermas, *Legitimation Crisis,* trans. Thomas McCarthy (Boston: Beacon, 1975).

17. Wolf, *Envisioning Power;* Eric R. Wolf, *Europe and the People without History* (Berkeley: University of California Press, 1982).

18. The societies of the Pacific offer particularly interesting forms and variations on kin-
ordered societies, especially as groups migrated from one island to another. The Bishop Museum
in Honolulu, Hawai'i, offers some interesting displays in this regard. See also John Edward Ter-
rell, Terry L. Hunt, and Chris Gosden, "The Dimensions of Social Life in the Pacific—Human Diversity and the Myth of the Primitive Isolate," *Current Anthropology* 38, no. 2 (April 1997): 155–95.

19. Wolf, *Europe,* 91.

20. Van der Pijl, *Nomads, Empires, States,* chap. 1.

21. One exploration of the elements of such "household pooling" can be found in Vu Tuan Anh,
Tran Thi Van Anh, and Terry G. McGee, "Household Economy under Impacts of Economic Reforms
in Viet Nam," 103–13, in *Socioeconomic Renovation in Viet Nam—The Origin, Evolution, and Impact of
Doi Moi,* ed. Peter Boothroyd and Pham Xuan Nam (Ottawa, Canada: International Development
Research Centre, 2000), at www.idrc.ca/openebooks/318-6/ (accessed February 7, 2008).

22. Robert D. Putnam, *Bowling Alone: The Collapse and Revival of American Community* (New
York: Simon and Schuster, 2000); Francis Fukuyama, *Trust: Social Virtues and the Creation of Prosperity* (New York: Free Press, 1995).

23. Putnam, *Bowling Alone,* 19.

24. Fukuyama, *Trust*.

25. Wolf, *Europe*, 79–88.

26. Feudalism lasted much longer in Eastern Europe and in Russia than in the West; serfs were not emancipated in Russia until the nineteenth century, while novels such as Thomas Hardy's *Tess of the d'Urbervilles* take place in a nineteenth-century Britain where tattered remnants of feudal relations were still visible in rural areas. Feudal relations continue to exist in some parts of the developing world.

27. Ruth Benedict, *The Chrysanthemum and the Sword: Patterns of Japanese Culture* (Boston: Houghton Mifflin, 1946).

28. Daniel Chirot and Anthony Reid, eds., *Essential Outsiders: Chinese and Jews in the Modern Transformation of Southeast Asia and Central Europe* (Seattle: University of Washington Press, 1997).

29. Ellen Meiksins Wood, *The Origins of Capitalism: A Longer View* (London: Verso, 2002), chap. 5. Also Barrington Moore Jr., *Social Origins of Dictatorship and Democracy: Lord and Peasant in the Modern World* (Boston: Beacon Press, 1966), chap. 1.

30. Christopher Dyer, *Making a Living in the Middle Ages: The People of Britain 850–1520* (New Haven, Conn.: Yale University Press, 2003).

31. In *An Inquiry into the Nature and Causes of the Wealth of Nations* (aka, *The Wealth of Nations* [1776], chap. 1), Adam Smith offered the famous parable of the pin factory:

> To take an example, therefore, from a very trifling manufacture; but one in which the division of labour has been very often taken notice of, the trade of the pin-maker. . . . One man draws out the wire, another straights it, a third cuts it, a fourth points it, a fifth grinds it at the top for receiving the head; to make the head requires two or three distinct operations; to put it on, is a peculiar business, to whiten the pins is another; it is even a trade by itself to put them into the paper; and the important business of making a pin is, in this manner, divided into about eighteen distinct operations. . . . Ten persons, therefore, could make among them upwards of forty-eight thousand pins in a day. . . . But if they had all wrought separately and independently, and without any of them having been educated to this peculiar business, they certainly could not each of them have made twenty, perhaps not one pin in a day.

32. A fascinating discussion of long-distance noncapitalist trade can be found in Amitav Ghosh, *In an Antique Land* (New York: Knopf, 1993).

33. This "labor theory of surplus value" is disputed by neoclassical economists, who argue that the value of any good is set merely by the local prevailing wage plus other variable and fixed costs. Profit represents the risk premium to capital and has no relationship to the value of labor inputs.

34. See, for example, Tim Di Muzio, "The 'Art' of Colonisation: Capitalising Sovereign Power and the Ongoing Nature of Primitive Accumulation," *New Political Economy* 12, no. 4 (December 2007): 517–39.

35. This practice is discussed in detail by Ramachandra Guha, *The Unquiet Woods: Ecological Change and Peasant Resistance in the Himalaya* (Berkeley: University of California Press, 2000; expanded edition). Another example of primitive accumulation is visible in the TV series *The Sopranos*, which offers the "deal you can't refuse."

36. This would be the case even if the fruit were obtained for free, since there are costs involved in transport, time, and building and operating the stand.

37. See, for example, Vance Packard, *The Hidden Persuaders* (New York: McCay, 1957); Michael Dawson, *The Consumer Trap: Big Business in American Life* (Urbana: University of Illinois Press, 2003).

38. Dawson, *Consumer Trap*.

39. This, however, is changing. The middle classes of India and China are estimated to be in the range of 200–300 million each; the 2008 rollout of the Tata Nano, a $2,500/100,000 rupee car likely to outsell foreign competitors is indicative of rapidly growing demand in both countries.

40. Gary Rivlin, "In Silicon Valley, Millionaires Who Don't Feel Rich," *New York Times*, August 5, 2007, at www.nytimes.com/2007/08/05/technology/05rich.html?scp=1&sq=silicon+valley+millionaires&st=nyt (accessed February 7, 2008).

41. Michael Pollan, *In Defense of Food: An Eater's Manifesto* (New York: Penguin, 2008).

42. Mark Rupert, *Producing Hegemony: The Politics of Mass Production and American Global Power* (Cambridge: Cambridge University Press, 1995).

43. As producers of the archetypal Fordist product, even the Ford Motor Company found it impossible to continue producing only black Model Ts. The General Motors Company began to sell different models of cars, in a range of colors, and with a variety of optional features. GM rapidly became the largest of many American automobile companies (of which there are only three left today), and Ford never managed to reclaim its dominance.

44. On the Great Depression, see Studs Terkel, *Hard Times* (New York: Pantheon, 1970) and Amity Shales, *The Forgotten Man: A New History of the Great Depression* (New York: HarperCollins, 2007).

45. Fred L. Block, *The Origins of International Economic Disorder: A Study of United States International Monetary Policy from World War II to the Present* (Berkeley: University of California Press, 1977).

46. Robert A. Pollard, *Economic Security and the Origins of the Cold War, 1945–1950* (New York: Columbia University Press, 1985); Ronnie D. Lipschutz, *When Nations Clash: Raw Materials, Ideology and Foreign Policy* (New York: Ballinger/Harper and Row, 1989).

47. Rupert, *Producing Hegemony*.

48. James R. Kurth, "The Political Consequences of the Product Cycle: Industrial History and Political Outcomes," *International Organization* 33, no. 1 (Winter 1979): 1–34.

49. Rupert, *Producing Hegemony*; also Leo Panitch, "The New Imperial State," *New Left Review* (March–April 2000): 5–20; Maier, *Among Empires*, chaps. 5–6.

50. Joseph Schumpeter, "The Process of Creative Destruction," in *Capitalism, Socialism, and Democracy* (New York: Harper and Row, 1975), 81–86; Katherine Boo, "The Churn: Creative Destruction in a Border Town," *New Yorker*, March 29, 2004, at www.newyorker.com/printable/?fact/040329fa_fact (accessed July 21, 2004); David Harvey, "Neoliberalism as Creative Destruction," *Annals of the American Academy of Political and Social Science* 610 (March 2007): 22–44.

51. Jonathan Nitzan and Shimshon Bichler, *The Global Political Economy of Israel* (London: Pluto Press, 2002).

52. See Ronnie D. Lipschutz, *After Authority: War, Peace and Global Politics in the 21st Century* (Albany, N.Y.: SUNY Press, 2000), chap. 2; also Kurth, "Political Consequences."

53. Mary Kaldor, *The Imaginary War: Understanding the East-West Conflict* (Oxford: Blackwell, 1990).

54. For an undertheorized discussion of this transformation, see Lipschutz, *After Authority*, chap. 2. A more detailed analysis can be found in Enrico Augelli and Craig Murphy, *America's Quest for Supremacy and the Third World: A Gramscian Analysis* (London: Pinter, 1988).

55. Boo, "The Churn"; Katherine Boo, "The Best Job in Town," *New Yorker*, July 5, 2004, 54–69; Karen Chapple, "Just-in-Time Intervention: Economic Development Policy for Apparel Manufacturing in San Francisco," *Economic Development Quarterly* 13, no. 1 (1999): 78–96.

56. For a historical discussion of this process, see Kurth, "Political Consequences"; Robert H. McGuckin, "Can Manufacturing Survive in Advanced Countries?" *Executive Action* (Conference Board) 93 (March 2004), at www.conference_board.org/pdf_free/EAReports/A_0093_04_EA .pdf (accessed July 26, 2004).

57. It no longer makes sense to speak simply of rich and poor countries. Within the former, there are growing numbers of poor and immigrants who, while not so badly off as their counterparts in the developing countries, have only limited access to goods and services. Within the latter, there are growing numbers of rich and powerful who, while not so well off as their counterparts in the industrialized countries, have high levels of access to goods and services. The term "Global South" recognizes that poverty is a structural phenomenon of global extent.

58. Boo, "The Best Job in Town." For a discussion of the benefits of such work, see Naila Kabeer, "Globalization, Labor Standards, and Women's Rights," *Feminist Economics* 10, no. 1 (March 2004): 3–35.

59. These billions do not have enough income to constitute much of a market for high-priced goods, so they tend to be ignored by companies that don't sell relatively inexpensive products (such as sodas and cigarettes). For a contrary view, see C. K. Prahalad and Allan Hammond, "Serving the World's Poor, Profitably," *Harvard Business Review* (September 2002): 4–11.

60. See, for example, John C. Cross, *Informal Politics: Street Vendors and the State in Mexico City* (Palo Alto, Calif.: Stanford University Press, 1998), chap. 4; Carolyn Nordstrom, "Shadows and Sovereigns," *Theory, Culture & Society* 17, no. 4 (2000): 35–54.

61. Stephen Gill, "Globalization, Market Civilization and Disciplinary Neo-Liberalism," in *Power and Resistance in the New World Order*, ed. Henk Overbeek (Houndsmill, Basingstoke: Palgrave Macmillan), 116–42; also Henk Overbeek, *Restructuring Hegemony in the Global Political Economy* (London: Routledge, 1993).

62. H. W. Arndt, "The 'Trickle-down' Myth," *Economic Development and Cultural Change* 32, no. 1 (October 1983): 1–10.

63. Joseph Kahn and David Barboza, "China Passes a Sweeping Labor Law," *New York Times*, June 30, 2007, at www.nytimes.com/2007/06/30/business/worldbusiness/30chlabor.html?sq= China (accessed June 30, 2007).

64. See Lipschutz, *Global Environmental Politics*, 63–68.

65. Boo, "The Churn" and "Best Job in Town."

66. NOW, "Benefits Denied," broadcast February 15, 2008, available at www.pbs.org/ now/shows/407/index.html (accessed February 15, 2008).

67. This also happens to musicians; in the San Francisco Bay Area, musicians may perform in as many as six orchestras, and these itinerants have come to be known as the "Freeway Philharmonic." See Joshua Kosman, "Freelance Musicians Have Violins, Will Travel," *San Francisco Chronicle*, January 26, 2008, at www.sfgate.com/cgi-bin/article.cgi?f=/c/a/2008/01/26/ MN81UJJ13.DTL&feed=rss.classical (accessed February 14, 2008). On "casual academic labor," see Ben Johnson and Tom McCarthy, "Casual Labor and the Future of the Academy," *NEA Higher Education Journal—Thought and Action* (Summer 2000): 107–20, at www2.nea.org/he/heta00/ images/s00p107.pdf (accessed February 14, 2008).

68. The classic expression of this dilemma is John Steinbeck, *The Grapes of Wrath* (New York: Viking, 1939). See also Jan Bremen and Ravi Agarwal, "Down and Out: Laboring under Global Capitalism," *Critical Asian Studies* 34, no. 1 (2002): 116–28.

69. Juliet B. Schor, "Prices and Quantities: Unsustainable Consumption and the Global Economy," *Ecological Economics* 55 (2005): 309–20.

70. J. Gary Taylor and Patricia J. Scharlin, *Smart Alliance: How a Global Corporation and Environmental Activists Transformed a Tarnished Brand* (New Haven, Conn.: Yale University Press, 2004); Edmund Conway, "Battle Lines Draw for Banana Wars Two," *money.telegraph.co.uk*, July 3, 2004, at www.telegraph.co.uk/money/main.jhtml?xml=/money/2004/07/03/ccban03.xml&s Sheet/ money/2004/07/03/ixcoms.html (accessed July 22, 2004).

71. Amartya Sen, "How to Judge Globalism," *American Prospect*, January 1, 2002, at www .prospect.org/print/V13/1/sen-a.html (accessed July 22, 2004). See also Amartya Sen, *Development as Freedom* (New York: Knopf, 1999).

72. Amartya Sen, "Food for Thought," *Guardian*, March 31, 2001, at www.guardian .co.uk/ saturday_review/story/0,3605,465796,00.html (accessed July 22, 2004).

73. Drahos, *Information Feudalism*.

74. Karl Polanyi, *The Great Transformation* (1944; repr., Boston: Beacon, 2001). It is also useful to distinguish between the "real" economy, in which we live our everyday lives, and the "virtual" economy, a real of speculation, corruption, spectacular profits and even more spectacular losses. Unfortunately, as is evident in the 2007–08 "mortgage meltdown," the bursting of a speculative bubble in the virtual economy has ramifications for the real economy that are quite serious and widespread.

75. Giddens, *Consequences of Modernity*.

Chapter 5: People and States

1. See, for example, Benedict Anderson, *Imagined Communities: Reflections on the Origins and Spread of Nationalism*, rev. ed. (London: Verso, 1991); Perry Anderson, *Lineages of the Absolutist State* (London: NLB, 1974); Basil Davidson, *The Black Man's Burden: Africa and the Curse of the Nation-State* (New York: Times Books, 1992); Hendrik Spruyt, *The Sovereign State and Its Competitors: An Analysis*

of Systems Change (Princeton, N.J.: Princeton University Press, 1994); Charles Tilly, "War Making and State Making as Organized Crime," in *Bringing the State Back In*, ed. Peter B. Evans, Dietrich Rueschemeyer, and Theda Skoçpol (New York: Cambridge University Press, 1985): 169–91; Charles Tilly, *Coercion, Capital and European States: AD 990–1992*, rev. ed. (Cambridge: Blackwell, 1992); Kenneth Waltz, *Theory of International Politics* (Reading, Mass.: Addison-Wesley, 1979); Ricardo Soares de Oliveira, *Oil and Politics in the Gulf of Guinea* (New York: Columbia University Press, 2007).

2. United Press International, "Vermont Town Decries Security Changes," August 24, 2008, at www.upi.com/Top_News/2008/08/24/Vermont_town_decries_security_changes/UPI-10471219609054/ (accessed September 13, 2008).

3. This outline of the change from the ancient to the medieval world comes from Henri Pirenne, *Mohammed and Charlemagne* (Mineola, N.Y.: Dover, 2001).

4. María Rosa Menocal, *The Ornament of the World: How Muslims, Jews, and Christians Created a Culture of Tolerance in Medieval Spain* (Boston: Little, Brown, 2002).

5. Thomas Cahill, *How the Irish Saved Civilization: The Untold Story of Ireland's Heroic Role from the Fall of Rome to the Rise of Medieval Europe* (New York: Doubleday, 1996).

6. Pirenne, *Mohammed and Charlemagne*, 235.

7. Charles Petit-Dutaillis, *The Feudal Monarchy in France and England from the Tenth to the Thirteenth Century*, trans. E. D. Hunt (New York: Harper Torchbooks, 1964). For a brief sketch of the struggles of the heirs of Louis the Pious, see Stuart Airlie, "Private Bodies and the Body Politic in the Divorce Case of Lothar II," *Past and Present* 161 (November 1998): 5–6.

8. Lucette Valensi, *The Birth of the Despot: Venice and the Sublime Porte*, trans. Arthur Denner (Ithaca, N.Y.: Cornell University Press, 1993); Lisa Jardine and Jerry Brotton, *Global Interests: Renaissance Art between East and West* (Ithaca, N.Y.: Cornell University Press, 2000).

9. Leo Braudy, *From Chivalry to Terrorism: War and the Changing Nature of Masculinity* (New York: Knopf, 2003), 59.

10. Barbara Tuchman, *A Distant Mirror: The Calamitous Fourteenth Century* (New York: Ballentine Books, 1987). Janet L. Abu-Lughod traces the spread of plague along fourteenth-century trade routes in *Before European Hegemony: The World System A.D. 1250–1350* (New York: Oxford University Press, 1989), esp. map on 173. Earlier epidemics also have been traced to trade and war—see, for example, Pirenne, *Mohammed and Charlemagne*, 95–96.

11. Joseph Strayer, *On the Medieval Origins of the Modern State* (Princeton, N.J.: Princeton University Press, 1970), 26–41.

12. Michael Herb, "Taxation and Representation," *Studies in Comparative International Development* 38, no. 3 (Fall 2003): 3–31.

13. Jardine and Brotton, *Global Interests*.

14. Abu-Lughod, *Before European Hegemony*, 181.

15. Abu-Lughod, *Before European Hegemony*, 59.

16. Aziz al-Azmeh, *Muslim Kingship: Power and the Sacred in Muslim, Christian and Pagan Politics* (London: I. B. Tauris, 1997).

17. William Cobbett, *History of the Protestant Reformation in England and Ireland* (Rockford, Ill.: TAN Books, 1988).

18. For the story of this interesting parallel to the more recent clash between (king) Bill Clinton and (archbishop) Kenneth Starr, see Airlie, "Private Bodies and the Body Politic."

19. This process is described by James C. Scott in *Seeing Like a State: How Certain Schemes to Improve the Human Condition Have Failed* (New Haven, Conn.: Yale University Press, 1998).

20. Donna J. Guy, "'White Slavery,' Citizenship and Nationality in Argentina," in *Nationalisms and Sexualities*, ed. Andrew Parker, Mary Russo, Doris Sommer, and Patricia Yaeger (New York: Routledge, 1992), 201–17.

21. Robert Frost, "The Death of the Hired Man," *Collected Poems of Robert Frost* (New York: Halcyon House, 1939).

22. Carolyn Bynum, *Holy Feast, Holy Fast: The Religious Significance of Food to Medieval Women* (Berkeley: University of California Press, 1987); W. J. Sheils and Diana Wood, eds., *Women in the Church, Studies in Church History*, vol. 27 (Oxford: Oxford University Press, 1990).

23. Braudy, *From Chivalry to Terrorism*, 63–80.

24. Isaiah Berlin, "Two Concepts of Liberty," in *Four Essays on Liberty* (Oxford: Oxford University Press, 1969), 118–72.

25. C. B. Macpherson, *The Political Theory of Possessive Individualism: Hobbes to Locke* (Oxford: Oxford University Press, 1964).

26. Karl Polanyi, *The Great Transformation* (1944; New York: Farrar and Rinehart, 2001).

27. Adam Smith, *An Inquiry into the Nature and Causes of the Wealth of Nations* (Edinburgh, 1776).

28. Early factory owners did provide housing for their mostly young female employees—if they had not, their parents would not have allowed them to work. But employer-provided housing is a trap. "Rent" accumulates, like debt at company stores, racking up interest charges that make it impossible for workers to try their luck elsewhere. This situation is called "debt peonage." It lasted well into the twentieth century in the United States. For example, see Linda Gordon, *The Great Arizona Orphan Abduction* (Cambridge, Mass.: Harvard University Press, 1999).

29. Polanyi, *The Great Transformation*. Americans are familiar with the result of dismantling government services such as federal supervision of lending practices, which resulted in the subprime loan debacle, and consumer products inspections whose elimination allowed the importation of lead-contaminated toys.

30. Robert N. Bellah, "American Civil Religion," in *American Civil Religion*, ed. R. E. Richey and D. G. Jones (New York: Harper, 1974), 255–72.

31. Garry Wills, *Under God: Religion and Politics in America* (New York: Simon and Schuster, 1990).

32. Cynthia Weber, *Simulating Sovereignty: Intervention, the State and Symbolic Exchange* (Cambridge: Cambridge University Press, 1995).

33. The growth of mercenary military forces is viewed with alarm by people who see state sovereignty as protective as well as coercive. For several perspectives on this issue, see P. W. Singer, *Corporate Warriors: The Rise of the Privatized Military Industry* (Ithaca, N.Y.: Cornell University Press, 2003); Patrick Radden Keefe, "Iraq: America's Private Armies," *New York Review of Books* August 12, 2004, 48–50; Jeremy Scahill, *Blackwater: The Rise of the World's Most Powerful Mercenary Army* (New York: Nation Books, 2007); and Braudy, *From Chivalry to Terrorism*. See also the last section in this chapter.

34. Robert Jackson, *Quasi-states: Sovereignty, International Relations and the Third World* (Cambridge: Cambridge University Press, 1990).

35. Jackson, *Quasi-states*; also Václav Havel, "Kosovo and the End of the Nation-State," trans. Paul Wilson, *New York Review of Books,* June 10, 1999, 4, 6.

36. Weber, *Simulating Sovereignty*.

37. Havel, "Kosovo and the End of the Nation-State."

38. T. H. Marshall,"Citizenship and Social Class," in *"Citizenship and Social Class" and Other Essays* (Cambridge: Cambridge University Press, 1950), 1–85.

39. Kurt Burch, *"Property" and the Making of the International System* (Boulder, Colo.: Lynne Rienner, 1998).

40. Immanuel Kant, "Perpetual Peace: A Philosophical Sketch," 1795, at www.mtholyoke.edu/acad/intrel/kant/kant1.htm (accessed January 4, 2008).

41. Richard Newhauser, *The Early History of Greed* (Cambridge: Cambridge University Press, 2000); also Albert O. Hirschman, *The Passions and the Interests: Political Arguments for Capitalism before its Triumph*, 20th anniversary ed. (Princeton, N.J.: Princeton University Press, 1997).

42. Tilly, "War Making and State Making"; also John Brewer, *War, Money and the English State, 1688–1783* (New York: HarperCollins, 1989); James MacDonald, *A Free Nation, Deep in Debt: The Financial Roots of Democracy* (New York: Farrar, Straus and Giroux, 2003).

43. Michael Walzer, *Revolution of the Saints* (Cambridge, Mass.: Harvard University Press, 1965); also Weber, *The Protestant Ethic*.

44. Mary Ann Tétreault, "Pleasant Dreams: The WTO as Kuwait's Holy Grail," *Critique: Critical Middle Eastern Studies* 12, no. 1 (Spring 2003): 75–93.

45. Peter J. Taylor, *Modernities: A Geohistorical Interpretation* (Minneapolis: University of Minnesota Press, 1999); Harold James, *The End of Globalization: Lessons from the Great Depression*

(Cambridge, Mass.: Harvard University Press, 2001). For a discussion of sensitivity and vulnerability, see Robert O. Keohane and Joseph S. Nye, *Power and Interdependence: World Politics in Transition* (Boston: Little, Brown, 1977), 11–19.

46. James, *End of Globalization*; Richard Rosecrance, *The Rise of the Trading State: Commerce and Conquest in the Modern World* (New York: Basic Books, 1987); Thomas Freedman, *The World Is Flat: A Brief History of the Twenty-first Century* (New York: Farrar, Straus and Giroux, 2006).

47. For example, Naomi Klein, *The Shock Doctrine: The Rise of Disaster Capitalism* (New York: Metropolitan Books, 2007).

48. Susan Strange, *The Retreat of the State: The Diffusion of Power in the World Economy* (Cambridge: Cambridge University Press, 1996); Ronen Palan, *The Offshore World: Sovereign Markets, Virtual Places, and Nomad Millionaires* (Ithaca, N.Y.: Cornell University Press, 2006).

49. Jackson, *Quasi-states*, chap. 2.

50. William Reno, *Warlord Politics and African States* (Boulder, Colo.: Lynne Rienner, 1999), esp. chap. 3.

51. Jill Crystal, *Oil and Politics in the Gulf: Rulers and Merchants in Kuwait and Qatar* (New York: Cambridge University Press, 1990); Michael Herb, *All in the Family: Absolutism, Revolution, and Democracy in the Middle Eastern Monarchies* (Albany, N.Y.: SUNY Press, 1999).

52. For African examples, see Jean-François Bayart, Stephen Ellis, and Béatrice Hibou, *The Criminalization of the State in Africa* (Bloomington: Indiana University Press, 1999). The concept of protected spaces is developed in Mary Ann Tétreault, "Civil Society in Kuwait: Protected Spaces and Women's Rights," *Middle East Journal* 47, no. 2 (Spring 1993): 178–91.

53. Misha Glenny, "The Age of the Parastate," *New Yorker,* May 8, 1995, 45–49, 52–53.

54. For a detailed examination of post-Saddam Iraq see Ali Allawi, *The Occupation of Iraq: Winning the War, Losing the Peace* (New Haven, Conn.: Yale University Press, 2007).

55. Clea Koff, *The Bone Woman: A Forensic Anthropologist's Search for Truth in the Mass Graves of Rwanda, Bosnia, Croatia, and Kosovo* (New York: Random House, 2004), 262.

56. Separatist movements are discussed in the following: Economist Intelligence Unit, "A Crucial Year at the Polls for Europe's Separatists," *Economist Intelligence Unit ViewsWire,* March 1, 2007, at www.economist.com/agenda/displaystory.cfm?story_id=8780153 (accessed January 7, 2008); Anthony Brown, "There Is a Massive Political and Economic Imbalance between England [and Scotland]," *The Sunday Herald,* November 4, 2007, at findarticles.com/p/articles/mi_qn4156/is_20071104/ai_n21088465 (accessed January 7, 2008); Andrew Rettman, "Kosovo Issue Inflaming Separatism in EU Neighbours," *EU Observer,* February 24, 2006, at www.iiss.org/whats-new/iiss-in-the-press/press-coverage-2006/february-2006/kosovo-issue-inflaming-separatism (accessed January 7, 2008); Gary J. Bass, "Independence Daze," *New York Times Magazine,* January 6, 2008, 28.

57. See Clive Thompson, "Can You Count On These Machines?" *New York Times Magazine,* January 6, 2008, 40–47, 68–71.

58. The first sustained critique along these lines is Polanyi, *The Great Transformation*. More recent ones can be found in Leo Panitch, Colin Leys, Alan Zuege, and Martijn Konings, eds., *The Globalization Decade: A Critical Reader* (New Delhi: Aakar Books, 2006). A gentle version is Joseph E. Stiglitz, *Globalization and Its Discontents* (New York: Norton, 2002).

59. Ronan Palan, "Tax Havens and the Commercialization of State Sovereignty," *International Organization* 56, no. 1 (Winter 2002): 151–76; Jim Morris, "'Flags of Convenience' Give Owners a Paper Refuge," *Houston Chronicle,* August 21, 1996, at www.chron.com/content/interactive/special/maritime/96/08/22/part5.html (accessed January 7, 2008).

60. John Keane, "Despotism and Democracy: The Origins and Development of the Distinction between Civil Society and the State, 1750–1850," in *Civil Society and the State,* ed. John Keane (London: Verso, 1988), 35–71; Alejandro Cólas, *International Civil Society: Social Movements in World Politics* (Cambridge, U.K.: Polity, 2002); Mary Kaldor, *Global Civil Society: An Answer to War* (Cambridge, U.K.: Polity, 2003); for a cautionary note, see Ronnie D. Lipschutz, with James K. Rowe, *Globalization, Governmentality and Global Politics—Regulation for the Rest of Us?* (London: Routledge, 2005).

61. Niall Ferguson, *The House of Rothschild: Money's Prophets, 1798–1848* (New York: Penguin, 1999); Herman M. Schwartz, *States Versus Markets: History, Geography, and the Development of International Political Economy,* 2nd ed. (New York: St. Martin's, 2000).

62. Edmund S. Morgan, "America's First Great Man," *New York Review of Books,* June 12, 1997, at www.nybooks.com/articles/1161 (accessed January 4, 2008). Also, Richard S. Dunn and Laetitia Yeandle, eds., *The Journal of John Winthrop, 1630–1649* (Cambridge, Mass.: Belknap, 1996), and Edmund S. Morgan, *The Puritan Dilemma: The Story of John Winthrop* (Boston: Little, Brown, 1958).

63. John Winthrop, quoted in Morgan, "America's First Great Man."

64. J. G. A. Pocock, ed., *Three British Revolutions, 1641, 1688, 1776* (Princeton, N.J.: Princeton University Press, 1980); Jack A. Goldstone, "The English Revolution: A Structural-Demographic Approach," in *Revolutions: Theoretical, Comparative, and Historical Studies,* ed. Jack A. Goldstone (New York: Harcourt, Brace, Jovanovich, 1986), 88–104; Lawrence Stone, "The Revolution over the Revolution," *New York Review of Books,* June 11, 1992, at www.nybooks.com/articles/article-preview?article_id=2894 (accessed January 4, 2008).

65. Colás, *International Civil Society.*

66. Aryeh Neier, *Taking Liberties: Four Decades in the Struggle for Rights* (New York: Public Affairs, 2003); Abigail Abrash, "Let Freedom Ring: Recharging and Consolidating 'Inside the Beltway' Activism," in *Partial Truths and the Politics of Community,* ed. Mary Ann Tétreault and Robin L. Teske (Columbia: University of South Carolina Press, 2003), 211–37; Michael Ignatieff, "The Rights Stuff," *New York Review of Books,* June 13, 2002, at www.nybooks.com/articles/article-preview?article_id=15465 (accessed January 4, 2008).

67. Ignatieff, "The Rights Stuff."

68. Zafar Bangash, "The Many Fronts of the West's War on Islam," *Media Monitors Network,* January 4, 2008, at usa.mediamonitors.net/content/view/full/48675 (accessed January 4, 2008).

69. Mark Danner, *Torture and Truth: America, Abu Ghraib, and the War on Terror* (New York: New York Review Books, 2004); Mark Danner, "We Are All Torturers Now," *New York Times,* January 6, 2005, at www.nytimes.com/2005/01/06/opinion/06danner.html?_r=1&oref=slogin (accessed January 4, 2008); Jack Goldsmith, *The Terror Presidency: Law and Judgment Inside the Bush Administration* (New York: Norton, 2007); Alfred W. McCoy, "Torture in the Crucible of Counterinsurgency," in *Iraq and the Lessons of Vietnam: Or How **Not** to Learn from the Past,* ed. Lloyd C. Gardner and Marilyn B. Young (New York: New Press, 2007), 230–62.

70. Charlie Savage, *Takeover: The Return of the Imperial Presidency and the Subversion of American Democracy* (Boston: Little, Brown, 2007).

71. For plenty of examples, see any issue of the *World Development Report,* an annual publication of the United Nations. Also, Gilbert Rist, *The History of Development: From Western Origins to Global Faith,* trans. Patrick Camiller (London: Zed Books, 1997); Amartya Sen, *Underdevelopment as Freedom* (New York: Doubleday Anchor, 2000); and Ronnie D. Lipschutz with James K. Rowe, *Globalization, Governmentality and Global Politics: Regulation for the Rest of Us?* (New York: Routledge, 2005).

72. Kevin Phillips, *Wealth and Democracy: A Political History of the American Rich* (New York: Broadway Books, 2002).

73. Phillips, *Wealth and Democracy.*

74. In her book on global climate change, Elizabeth Kolbert looks at the influence of big energy companies on Bush administration environmental policy—see *Field Notes from a Catastrophe* (New York: Bloomsbury USA, 2006). Both the executive and Congress protect industrial agriculture at the expense of the health of Americans—see Michael Pollan, *The Omnivore's Dilemma: A Natural History of Four Meals* (New York: Penguin, 2006).

75. For information on the work of these organizations, check their websites: www.amnesty.org/ and fp.arizona.edu/mesassoc//cafmena.htm (both accessed January 4, 2008).

76. Singer, *Corporate Warriors.* On costs, see, for example, Bill Buzenberg, "Bagdad Bonanza," Center for Public Integrity, n.d., at www.publicintegrity.org/WOWII/ (accessed March 15, 2008); Walter Pincus, "U.S. Pays Steep Price for Private Security in Iraq," *Washington Post,* October 1, 2007, at www.washingtonpost.com/wp-dyn/content/article/2007/09/30/AR2007093001352.html (accessed March 15, 2008).

77. For a *New York Times* bibliography on military contracting in general, see topics.nytimes
.com/top/reference/timestopics/subjects/p/private_military_companies/index.html?8qa; for
one specializing in stories about Blackwater, see topics.nytimes.com/top/news/business/
companies/blackwater_usa/index.html?inline=nyt-org (both accessed January 4, 2008).

78. See, for example, Justin Rood, "Pentagon Won't Probe KBR Rape Charges," *ABC News*, January 8, 2008, at abcnews.go.com/Blotter/story?id=4099514&page=1 (accessed January 9, 2008).

79. John M. Broder and James Risen, "Armed Guards in Iraq Occupy a Legal Limbo," *New York
Times*, September 20, 2007, at www.nytimes.com/2007/09/20/world/middleeast/20blackwater
.html?pagewanted=print; and Elizabeth Newell, "House Backs Expansion of Law Governing
Wartime Contractors," *GovernmentExecutive.com*, October 4, 2007, at www.govexec.com/
dailyfed/1007/100407e1.htm (both accessed January 4, 2008).

80. Richard Harding, *Private Prisons and Public Accountability* (New Brunswick, N.J.: Transaction Publishers, 1997); Douglas McDonald et al., "Private Prisons in the United States," Executive
Summary (Cambridge, Mass.: Abt Associates, July 16, 1998), at www.abtassociates.com/
reports/ES-priv-report.pdf (accessed January 6, 2008); Education Week Research Center, "Charter Schools," *Education Week*, n.d., at www.edweek.org/rc/issues/charter-schools/ (accessed January 6, 2008); Andrew MacCloud, "Welfare Reform's Public-Private Partnerships," *The Tyee.ca*,
July 13, 2004, at thetyee.ca/News/2004/07/13/Welfare_Reforms_Public-Private_Partnerships/
(accessed January 6, 2008).

81. Janine R. Wedel, *Collision and Collusion: The Strange Case of Western Aid to Eastern Europe,
1989–1998* (New York: St. Martin's Press, 1998).

82. Tony Allison, "Enron's Eight-Year Power Struggle in India: Special Report," *Asia Times*, January 18, 2001, at www.atimes.com/reports/CA13Ai01.html (accessed January 6, 2008; Richard Ripley, "Enron's Fallout Hits Avista," *Spokane Journal of Business*, April 5, 2002, at www.spokanejournal
.com/index.php?id=article&sub=96&keyword= (accessed January 6, 2008). These shady arrangements have not disappeared. See Floyd Norris, "Securities, in a Swoon, Come Home," *New York
Times*, January 4, 2008, C1, C6.

83. Souphala Chomsisengphet and Anthony Pennington-Cross, "The Evolution of the Subprime Mortgage Market," *Federal Reserve Bank of St. Louis Review*, January/February 2006, at research.stlouisfed.org/publications/review/06/01/ChomPennCross.pdf (accessed January 6,
2008); Ruth Simon, James R. Hagerty, and James T. Areddy, "Housing-Bubble Talk Doesn't Scare Off
Foreigners," *Wall Street Journal*, August 24, 2005, 1; Gretchen Morgenson, "Investors in Mortgage-Backed Securities Fail to React to Market Plunge," *International Herald Tribune*, February 18, 2007, at
www.iht.com/articles/2007/02/18/yourmoney/morgenson.php (accessed January 6, 2008).

84. On the lack of transparency in public-private partnerships see, for example, Steven
Rathgeb Smith, "Hybrid Organizations and the Diversification of Policy Tools: The Governance
Challenge" (paper prepared for delivery at the biennial meeting of the Public Management Research Association conference, Tucson, Ariz., October 26–27, 2007).

85. Anne Farris, Richard P. Nathan, and David J. Wright, "The Expanding Administrative Presidency: George W. Bush and the Faith-Based Initiative," New York: Rockefeller Institute, August
2004, at www.religionandsocialpolicy.org/docs/policy/FB_Administrative_Presidency_
Report_10_08_04.pdf (accessed January 6, 2008). Religious partners are permitted to apply their
own standards to clients and employees, leading to proselytizing in prison ministries and such
matters as providing insurance that does not cover family planning services, denying employment to gay, lesbian, and transgendered persons, and denying employees equal protection under
U.S. civil rights laws.

86. Karen Ordahl Kupperman, *Indians and English: Facing Off in Early America* (Ithaca, N.Y.:
Cornell University Press, 2000)—but the natives did not give up without a fight. See Linda Colley, *Captives: The Story of Britain's Pursuit of Empire and How Its Soldiers and Civilians Were Held Captive by the Dream of Global Supremacy, 1600–1850* (New York: Pantheon, 2002).

87. Thomas Carothers, *U.S. Democracy Promotion During and After Bush* (Washington, D.C.:
Carnegie Endowment for International Peace, September 2007).

Chapter 6: People and Borders

1. As in the old quip, "The equator is an imaginary lion running around the earth."

2. William Mallinson, "US Interests, British Acquiescence and the Invasion of Cyprus," *British Journal of Politics and International Relations* 9, no. 3 (2007): 494–508.

3. Adamantia Pollis, "The Social Construction of Ethnicity and Nationality: The Case of Cyprus," *Nationalism and Ethnic Politics* 2, no. 1 (1996): 67–90.

4. *Civilization and Its Discontents*, ed. and trans. James Strachey (New York: Norton, 2005), 108.

5. *The American Heritage Dictionary of the English Language*, 4th ed. (Boston: Houghton Mifflin, 2000), at www.bartleby.com/61/6/R0120600.html (accessed July 15, 2008).

6. Margaret Gruter and Roger D. Masters, "Ostracism as a Social and Biological Phenomenon: An Introduction," *Ethology and Sociobiology* 7 (1986): 149–58.

7. Carl Schmitt, *Political Theology: Four Chapters on the Concept of Sovereignty* (Chicago: University of Chicago Press, 2006).

8. Irving Janis, *Groupthink: Psychological Studies of Policy Decisions and Fiascoes* (Boston: Houghton Mifflin, 1982); U.S. Senate, Select Committee on Intelligence, *Report on the U.S. Intelligence Community's Prewar Intelligence Assessments on Iraq*, July 7, 2004, 272–83, 357–65 (note that portions of the latter have been blacked out for security reasons), at intelligence.senate.gov/iraqreport2.pdf (accessed July 23, 2004).

9. Kees van der Pijl, *Nomads, Empires, States—Modes of Foreign Relations* (London: Pluto Press, 2007), esp. chaps. 1 and 2.

10. See Hillary Mayell, "Thousands of Women Killed for Family 'Honor,'" *National Geographic News*, February 12, 2002, at news.nationalgeographic.com/news/2002/02/0212_020212_honorkilling.html. Although these killings tend to take place in developing countries, places such as Germany and the United States, where such populations reside together, may also experience honor killing.

11. Eric R. Wolf, *Europe and the People without History* (Berkeley: University of California Press, 1982), chap. 3.

12. Van der Pijl notes that the exact borders we know today did not exist historically; see *Nomads, Empires, States*, chap. 3.

13. For example, Henry II of England married Eleanor of Aquitaine in 1152—their stories are quite complicated and worth looking up—giving him some degree of control over much of present-day France. In 1167, the two separated.

14. Among those in dispute are borders between Ethiopia and Eritrea; and in Kashmir, among India, China, and Pakistan. A few yet to be drawn may be found in the "empty quarter" of the Saudi peninsula.

15. See, for example, John Torpey, *The Invention of the Passport: Citizenship, Surveillance and the State* (Cambridge: Cambridge University Press, 2000); N. W. Sibley, "The Passport System," *Journal of the Society of Comparative Legislation*, New Series, 7, no. 1 (1906), 26–33, at www.jstor.org/stable/pdfplus/752152.pdf (accessed May 23, 2008).

16. George Katsiaficas, "Comparing the Paris Commune and the Gwangju Uprising," *New Political Science* 25, no. 2 (2006): 261–70.

17. James C. Scott, *Seeing Like a State: How Certain Schemes to Improve the Human Condition Have Failed* (New Haven, Conn.: Yale University Press, 1998).

18. Donna J. Guy, *White Slavery and Mothers Alive and Dead: The Troubled Meeting of Sex, Gender, Public Health and Progress in Latin America* (Lincoln: University of Nebraska Press, 2000); Rhacel Salazar Parreñas, *Servants of Globalization: Women, Migration and Domestic Work* (Stanford, Calif.: Stanford University Press, 2001); Dennis Altman, *Global Sex* (Chicago: University of Chicago Press, 2001).

19. Claudia Goldin, "The Political Economy of Immigration Restriction in the United States, 1890–1921," NBER Working Paper No. 4345, April 1993, at www.nber.org/papers/w4345.pdf ?new_window=1 (accessed June 9, 2008).

20. Kenichi Ohmae, *The End of the Nation State: The Rise of Regional Economies* (New York: The Free Press, 1995).

21. Paul Q. Hirst and Grahame Thompson, *Globalization in Question: The International Economy and the Possibilities of Governance,* 2nd ed. (Cambridge, U.K.: Polity, 2000).

22. Benedict Anderson, *Imagined Communities: Reflections on the Origins and Spread of Nationalism* (London: Verso, 1991).

23. See, for example, Chris Brown, "Borders and Identity in International Political Theory," in *Identities, Borders, Orders—Rethinking International Relations Theory,* ed. Mathias Albert, David Jacobson, and Yosef Lapid (Minneapolis: University of Minnesota Press, 2001), 117–36; Mary Bernstein, "Identity Politics," *Annual Review of Sociology* 31 (2005): 47–74.

24. See, for example, Beverly Crawford and Ronnie D. Lipschutz, eds., *The Myth of "Ethnic Conflict": Politics, Economics, and "Cultural" Violence* (Berkeley: UC Berkeley International and Area Studies Press, 1998); Philip Gourevitch, *We Wish to Inform You That Tomorrow We Will Be Killed with Our Families* (New York: Farrar, Straus and Giroux, 1998).

25. Eric Lipton, "Hurdles for High-Tech Efforts to Track Who Crosses Borders," *New York Times,* August 10, 2005, at www.nytimes.com/2005/08/10/politics/10biometrics.html (accessed August 8, 2005); Ronnie D. Lipschutz, "Imperial Warfare in the Naked City—Sociality as Critical Infrastructure," *International Political Sociology* 2, no. 3 (September 2008); on money laundering, see Raymond W. Baker, *Capitalism's Achilles Heel—Dirty Money and How to Renew the Free Market System* (New York: Wiley, 2005).

26. At this writing (June 2008), the price of oil has soared to unprecedented levels, while it is estimated that one in ten home mortgages in the United States are in or near foreclosure. Paul Krugman has offered a series of fairly pessimistic views of the global economy's near-term prospects; see *Conscience of a Liberal* (New York: Norton, 2007); "After the Money's Gone," *New York Times,* December 14, 2007, at www.nytimes.com/2007/12/14/opinion/ 14krugman.html?_r=1&ref=opinion& (accessed December 14, 2007); and "The B Word," *New York Times,* March 17, 2008, at www.nytimes.com/2008/03/17/opinion/17krugman.html? (accessed March 17, 2008). More recently, he has expressed some optimism that the "worst" might be over—but there are many good reasons to be skeptical of his prognostications.

27. In dollar terms, the U.S. economy totaled almost $13.5 trillion in 2006; the second largest national economy by this measure was Japan's at $4.9 trillion. As a unit, the EU's economy totaled $14.6 trillion in 2006, but only $11.8 trillion in terms of "purchasing power parity" (PPP; the comparable U.S. figure was $13.2 trillion). In 2006, China's economy came in third in terms of PPP, at $10.15 trillion. See World Bank, "Selected World Development Indicators," *Agriculture for Development—World Development Report 2008* (Washington, D.C.: World Bank Publications, 2007), 334–35, at siteresources.worldbank.org/INTWDR2008/Resources/2795087-1192112387976/WDR08_24_SWDI.pdf (accessed June 9, 2008).

28. Chalmers Johnson, *The Sorrows of Empire: Militarism, Secrecy, and the End of the Republic* (New York: Metropolitan Books, 2004), 24.

29. Matthew Paterson, *Consumption and Everyday Life* (London: Routledge, 2005).

30. Leslie Sklair, *The Transnational Capitalist Class* (Oxford: Blackwell, 2001).

31. See, for example, Somini Sengupta, "Inside Gate, India's Good Life; Outside, the Servants' Slums," *New York Times,* June 6, 2009, at www.nytimes.com/2008/06/09/world/asia/09gated.html? (accessed June 8, 2008).

32. According to Walker Conner, at least 90 percent of a state's population must be of a single ethnic group for it to qualify as an actual nation-state; see Walker Conner, *Ethnonationalism: The Quest for Understanding* (Princeton, N.J.: Princeton University Press, 1994).

33. Andre Gingrich, "Concepts of Race Vanishing, Movements of Racism Rising? Global Issues and Austrian Ethnography," *Ethnos* 69, no. 2 (June 2004): 156–76.

34. Charles Tilly, "War Making and State Making as Organized Crime," in *Bringing the State Back In,* ed. Peter B. Evans, Dietrich Rueschemeyer, and Theda Skoçpol (Cambridge: Cambridge University Press, 1985), 169–91.

35. Anderson, *Imagined Communities*.

36. The literature on the breakup of Yugoslavia is voluminous. A good starting point is Misha Glenny, *The Fall of Yugoslavia: The Third Balkan War* (London: Penguin, 1995).

37. Basil Davidson, *The Black Man's Burden: Africa and the Curse of the Nation-State* (New York: Times Books, 1992).

38. An interesting and current example of this can be found in the North–South peace agreement signed in 2005 by warring parties in the Sudan. This agreement specifies that, in 2011, the government of the southern region will conduct a referendum on secession and independence. See "The Implementation Modalities of the Protocol on Power Sharing, dated 26th May, 2004, Naivasha, Kenya, 31st December 2004," U.S. Institute of Peace, Peace Agreements Digital Collection, at www.usip.org/library/pa/sudan/cpa01092005/implementation_agreement.pdf (accessed June 9, 2008).

39. Beverly Crawford, "Explaining Defection from International Cooperation: Germany's Unilateral Recognition of Croatia," *World Politics* 48, no. 4 (1996): 482–521.

40. One of the best illustrations of these points can be seen in the case of Rwanda; one excellent history is Gérard Prunier, *The Rwanda Crisis—History of a Genocide* (New York: Columbia University Press, 1995); another is Romeo Dalliére, with Brent Beardsley, *Shake Hands with the Devil—The Failure of Humanity in Rwanda* (New York: Carroll & Graf, 2005).

41. Paul Magnarella, "Explaining Rwanda's 1994 Genocide," *Human Rights & Human Welfare* 2, no. 1 (Winter 2002): 25–34, at www.du.edu/gsis/hrhw/volumes/2002/2-1/magnarella2-1.pdf (accessed June 9, 2008); Gourevitch, *We Wish to Inform You That Tomorrow We Will Be Killed*.

42. Réne Lemarchand, *Burundi: Ethnic Conflict and Genocide* (Cambridge: Cambridge University Press, 1996); Alan J. Kuperman, "Provoking Genocide: A Revised History of the Rwandan Patriotic Front," *Journal of Genocide Research* 6, no. 1 (2004): 61–84. Apparently, there is some evidence that it was the mostly Tutsi Rwandan Patriotic Front that shot down the plane; see Réne Lemarchand, "Controversy within the Cataclysm," *African Studies Review* 50, no. 1 (2007): 140–44.

43. Gourevitch, *We Wish to Inform You That Tomorrow We Will Be Killed*; Mahmood Mamdani, *When Victims Become Killers: Colonialism, Nativism, and the Genocide in Rwanda* (Princeton, N.J.: Princeton University Press, 2001); Linda Melvern, *Conspiracy to Murder: The Rwandan Genocide* (London: Verso, 2004).

44. For an especially harrowing example see Peter Landesman, "A Woman's Work," *New York Times Magazine*, September 15, 2002, 82–89, 116, 125, 130, 132, 134. This article is about Pauline Nyiramasuhuko, Rwanda's minister of rape.

45. Jeff Weintraub and Krishnan Kumar, eds., *Public and Private in Thought and Practice: Perspectives on a Grand Dichotomy* (Chicago: University of Chicago Press, 1997).

46. Phillippe Ariès, Georges Duby, Michelle Perrot, and Arthur Goldhammer, *A History of Private Life—From the Fires of Revolution to the Great War, Volume IV* (Cambridge, Mass.: Belknap, Press, 2006).

47. Sandra Halperin, *In the Mirror of the Third World: Capitalist Development in Modern Europe* (Ithaca, N.Y.: Cornell University Press, 1997); Sandra Halperin, *War and Social Change in Modern Europe: The Great Transformation Revisited* (Cambridge: Cambridge University Press, 2004).

48. Emma Rothschild, "Adam Smith and the Invisible Hand," *The American Economic Review* 84, no. 2 (May 1994): 319–22; Friedrich A. von Hayek, "Economics and Knowledge," *Economica*, New Series, 4, no. 13 (February 1937): 33–54.

49. Boyd Hilton, *A Mad, Bad, and Dangerous People? England, 1783–1846* (Oxford: Oxford University Press, 2006).

50. To cite only one example: in 1832, the British Parliament passed the "Reform Act of 1832, which increased the size of the electorate by some 45 percent, a figure that seems less impressive when we realize that it still enfranchised only 4.7 percent of the population" (John Brewer, "England: The Big Change," *New York Review of Books* 55, no. 11, June 26, 2008.

51. Karl Polanyi, *The Great Transformation* (1944; Boston: Beacon, 2001); Halperin, *War and Social Change*.

52. For an interesting discussion of the fears of too much democracy in late nineteenth century Britain, see Matthew Beaumont, "Cacotopianism, The Paris Commune, and England's Anti-Communist Imaginary, 1870–1900," *English Literary History* 73 (2006): 465–87.

53. The classic debate along these lines took place between Alexander Hamilton and James Madison, pitting Federalists against Anti-Federalists. See Colleen A. Sheehan, "Madison v. Hamilton: The Battle Over Republicanism and the Role of Public Opinion," *American Political Science Review* 98, no. 3 (August 2004): 405–24; and Albert O. Hirschmann, *The Passions and the Interests: Political Arguments for Capitalism before Its Time* (Princeton, N.J.: Princeton University Press, 1997).

54. Garry Wills, *"Negro President": Jefferson and the Slave Power* (Boston: Houghton Mifflin, 2003).

55. Keller Morton, *Regulating a New Economy: Public Policy and Economic Change in America, 1900–1933* (Cambridge, Mass.: Harvard University Press, 1990). Today, rule by experts has replaced regulatory administration; see chap. 10, as well as Ulrich Beck, *Risk Society: Towards a New Modernity* (Beverly Hills, Calif.: Sage, 1992), and Timothy W. Luke, *Capitalism, Democracy, and Ecology: Departing from Marx* (Urbana: University of Illinois Press, 1999), chap. 2.

56. Deborah Avant, "The Privatization of Security and Change in the Control of Force," *International Studies Perspectives* 5, no. 2 (2004): 153–57; Peter W. Singer, *Corporate Warriors: The Rise of the Privatized Military Industry* (Ithaca, N.Y.: Cornell University Press, 2003).

57. Cheryl I. Harris, "Whiteness as Property," *Harvard Law Review* 106, no. 8 (June 1993): 1707–91; George Lipsitz, *The Possessive Investment in Whiteness: How White People Profit from Identity Politics* (Philadephia: Temple University Press, 2006).

58. See, for example, T. J. Bouchard et al., "Sources of Human Psychological Differences: The Minnesota Study of Twins Reared Apart," *Science* 250, no. 4978 (October 12, 1990): 223–28. Judith Butler addresses gender fluidity in *Gender Trouble: Feminism and the Subversion of Identity* (London: Routledge, 1990).

59. Jack Balkin, "The Constitution of Status," *Yale Law Journal* 106, no. 8 (June 1997): 2313–74.

60. See, for example, Karen Harvey, "The History of Masculinity, circa 1650–1800," *Journal of British Studies* 44, no. 2 (2005): 296–311.

61. Amy Dru Stanley, *From Bondage to Contract: Wage Labor, Marriage and the Market in the Age of Slave Emancipation* (Cambridge: Cambridge University Press, 1998); Cynthia Enloe, *Bananas, Beaches and Bases* (Berkeley: University of California Press, 1990); Fatima Mernissi, *Islam and Democracy: Fear of the Modern World*, trans. Mary Jo Lakeland (Reading, Mass.: Addison-Wesley, 1992).

62. V. Spike Peterson, "An Archeology of Domination: Historicizing Gender and Class in Early Western State Formation" (PhD diss., Department of Political Science, American University, 1988).

63. See, for example, Luigi Cavalli-Sforza, *Genes, Peoples, and Languages*, trans. Mark Seielstad (New York: North Point, 2000).

64. Stephen Jay Gould, *The Mismeasure of Man* (New York: Norton, 1981).

65. Balkin, "The Constitution of Status." For a historical discussion of how such perceived threats have played a role in American politics since the 1960s, see Rick Pearlstein, *Nixonland: The Rise of a President and the Fracturing of America* (New York: Scribner, 2008).

66. David Brion Davis, "The Terrible Cost of Reconciliation," *New York Review of Books*, July 18, 2002, 50–52. It is not that this is a new strategy for eliding class differences. Aristotle made similar observations in *Politics*, asserting the superiority of Greek men over "barbarians" and persons he insisted were "slaves by nature," including women.

67. Schmitt, *Political Theology*.

68. Kees van der Pijl discusses borderlands ("frontiers") in history; see *Nomads, Empires, States*, chap. 3.

69. Martin Pratt and Janet Allison Brown, eds., *Borderlands under Stress* (The Hague: Kluwer Law International, 2000); Carlos G. Vélez-Ibáñez, *Border Visions: Mexican Cultures of the Southwest United States* (Tucson: University of Arizona Press, 1996).

70. Linda Gordon, *The Great Arizona Orphan Abduction* (Cambridge, Mass.: Harvard University Press, 1999).

71. See, for example, Geroge J. Borjas, *Mexican Immigration to the United States* (Chicago: University of Chicago Press).

72. See, for example, Julia Preston, "Immigrants' Families Figuring Out What to Do After Federal Raids," *New York Times*, December 16, 2006, at www.nytimes.com/2006/12/16/washington/16immig.html (accessed June 10, 2008).

73. See, for example, James Lowry, Alex Ulanov, and Thomas Wenrich, "Advancing to the Next Level of Latino Marketing: Strike First, Strike Twice," Boston Consulting Group, February 15, 2003, at www.bcg.com/publications/publication_view.jsp?pubID=791&language=English (accessed December 20, 2005); "Services: Latino Marketing," Pluribus Media, n.d., at www.pluribusmedia.com/serv_spanish.htm (accessed May 2, 2007).

74. Randal C. Archibold and Julia Preston, "Homeland Security Stands by Its Fence," *New York Times*, May 21, 2008, at www.nytimes.com/2008/05/21/washington/21fence.html (accessed June 10, 2008).

75. "U.S. Mexicans Gain Dual Citizenship," *New York Times*, March 20, 2003, at query.nytimes.com/gst/fullpage.html?res=9800E6DA1331F933A15750C0A9659C8B63&scp=1&sq=mexico+dual+citizenship&st=nyt (accessed June 10, 2008); James C. McKinley, "Lawmakers in Mexico Approve Absentee Voting for Migrants," *New York Times*, June 29, 2005, at www.nytimes.com/2005/06/29/international/americas/29mexico.html? (accessed June 10, 2008); personal communication with Professor Jorge Gonzalez, Trinity University, September 2008.

76. Marc Lacey, "Filipe Calderón: A Politician at Birth," *New York Times*, September 6, 2006, at www.nytimes.com/2006/09/06/world/americas/06calderon.html (accessed June 10, 2008).

77. Louis Sheldon, "Constitutional Attorney Sees Polygamy as Next Stage of Sexual Revolution," Traditional Values Coalition Press Release, October 5, 2004, at traditionalvalues.org/modules.php?sid=1935 (accessed September 22, 2005); Stanley Kurtz, "Beyond Gay Marriage—The Road to Polyamory," *Weekly Standard* 8, no. 45, August 4, 2003, at www.weeklystandard.com/Content/Public/Articles/000/000/002/938xpsxy.asp (accessed September 23, 2005); Allan C. Carlson and Paul T. Mero, "The Natural Family: A Manifesto," The Howard Center for Family, Religion and Society, 2005, at www.familymanifesto.net (accessed September 23, 2005).

78. Schmitt, *Political Theology*.

Chapter 7: People and War

1. We make this argument despite the rhetoric of the Bush administration that describes a policy it calls a "war against terrorism."

2. For a discussion of structural violence, see Johan Galtung, *Human Rights in Another Key* (Cambridge, U.K.: Polity Press, 1994).

3. Wolfgang Schivelbusch, *The Culture of Defeat: On National Trauma, Mourning, and Recovery,* trans. Jefferson Chase (New York: Metropolitan Books, 2003), 5.

4. Thucydides, *The Peloponnesian War*. There are many editions of this work, which is over two thousand five hundred years old and has attracted many famous translators. One of the earliest English translations was prepared by our old friend, Thomas Hobbes.

5. Immanuel Kant, "Perpetual Peace"; Carl von Clausewitz, *On War*. Both are widely available in many different editions.

6. See, for example, W. Michael Reisman and Chris T. Antoniou, eds., *The Laws of War: A Comprehensive Collection of Primary Documents on International Laws Governing Armed Conflict* (New York: Vintage, 1994).

7. Anatol Rapoport, introduction to *On War*, by Carl von Clausewitz (New York: Penguin, 1968), 19.

8. The Americans also had substantial help from France, including troops and money. See Simon Schama, *Citizens: A Chronicle of the French Revolution* (New York: Knopf, 1989), 25–26, 38–40, 47–49, 61. Schama argues that French financial support for the American Revolution undermined the state and helped bring on the French Revolution in 1789.

9. Schivelbusch, *Culture of Defeat,* 107–12.

10. Alan Kramer, *Dynamic of Destruction: Culture and Mass Killing in the First World War* (Oxford: Oxford University Press, 2007).

11. The literature on this long and bitter war is enormous. Examples that reveal the strange combination of limited and total war from the U.S. perspective include Leslie Gelb and Richard K. Betts, *The Irony of Vietnam: The System Worked* (Washington, D.C.: Brookings, 1979); Jeffrey Record, *The Wrong War: Why We Lost in Vietnam* (Annapolis, Md.: Naval Institute Press, 1998). For examples from the Vietnamese perspective, see Truong Nhu Tang, *A Viet Cong Memoir* (New York: Vintage, 1985); Tam Vu, "People's War against Special War"; and Le Tan Danh, "The South Vietnam National Front for Liberation during the Period from 1961 to 1965," both in *Vietnamese Studies* 11, "The Failure of 'Special War'" (Hanoi: English language reprint, n.d.). Works that focus on the disjunction explicitly include Tom Mangold and John Penycate, *The Tunnels of Cu Chi* (New York: Berkeley, 1985); and James William Gibson, *The Perfect War: The War We Couldn't Lose and How We Did* (New York: Vintage, 1988).

12. Noel Perrin, *Giving Up the Gun: Japan's Reversion to the Sword, 1543–1879* (Boulder, Colo.: Shambhala, 1980).

13. Kramer, *Dynamic of Destruction;* also Niall Ferguson, *War of the World* (New York: Penguin Books, 2006).

14. *The Fog of War* (Errol Morris, 2003). This film is structured around interviews with former defense secretary Robert S. McNamara. One compelling scene shows the cities firebombed in WWII paired with U.S. cities of the same size, to give viewers a sense of the physical and moral extent of the damage.

15. Zygmunt Bauman, *Modernity and the Holocaust* (Ithaca, N.Y.: Cornell University Press, 2000); Irving Louis Horowitz, *Taking Lives: Genocide and State Power* (New Brunswick, N.J.: Transaction Books, 1980). The "body count" amassed between 1900 and 1987 by states that targeted specific populations for extermination, a period that omits notorious genocidal campaigns in Bosnia, Rwanda, and Darfur, and smaller-scale efforts in Kosovo, Uganda, Burundi, Chechnya, and elsewhere, reached about 169,198,000 persons. See R. J. Rummel, *Death by Government* (New Brunswick, N.J.: Transaction Books, 1994).

16. Mary Ann Tétreault and Harry W. Haines, "Postmodern War and Historical Memory" (paper presented at the annual meeting of the International Studies Association, Montreal, March 2004).

17. See Convention on the Prevention and Punishment of the Crime of Genocide, United Nations, 1948, at www.preventgenocide.org/law/convention/text.htm.

18. Carol Cohn, "Nuclear Language and How We Learned to Pat the Bomb," *Bulletin of the Atomic Scientists* 43, no. 5 (June 1987): 17–24, at www.thebulletin.org/pdf/temp/043_005_013.pdf.

19. Simon Chesterman, ed., *Civilians in War* (Boulder, Colo.: Lynne Rienner, 2001).

20. Eric Schmitt and Tom Shanker, "A Nation Challenged: Body Count; Taliban and Qaeda Death Toll in Mountain Battle Is a Mystery," *New York Times,* March 14, 2002, at query.nytimes.com/gst/fullpage.html?res=9A02E7DB1039F937A25750C0A9649C8B63 (accessed July 15, 2008).

21. Refugees International, "Iraq: U.S. Response to Displacement Remains Inadequate," August 5, 2007, at www.refugeesinternational.org/content/article/detail/9993 (accessed July 15, 2008). "From 2003 to early 2007, the U.S. resettled only 466 Iraqis," see "The Iraqi Displacement Crisis," March 3, 2008, at www.refugeesinternational.org/content/article/detail/9679 (accessed July 15, 2008). By mid-2007, almost five million Iraqis were displaced, with about half having fled abroad and half living in Iraq but not in their homes.

22. Theda Skoçpol, *Protecting Soldiers and Mothers: The Political Origins of Social Policy in the United States* (Cambridge, Mass.: Belknap, 1995).

23. Washington Headquarters Services, Directorate for Information Operations and Reports, U.S. Department of Defense Records, "Principal Wars in Which the US Participated: US Military Personnel Serving and Casualties," table 2–23, at www.cwc.lsu.edu/cwc/other/stats/warcost.htm (accessed August 8, 2004).

24. This is the message of psychiatrist Jonathan Shay in two books about American veterans and combat trauma: *Achilles in Vietnam: Combat Trauma and the Undoing of Character* (New York: Touchstone, 1994); and, with Max Cleland and John McCain, *Odysseus in America* (New York: Scribner, 2002).

25. Elaine Showalter, "Male Hysteria," in *The Female Malady: Women, Madness, and English Culture, 1830–1980* (New York: Penguin, 2002). Showalter argues that part of the resistance to admitting that men could experience "hysteria" was that it denied the masculinity of war as an enterprise. The other reason was that officers were afraid that if men could get out of combat by claiming mental illness, practically everyone would do it. That is the premise of Joseph Heller's famous WWII novel, *Catch 22*. Pat Barker has written a trilogy of novels that focus on combat trauma in WWI and its class-differentiated treatment by British medical personnel. See her *Regeneration, The Eye in the Door*, and *Ghost Road*, all available in multiple editions.

26. Jason Epstein, "Always Time to Kill," *New York Review of Books*, November 4, 1999, at www.nybooks.com. A recent review of books by U.S. military personnel serving in Iraq reveals a wide range of reactions to fighting, killing, and torturing prisoners. See Michael Massing, "Iraq: The Hidden Human Costs," *New York Review of Books*, December 20, 2007, at www.nybooks .com/articles/20906 (accessed July 16, 2008). How low-level military personnel adapted to the torture of prisoners at Abu Ghraib is the subject of a new book by Philip Gourevitch and Errol Morris, *Standard Operating Procedure* (New York: Penguin, 2008).

27. P. W. Singer, *Corporate Warriors: The Rise of the Privatized Military Industry* (Ithaca, N.Y.: Cornell University Press, 2003), 53.

28. This is the message of Chris Hedges's book *War Is a Force That Gives Us Meaning* (New York: PublicAffairs, 2002), and it afflicts women as well as men. Compare Lynda Van Devanter, *Home Before Morning* (New York: Warner Books, 1983) and Philip Caputo, *A Rumor of War* (New York: Holt, Rinehart and Winston, 1977).

29. Ronnie D. Lipschutz, "Imperial Warfare in the Naked City—Sociality as Critical Infrastructure," *International Political Sociology* 3, no. 3 (September 2008): 204–18.

30. Christopher S. Kelley, "Rethinking Presidential Power: The Unitary Executive and the George W. Bush Presidency" (paper delivered at the annual meeting of the Midwest Political Science Association, Chicago, April 2005); Charlie Savage, *Takeover: The Return of the Imperial Presidency and the Subversion of American Democracy* (Boston: Little, Brown, 2007).

31. Charles Tilly, "War Making and State Making as Organized Crime," in *Bringing the State Back In*, ed. Peter Evans, Dietrich Rueschemeyer, and Theda Skoçpol (New York: Cambridge University Press, 1985), 169–91.

32. Tilly, "War Making"; also Frederic C. Lane, "The Economic Meaning of War and Protection," in *Venice and History: The Collected Papers of Frederic C. Lane* (Baltimore: Johns Hopkins University Press, 1966).

33. Robert Gilpin, *War and Change in World Politics* (New York: Cambridge University Press, 1981).

34. Kevin Phillips, *American Dynasty: Aristocracy, Fortune, and the Politics of Deceit in the House of Bush* (New York: Viking, 2004); and Ron Suskind, *The Price of Loyalty: George W. Bush, the White House, and the Education of Paul O'Neill* (New York: Simon and Schuster, 2004). A similar analysis of cold war resource redistribution can be found in Kees van der Pijl, *The Making of an Atlantic Ruling Class* (London: Verso, 1984).

35. Kenneth N. Waltz, *Man, the State, and War: A Theoretical Analysis* (New York: Columbia University Press, 1965).

36. Kenneth N. Waltz, *Theory of International Relations* (Reading, Mass.: Addison-Wesley, 1979), 18.

37. Different ways to interpret "balance of power" are discussed in Karl Polanyi, *The Great Transformation* (New York: Farrar and Rinehart, 1944), 259–64.

38. Niall Ferguson, *The Pity of War: Explaining World War I* (New York: Basic Books, 1998).

39. Robert Jervis, *Perception and Misperception in International Politics* (Princeton, N.J.: Princeton University Press, 1976).

40. This is the conclusion of Joshua S. Goldstein from an exhaustive literature survey seeking evidence of cultures without war. See his *War and Gender* (New York: Cambridge University Press, 2001), chap. 1.

41. Thomas Hobbes, *Leviathan* (Chicago: Encyclopedia Britannica, 1952), 86.

42. Hans J. Morgenthau, *Politics among Nations: The Struggle for Power and Peace*, 5th ed. (New York: Knopf, 1973).

43. George W. Bush, "The National Security Strategy of the United States," White House, Washington, September 17, 2002, at www.whitehouse.gov/nsc/nss.html (accessed February 17, 2008).

44. Former U.S. treasury secretary Paul O'Neill says that even at the first meeting of the principals of the Bush national security team, January 30, 2001, "it was all about Iraq." By February 2001, the Defense Intelligence Agency was "mapping Iraq's oil fields and . . . listing companies that might be interested in leveraging the precious asset." Suskind, *The Price of Loyalty*, 75, 96.

45. Gilpin, *War and Change;* Robert O. Keohane and Joseph S. Nye, *Power and Interdependence: World Politics in Transition* (Boston: Little, Brown, 1977). The most spirited defense of the soft version of hegemonic stability theory can be found in Robert O. Keohane, *After Hegemony: Cooperation and Discord in the World Political Economy* (Princeton, N.J.: Princeton University Press, 1984). See below in the text.

46. Keohane, *After Hegemony*, 34.

47. Alejandro Colás, *International Civil Society: Social Movements in World Politics* (Cambridge, U.K.: Polity, 2002); John Keane, *Civil Society: Old Images, New Visions* (Stanford, Calif.: Stanford University Press, 1998); Martha Nussbaum, "Kant and Stoic Cosmopolitanism," *Journal of Political Philosophy* 5, no. 1 (March 1977); Robin L. Teske, "Political Space: The Importance of the Inbetween," in *Conscious Acts and the Politics of Social Change*, ed. Mary Ann Tétreault and Robin L. Teske (Columbia: University of South Carolina Press, 2000), 72–90.

48. Nussbaum, "Kant and Stoic Cosmopolitanism," 2, emphasis in the original.

49. Nussbaum, "Kant and Stoic Cosmopolitanism," 3.

50. Nussbaum, "Kant and Stoic Cosmopolitanism."

51. *Kant: Political Writings*, 2nd ed., ed. Hans Reiss, trans. H. B. Nisbet (Cambridge: Cambridge University Press, 1944), 104.

52. J. Ann Tickner, *Gender in International Relations: Feminist Perspectives on Achieving Global Security* (New York: Columbia University Press, 1992); V. Spike Peterson, *A Critical Rewriting of Global Political Economy: Integrating Reproductive, Productive, and Virtual Economies* (London: Routledge, 2003). This perspective also can be derived from constructivist theories of IR. See Cynthia Weber, *International Relations Theory: A Critical Introduction* (London: Routledge, 2001), chap. 4.

53. Chris Hables Gray, *Postmodern War: The New Politics of Conflict* (New York: Guilford, 2003), 245.

54. See Gray, *Postmodern War;* James William Gibson, *Warrior Dreams: Paramilitary Culture in Post-Vietnam America* (New York: Hill and Wang, 1994); James Der Derian, *Virtuous War: Mapping the Military-Industrial-Media-Entertainment Network* (Boulder, Colo.: Westview, 2001).

55. Tétreault and Haines, "Postmodern War."

56. Fairness and Accuracy in Reporting (FAIR), "What a Difference Four Years Makes: Why U.N. Inspectors Left Iraq—Then and Now," October 2002, at www.fair.org/index.php?page=1123 (accessed July 16, 2008).

57. How this was done is detailed in Michael Massing, "Now They Tell Us," *New York Review*, February 26, 2004, at www.nybooks.com/articles/16922 (accessed August 5, 2008).

58. "The Secret Downing Street Memo," from David Manning to Michael Rycroft, sent July 23, 2002, at www.downingstreetmemo.com/docs/memotext.pdf (accessed August 5, 2008). For an analysis of the memo and what it reveals about how these two leaders planned to invade Iraq regardless of whatever the United Nations might do, see Mark Danner, *The Secret Way to War: The Downing Street Memo and the Iraq War's Buried History* (New York: New York Review Books, 2006). The Danner book includes a copy of the memo.

59. Alan Cowell, "For Blair, Iraq Issue Just Won't Go Away," *New York Times*, May 2, 2005, at www.nytimes.com/2005/05/02/international/europe/02britain.html?_r=1&oref=slogin (accessed August 5, 2008).

60. Clark Hoyt, "New Public Editor Looks at 'Downing Street Memo' Coverage," *New York Times*, May 24, 2005, at publiceditor.blogs.nytimes.com/2005/05/24/new-public-editor-looks-at-downing-street-memo-coverage/?scp=2&sq=Downing%20Street%20Memo&st=cse (accessed August 5, 2008).

61. Mark Danner, "The Secret Way to War," *New York Review,* June 9, 2005, at www.nybooks.com/articles/18034 (accessed August 5, 2008).

62. Mark Danner, "Words in a Time of War: Taking the Measure of the First Rhetoric-Major President" (commencement address to graduates of the Department of Rhetoric at Zellerbach Hall, University of California, Berkeley, May 10, 2007), at www.markdanner.com/articles/show/words_in_a_time_of_war (accessed August 5, 2008).

63. W. Lance Bennett, *News: The Politics of Illusion,* 4th ed. (New York: Longman, 2001); also Pierre Bourdieu, *On Television,* trans. Priscilla Parkhurst Ferguson (New York: New Press, 1998).

64. Daniel C. Hallin, "The Media, the War in Vietnam, and Political Support: A Critique of the Thesis on an Oppositional Media," *Journal of Politics* 46, no. 1 (February 1984): 2–24.

65. Terese A. Thompson, "The Political and Ideological Context of Broadcast News: CBS Nightly News Coverage of Eastern Europe" (MA thesis, Old Dominion University, 1991). An example from popular culture can be found in *Rambo, First Blood*. Rambo's captors in Vietnam look suspiciously like Japanese and Germans in WWII. See Ronnie D. Lipschutz, *Cold War Fantasies: Film, Fiction, and Foreign Policy* (Lanham, Md.: Rowman & Littlefield, 2001), 146–47.

66. Jürgen Habermas, *The Structural Transformation of the Public Sphere: An Inquiry into a Category of Bourgeois Society,* trans. Thomas Burger with Frederick Lawrence (Cambridge, Mass.: MIT Press, 1991).

67. The three Gulf Wars are Iran–Iraq (1980–1988), Kuwait (1990–1991), and the ongoing war that began in March 2003.

68. Steven Kull (principal investigator) et al., "Misperceptions, the Media, and the Iraq War," Program on International Policy Attitudes and Knowledge Networks, October 2, 2003, at 65.109.167.118/pipa/pdf/oct03/IraqMedia_Oct03_rpt.pdf (accessed July 16, 2008).

69. Compare Susan Sontag, "Looking at War," *New Yorker*, December 9, 2002, 82–98; Douglas Kellner, *The Persian Gulf TV War* (Boulder, Colo.: Westview, 1992), 160. Philip Taylor also finds video-game analogues in coverage of GWII in *War and the Media: Propaganda and Persuasion in the Gulf War* (Manchester: Manchester University Press, 1993).

70. Bill Katovsky and Timothy Carlson, *Embedded: The Media at War in Iraq* (Guilford, Conn.: Lyons, 2003). Compare the experiences recounted here with Anne Garrels's account of her unembedded coverage of the Iraq war in *Naked in Baghdad* (New York: Farrar, Straus and Giroux, 2003).

71. Michael Massing, "Embedded in Iraq," *New York Review of Books,* July 17, 2008, at www.nybooks.com/articles/21617 (accessed July 16, 2008).

72. Julian E. Barnes, "The Iraq War Movie: Military Hopes to Shape Genre," *Los Angeles Times*, July 7, 2008, at www.latimes.com/news/la-na-armyfilms7-2008jul07,0,2707554.story?track=ntothtml (accessed July 7, 2008). For a partial list of films the military has "helped with," including films dealing with earlier wars, see www.latimes.com/news/nationworld/nation/la-na-armyfilmsbox7-2008jul07,0,5412172.story?track=ntothtml. An interesting omission from this list is *The Sands of Iwo Jima* (Allan Dwan, 1949), which was made with the extensive cooperation of the U.S. Marines—much of it was filmed at Camp Pendleton—at a time when Congress was considering its abolition as an independent force.

73. Adam Smith, "Normalizing Torture on '24,'" *New York Times*, May 22, 2005, at www.nytimes.com/2005/05/22/arts/television/22gree.html (accessed July 16, 2008).

74. World Public Opinion, "World Citizens Reject Torture, BBC Global Poll Reveals," October 18, 2006, at www.worldpublicopinion.org/pipa/articles/btjusticehuman_rightsra/261.php?nid=&id=&pnt=261 (accessed July 16, 2008).

75. See, for example, R. Po-Chia Hsia, *Trent 1475: Stories of a Ritual Murder Trial* (New Haven, Conn.: Yale University Press, 1992).

76. Elaine Scarry, *The Body in Pain: The Making and Unmaking of the World* (New York: Oxford University Press, 1985), 28 (emphasis in the original).

77. The orchestration of the spectacle is discussed in Mary Ann Tétreault, "The Sexual Politics of Abu Ghraib: Hegemony, Spectacle, and the Global War on Terror," *National Women's Studies Association Journal* 18, no. 3 (Fall 2006): 33–50.

78. Mary Ann Tétreault, "The Politics of Abu Ghraib, Part One: Paved with . . . Intentions" (paper presented at the annual meeting of the International Studies Association, March 2005); Tétreault, "Sexual Politics of Abu Ghraib."

79. Jane Mayer, *The Dark Side: The Inside Story of How the War on Terror Turned into a War on American Ideals* (New York: Doubleday, 2008).

80. Robert Jervis, "Cooperation under the Security Dilemma," *World Politics* 30, no. 2 (January 1978): 167–214; and Ronnie D. Lipschutz, *After Authority: War, Peace, and Global Politics in the 21st Century* (Albany, N.Y.: SUNY Press, 2000), 33–62.

81. Economist Mehrdad Valibeigi, personal communication to Mary Ann Tétreault, September 2003.

82. Vera Brittain, *Testament of Youth* (1933; New York: Seaview Books, 1980).

83. Brittain, *Testament of Youth*, 637–38.

84. James J. Sheehan, *Where Have All the Soldiers Gone? The Transformation of Modern Europe* (Boston: Houghton Mifflin, 2008).

85. Hedges, *War Is a Force*, 184–85.

Chapter 8: People and Justice

1. Presidential claims regarding the torture and abuse of prisoners at Iraq's Abu Ghraib prison, and protests by the families of soldiers charged with these activities, illustrate the widely held notion that injustice is committed by "bad apples." See, for example, Eric Scmitt, "Army Report Says Flaws in Detention Didn't Cause Abuse," *New York Times*, July 23, 2004, at www.nytimes.com/2004/07/23/politics/23abus.html?th (accessed July 23, 2004). For discussions of this point, see Anthony Lewis, "Making Torture Legal," *New York Review of Books* 51, no. 12 (July 15, 2004); and Mark Danner, "The Logic of Torture," *New York Review of Books* 51, no. 11 (June 24, 2004). That torture was a systematic policy instigated at the highest level of government is meticulously documented by Jane Mayer in *The Dark Side: The Inside Story of How the War on Terror Turned into a War on American Ideals* (New York: Doubleday, 2008).

2. Consider, for example, the commutation of prison time granted by President Bush to Lewis "Scooter" Libby who was convicted of obstruction of justice and perjury.

3. Peter Singer, "Famine, Affluence, and Morality," *Philosophy and Public Affairs* 1 (1972): 229–44.

4. This is a contested viewpoint. The moral competence of charities to deliver assistance to the suffering is very much in doubt, according to William Shawcross, *The Quality of Mercy: Cambodia, Holocaust, and the Modern Conscience* (New York: Simon and Schuster, 1984); and Peter Uvin, *Aiding Violence: The Development Enterprise in Rwanda* (West Hartford, Conn.: Kumarian, 1998).

5. Shawcross, *Quality of Mercy*; and Uvin, *Aiding Violence*.

6. Garrett Hardin, "Life Boat Ethics: The Case against Helping the Poor," *Psychology Today* (September 1974), 126.

7. See Eric Ross, *The Malthus Factor* (London: Zed, 1998).

8. Thomas Robert Malthus, "An Essay on the Principle of Population; or, A View of Its Past and Present Effects on Human Happiness; with an Inquiry into Our Prospects Respecting the Future Removal or Mitigation of the Evils Which It Occasions (1778; repr., London: printed for J. Johnson by T. Bensley, 1803).

9. Hardin, "Life Boat Ethics."

10. John Rawls, *A Theory of Justice* (Cambridge, Mass.: Harvard University Press, 1971).

11. In economics, this is often described in terms of "Pareto optimality."

12. Martha Nussbaum, "The Enduring Significance of John Rawls," *Chronicle of Higher Education*, July 20, 2001, B7; Peter Berkowitz, "John Rawls and the Liberal Faith," *Wilson Quarterly* (Spring 2002) at wwics.si.edu/index.cfm?fuseaction_wq.print&essay_id_8468&stoplayout_true; Susan Moeller Okin, *Justice, Gender and the Family* (New York: Basic Books, 2001); Brian C. Anderson, "The Antipolitical Philosophy of John Rawls," *Public Interest* (Spring 2003) at www.findarticles.com/p/articles/mi_m0377/is_2003_Spring/ai_100388979; Michael Sandel, *Liberalism and the Limits of Justice* (Cambridge: Cambridge University Press, 1983); Iris Marion Young, *Justice and the Politics of Difference* (Princeton, N.J.: Princeton University Press, 1990).

13. See, for example, Thomas W. Pogge, *World Poverty and Human Rights* (Cambridge, U.K.: Polity, 2002). For an interesting extension of this principle, see Donald G. McNeil Jr., "When Human Rights Extend to Nonhumans," *New York Times*, July 13, 2008, at www.nytimes.com/2008/07/13/weekinreview/13mcneil.html (accessed July 15, 2008).

14. Isaiah Berlin, *Four Essays on Liberty* (London: Oxford University Press, 1969).

15. Alice Walker and Pratibha Parmar, *Warrior Marks: Female Genital Mutilation and the Sexual Blinding of Women* (New York: Harvest Books, 1996).

16. On male circumcision, see, for example, Marie Fox and Michael Thompson, "A Covenant with the Status Quo? Male Circumcision and the New BMA Guidance to Doctors," *Journal of Medical Ethics* 31 (2005): 463–69. On female circumcision, see Agda Rossel, "Human Rights and the Rights of Women: Retrospects and Perspectives on Work in the United Nations," in *Partial Truths and the Politics of Community*, ed. Mary Ann Tétreault and Robin L. Teske (Columbia: University of South Carolina Press), 265–74. Agda Rossel was the first female ambassador to the United Nations—from Sweden—and she was the first to bring this issue to the Economic and Social Council, but it took many years before UN agencies attempted to halt the practice.

17. See, for example, Anatole Lieven, *America Right or Wrong: An Anatomy of American Nationalism* (Oxford: Oxford University Press, 2004).

18. United Nations, Department of Public Information, "Fiftieth Anniversary of the Declaration of Human Rights," 1998, at www.un.org/rights/50/decla.htm (accessed July 23, 2004).

19. United Nations, "International Covenant on Civil and Political Rights," July 7, 1994, at www.hrweb.org/legal/cpr.html (accessed July 23, 2004).

20. United Nations, "International Covenant on Economic, Social, and Cultural Rights," July 7, 1994, at www.hrweb.org/legal/escr.html (accessed July 23, 2004).

21. For example, although the U.S. Department of State issues an annual report on human rights violations, it never lists the United States among countries committing them.

22. Amnesty International, www.amnesty.org; Human Rights Watch, www.hrw.org.

23. Jennifer Hadden and Sidney Tarrow, "Spillover or Spillout? The Global Justice Movement in the United States after 9/11," *Mobilization: An International Quarterly* 12, no. 4 (2007): 359–76.

24. Amartya Sen, *Development as Freedom* (New York: Anchor, 2000).

25. Sen, *Development as Freedom*, 36.

26. Not everyone would agree, however, that Western-funded development projects are actually intended to expand such substantive freedoms; see, for example, Gilbert Rist, *The History of Development—From Western Origins to Global Faith,* trans. Patrick Camiller (London: Zed Books, 2002).

27. Sen, *Development as Freedom*, 18.

28. Sen, *Development as Freedom*, esp. chaps. 8 and 9.

29. Ashutosh Varshney, "Ethnic Conflict and Civil Society: India and Beyond," *World Politics* 53, no. 3 (April 2001): 262–98.

30. John Isbister, *Capitalism and Justice: Envisioning Social and Economic Fairness* (Bloomfield, Conn.: Kumarian, 2001), 15. This is one of the best introductions available to the problems of distributive and social justice.

31. Isbister, *Capitalism and Justice*, 14.

32. Philippe Van Parijs, quoted in Isbister, *Capitalism and Justice*, 16.

33. Isbister, *Capitalism and Justice*, 70–71.

34. Isbister, *Capitalism and Justice*, chap. 5.

35. A detailed discussion of these statistics can be found in Moya K. Mason, "Small Businesses," at www.moyak.com/researcher/resume/papers/businesses2.html (accessed July 16, 2008).

36. Richard L. Abel, *Speaking Respect, Respecting Speech* (Chicago: University of Chicago Press, 1998).

37. Abel, *Speaking Respect, Respecting Speech*.

38. Remember, if Bill Gates is drinking in a bar with twenty-five bums, they are, on average, all billionaires.

39. In other words, and to be very specific, the elevation of Clarence Thomas to the U.S. Supreme Court almost certainly came at the expense of other, equally qualified African American, Latino, Asian American, white, Jewish, and so on, lawyers and judges. But, so did the appointment of Antonin Scalia and John Roberts. Moreover, such selection, at best, raises the average of a specific social group; it does not lift individual capabilities of the entire group. The individualist approach used in the United States should be compared with state policy in Malaysia during the late 1960s and 1970s, where the more prosperous Chinese population was, in effect, made to yield a portion of their wealth and property to the Malay population. See, for example, Firdaus Hj. Abdullah, "Affirmative Action Policy in Malaysia: To Restructure Society, to Eradicate Poverty," *Ethnic Studies Report* 15, no. 2 (July 1997): 189–221, at www.ices.lk/publications/esr/articles_jul97/Esr-Abdullah.PDF (accessed July 16, 2008).

40. Howard Ball, *The Bakke Case: Race, Education, and Affirmative Action* (Lawrence: University Press of Kansas, 2000).

41. Barbara A. Perry, *The Michigan Affirmative Action Cases* (Lawrence: University Press of Kansas, 2007).

42. This point makes for odd bedfellows: conservatives, such as U.S. Supreme Court Justice Scalia, make a similar argument, confident that the public and its representatives will go for the more restrictive outcome (e.g., ban all race-based affirmative action).

43. Nancy Fraser, "Social Justice in the Age of Identity Politics: Redistribution, Recognition, Participation" (lecture given at the Wissenschaftszentrum Berlin für Sozialforschung, December 1998), at skylla.wz_berlin.de/pdf/1998/i98_108.pdf (accessed July 23, 2004). For a comparison of six rights movements motivated by the desire of activists for justice as respect, see Doron Shultziner, "Struggles of Recognition: The Psychological Causes of Democratization" (PhD diss., Department of Politics and International Relations, University of Oxford, Oxford, U.K., 2007).

44. Actually, Singer's position is a good deal more complex than this, for he is primarily concerned with minimizing pain and suffering. He is not interested in the welfare or fate of those who lack awareness of pain, including not only lower forms of life but also certain humans without sensory awareness. On Marx's view, see "On the Jewish Question," *Deutsch-Französische Jahrbucher*, February 1844, at www.marxists.org/archive/marx/works/1844/jewish_question/ (accessed July 23, 2004).

45. Chris Brown, *International Relations Theory: New Normative Approaches* (New York: Columbia University Press, 1992), esp. chap. 2.

46. See, for example, Charles Jones, *Global Justice: Defending Cosmopolitanism* (Oxford: Oxford University Press, 1999), esp. chaps. 2–4.

47. Onora O'Neill, *Bounds of Justice* (Cambridge: Cambridge University Press, 2000), chap. 10.

48. This was the apparent response of the Bush administration as the full scope became clear of the injury, death, and damage done in and to New Orleans by Hurricane Katrina.

49. For a detailed discussion of communitarianism, see Amitai Etzioni, *The New Golden Rule: Community and Morality in a Democratic Society* (New York: Basic, 1997).

50. O'Neill, *Bounds of Justice*, 199.

51. Arlo Guthrie, "Alice's Restaurant," copyright 1966, 1967 (renewed) by Appleseed Music, Inc., all rights reserved.

52. Abel, *Speaking Respect, Respecting Speech.*

53. Raymond A. Winbush, ed., *Should America Pay? Slavery and the Raging Debate Over Reparations* (New York: Amistad, 2003): Lawrie Balfour, "Unreconstructed Democracy: W. E. B. Du Bois and the Case for Reparations," *American Political Science Review* 97 (2003): 33–44.

54. Assume one million slaves working ten hours per day, three hundred days per year, for two hundred years, being paid minimum wage (in current dollars). Total wages would exceed $3.5 trillion in today's dollars.

55. This is discussed in Stephen Winter, "What's So Bad about Slavery? Assessing the Grounds for Reparations," *Patterns of Prejudice* 41, no. 3 (2007): 373–93.

56. Hardin, "Life Boat Ethics," 126.

57. Carol S. Robb, *Equal Value: An Ethical Approach to Economics and Sex* (Boston: Beacon, 1995), 145.

58. Thorstein Veblen, "The Beginning of Ownership," *American Journal of Sociology* 4, no. 3 (November 1898): 352–65, at socserv2.socsci.mcmaster.ca/_econ/ugcm/3ll3/veblen/ownersh (accessed July 23, 2004).

59. O'Neill, *Bounds of Justice*, 140, 141.

Chapter 9: People and Globalization

1. Joseph E. Stiglitz, *Globalization and Its Discontents* (New York: Norton, 2002), 9.

2. James H. Mittelman, "The Dynamics of Globalization," in *Globalization: Critical Reflections*, ed. James H. Mittelman (Boulder, Colo.: Rienner, 1997), 3.

3. Harris Collingwood, "The Sink-or-Swim Economy," *New York Times Magazine*, June 8, 2003, 42–45; Rodrigue Tremblay, "Financial Bankruptcy, the US Dollar and the Real," *Canadian Dimension*, February 1, 2008, at canadiandimension.com/articles/2008/02/01/1295/ (accessed August 5, 2008).

4. Karl Marx and Friedrich Engels, *The Communist Manifesto* (New York: Pocket Books, 1964), 63.

5. Karl Polanyi, *The Great Transformation* (Boston: Beacon, 1944, 2000), 159.

6. Anthony Giddens, *Runaway World: How Globalization Is Reshaping Our Lives* (London: Routledge, 1999), 33–34.

7. Plague transmission followed market routes worldwide in the Middle Ages. See Janet Abu-Lughod, *Before European Hegemony: The World System A.D. 1250–1350* (New York: Oxford University Press, 1989), 173–74; Christopher Dyer, *Making a Living in the Middle Ages: The People of Britain, 850–1520* (New Haven, Conn.: Yale University Press, 2002), 271–77.

8. Eric R. Wolf, *Europe and the People without History* (Berkeley: University of California Press, 1982).

9. Mike Davis, *Late Victorian Holocausts: El Niño Famines and the Making of the Third World* (London: Verso, 2001). Davis looks at societies dominated by foreigners. Where native populations adjusted on their own, without the assistance to local elites that characterized adjustment in imperial dependencies, those local elites could occasionally be beaten back. See Dyer, *Making a Living*, 286–93.

10. For the political economy of the Irish potato famine, see Herman M. Schwartz, *States versus Markets: History, Geography, and the Development of the International Political Economy*, 2nd ed. (New York: St. Martin's, 2000); and www.people.Virginia.EDU/_eas5e/Irish/Famine.html. It should be noted that "Irish" landlords were mostly British, putting Ireland among the imperial dependencies referred to above. For the El Niño famines, see Davis, *Late Victorian Holocausts*. Davis stresses the importance of globalization in the spread of famine during these droughts. One example is that areas not served by railroads had lower food prices because there was no alternative external market, while regions connected by rail experienced skyrocketing prices even if their crops were not affected by drought. The integration of Ireland into European markets had the same effect. A similar situation exists today in Sudan, where food crops are grown for foreign buyers while domestic

populations, especially groups the government would like to get rid of, are literally starving. See Jeffrey Gettleman, "The Food Chain: Darfur Withers as Sudan Sells Food," *New York Times,* August 90, 2008, at www.nytimes.com/2008/08/10/world/africa/10sudan.html?_r=1&scp=1&sq=Sudan %20agriculture&st=cse&oref=slogin (accessed August 11, 2008).

11. Edmund Burke questioned the operation of the British East India Company in 1783, challenging assertions of its financial soundness and the involvement of court and Parliament in skimming profits from its activities. "Ninth Report of the Select Committee," June 25, 1783, in *The Writings and Speeches of Edmund Burke,* vol. 5, *India: Madras and Bengal, 1774–1785,* ed. P. J. Marshall (Oxford: Oxford University Press, 1985).

12. Linda Colley, *Captives: The Story of Britain's Pursuit of Empire and How Its Soldiers and Civilians Were Held Captive by the Dream of Global Supremacy, 1600–1850* (New York: Pantheon, 2002), chap. 9; John S. Galbraith, "The 'Turbulent Frontier' as a Factor in British Expansion," *Comparative Studies in Society and History* 2, no. 2 (1960): 150–68. We saw a similar loss of command and control in chapter 5, when we looked at the Massachusetts Bay Company. In that case, the crown found itself the unwitting (and unwilling) sponsor of a democratic political regime. It took fifty years for Britain to reimpose "normal" authoritarian rule in Massachusetts, given the command and control technologies of that time.

13. By then, the BEIC controlled all of India and was training local troops—Sepoys—to augment its need for military manpower. "The mutiny . . . began . . . when Indian soldiers who had been placed in irons for refusing to accept new cartridges were rescued by their comrades. The greased cartridges had to be bitten off before use, and the manufacturers had [packed them in a mixture of the] fat of beef and pork—repulsive to both Hindus and Moslems." See www.hyperhistory.com/online_n2/civil_n2/histscript6_n2/sepoy.html. Also see Christopher Hibbert, *The Great Mutiny of 1857* (New York: Viking, 1978); and Colley, *Captives.*

14. George R. Fay, "AR 15-6 Investigation of the Abu Ghraib Detention Facility and 205th Military Intelligence Brigade (U)," reprinted in *Torture and Truth: America, Abu Ghraib, and the War on Terror,* ed. Mark Danner (New York: New York Review Books, 2004), 514.

15. "Palace and Mosque: Islamic Art from the Victoria and Albert Museum," National Gallery of Art, Washington, D.C., July 18, 2004–February 6, 2005.

16. The classic work in this field is Theodor Adorno, "The Culture Industry: Enlightenment as Mass Deception," in *Dialectic of Enlightenment,* ed. Max Horkheimer and Theodor Adorno (New York: Herder and Herder, 1972), 120–67.

17. Barbara Jenkins, "Creating Global Hegemony: Culture and the Market," in *Rethinking Global Political Economy: Emerging Issues and Unfolding Odysseys,* ed. Mary Ann Tétreault, Robert A. Denemark, Kenneth P. Thomas, and Kurt Burch (London: Routledge, 2003), 65–85. Also, Ien Ang, *Watching Dallas: Soap Opera and the Melodramatic Imagination,* trans. Della Couling (London: Methuen, 1985).

18. Mary Ann Glendon, *A World Made New: Eleanor Roosevelt and the Universal Declaration of Human Rights* (New York: Random House, 2001); Robert A. Pape, *Dying to Win: The Strategic Logic of Suicide Terrorism* (New York: Random House, 2005).

19. Davis, *Late Victorian Holocausts,* chap. 1.

20. Davis, *Late Victorian Holocausts,* 36, 43–44.

21. On the joint contributions of agents and structures to structural violence, see Johan Galtung, *Human Rights in Another Key* (Cambridge, U.K.: Polity, 1994), 27–38.

22. The model was constructed to explain the impact of transportation costs on land rents and the location of production around a central market. See *Von Thünen's Isolated State: An English Edition of Der Isolierte Staat by Johann Heinrich von Thünen,* ed. Peter Hall, trans. Carla M. Wertenberg (Oxford: Pergamon, 1966). The current far-flung supply chains of global production are at the mercy of rising oil prices, and corporations are rethinking where to locate new sites for manufacturing heavy equipment. See, for example, Larry Rohter, "Shipping Costs Start to Crimp Globalization," *New York Times,* August 3, 2008, at www.nytimes.com/2008/08/03/business/worldbusiness/03global.html?_r=1&oref=slogin (accessed August 5, 2008).

23. *Von Thünen's Isolated State.* Also Schwartz, *States versus Markets,* chaps. 1–2.

24. Abu-Lughod, *Before European Hegemony*, 175–82.

25. The connection between national economic integration and state finance was a matter of great controversy. Outside of England it proceeded slowly, in fits and starts. See, for example, Simon Schama, *Citizens: A Chronicle of the French Revolution* (New York: Knopf, 1989), chap. 2.

26. Barrington Moore, *The Social Origins of Dictatorships and Democracies: Lord and Peasant in the Making of the Modern World* (Boston: Beacon, 1966).

27. James Macdonald, *A Free Nation Deep in Debt: The Financial Roots of Democracy* (New York: Farrar, Straus and Giroux, 2003); also John Brewer, *The Sinews of Power: War and the English State, 1688–1783* (London: HarperCollins, 1989).

28. The leadership of peasants in spreading market relations in feudal Britain is one of the theses of Dyer's *Making a Living*.

29. Adam Hochschild, *King Leopold's Ghost* (Boston: Houghton Mifflin, 1999). We thank geographer Bernard Logan for pointing out the consequences back in the 1980s (personal communication with Mary Ann Tétreault).

30. James R. Kurth, "The Political Consequences of the Product Cycle: Industrial History and Political Outcomes," *International Organization* 33, no. 1 (Winter 1979): 1–34.

31. Davis reports that the British made the Indians pay the full cost of Britain's occupation. Stanley Karnow reports a similar policy by the French in Vietnam—see his *Vietnam: A History* (New York: Penguin, 1997). Africans were even more brutally exploited. Hochschild tells how King Leopold of Belgium extracted the costs of looting the Congo from native Africans; Edward Hooper reports that the Belgian government was paid by entrepreneurs developing polio vaccines for the right to test the vaccines on the native peoples, a token of the status of the Congo as an "estate" of the Belgian government rather than an autonomous entity. Edward Hooper, *The River: A Journey to the Source of HIV and AIDS* (Boston: Little, Brown, 1999).

32. See, for example, Anthony Sampson, *The Seven Sisters: The Great Oil Companies and the World They Shaped* (New York: Viking, 1975); also Robert W. Tolf, *The Russian Rockefellers: The Saga of the Nobel Family and the Russian Oil Industry* (Stanford, Calif.: Hoover Institute, 1977).

33. Phebe Marr, *The Modern History of Iraq* (Boulder, Colo.: Westview, 1985); Mary Ann Tétreault, "Independence, Sovereignty, and Vested Glory: Oil and Politics in the Second Gulf War," *Orient* 34, no. 1 (March 1993): 87–103; interview by Terry Gross of Charles Lewis, director of the Center for Public Integrity, on Fresh Air, National Public Radio, June 17, 2003; Alan Greenspan, *The Age of Turbulence: Adventures in a New World* (New York: Penguin, 2007), 463.

34. Pietra Rivoli, *The Travels of a T-Shirt in the Global Economy: An Economist Examines the Markets, Power, and Politics of World Trade* (Hoboken, N.J.: John Wiley & Sons, 2005).

35. For example, Ikea opened a factory in Danville, Virginia, to ship furniture to stores in the eastern United States because the rising cost of fuel has increased transport charges, making producing these products abroad too expensive. See Ylan Q. Mui, "Ikea Helps a Town Put It Together: Manufacturing Jobs Come Back to Southern Va.," *Washington Post*, May 13, 2008, A01.

36. Clark A. Miller, "The Globalization of Human Affairs: A Reconsideration of Science, Political Economy, and World Order," in *Rethinking Global Political Economy*, ed. Tétreault, Denemark, Thomas, and Burch, 216–17.

37. Naomi Sakr, *Satellite Realms: Transnational Television, Globalization, and the Middle East* (London: I. B. Tauris, 2001), esp. chap. 3.

38. N. Janardhan, "New Media: In Search of Equilibrium," in *After Saddam: Political Development in the Arab Gulf*, ed. Mary Ann Tétreault and Andrzej Kapiszewski (Boulder, Colo.: Lynne Rienner, forthcoming).

39. Mary Ann Tétreault and Harry W. Haines, "Postmodern War and Historical Memory" (paper presented at the annual meeting of the International Studies Association, Montréal, March 2004); also W. Lance Bennett, *News: The Politics of Illusion*, 4th ed. (New York: Longman, 2001); also Pierre Bourdieu, *On Television*, trans. Priscilla Parkhurst Ferguson (New York: New Press, 1998).

40. Olivier Roy, "Bin Laden et ses frères," *Politique International* 93, 67–81; "Bin Laden: An Apocalyptic Sect Severed from Political Islam," *East European Constitutional Review* 10, no. 4 (Fall): 108–14.

41. Olivier Roy, "Changing Patterns among Radical Islamist Movements," *Brown Journal of World Affairs* 6, no. 1 (Winter/Spring 1999): 109–20; also Roy, "Bin Laden et ses frères."

42. Carolyn Nordstrom, *Girls and Warzones* (Uppsala, Sweden: Life and Peace Institute, 1997); see also her *Shadows of War: Violence, Power, and International Profiteering in the Twenty-first Century* (Berkeley: University of California Press, 2004).

43. Mary Ann Tétreault heard about this in interviews conducted in Kuwait in December 2004.

44. Ahmad Rashid, *Taliban* (New Haven, Conn.: Yale Nota Bene, 2000).

45. Rashid, *Taliban*; also Craig Unger, "Saving the Saudis," *Vanity Fair*, October 2003, 162, 164–66, 175–76, 178–79; and Steve Coll, *The Bin Ladens: An Arabian Family in the American Century* (New York: Penguin, 2008).

46. See, for example, T. J. Stiles, *Jesse James: Last Rebel of the Civil War* (New York: Vintage, 2003).

47. Roberto Saviano, *Gomorrah: A Personal Journey into the Violent International Empire of Naples' Organized Crime System*, trans. Virginia Jewiss (New York: Farrar, Straus and Giroux, 2007).

48. Misha Glenny, *McMafia: A Journey through the Global Criminal Underworld* (New York: Knopf, 2008), 53.

49. Glenny, *McMafia*, 80, and see the chart tracing relationships among the leading actors on 81. Their various nationalities illustrate the frontier qualities of multinational business operations more generally.

50. Robin Wright, *Dreams and Shadows: The Future of the Middle East* (New York: Penguin, 2008), 67–68.

51. See, for example, Alfred W. McCoy, *The Politics of Heroin: CIA Complicity in the Global Drug Trade* (Chicago: Lawrence Hill Books, 1991).

52. Tamar Gabelnick, William D. Hartung, and Jennifer Washburn, with research assistance by Michelle Ciarrocca, "Arming Repression: U.S. Arms Sales to Turkey During the Clinton Administration," A Joint Report of the World Policy Institute and the Federation of American Scientists, October 1999, at www.fas.org/asmp/library/reports/turkeyrep.htm#kurds (accessed August 9, 2008).

53. David S. Meyer, "Protest Cycles and Political Process: American Peace Movements in the Nuclear Age," *Political Research Quarterly* 47, no. 3 (1993): 451–79; and "Social Movements: Creating Communities of Change," in *Conscious Acts and the Politics of Social Change*, ed. Robin L. Teske and Mary Ann Tétreault (Columbia: University of South Carolina Press, 2000), 35–55.

54. David Ronfeldt and John Arquilla, "Networks, Netwars, and the Fight for the Future," *First Monday* 6, no. 10 (2001), at www.firstmonday.org/issues/issue6_10/ronfeldt/index.html (accessed June 2002). This is the same kind of activity that nonviolent—and legal—groups pursue, such as the coalition Let Freedom Ring, mentioned in chapter 5, which held demonstrations protesting China's human rights record during the 1997 state visit of the president of China to the United States.

55. Michael Hardt and Antonio Negri, *Empire* (Cambridge, Mass.: Harvard University Press, 2000).

56. Kirin Aziz Chaudhry, *The Price of Wealth: Economies and Institutions in the Middle East* (Ithaca, N.Y.: Cornell University Press, 1997), 241–50. These little financial organizations are primary targets of antiterrorism efforts, even though larger sums are transferred internationally through far larger enterprises.

57. Thomas Friedman, "Where Freedom Reigns," *New York Times*, August 14, 2002, A29.

58. Ashutosh Varshney, "Ethnic Conflict and Civil Society: India and Beyond," *World Politics* 53, no. 3 (April 2001): 362–98.

59. Varshney, "Ethnic Conflict"; and Amartya Sen, *Underdevelopment as Freedom* (New York: Doubleday Anchor, 2000).

60. Stiglitz, *Globalization and Its Discontents*; George Soros, *George Soros on Globalization* (New York: Public Affairs, 2002).

61. Sen agrees, and argues that this involves systematic misinterpretation and suppression of all but a narrow segment from the canonical works of Adam Smith—see *Underdevelopment as Freedom*, 271–72.

62. Stiglitz, *Globalization and Its Discontents*, 13, 74, 78, quote from 74.

63. Emma Rothschild, "The Bloody and Invisible Hand," in *Economic Sentiments: Adam Smith, Condorcet, and the Enlightenment* (Cambridge, Mass.: Harvard University Press, 2001), chap. 5, 115–156, at www.compilerpress.atfreeweb.com/Anno%20Rothschild%20Bloody%20&%20Invisible%201.htm (accessed November 2, 2007).

64. See Polanyi, *The Great Transformation*, 148. Such contradictions permeate formal clashes between proponents of these two incompatible tenets. For another example, see Ken Auletta, *World War 3.0: Microsoft and Its Enemies* (New York: Random House, 2001), which looks at the contradiction as it affects antitrust regulation.

65. Polanyi, *The Great Transformation*, 148.

66. Tony Clarke, "Priming the Pump: The Emerging Debate over Water Privatization in North America," *Cross Border Perspectives*, November 2002, at www.maxwell.syr.edu/campbell/XBorder/Clarke%20oped.pdf (accessed September 2003).

67. Glenny, *McMafia*, chaps. 1–4.

68. PBS's *Frontline* showed how the 1995 decision by the G-7 to change the dollar–yen exchange rate touched off the Asian economic crisis. *Frontline*, "The Crash," broadcast June 29, 1999. Transcript at www.pbs.org/wgbh/pages/frontline/shows/crash/etc/script.html (accessed July 2008).

69. Nicholas Bakalar, "Rise in TB Is Linked to Loans from I.M.F.," *New York Times*, July 22, 2008, at www.nytimes.com/2008/07/22/health/research/22tb.html?_r=2&adxnnl=1&oref=slogin&adxnnlx=1218308557-UbaeDi19zsxVi5OM2iDDqA (accessed August 9, 2008).

70. Peter Uvin, *Aiding Violence: The Development Enterprise in Rwanda* (West Hartford, Conn.: Kumarian, 1998).

71. UN News Centre, "Collapse of Doha Round of Global Trade Talks Disappointing, Says Ban," July 30, 2008, at www.un.org/apps/news/story.asp?NewsID=27534&Cr=WTO&Cr1=trade (accessed August 9, 2008).

72. Joseph Stiglitz, "The Broken Promise of NAFTA," *New York Times*, January 6, 2004, A27.

73. Western Organization of Resource Councils, "Fact Sheet: Investor to State Provisions: Putting Profit Before People," May 2005, at www.worc.org/pdfs/Chapter11.pdf (accessed August 9, 2008).

74. But for a more skeptical view, see Ronnie D. Lipschutz, with James K. Rowe, *Globalization, Governmentality and Global Politics—Regulation for the Rest of Us?* (London: Routledge, 2005).

75. Robert O. Keohane and Joseph S. Nye, *Power and Interdependence: World Politics in Transition* (Boston: Little, Brown, 1977).

76. This is David Ricardo's famous theory of comparative advantage.

77. Hochschild, *King Leopold's Ghost*, 28, 42.

78. Sandra G. Boodman, "Raw Menace: Major Hepatitis A Outbreak Tied to Green Onions," *Washington Post*, November 25, 2003, HE01; and also see www.agriculturelaw.com/archive/nov03.html.

79. U.S. Food and Drug Administration, "Salmonella Saintpaul Outbreak: Updated: August 1, 2008," at www.fda.gov/oc/opacom/hottopics/tomatoes.html (accessed August 9, 2008); Centers for Disease Control and Prevention, "Investigation of Outbreak of Infections Caused by Salmonella Saintpaul," *CDC-Info*, August 8, 2008, at www.cdc.gov/Salmonella/saintpaul/ (accessed August 9, 2008).

80. Susan Lindquist, "From Mad Cows to Nanoscale Technology" (Trinity University Distinguished Scientist Lecture, San Antonio, April 5, 2004).

81. John Darnton, "Britain Ties Deadly Brain Disease to Cow Ailment," *New York Times*, March 21, 1996, A1, A7.

82. "Japan Deems Beef Standards Lax in Canada and U.S.," *New York Times*, January 20, 2004, D3.

83. Voice of America, "Tens of Thousands Join Korean Demonstration Against US Beef," July 5, 2008, at www.voanews.com/english/2008-07-05-voa18.cfm (accessed August 9, 2008).

84. Robert G. Webster, "Influenza: An Emerging Disease," *Emerging Infectious Diseases* 4, no. 3 (July–September 1998), at www.cdc.gov/ncidod/eid/vol4no3/webster.htm (accessed January 2004).

85. Quote from Andrew Pollack, "No Foolproof Way Is Seen to Contain Altered Genes," *New York Times*, January 21, 2004, A10; also Carol Kaesuk Yoon, "Genetic Modification Taints Corn in Mexico," *New York Times*, October 2, 2001, at www.biotech_info.net/mexico_corn.html.

86. United Nations Intergovernmental Panel on Climate Change, Fourth Assessment Report," 2007, at www.ipcc.ch/ipccreports/ar4-wg1.htm (accessed August 9, 2008).

87. Elizabeth Kolbert, *Field Notes from a Catastrophe* (New York: Bloomsbury, 2006).

88. Mike Davis, "Living on the Ice Shelf: Humanity's Meltdown," *TomDispatch.com*, posted June 26, 2008, at www.tomdispatch.com/post/174949 (accessed August 9, 2008).

89. See, for example, Kolbert, *Field Notes*; also Stephen Gill, "Globalization, Democratization, and the Politics of Indifference," in *Globalization: Critical Reflections*, ed. James H. Mittelman (Boulder, Colo.: Lynne Rienner, 1996), 205–28; Don Van Natta Jr., and Neela Banerjee, "Top G.O.P. Donors in Energy Industry Met Cheney Panel," *New York Times*, March 1, 2002, A1, A15; Andrew C. Revkin, "Bush Aide Softened Greenhouse Gas Links to Global Warming," *New York Times*, June 8, 2005, at www.nytimes.com/2005/06/08/politics/08climate.html.

90. James Hansen, "Global Warming Twenty Years Later: Tipping Points Near," Briefing to the House Select Committee on Energy Independence & Global Warming, June 23, 2008, at www.columbia.edu/~jeh1/2008/TwentyYearsLater_20080623.pdf (accessed August 9, 2008).

91. George W. Bush, "National Energy Policy," 2001, "Overview," at www.whitehouse.gov/energy/Overview.pdf and Summary of Recommendations, at www.whitehouse.gov/energy/summaries.pdf; Kevin C. Armitage, "State of Denial: The United States and the Politics of Global Warming," *Globalizations* 2, no. 3 (December 2005): 417–27.

92. S. W. Verstegen and J. C. Hanekamp, "The Sustainability Debate: Idealism versus Conformism—the Controversy over Economic Growth," *Globalizations* 2, no. 3 (December 2005): 349–62; Björn-Ola Linnér and Merle Jacob, "From Stockholm to Kyoto and Beyond: A Review of the Globalization of Global Warming Policy and North-South Relations," *Globalizations* 2, no. 3 (December 2005): 403–15; Hugh Dyer, "Environmental Imperialism: Theories of Governance and Resistance" (paper presented at the International Studies Association annual convention, Honolulu, March 2003).

93. For example, Kolbert, *Field Notes*; also "Renewable Energy Sources and Low Wastage Make Denmark a Net Exporter of Energy While Its Economy Grows By 50 Percent," *Horizon Solutions Site*, posted October 29, 2006, at www.solutions-site.org/artman/publish/article_288.shtml (accessed August 9, 2008).

94. Bill McKibben, "A Special Moment in History," May 1998, at www.theatlantic.com/issues/98may/special1.htm (accessed August 9, 2008). McKibben wrote the first book about global warming for a popular audience: *The End of Nature* (New York: Random House, 1989).

95. This trend was visible as early as the nineteenth century, but nongovernmental agents were appreciably smaller in capacity and reach as compared to states than at least a few such agents are today. See Craig N. Murphy, *International Organization and Industrial Change: Global Governance since 1850* (Cambridge, U.K.: Polity, 1994).

Chapter 10: People Matter

1. Sheldon Wolin, "Fugitive Democracy," in *Democracy and Difference*, ed. Seyla Benhabib (Princeton, N.J.: Princeton University Press, 1996), 31–45.

2. Hannah Arendt, *On Revolution* (New York: Viking, 1963).

3. Ronnie D. Lipschutz, with James K. Rowe, *Globalization, Governmentality and Global Politics—Regulation for the Rest of Us?* (London: Routledge, 2005).

4. *American Heritage Dictionary of the English Language* (Boston: Houghton Mifflin, 1981), 436.

5. Lewis Mumford, *The Human Prospect* (London: Secker and Warburg, 1955), and *The Transformations of Man* (New York: Harper, 1956).

6. Kees van der Pijl, *Nomads, Empires, States—Modes of Foreign Relations* (London: Pluto Press, 2007).

7. The "great man" theory of history is usually attributed to the Scottish historian Thomas Carlyle, who wrote that "the history of the world is but the biography of great men."

8. Hannah Arendt, *The Human Condition: A Study of the Central Dilemmas Facing Modern Man* (New York: Doubleday Anchor, 1959), 10–11.

9. Which is 42; see Douglas Adams, *The Hitchhiker's Guide to the Galaxy* (London: Pan Books, 1979).

10. See, for example, Jerry Harris, "To Be Or Not To Be: The Nation-Centric World Order Under Globalization," *Science and Society* 69, no. 3 (July 2005): 329–40.

11. Elsa V. Artadi and Xavier Sala-i-Martin, "The Economic Tragedy of the XXth Century: Growth in Africa," Working Paper 9865 (Cambridge, Mass: National Bureau of Economic Research, July 2003), at www.nber.org/papers/w9865 (accessed September 14, 2008).

12. Bill McKibben, *The End of Nature* (New York: Anchor, 1999).

13. Amartya Sen, *Development as Freedom* (New York: Knopf, 1999).

14. Karen Walch, "Feminist Ideas on Cooperation and Self-Interest for International Relations," in *Partial Truths and the Politics of Community*, ed. Mary Ann Tétreault and Robin L. Teske (Columbia: University of South Carolina Press, 2003), 161–78.

15. Michel Foucault, *Power/Knowledge*, trans. Colin Gordon (New York: Pantheon, 1980), 119.

16. Daniel J. Goldhagen, *Hitler's Willing Executioners: Ordinary Germans and the Holocaust* (New York: Knopf, 1996).

17. Lynn Hunt, *The Family Romance of the French Revolution* (Berkeley: University of California Press, 1992).

18. Although many on the American Right seem to regard same-sex marriage as a "liberal" issue, insofar as all marriages involve protection of property, same-sex marriage can also be seen as a conservative phenomenon.

19. International Campaign to Ban Landmines, at www.icbl.org (accessed July 18, 2008).

20. "Help Ban Cluster Bombs Now!" at www.icbl.org/news/cm_peoplestreaty (accessed July 18, 2008); Cluster Munitions Coalition, at www.stopclustermunitions.org/ (accessed July 18, 2008); "Campaigners Launch People's Treaty to Hold Governments to Their Word," at www.stopclustermunitions.org/news/?id=296 (accessed July 18, 2008).

21. International Campaign to Ban Landmines.

22. Margaret Keck and Kathryn Sikkink, *Activists Beyond Borders: Advocacy Networks in International Politics* (Ithaca, N.Y.: Cornell University Press, 1998); Richard Price, "Reversing the Gun Sights: Transnational Civil Society Targets Land Mines," *International Organization* 52 (1998): 613–44.

23. Katherine Boo, "The Churn: Creative Destruction in a Border Town," *New Yorker*, March 29, 2004, at www.newyorker.com/printable/?fact/040329fa_fact (accessed July 21, 2004); W. Michael Cox and Richard Alm, "The Churn—The Paradox of Progress," Federal Reserve Bank of Dallas, reprint from 1992 Annual Report, at www.dallasfed.org/fed/annual/1999p/ar92.pdf (accessed December 6, 2005); William J. Baumol, Alan S. Blinder, and Edward N. Wolfe, *Downsizing in America: Reality, Causes, and Consequences* (New York: Russell Sage Foundation, 2003).

24. Peter Dombrowski, ed., *Guns and Butter: The Political Economy of International Security* (Boulder, Colo.: Lynne Rienner, 2005).

25. We presume that Iranian rhetoric about the destruction of Israel is exactly that, although we should never underestimate the potential of inflammatory speeches to create "real" facts on the ground and in the air. See, for example, Benny Morris, "Using Bombs to Stave Off War," *New York Times*, July 19, 2008, at www.nytimes.com/2008/07/18/opinion/18morris.html (accessed July 18, 2008).

26. Ronnie D. Lipschutz, *Global Environmental Politics: Power, Perspectives, and Practice* (Washington, D.C.: Congressional Quarterly, 2003), chap. 3; Mark Paterson, *Consumption and Everyday Life* (London: Routledge, 2005).

27. The perils of staying inside the box are explored in Arthur Kopit's 1984 play about the new cold war. See *End of the World* (New York: Hill and Wang, 1984).

28. Sarah Babb, "The Social Consequences of Structural Adjustment: Recent Evidence and Current Debates," *Annual Review of Sociology* 31 (2005): 199–222.

29. For example, see Mark D. Harmon, *The British Labour Government and the 1976 IMF Crisis* (New York: St. Martin's, 1997). The United States has, so far, escaped any form of SAP, although that could change in the future.

30. Deborah Stone, *Policy Paradox: The Art of Political Decision Making* (New York: Norton, 1997).

31. Hans Blix, *Disarming Iraq* (New York: Pantheon, 2004); Mark Danner, *The Secret Way to War: The Downing Street Memo and the Iraq War's Buried History* (New York: New York Review Books, 2006).

32. "Powell Regrets UN Speech on Iraq WMDs," ABC News Online, September 9, 2005, at www.abc.net.au/news/newsitems/200509/s1456650.htm (accessed July 18, 2008).

33. The White House, "U.S. Secretary of State Colin Powell Addresses the U.N. Security Council" (transcript), February 5, 2003, at www.whitehouse.gov/news/releases/2003/02/20030205-1 .html (accessed July 18, 2008).

34. Danner, *The Secret Way to War*.

35. James Risen, *State of War: The Secret History of the CIA and the Bush Administration* (New York: Free Press, 2006).

36. Danner, *Secret Way to War*; Risen, *State of War*. How and why so many went along with the plan is detailed in Bob Woodward, *State of Denial: Bush at War, Part II* (New York: Simon and Schuster, 2006). Woodward castigates himself for being part of the pack.

37. Seymour M. Hersh, "The Redirection," *New Yorker*, March 5, 2007, 54–60, 62–65.

38. Intergovernmental Panel on Climate Change (IPCC), Climate Change 2007—Synthesis Report (Geneva: IPCC Secretariat, World Meteorological Organization, 2007), at www.ipcc.ch/pdf/assessment-report/ar4/syr/ar4_syr.pdf (accessed April 29, 2008); Intergovernmental Panel on Climate Change, Climate Change 2007—Synthesis Report—Summary for Policymakers (Geneva: IPCC Secretariat, World Meteorological Organization, 2007), at www.ipcc.ch/pdf/assessment-report/ar4/syr/ar4_syr_spm.pdf (accessed April 29, 2008).

39. Elizabeth Kolbert's analysis in *Field Notes from a Catastrophe: Man, Nature, and Climate Change* (New York: Bloomsbury, 2006).

40. Volker Mrasek, "A Storehouse of Greenhouse Gases Is Opening in Siberia," Spiegel International Online, April 17, 2008, at www.spiegel.de/international/world/0,1518,547976,00.html (accessed September 5, 2008).

41. S. Fred Singer and D. T. Avery, *Unstoppable Global Warming: Every 1500 Years* (Lanham, Md.: Rowman & Littlefield, 2006).

42. The drama of the many-fronted Bush rejection of the science on climate change is part of Elizabeth Kolbert's analysis in *Field Notes from a Catastrophe*.

43. James Hansen, "Timeline for Irreversible Climate Change," *Policy Innovations*, April 22, 2008 (New York: Carnegie Council), at www.policyinnovations.org/ideas/commentary/data/000049. Hansen is the head of the Goddard Space Center and was one of the first nationally renowned scientists to identify climate change and some of the mechanisms driving it.

44. A macabre example is recounted in Jane Mayer, *The Dark Side: The Inside Story of How the War on Terror Turned into a War on American Ideals* (New York: Doubleday, 2008), 155–74, on the Bush administration's search for satisfactory experts on interrogation and torture.

45. Kolbert, *Field Notes for a Catastrophe*; Bill McKibben, *Deep Economy: The Wealth of Communities and the Durable Future* (New York: Times Books, 2007), 162–64.

46. Mancur Olson, *The Logic of Collective Action* (Cambridge, Mass.: Harvard University Press, 1965).

47. Local Governments for Sustainability, at www.iclei.org/ (accessed July 18, 2008).

48. "Mayors Climate Protection Center: List of Participating Mayors," U.S. Conference of Mayors, at www.usmayors.org/climateprotection/list.asp (accessed January 8, 2008).

49. This information, and more, can be found on The California Climate Change Portal, at www.climatechange.ca.gov/ (accessed July 18, 2008).

50. The Cato Institute (www.cato.org/), which subscribes to a form of economic libertarianism, often makes such claims. For a critique of such market logic, see Lipschutz, *Globalization, Governmentality and Global Politics*.

51. Tony Boivaird, "Public-Private Partnerships: From Contested Concepts to Prevalent Practice," *Int'l Review of Administrative Sciences* 70, no. 2 (2004): 199–215; Bernardo Bortolotti and Enrico Perotti, "From Government to Regulatory Governance: Privatization and the Residual Role of the State," *The World Bank Research Observer* 22, no. 1 (Spring 2007): 53–66.

52. The literature on replacement jobs is large and growing. See, for example, Rich Reinhold, "How Laid Off Workers Fared in Their Reemployment Efforts," *Illinois Labor Market Review* 4, no. 1 (Spring 1998), at lmi.ides.state.il.us/lmr/article1.htm (accessed August 20, 2004).

53. Shelley Hurt, "Science, Power, and the State: U.S. Foreign Policy, Intellectual Property Law, and the Origins of the World Trade Organization, 1969–1994" (New York: PhD diss., Department of Political Science, The New School for Social Research, 2008).

54. A recent controversy in the United States pits health economists against health advocates as to whether "a vaccine that could save the lives of nearly 3,000 people, many of them teenagers, from deaths caused" by bacterial meningitis will be provided because the cost to the government is estimated at $3.5 billion, or "more than $1 million a life spared, far more than health officials are normally willing to spend." See Gardiner Harris, "Panel Reviews New Vaccine That Could Be Controversial," *New York Times*, October 27, 2004, A12.

55. For instance, the U.S. Environmental Protection Agency puts the value of a "statistical life" in the United States at $6.9 million (reduced from $7.8 million in 2003); see Seth Borenstein, "An American Life Worth Less Today," *San Francisco Chronicle*, July 10, 2008, at www.sfgate.com/cgi-bin/article.cgi?f=/n/a/2008/07/10/national/a110546D37.DTL (accessed July 18, 2008).

56. Neta Crawford and Audie Klotz, *How Sanctions Work: Lessons from South Africa* (New York: Macmillan, 1999).

57. Such a project devastated many communities in Haiti. See Tracy Kidder, *Mountains Beyond Mountains: The Quest of Dr. Paul Farmer, A Man Who Would Cure the World* (New York: Random House, 2004).

58. Michel Foucault, "Governmentality," in *The Foucault Effect: Studies in Governmentality*, ed. Graham Burchell, Colin Gordon, and Peter Miller (Chicago: University of Chicago Press, 1991), 87–104; quote on 102.

59. Mitchell Dean, *Governmentality: Power and Rule in Modern Society* (London: Sage, 1999), 99.

60. Vladimir Ilyich Lenin, *What Is to Be Done? Burning Questions of Our Movement* (New York: International, 1929). In Russian, "Shto delat?" (Что делать?) has appeared in the titles of works by Tolstoy, Chernyshevsky, and others.

61. Stone, *Policy Paradox*, 26.

62. This is the famous formulation of Harold Lasswell, who asserted that "politics is who gets what, when, and how." See his book, *Politics: Who Gets What, When, How* (New York: Peter Smith, 1936).

63. James C. Scott, *Seeing Like a State: How Certain Schemes to Improve the Human Condition Have Failed* (New Haven, Conn.: Yale University Press, 1999). The Bush administration's project to "transform" the Middle East is an example of the folly of such plans.

64. Foucault, *Power/Knowledge*, 119.

65. Hannah Arendt, *The Human Condition*, 2nd ed. (Chicago: University of Chicago Press), 198.

66. Arendt, *The Human Condition*, 200.

67. Arendt, *The Human Condition*, 199.

68. Arendt, *The Human Condition*, 198.

69. See, for example, David Harvey, *A Brief History of Neoliberalism* (Oxford: Oxford University Press, 2005).

70. See, for example, Bruno Latour, *Pandora's Hope: Essays on the Reality of Science Studies* (Cambridge, Mass.: Harvard University Press, 1999), chap. 2.

71. One discussion of political space can be found in Robin L. Teske, "Political Space: The Importance of the Inbetween," in *Conscious Acts and the Politics of Social Change*, ed. Robin L. Teske and Mary Ann Tétreault (Columbia: University of South Carolina Press, 2000), 72–90.

72. Even earlier than that—in medieval Britain, for example—unskilled workers were not permitted to associate. They couldn't form workers' organizations or groups, or even meet together regularly as a social club or a religious fraternity. The power of association to generate politics and the desire of status quo forces to repress that power explain why the right of association is part of the First Amendment to the U.S. Constitution, a position that announces its bedrock importance to democratic life. On medieval restrictions on associations in Britain see Christopher Dyer, *Making a Living in the Middle Ages: The People of Britain, 850–1520* (New Haven, Conn.: Yale University Press, 2002), on women's movements, see suffragist writings such as those by Susan B. Anthony, Elizabeth Cady Stanton, Emmeline Pankhurst, Doris Stevens, and others.

73. See, for example, Ian Welsh, "In Defence of Civilisation: Terrorism and Environmental Politics in the 21st century," *Environmental Politics* 16, no. 2 (2007): 356–75.

74. Lipschutz, *Globalization, Governmentality and Global Politics.*

75. Norman Long, "From Paradigm Lost to Paradigm Regained? The Case for an Actor-Oriented Sociology of Development," in *Battlefields of Knowledge: The Interlocking of Theory and Practice in Social Research and Development*, ed. Norman Long and Ann Long (London: Routledge, 1992), 23–24 (emphasis added).

76. Ronnie D. Lipschutz, *After Authority: War, Peace and Global Politics in the 21st Century* (Albany, N.Y.: SUNY Press, 2000), chap. 8.

77. Mary Ann Tétreault and Robin L. Teske, "Framing the Issues," in Teske and Tétreault, *Conscious Acts*, 6.

78. This observation is laid out with great elegance in Graham Allison's classic work, *Essence of Decision: Explaining the Cuban Missile Crisis* (Reading, Mass.: Addison-Wesley, 1972).

79. The joke is rather too long to tell here. Suffice it to say that it involves a physicist modeling a cow's failure to produce milk by "assuming a spherical cow." See John Harte, *Consider a Spherical Cow: A Course in Environmental Problem Solving* (Los Altos, Calif.: Kaufman, 1985).

80. That globalization has effects that produce reactions in the form of religious social movements is the premise of a set of case studies in Mary Ann Tétreault and Robert A. Denemark, eds., *Gods, Guns, and Globalization: Religious Radicalism and International Political Economy*, vol. 13, *The International Political Economy Yearbook* (Boulder, Colo.: Lynne Rienner, 2004).

81. Olson, *The Logic of Collective Action.*

82. Sidney Tarrow, *Power in Movement: Social Movements and Contentious Politics*, 2nd ed. (Cambridge: Cambridge University Press, 1998); Doug McAdam, John D. McCarthy, and Meyer N. Zald, *Comparative Perspectives on Social Movements: Political Opportunities, Mobilizing Structures, and Cultural Framings* (Cambridge: Cambridge University Press, 1996).

83. Chantal Mouffe, *The Democratic Paradox* (London: Verso, 2000).

84. Eric R. Wolf, *Europe and the People without History* (Berkeley: University of California Press, 1982), 388.

85. Although recent events suggest that those in the great capitals do worry about what small groups might do, especially if they unite together in national form. Chinese suppression of Falun Gong and the U.S. FBI's search for "home-grown terrorists" both demonstrate fear of social power, however small or fragmented such groups might be.

Index

About the Authors

Mary Ann Tétreault is the Una Chapman Cox Distinguished Professor of International Affairs at Trinity University in San Antonio, Texas. Her publications include books and articles about social movements, gender, oil markets, war crimes, international political economy, world politics, and American foreign policy. At Trinity, she teaches courses on world politics, violent conflict, gender, energy, and development. Her regional specialization is the Middle East, especially Kuwait and the Persian Gulf.

Ronnie D. Lipschutz is professor of politics and codirector of the Center for Global, International and Regional Studies at the University of California, Santa Cruz. His primary areas of research and teaching include international politics, global environmental affairs, U.S. foreign policy, globalization, international regulation, and film, fiction, and politics. His most recent books include *The Constitution of Imperium* (2008) and *Globalization, Governmentality and Global Politics: Regulation for the Rest of Us?* (2005).